Geo. F. Pentecost

Bible Studies

studies in the Pentateuch, II. studies in the life of Christ

Geo. F. Pentecost

Bible Studies
studies in the Pentateuch, II. studies in the life of Christ

ISBN/EAN: 9783337100308

Printed in Europe, USA, Canada, Australia, Japan

Cover: Foto ©Lupo / pixelio.de

More available books at **www.hansebooks.com**

BIBLE STUDIES

I. STUDIES IN THE PENTATEUCH
II. STUDIES IN THE LIFE OF CHRIST

THE INTERNATIONAL SUNDAY-SCHOOL LESSONS FOR 1894

By GEO. F. PENTECOST, D. D.

AUTHOR OF
"IN THE VOLUME OF THE BOOK," "OUT OF EGYPT," "A SOUTH WINDOW," ETC.

FLEMING H. REVELL COMPANY
NEW YORK   CHICAGO   TORONTO
Publishers of Evangelical Literature

PREFACE.

WITH this volume of Bible Studies a new series begins. It is the plan of these Studies to cover substantially the whole Bible in the course of seven years. The measure of favor with which both the American and British Christian public have received the preceding volumes warrants the beginning of another series. There is nothing new for the author to say by way of preface, except to cordially introduce his new publishers, Messrs. Fleming H. Revell Company, whose well-known firm is a guarantee for the publisher's department. The volumes as they may successively appear will come to their readers in their old typographical dress, and the general plan of the Studies has been unchanged. In this volume there are several reprints from preceding ones, inasmuch as the new series in part overlaps the last series. This the author trusts will be no blemish on the present volume.

The last two volumes were written in India, amidst a laborious evangelistic campaign. This has been written amid the confusion incident to a settlement over a new pastoral field in this great city of London. The writing of the volume has afforded me almost the only quiet hours I have had during the past year. May the Gracious Spirit, whose constant help the author has invoked, be present to bless his many readers.

G. F. P.

MARYLEBONE PRESBYTERIAN CHURCH,
    LONDON, ENGLAND, July 1, 1893.

GOOD BOOKS TO CONSULT IN THE STUDY OF THE SUNDAY SCHOOL LESSONS FOR 1894.

EACH BOOK IS BOUND IN CLOTH.

General Works of Reference.

MATTHEW HENRY'S COMMENTARY. 6 vols.................................. $15.00
JAMIESON, FAUSSETT & BROWN'S COMMENTARY, 4 vols................. 8.00
POCKET COMMENTARY. Compiled from Matthew Henry, Scott, and others. 3 vols...... .... 1.50
FRESH LIGHT ON BIBLICAL RACES. By Prof. A. H. Sayce. 6 vols,.... 6.00
THE BIBLE HISTORY. By Rev. Alfred Edersheim, D.D. 7 vols........ 6.00
MY SERMON NOTES. By Rev. C. H. Spurgeon, 4 vols............. 4.00
THE TREASURY OF SCRIPTURE KNOWLEDGE.......................... 2.00
THE BIBLE TEXT CYCLOPEDIA. A Complete Classification of Scripture Texts. By Rev. James Inglis........ 1.75
THE BIBLE HANDBOOK. By Joseph Angus, M.A............. .... 2.00
THE BIBLE REMEMBRANCER—containing an analysis of the Whole Bible.. 1.25
BIBLICAL THEOLOGY OF THE NEW TESTAMENT. Volume I. and II. By Prof. R. F. Weidner, M.A......each 1.50

Special Helps.
First and Second Quarters.

MOSES, THE SERVANT OF GOD. By F. B. Meyer, B.A.................... 1.00
ABRAHAM; OR, THE OBEDIENCE OF FAITH. By F. B. Meyer, B.A.. 1.00
ISRAEL, A PRINCE WITH GOD. By F. B. Meyer, B.A............... 1.00
JOSEPH, BELOVED, HATED, EXALTED. By F. B. MEYER, B.A.......... 1.00
NOTES ON THE BOOK OF GENESIS. By C. H. McIntosh............... .75
NOTES ON THE BOOK OF EXODUS. By C. H. McIntosh.. ..... .75
GOSPEL ACCORDING TO MOSES AS SEEN IN THE TABERNACLE. By Geo. Rodgers... .... .75
THE HISTORY OF THE JEWS FROM THE WAR WITH ROME TO THE PRESENT TIME. By Rev. H. C. ADAMS.. 3.20
SERMON NOTES ON GENESIS. By Rev. C. H. SPURGEON............. 1.00
STUDIES IN THE BOOK—GENESIS. *Interleaved.* By Prof. R. F. Weidner 1.00
THE LIFE AND TIMES OF JOSEPH. By Rev. H. G. Tomkins........ ... 1.00

A SYLLABUS OF OLD TESTAMENT HISTORY. Outlines and Literature. *Interleaved.* By Ira M. Price.... 1.50
TEN YEARS DIGGING IN EGYPT. 1881-1891. Illustrated. By W. M. Flinders Petrie 1.50
EGYPT AND SYRIA. Their Physical Features in Relation to Bible History. By Sir J. W. Dawson.......... 1.20
THE RACES OF THE OLD TESTAMENT. By Prof. A. H. Sayce 1.20
EARTH'S EARLIEST AGES, AND THEIR CONNECTION WITH MODERN SPIRITUALISM AND THEOSOPHY. By G. H. Pember, M.A..................... 1.50
BIBLE CHARACTERS. By D. L. Moody. cloth... .... .60
PHILOSOPHY OF THE PLAIN OF SALVATION. By Dr. Walker............ .25
THE MOSAIC RECORD. By A. G. Jennings............................ .40
THE WORKS OF FLAVIUS, JOSEPHUS. Translated by Wm. Whiston.... 1.50

Third and Four Quarters.

THE EARTHLY FOOTPRINTS OF OUR RISEN LORD, ILLUMINED. *net..* $1.50
A Continous Narrative of the Four Gospels according to The Revised Version, with introduction by Rev. John Hall, D.D. Illustrated by 113 full-page half-tone reproductions.
THE LIFE OF JESUS CHRIST. By Rev. James Stalker, D.D.............. .60
THE LIFE AND LIGHT OF MEN—EXPOSITIONS OF JOHN I—XII. By F. B. Meyer, B.A...... .... 1.00
NOTES ON THE GOSPELS, principally designed for the use of Sunday School Teachers and Bible Classes. By Albert Barnes. 2 vols.... ..... 1.60
NOTES ON THE PARABLES AND MIRACLES OF OUR LORD. By Richard C. Trench........................ 2.00
MEDITATIONS ON THE MIRACLES OF CHRIST. By J. S. Howson, D.D. 1.20
GALILEE IN THE TIME OF CHRIST. By Rev. Selah Merrill, D.D........ 1.00
THE TEMPLE: Its Ministry and Services at the Time of Jesus Christ. By Rev. Dr. Edersheim............. 1.25
OUTLINES OF THE LIFE OF CHRIST. By E. R. Conder, M.A., D.D. Cheap edition. 18mo..... .... .25

CONTENTS.

LESSONS AND GOLDEN TEXTS.

FIRST QUARTER.

LESSON   PAGE

I.—Jan. 7.—**The First Adam.** Gen. i, 26-31; ii, 1-3. Memory verses, 26-28 1
    GOLDEN TEXT: So God created man in his own image.—Gen. i, 27.

II.—Jan. 14.—**Adam's Sin and God's Grace.** Gen. iii, 1-15. Memory verses, 13-15 11
    GOLDEN TEXT: For as in Adam all die, even so in Christ shall all be made alive.—I. Cor. xv, 22.

III.—Jan. 21.—**Cain and Abel.** Gen. iv, 3-13. Memory verses, 3-5 20
    GOLDEN TEXT: By faith Abel offered unto God a more excellent sacrifice than Cain.—Heb. xi, 4.

IV.—Jan. 28.—**God's Covenant with Noah.** Gen. ix, 8-17. Memory verses, 11-13. 30
    GOLDEN TEXT: I do set my bow in the cloud, and it shall be for a token of a covenant between me and the earth.—Gen. ix, 13.

V.—Feb. 4.—**Beginning of the Hebrew Nation.** Gen. xii, 1-9. Memory verses, 1-3 37
    GOLDEN TEXT: I will bless thee, and make thy name great; and thou shalt be a blessing.—Gen. xii, 2.

VI.—Feb. 11.—**God's Covenant with Abraham.** Gen. xvii, 1-9. Memory verses, 7, 8 45
    GOLDEN TEXT: He believed in the Lord; and he counted it to him for righteousness.—Gen. xv, 6.

VII.—Feb. 18.—**God's Judgment on Sodom.** Gen. xviii, 22-33. Memory verses, 23-26 53
    GOLDEN TEXT: Shall not the Judge of all the earth do right?—Gen. xviii, 25.

VIII.—Feb. 25.—**The Trial of Abraham's Faith.** Gen. xxii, 1-13. Memory verses, 41-43 61
    GOLDEN TEXT: By faith Abraham, when he was tried, offered up Isaac.—Heb. xi, 17.

CONTENTS.

LESSON	PAGE

IX.—MARCH 4.—**Selling the Birthright.** Gen. xxv, 27–34. Memory verses, 31–34 69
  GOLDEN TEXT: The life is more than meat, and the body is more than raiment.—Luke xii, 23.

X.—MARCH 11.—**Jacob at Bethel.** Gen. xxviii, 10–22. Memory verses, 12–14 78
  GOLDEN TEXT: Behold, I am with thee, and will keep thee.—Gen. xxviii, 15.

XI.—MARCH 18.—**The Resurrection of Christ.** Mark xvi, 1–8. Memory verses, 6, 7 86
  GOLDEN TEXT: But now is Christ risen from the dead.—I. Cor. xv, 20.

XII.—MARCH 25.—**Review.** 95
  GOLDEN TEXT: I am the God of Abraham, and the God of Isaac, and the God of Jacob; God is not the God of the dead, but of the living.—Matt. xxii, 32.

SECOND QUARTER.

XIII.—APRIL 1.—**Jacob's Prevailing Prayer.** Gen. xxxii, 9–12; 24–30. Memory verses, 28–30 96
  GOLDEN TEXT: I will not let thee go except thou bless me.—Gen. xxxii, 26.

XIV.—APRIL 8.—**Discord in Jacob's Family.** Gen. xxxvii, 1–11. Memory verses, 3, 4 104
  GOLDEN TEXT: See that ye fall not out by the way.—Gen. xlv, 24.

XV.—APRIL 15.—**Joseph Sold into Egypt.** Gen. xxxvii, 23–36. Memory verses, 26–28 112
  GOLDEN TEXT: Ye thought evil against me; but God meant it unto good.—Gen. l, 20.

XVI.—APRIL 22.—**Joseph Ruler in Egypt.** Gen. xli, 38–48. Memory verses, 38–40 121
  GOLDEN TEXT: Them that honor me I will honor.—I. Sam. ii, 30.

XVII.—APRIL 29.—**Joseph Forgiving His Brethren.** Gen. xlv, 1–15. Memory verses, 3–5 130
  GOLDEN TEXT: If thy brother trespass against thee, rebuke him; and if he repent, forgive him.—Luke xvii, 3.

XVIII.—MAY 6.—**Joseph's Last Days.** Gen. l, 14–26. Memory verses, 24–26 138
  GOLDEN TEXT: The path of the just is as the shining light, that shineth more and more unto the perfect day.—Prov. iv, 18.

XIX.—MAY 13.—**Israel in Egypt.** Ex. i, 1–14. Memory verses, 8–10 147
  GOLDEN TEXT: Our help is in the name of the Lord.—Ps. cxxiv, 8.

CONTENTS.

LESSON	PAGE

XX.—MAY 20.—The Childhood of Moses. Ex. ii, 1-10. Memory verses, 8-10 156
> GOLDEN TEXT: I will deliver him, and honour him.—Ps. xci, 15.

XXI.—MAY 27.—Moses sent as a Deliverer. Ex. iii, 10-20. Memory verses, 10-12 165
> GOLDEN TEXT: Fear thou not, for I am with thee.—Is. xli, 10.

XXII.—JUNE 3.—The Passover Instituted. Ex. xii, 1-14. Memory verses, 13, 14 174
> GOLDEN TEXT: Christ our passover is sacrificed for us.—I. Cor. v, 7.

XXIII.—JUNE 10.—Passage of the Red Sea. Ex. xiv, 19-29. Memory verses, 27-29 189
> GOLDEN TEXT: By faith they passed through the Red Sea.—Heb. xi, 29.

XXIV.—JUNE 17.—The Woes of the Drunkard. Prov. xxiii, 29-35. Memory verses, 29-32 196
> GOLDEN TEXT: Look not thou upon the wine when it is red.—Prov. xxiii, 31.

XXV.—JUNE 24.—Review 205
> GOLDEN TEXT: The Lord's portion is his people.—Deut. xxxii, 9.

THIRD QUARTER.

XXVI.—JULY 1.—The Birth of Jesus. Luke ii, 1-20. Memory verses, 10-14.......................... 206
> GOLDEN TEXT: Unto you is born this day in the city of David a Saviour, which is Christ the Lord.—Luke ii, 11.

XXVII.—JULY 8.—Presentation in the Temple. Luke ii, 25-38. Memory verses, 27-32 214
> GOLDEN TEXT: A light to lighten the Gentiles, and the glory of thy people Israel.—Luke ii, 32.

XXVIII.—JULY 15.—Visit of the Wise Men. Matt. ii, 1-12. Memory verses, 9-11 223
> GOLDEN TEXT: They saw the young child with Mary his mother, and fell down, and worshipped him.—Matt. ii, 11.

XXIX.—JULY 22.—Flight into Egypt. Matt. ii, 13-23. Memory verses, 13-15......................... 233
> GOLDEN TEXT: The Lord shall preserve thy going out and thy coming in.—Ps. cxxi, 8.

XXX.—JULY 29.—The Youth of Jesus. Luke ii, 40-52. Memory verses, 46-49......................... 241
> GOLDEN TEXT: And Jesus increased in wisdom and stature, and in favour with God and man.—Luke ii, 52.

LESSON	PAGE

XXXI.—Aug. 5.—**The Baptism of Jesus.** Mark i, 1-11. Memory verses, 9-11 248
 GOLDEN TEXT: Thou art my beloved Son, in whom I am well pleased.—Mark i, 11.

XXXII.—Aug. 12.—**The Temptation of Jesus.** Matt. iv, 1-11. Memory verses, 1-4 256
 GOLDEN TEXT: In all points tempted like as we are, yet without sin.—Heb. iv, 15.

XXXIII.—Aug. 19.—**First Disciples of Jesus.** John i, 34-49. Memory verses, 40-42 263
 GOLDEN TEXT: We have found the Messias, which is, being interpeted, the Christ.—John i, 41.

XXXIV.—Aug. 26.—**The First Miracle of Jesus.** John ii, 1-11. Memory verses, 1-5 271
 GOLDEN TEXT: This beginning of miracles did Jesus in Cana of Galilee, and manifested forth his glory.—John ii, 11.

XXXV.—Sept. 2.—**Jesus Cleansing the Temple.** John ii, 13-25. Memory verses, 13-16 280
 GOLDEN TEXT: Make not my Father's house a house of merchandise.—John ii, 16.

XXXVI.—Sept. 9.—**Jesus and Nicodemus.** John iii, 1-16. Memory verses, 1-3 288
 GOLDEN TEXT: God so loved the world, that he gave his only begotten Son, that whosoever believeth in him should not perish, but have everlasting life.—John iii, 16.

XXXVII.—Sept. 16.—**Jesus at Jacob's Well.** John iv, 5-26. Memory verses, 11-14 296
 GOLDEN TEXT: Whosoever drinketh of the water that I shall give him shall never thirst.—John iv, 14.

XXXVIII.—Sept. 23.—**Daniel's Abstinence.** Dan. i, 8-20. Memory verses, 8, 9 305
 GOLDEN TEXT: Daniel purposed in his heart that he would not defile himself.—Dan. i, 8.

XXXIX.—Sept. 30.—**Review** 314
 GOLDEN TEXT: The kingdom of God is at hand: repent ye, and believe the gospel.—Mark i, 15.

FOURTH QUARTER.

XL.—Oct. 7.—**Jesus at Nazareth.** Luke iv, 16-30. Memory verses, 16-19 31
 GOLDEN TEXT: See that ye refuse not him that speaketh.—Heb. xii, 25.

XLI.—Oct. 14.—**The Draught of Fishes.** Luke v, 1-11. Memory verses, 4-6 3
 GOLDEN TEXT: Come ye after me and I will make you to become fishers of men.—Mark i, 17.

CONTENTS.

LESSON		PAGE

XLII.—Oct. 21.—**A Sabbath in Capernaum.** Mark i, 21-34. Memory verses, 27, 28 331
  Golden Text: He taught them as one that had authority, and not as the scribes.—Mark i, 22.

XLIII.—Oct. 28.—**A Paralytic Healed.** Mark ii, 1-12. Memory verses, 9-12 339
  Golden Text: The Son of man hath power on earth to forgive sins.—Mark ii, 10.

XLIV.—Nov. 4.—**Jesus Lord of the Sabbath.** Mark ii, 23-28. Memory verses, 3-5 347
  Golden Text: The Son of man is Lord also of the sabbath.—Mark ii, 28.

XLV.—Nov. 11.—**The Twelve Chosen.** Mark iii, 6-19. Memory verses, 13-15 355
  Golden Text: I have chosen you, and ordained you, that ye should go and bring forth fruit.—John xv, 16.

XLVI.—Nov. 18.—**The Sermon on the Mount.** Luke vi, 20-31. Memory verses, 27-31 364
  Golden Text: As ye would that men should do to you, do ye also to them likewise.—Luke vi, 31.

XLVII.—Nov. 25.—**Opposition to Christ.** Mark iii, 22-35. Memory verses, 23-26 374
  Golden Text: He came unto his own, and his own received him not.—John i, 11.

XLVIII.—Dec. 2.—**Christ's Testimony to John.** Luke vii, 24-35. Memory verses, 27, 28 383
  Golden Text: Behold, I send my messenger before thy face.—Luke vii, 27.

XLIX.—Dec. 9.—**Christ Teaching by Parables.** Luke viii, 4-15. Memory verses, 11-15 391
  Golden Text: The seed is the word of God.—Luke viii, 11.

L.—Dec. 16.—**The Twelve Sent Forth.** Matt. x, 5-16. Memory verses, 7-10 399
  Golden Text: As ye go, preach, saying, The kingdom of heaven is at hand.—Matt. x, 7.

LI.—Dec. 23.—**The Prince of Peace.** Is. ix, 2-7. Memory verses, 6, 7 407
  Golden Text: Of the increase of his government and peace there shall be no end.—Is. ix, 7.

LII.—Dec. 30.—**Review** 416
  Golden Text: Jesus Christ the same yesterday, and to-day, and forever.—Heb. xiii, 8.

I.

THE FIRST ADAM.—Genesis i, 26-31; ii, 1-3.

(26) And God said, Let us make man in our image, after our likeness: and let them have dominion over the fish of the sea, and over the fowl of the air, and over the cattle, and over all the earth, and over every creeping thing that creepeth upon the earth. (27) So God created man in his own image, in the image of God created he him; male and female created he them. (28) And God blessed them, and God said unto them, Be fruitful, and multiply, and replenish the earth, and subdue it: and have dominion over the fish of the sea, and over the fowl of the air, and over every living thing that moveth upon the earth. (29) And God said, Behold, I have given you every herb bearing seed, which is upon the face of all the earth, and every tree, in the which is the fruit of a tree yielding seed; to you it shall be for meat. (30) And to every beast of the earth, and to every fowl of the air, and to every thing that creepeth upon the earth, wherein there is life, I have given every green herb for meat: and it was so. (31) And God saw every thing that he had made, and, behold, it was very good. And the evening and the morning were the sixth day. (1) Thus the heavens and the earth were finished, and all the host of them. (2) And on the seventh day God ended his work which he had made; and he rested on the seventh day from all his work which he had made. (3) And God blessed the seventh day, and sanctified it: because that in it he had rested from all his work which God created and made.—Genesis i, 26-31; ii, 1-3.

More than two thirds of the studies for the first quarter of this year are taken from the first book of the Bible. Naturally it would suggest itself to any writer to begin this course of study by some general remarks concerning the Book of Genesis. But the limited space we have for our lessons precludes the possibility of any adequate observations on this sublime book. We must therefore content ourselves with simply remarking that Genesis is without doubt the "seed book" of the Bible. Whatever great truth or doctrine appears in any subsequent book of Holy Scripture may be traced back to this book. It is said by naturalists that there is a slender thread of fiber attaching itself to even the outermost leaves of every tree and passing down through twig, branch, limb, and trunk until it finds a place for itself in the network of roots buried in the ground from which the whole tree draws its life; that indeed the sum of these myriad fibers makes up the wood of the tree. Thus it is with the revelation of God. The roots of it all may be found in Genesis; thence stretching upward and outward, it rises into the splendid tree whose healing leaves display themselves against the sky in the last book of the Bible, called "Revelation."

The character of this book as to literature is incomparable—the most authentic as it is the most ancient and complete history of the creation extant. Its style is sublimely above compare with any other of the many ancient speculations as to the creation of the world. As to the questions of criticism now raging about this book, it is sufficient for our purpose to say, that, while it may not in every detail of its account of the creation be exactly in harmony with the latest dicta, in its general outlines it is yet in harmony with the two great sciences of geology and biology, and is at least singularly free from those grotesque errors into which all other ancient writings which deal with this great subject have fallen. It would not be fair, even from the most advanced point of scientific criticism, to say that the Mosaic account of creation was *un*scientific; at most it may be said that it is not scientific. In its record of the history of man in his progressive development on the earth, the book is full of pathetic simplicity in its details of family and patriarchal life. In it account of the revelation of God to man, the story is natural and simple, containing nothing that outrages the moral sense or shocks the imagination, as do the mythological and grotesque accounts of the intercourse of "the gods" with man (found in other religious writings, such as in India or even in Greece and Rome). Dr. Parker has well said of this account of the creation that it is (1) simple, (2) sublime, (3) sufficient.

As to the authorship of this book, we are still not ashamed to hold fast by the belief that Moses was the author of Genesis. We are content to stand with the Master in thus ascribing to Moses the work of this book. This does not forbid the possibility of the truth of the suggestion that it may be largely the work of an editor; that is, in the composition of this book Moses may have used and incorporated with his own original work traditions already extant either as stories told or preserved in writing. Certainly it is a more difficult task for the critic to point out *who* was the author of Genesis, if not Moses, than for us who cleave (not superstitiously but intelligently) to the Mosaic authorship to defend the received opinion. But whoever may have been the author or editor of the book, of this we are sure, that it was written and compiled by some man or men who wrote, wrought, and "spake as they were moved by the Holy Ghost."

Having detailed the results of the first five days of creation, and the first half of the sixth day's work, Moses approaches the climax of his preliminary account in the creation of man. The material universe is spread out before us: the earth and the water; the sun, moon, and stars; light and darkness; trees, birds, fishes, and all creeping things; also the beasts of the field. The world is made ready for man's appearance; and we now have the account of his creation.

I.—THE COUNCIL OF ELOHIM.

Hitherto the formula in which God is described as expressing his intention toward creation had been, "Let there be," etc.; but here it is changed to words more sublime, more intense, more mysterious —"Let *us* make man." This is undoubtedly remarkable as a great step in advance of anything that has before gone forth from the creative will of God. It prepares us for a climax, and as we read on we are not surprised, though we are filled with adoration by what follows.

1.—The plurality of the Godhead.—The first thing that strikes the student in this pregnant sentence is the plural form of the name of God and the corresponding parts of speech, especially the pronouns. "Let us make man in our image and after our likeness." It is true that heretofore the proper noun "Elohim" used hitherto in this chapter is also in the plural form, but it does not appear associated with plural pronouns as here. The name Elohim is the most common name given to God in the Old Testament Scriptures, being used more than two thousand times, and exclusively in this section of Genesis. Many speculations have been indulged in by scholars as to why the name is used in the plural, as it would be quite proper (unless there was a special reason) to use the singular form of the noun. Without reviewing the many learned discussions on this point, I will simply point out what seems to me the most natural and true conclusion. Having completed the inferior creation, and being now about to finish and crown the whole with a being made "in the image and likeness of God," God especially begins to give intimation as to the mysterious mode of his own being. In other words, the name and the whole form of the sentence is designed to express at once the infinite fullness of the divine Being, and also that there is a plurality of persons in the Godhead. It is certainly clear that it is foreign to Hebrew usage to adopt what we might call the dignified form of expression used by modern kings who style themselves "we," and speak of themselves as "us," and of their acts and possessions as "our." It was early believed by the Jews that there was a plurality in God, though it was not until New Testament times that the clear discovery of the triunity of the Godhead was made. But like so many other truths common to both Testaments, the imbedded truth in the Old Testament was not fully brought out till the same truth in fuller development was announced by our Lord and his apostles. We are reminded of the saying of one of the fathers, that "the Old Testament *in*folds the New, and the New Testament *un*folds the Old." The suggestion that this passage teaches the plurality of the Godhead does not stand alone upon the peculiar plural form of the noun and its pronouns. There are other intimations running all through this book. For instance, we read that "the Spirit of God moved upon the face of the waters." (i, 2.) And again we read of the "Angel of Jehovah." (Gen. xvi, 10; xxii, 11, 15, 16; xxxi, 11-13.) The truth of the triunity of "Elohim" is suggested in the beautiful benediction prescribed in Num. vi, 24-26. Here we have three times over: "The Lord bless thee;" "The Lord make his face to shine upon thee;" "The Lord lift up his countenance upon thee." The Trinity is seen in creation as well as in redemption, though it shines out more conspicuously in redemption. Still, it is of deep significance that this sublime truth is first revealed in the creation of man, as showing that redemption was not an afterthought, but was in the mind of God from the beginning. It is no argument against the doctrine of the Trinity that we cannot explain the mystery of a triune being. For that matter we are as helpless in our attempts to explain the eternity and infinity of God's existence. To say that it is irrational to think or speak of a "tripersonality" in the Godhead is equally absurd, especially when the reason for this declaration is simply that we have no experience of such a fact by which to verify the revelation. Inherently, so far as we know, there is no more reason why there should not be a tripersonality in being, than there is length, breadth, and thickness, or any other number of qualities in matter. But we have not space to discuss further this interesting and fascinating theme.

2.—The divine council.—"Let us make man in our image and after our likeness." Here is council and determination, as it were, after deliberation; and the whole form of speech intimates that an act of supremest importance is about to take place. Matthew Henry quaintly remarks that in the previous formula, "Let there be," etc., we have a declaration of authority, but in this "Let us make," etc., we have a declaration of affection. All created things belong to God: "The earth is the Lord's and the fullness thereof;" but there is a peculiar sense in which man belongs to God. He was made in his image and after his likeness. The highest mode of his existence is revealed in connection with man's creation, and on him all the wealth of God's being was lavished. Hence, when man, redeemed by the common action of Father, Son, and Holy Ghost, is converted and reconciled to God, he is baptized into the triune name of God— the Father, the Son, and the Holy Ghost. This divine council of God in connection with the creation of man easily suggests to us that man from the very beginning is the object of the greatest and tenderest care. A being brought into the world as a result of such a council will not be left to the buffets of lawless and irresponsible circumstance. God has by this very act, so to speak, bound himself to take care of man. His image stamped upon him is still there, however marred and broken by man's deliberate sin, and marks him out for God's peculiar care. Hence not a "hair of his head but what is numbered," and he is of much "more value to God than many sparrows" or the "flower of the field." How far and to what extent that care extends both in time and eternity, let the boundless mercy and much more abounding grace of God determine.

II.—THE CREATION OF MAN.

Whatever the "mistakes of Moses" may be from the scientist's point of view, it is perfectly clear that he teaches us that man as he first appeared on this globe of ours was a new creation, and not an evolution from some preëxisting creature. So far as his physical structure is concerned, there certainly are many points of similarity between him and the lower orders of the animal kingdom; but this is only another evidence that the Creator who devised the one order was also the Creator of the other. That there is unity of design throughout the whole creation does not in the least show that the modern doctrine of evolution is true, especially as applied to man. Moses teaches that man is a new creation and has no antecedent connection with the animals created in the first half of the sixth day. In the twenty-seventh verse it is distinctly stated (and that three times over) that God created (*bara*) man. This word (*bara*), the same as used in the first verse of the Bible, is never used except in the sense of calling something into existence which was not in existence before. It is, however, stated that, so far as man's body was concerned, it was formed of the dust of the ground, but not evolved out of previously existing animal life. Later scientists of the Darwinian school have now very considerably modified their conclusions as to man. Professor Allman (of the British Association) some years ago distinctly gave up the claim that the consciousness of man could be accounted for by an evolution from a physical basis; and still more recently Mr. Wallace, one of the stoutest and most radical disciples of Darwin, has admitted that there is no evidence of an evolutionary link between man and the lower animal orders, but concludes that man must be a distinct and separate creation. At any rate, so far as science can demonstrate, Moses has made no mistake in declaring that man is a creation by himself, and not an evolution.

1.—The constitution of man.—It seems clear that man is a being allied to both heaven and earth. As to his body, he was "formed out of the dust of the ground." As to his soul, it was formed of the breath of God (ii, 7); that is, even his spiritual part seems to have been a creation different in kind from the sentient nature of the lower animal creation. In this sense he is more directly the offspring of God. Certain it is that his intelligence is of a higher order than that of the beasts of the field, differing not only in degree but in kind. The spirituality of his intelligence marks him off from the beast. The moral nature of man, of which the conscience is the most marked feature, distinguishes him absolutely from the lower creatures both in degree of greatness as well as kind. But this marked distinction of man from all other creatures on this earth is fully explained in the following clause.

2.—The likeness of God.—When God announced his purpose to make man, he said, "Let us make man in our image and after our likeness." This was an honor not conferred on any other creature. So far as we know, it is an honor not heretofore conferred even on the highest angels. It is true that for a little while man was made lower than the angels (Ps. viii), that is, to occupy a lower place than angels; but it certainly was in the purpose of God that, "crowned with glory and honor," he should ultimately take his place at the very top and crown of creation. This is clearly brought out in the second chapter of Hebrews, where man and Jesus are set together and Jesus is declared to be the true type and the illustration of God's purpose in the creation of man.

"The *image* of God." What does the "image of God" mean as in distinction from "the likeness of God"? It is, I believe, the opinion of the most spiritual interpreters that "the image of God" rather refers to the ideal which God had in mind when he created man, while the likeness refers to the appearance of man or the realization of the ideal. It is utterly impossible for us to apprehend by what we know of man now what that image and likeness originally was. It has been lost in man's fall. "God created him upright, but man has sought out many inventions." Man is a temple in ruins, in which indeed there are fragments of beauty left from which we may infer a former glory now wholly departed. But it is not true *now* that man is in the image and likeness of God. That is a standing difficulty with unbelievers of a certain sort. But when they point to the idiotic face of the demented man, to the gross face of the glutton, to the sinister face of the libertine, to the half hidden smile of the hypocrite, and say, "Is this the image and likeness of God?" we answer, "No, a thousand times no." "Then what did Moses mean?" "Moses meant that man, as he came from his Creator's hand and arose from his Creator's kiss which awakened him into life and spiritual being, was in the image and likeness of God in spirituality, righteousness, and true holiness, in glorious freedom of will, and in the possession of a moral nature so unsullied and obedient that the conscience latent in that nature had not been awakened by the least wrong-doing." David was amazed that man should be assigned so high a place in the favor and purpose of God. He wondered at God's mindful care, and that he should be crowned with glory and honor. (Ps. viii.) But the author of the Epistle to the Hebrews sets the matter right when he says (quoting David's language): "We see not yet all things put under him, but *we see Jesus*, who" for the sake of man's redemption "was made" for the time being "lower than the angels, . . . crowned with glory and honor." He further declares that there exists in Jesus, "who is the brightness of" God's "glory and the express image of his person" (Heb. i, 3), a character which shall be manifested at last in every man who is recovered to God from sin and ruin, through faith in Jesus Christ, the second Adam, who himself is God's original ideal completely set forth. For the image and likeness of God we must look to Jesus and not to fallen man. God says, "This is my beloved Son. He is the firstfruits of the new redemption race, in whom my thought and purpose in the creation of man are fully realized." If, therefore, we hope to rise into the image and likeness of God, it must be through faith and living union with Jesus, and not by any self-effort to restore in our fallen nature the lost and broken image. That image can only be restored through redemption, regeneration, and sanctification, and finally by resurrection. (John iii, 5; II. Cor. iii, 18; Phil. iii, 20, 21; I. John iii, 1–4.)

3.—Man's dual nature.—Moses uses language in connection with his account of man's creation which implies that while he is one being, he is in a sense a dual being. "God created man in his own image, in the image of God created he him; male and female created he them." In the second chapter we have a detailed account of how out of the side of the man God brought forth the woman—that is, the female man was separated from the male man and placed beside him as an individual helpmeet for him. From this wonderful method of creation and final separation we have some very striking lessons. (1) That man is only complete as he is united by holy ties of marriage to woman. The twain shall be one flesh in marriage, as they were originally created one. (2) That God contemplated marriage for the purpose of replenishing or peopling the earth. (3) That marriage is an indissoluble union between one man and one woman. (4) And finally, in that God made only one man (male and female) we see the solidarity of the race. Of animals he made many kinds, but of man he only created one man, from whom he brought forth one woman, and gave to them together the sovereignty of the world.

This Paul affirms when he says that God "hath made of one blood all nations of men, for to dwell on all the face of the earth." (Acts xvii, 26.) Man scattered and divided by sin, and the antagonisms it has generated, is gathered again into oneness and common fellowship through Jesus Christ, the new head of the race. "Babel confusion is set right at Pentecost."

4.—Man's sovereignty.—This is declared to be universal over the earth, and all that dwell upon it, as well as the fish in the sea and the birds in the air. Along with this sovereignty is imposed the obligation to "subdue" the earth—that is, God gave man a commission of universal lordship over all the earth, both the animate and the inanimate creation. In part, man has fulfilled this mission, and is still fulfilling it. He is the recognized master of all living creatures. There is no beast, bird, or fish that man has not subdued to his will. The treasures of earth, buried for his use centuries and millenniums before his creation, are being made to yield themselves up to his ingenuity; the mysterious forces of nature are opening their secrets to his study and submitting themselves to his harness to do his will. No doubt sin has interfered with his perfect sovereignty, but when man comes again with the second Adam into the "new heavens and the new earth," then will this commission be fulfilled and the eighth Psalm no longer seem a mystery.

5.—Man's food.—It seems from this account that from the

beginning neither man nor beast were flesh-eating animals. God appointed for man's food everything that grew on the face of the earth—that is, every seed-bearing plant and every fruit-bearing tree as man's portion, while the leaves and grass were appointed for the other living creatures. The carnivorous habits of both man and beast seem to have been acquired after the Fall, though this is not absolutely certain.

III.—THE FINISHED CREATION.

After man's creation there was nothing more lacking in order to complete God's great work. God looked down upon the earth and "saw everything that was made, and, behold, it was very good." Hitherto, at the close of every day's work God said, "It was good;" but now that all is finished he declared it to be "good, good" (that is, very good). His finished work gave rise to a divine complacency in God. He had delight in his work, and especially in the last act of creation, for from of old "his delights have been with the sons of men." (Prov. viii, 31.) When it is said that God's work was finished, we are not to understand that God ceased to be active in the midst of creation, but only that he ceased to create new orders. If other creatures, different species, have arisen on the earth since, then they have not come by creation, but rather by generation, "natural selection," and climatic changes. So far, there may be truth in what is known as "evolution"; but of that we know not.

IV.—THE SABBATH.

"Thus were the heavens and the earth finished, and all the host of them. And on the seventh day God ended his work, . . . and rested on the seventh day, . . . and blessed the seventh day, and sanctified it." In this we have the origin of the Sabbath. We are not to understand that God rested in the sense that he was weary with his work, but that, having finished his creation, he ceased from working. This seventh day he blessed and sanctified. From that time the seventh of time became an ordinance, as the bread and wine was made into an ordinance by Jesus blessing them. God sanctified the day—that is, set it apart from ordinary days to be wholly given to him, and for man's sake. Later on, when the Sabbath-day was incorporated into the Jewish economy, the thought and fact of redemption was added to it, as we learn from Deuteronomy v, 15. Still later, when Jesus finished his divine redemption work and rose from the dead, the Sabbath-day was still further sanctified and merged into the day of resurrection and made holy to God's people.

It has been observed that it is not said of the seventh day that there was an evening to it as to the other days. This may mean that God ultimately intended all time to be the length of this Sabbath-day. Therefore, there remains unto the people of God a rest (Sabbath) (Heb. iv, 9-11), and "we which have believed do enter into it." These three great thoughts cluster about the Sabbath: Creation; Redemption; Heaven. "The Sabbath was made for man, and not man for the Sabbath." Let us therefore use the Sabbath without abusing it, and come into fellowship with God's finished work, both of creation and redemption.

II.

ADAM'S SIN AND GOD'S GRACE.—Genesis iii, 1-15.

(1) Now the serpent was more subtile than any beast of the field which the Lord God had made. And he said unto the woman, Yea, hath God said, Ye shall not eat of every tree of the garden? (2) And the woman said unto the serpent, We may eat of the fruit of the trees of the garden: (3) But of the fruit of the tree which is in the midst of the garden, God hath said, Ye shall not eat of it, neither shall ye touch it, lest ye die. (4) And the serpent said unto the woman, Ye shall not surely die: (5) For God doth know that in the day ye eat thereof, then your eyes shall be opened, and ye shall be as gods, knowing good and evil. (6) And when the woman saw that the tree was good for food, and that it was pleasant to the eyes, and a tree to be desired to make one wise, she took of the fruit thereof, and did eat, and gave also unto her husband with her; and he did eat. (7) And the eyes of them both were opened, and they knew that they were naked; and they sewed fig leaves together, and made themselves aprons. (8) And they heard the voice of the Lord God walking in the garden in the cool of the day: and Adam and his wife hid themselves from the presence of the Lord God amongst the trees of the garden. (9) And the Lord God called unto Adam, and said unto him, Where art thou? (10) And he said, I heard thy voice in the garden, and I was afraid, because I was naked; and I hid myself. (11) And he said, Who told thee that thou wast naked? Hast thou eaten of the tree, whereof I commanded thee that thou shouldest not eat? (12) And the man said, The woman whom thou gavest to be with me, she gave me of the tree, and I did eat. (13) And the Lord God said unto the woman, What is this that thou hast done? And the woman said, The serpent beguiled me, and I did eat. (14) And the Lord God said unto the serpent, Because thou hast done this, thou art accursed above all cattle, and above every beast of the field; upon thy belly shalt thou go, and dust shalt thou eat all the days of thy life: (15) And I will put enmity between thee and the woman, and between thy seed and her seed; it shall bruise thy head, and thou shalt bruise his heel.—Genesis iii, 1-15.

Genesis opens with an account of the devil's triumph over man, and so, in a certain sense, his triumph also over God; but Revelation, the last book of the Bible, closes with an account of the final overthrow of the devil, the glorious deliverance and exaltation of man, and the glory of God. The intervening books of the Bible contain an account of the progress of the conflict between the "seed of the woman and the seed of the serpent." Innumerable questions have arisen as to whether the scenes depicted before us in these verses are historical or allegorical. However this question is decided, it is clear that no canon of interpretation will allow us to compromise and say that which refers to man is matter of fact, while that which refers to the devil is allegorical. The whole must be either matter of fact or allegorical. I can see no escape (even if such an escape were desirable on any grounds) from the conclusion that the whole is the record of literal fact, any more than I see any escape from the conclusion that the temptation of Christ in the wilderness was historical and not allegorical. It does not follow that because the devil does not *now* appear before us in some physical form, that he did not so appear to our first parents, or to Christ, any more than that because we hold communion with God now by means of his written Word and prayer, that he did not in earlier days appear as the Angel of the Lord to Abraham and to Moses. That you and I were converted without a bodily appearance of Jesus before us does not impeach the truth of the story of Saul's conversion on his way to Damascus. It seems to me that the best and simplest rule of interpretation is that everything we read in the Bible is to be understood literally, unless there is something in the context which plainly intimates that the account is allegorical.

Two considerations are enough to confirm the truth of this wondrous story. First, the account here given of the origin of sin, so far as we are concerned, is so consistent with our own experience that we cannot doubt the truth of this record. Second, this story gives powerful support to, and explains the wonderful consistency of, the traditions which have been preserved among all the ancient peoples of the earth. The early Assyrians, the Chinese, the Persians, the Indians, the Arabs, the ancient Greeks, and even the Egyptians, all have their legends of the serpent tempter, and of the trees of life and knowledge. In answer to the suggestion that this Bible account has been borrowed from these ancient traditions, it is sufficient to say that any comparison of the traditions and this recorded account abundantly testifies that their traditional stories of the temptation and fall of man are but perverted accounts of that sad event, while the Mosaic account is the authentic and true one. In my recent studies of the traditions of the Hindu religion, my close and minute examination of their idols has shown to me beyond doubt that that wonderful system is all based on ancient traditions brought down from the beginning, and have in them many original elements of truth, all obscured and overlain with the grossest superstition. It is impossible for me to say more than this on these moot-points; so, accepting the story as being literally true, let us now proceed to examine it and to learn its lessons.

I.—THE TEMPTER.

This account does not pretend to solve the mystery of the origin of sin. It is evident that sin did not originate with man. It was in the universe before man's creation. This tempter, who probably approached man almost as soon as he was created, was evidently a sinner. We are not altogether ignorant of his previous history. That he was once a glorious spirit, who through sin fell from his high estate, dragging down myriads of other angels with him, is more than hinted in the Bible (see Jude, 6th verse, etc.); but this does not come within the range of our study. We have only to do with the fact of man's temptation and fall, and here we are on plain and solid ground. Man's sin was the result of a suggestion from without, i.e., by the devil, and his unhappy yielding to it from an inward impulse which responded to the outward temptation. Sin has been described as "the free and voluntary substitution of the intelligent being of his own will for the will of God." This story bears out this definition.

1.—**The serpent.**—The tempter is here called the serpent, and this serpent seems to have been one of the beasts of the field which God had created. But we are sure that the serpent, the dumb reptile, was not the real tempter. It was "the great dragon, that old serpent, called the devil and Satan, which deceiveth the whole earth." (Rev. xii, 9.) It is pretty clear, however, that this evil spirit had for the time taken possession of the serpent in order that, thus embodied, he might approach the woman to deceive her. The serpent, before the curse which fell upon it for this transgression, was likely more fascinating, insinuating, and beautiful than it is now—its powers of locomotion evidently quite unlike what they are now. However that may be, Satan got possession of the serpent and used it as his instrument. As to how the devil could get possession of the serpent, is a question that belongs to all those mysteries with which we are familiar in connection with Bible history. How did the devil enter into Judas? (John xiii, 27.) How did the demons enter into the people who were possessed in the days of our Saviour's earthly ministry? How did they enter into the demoniac, a whole legion of them, and subsequently into the herd of swine?

How will he in the latter days enter into the great Antichrist and fill him with Satanic ability, clothe him with Satanic power, and direct him in all diabolical blasphemy and wickedness? These are questions which we cannot answer, but they do not hinder us from believing the statement of fact, any more than the mystery which hangs about and over all phenomena hinders us from accepting the ascertained relative facts. There was something in the nature of the serpent which suited well the devil's purpose. He was "subtle" (clever), shrewd, insinuating, plausible, and so peculiarly available for the end in view.

2.—**Satan's method of procedure.**—Paul says in one of his epistles (warning his disciples against the devil), "We are not ignorant of his devices." (II. Cor. ii, 11.) He probably had the original temptation (by means of which he accomplished the ruin of our first parents) in his mind at the time he made use of this expression. He probably found the woman separated from Adam, possibly looking upon the forbidden tree. This was his opportunity, just as it is his opportunity now with many a young man and woman who has either strayed from or deliberately left the companionship of their natural protectors and wandered alone into the neighborhood of forbidden things which are still "pleasant to the carnal eye." "Lead us not into temptation" is a prayer which becomes suggestive as we read this story. "He said unto the woman." How could a serpent speak? And if it could by any possible means speak, why was not the woman affrighted at such a phenomenon? In answer, we suggest that it was also possible for God to confer the power of speech upon the ass that rebuked Balaam. (Num. xxii, 28; II. Pet. ii, 16.) It is not improbable that the devil can work such a miracle as this, just as he through the magicians imitated the miracles of Moses in Egypt. That Eve was not surprised or affrighted may be sufficiently accounted for by supposing that, being yet so young herself in the knowledge of the creation, it may not have seemed a strange thing that the beasts should speak as well as herself. She probably had as yet "no adequate knowledge of the settled laws of nature."

(i) *The suggestion of a doubt.* "Yea, hath God said, Ye shall not eat of every tree of the garden?" We may well suppose that there had been talk preliminary to this, but Moses has simply given us so much of the conversation as is essential to our understanding of the matter. The first move evidently was to shake her knowledge of God's word,—the suggestion that probably she was mistaken in her understanding of God's prohibition. How often it is now suggested to men and women, and especially to young Christians: "Are you sure that God forbids this or that?" "Is there any commandment in the Bible bearing on this matter?" "Or, if there is, are you sure that your understanding of it is the true one?" In the light of this device of Satan it behooves us to know our Bibles well, and to be so *sure* of what God says, that no insinuation, doubt, or suggestion from the enemy may upset us. How happy it would have been for Eve if she had just boldly said, "There is no doubt of it at all: God has positively forbidden us to eat this fruit." It is true that she did make an answer somewhat like this, but she added to the original commandment, thus showing that she was not clear as to the exact nature of the prohibition. Exact words of Scripture are most important. The ten commandments (Ex. xx) are models in this respect. There can be no doubt as to what God says in these or as to what he means.

(ii) *The denial of the truth of God's word.* Eve's answer was a fair parry to the first pass of Satan. He proceeds to another thrust at her. "Ye shall not surely *die*." This is an absolute denial of the truth of God's word. First a question as to what God has said, then a denial of the truth of his word. How we are reminded of the present condition of things in respect to the Bible! A host of men are now busily engaged in asking the question, "Yes, hath God said? Are you sure what is written in Moses and the prophets are *God's words?* Nay, are ye even sure that Moses wrote what is ascribed to him, or Isaiah, Daniel, David, or Solomon wrote what is ascribed to them, or whether John or Peter wrote the gospel and epistles ascribed to them? You certainly will not be bound by words or commands when you are not sure that God has spoken them?" We are not ignorant of his devices. When the flesh is appealed to, and when Satan's words are listened to, doubt of God's word is almost certain to be followed by a denial of it. But here is a deeper device. There is the use of a half-truth or the perversion of a truth by juggling with words. "Ye shall not surely die" in the sense of immediately ceasing to live in the body. By magnifying natural or physical death, the devil covered from Eve's eyes that more terrible death, the death of the soul, by reason of sin. What multitudes of people who are living in the fullness of physical health are going about with souls "dead in trespasses and sins" because they deliberately choose to believe and follow Satan's lie rather than God's truth.

(iii) *Attacking God's character.* The third move was to undermine the confidence and faith of the woman in the character of God.

It is certain that the woman did not fully accept Satan's view of the matter thus far, but was yet holding her ground, though, alas! still parleying with the tempter. So now he returns to the attack thus: "Suppose God has forbidden you the fruit of this tree, and even suppose that there may be a sense in which ye shall die, by throwing off the yoke of obedience to your God. It is evident that the prohibition does not rest upon his love and care for you, but is dictated by jealousy and fear of you. God is withholding good from you; he wishes to keep you in bondage to ignorance and to limit your powers; and so he frightens you by a threat of death. It is not that he wishes to protect your life, but that he wishes to deprive you of some good." Thus the argument goes. First doubt is thrown upon the word of God, then upon his truth, and finally upon the character of God, especially upon his goodness. Is not this what is whispered in the heart of every man and woman who is tempted to take of things forbidden? "Why should God forbid this? Surely it is pleasant to see, and good for food or pleasure. God is not kind to set things before us that are good and then forbid us the use and pleasure of them." "If he does so he is not a good God, and if he is not a good God I will not obey and serve him." So goes the road down to ruin. With more half-truths (which are the worst lies) Satan goes on to ply Eve with arguments. First, God knows that in the moment you eat this fruit your eyes will be opened. Yes, but to open one's eyes does not necessarily add to our happiness. How many times sin has opened our eyes to a state of misery which we did not dream of before. "Ye shall be as gods, knowing good and evil." Yes, as the angels who fell. They had been, indeed, for the time being, higher than men, and they came to know good and evil, and the end of it was that they fell from their first estate. To know good and evil no doubt seems desirable. To know good and evil as the devil knows it—a good that is forever lost, and an evil that is eternally present—is one way of knowing good and evil; to know good and evil as God knows it is another way. Divine knowledge is what God has in reserve for obedience. Satanic knowledge is the mess of pottage for which we sell our birthright when we hearken to the devil. These are the devil's arguments to this day: an appeal to "the lust of the eye, the pride of life, and to the lusts of the flesh," open eyes, to be as gods, and to know evil as well as good. Thus Satan assaulted even the Son of God in the wilderness. If we would stand against his fiery darts, let us be sure of what God says, rely implicitly on the truth, on the written Word, and in no case doubt his goodness. The devil is a liar and the father of lies, and all who hearken to him "shall surely die."

II.—THE FALL OF MAN.

We need say but little upon this subject, as the sad truth has already been essentially pointed out. But we notice briefly the following points.

1.—The progress of temptation to the end.—Through "ear gate and eye gate" Satan entered into the citadel of the human heart. First Eve hearkened to the tempter; dared to stand and parley with him, and listened to his slanderous impeachments of God's word and character; added to this, she lent her awakening desires to his tale and to his false promises. "When she saw that the tree was good for food and pleasant to the eyes, and a tree to be desired to make one wise, she took of the fruit of it and did eat." When did the devil ever tempt us with things which were repulsive to the eyes and taste, and that had in them the promise of degradation? God's "ways are ways of pleasantness, and all his paths are peace"; but the approach into these ways and paths is through obedience and the denial of the flesh. The devil's way is a hard one, and the way into it is through things pleasant to the eyes, to the flesh, and that minister to our pride. Think on these things. Whether will ye travel, over a rough way into pleasantness, or over a smooth way into roughness?

2.—She corrupts her husband.—"She did eat, and gave also unto her husband." Sin seeks companionship, and so the woman no sooner transgressed God's law than she sought to corrupt her husband, which she seems to have accomplished all too easily. At any rate, this is true, that sinners are always ready to entice the virtuous. "My son, when sinners entice thee, consent thou not." (Prov. i, 10.)

3.—The effect of the sin upon the unhappy pair.—(i) *The first effect was indeed to open their eyes to see not some thing of beauty but their own nakedness.* It was not the nakedness of the body that first overwhelmed them; that was but a reflex of the nakedness of soul which they experienced. For their guilty disobedience had torn from their souls that pure and perfect clothing of innocence and unsullied righteousness with which they were clothed at their creation. Light upon this may be found in this saying: "Neither is there any creature that is not manifest in his sight; but all things are naked and open unto the eyes of him with whom we have to do." (Heb. iv, 13.) A sense of guilt or wrong-doing always leaves us naked before God. (ii) *The second effect was that they sought to cover their nakedness: probably not from their own and each other's eyes, but* *from God.* Or it may have been, ostrich-like, they thought if they could but cover their nakedness from each other, God would not discover it. This has been the vain conceit and endeavor of sinful man ever since the Fall. Sewing together fig-leaves, or clothing ourselves in good works, such as they are, we have vainly supposed that we could hide our nakedness and cover up our sins. (iii) *They were afraid.* Why? Do not we find the answer in our own hearts? We have been brave to do wrong, and then we are afraid to meet God. "Conscience makes cowards of us all." "I was afraid because I was naked." (iv) *They hid themselves.* They first sought to cover their nakedness, and then, because they were still deeply conscious of it in spite of their fig-leaves, they were full of fear at the sound of God's voice, and they fled to hide out of his sight and get away from him. So will all sinners do in that day when they shall call upon the rocks to fall upon them and hide them from the face of the Lamb. (Rev. vi, 16.)

III.—THE CALL TO JUDGMENT AND MERCY.

These guilty sinners fled from the voice of God, whom before they had run to meet. For they had lost their innocence, their standing with God. Communion, therefore, was no longer their privilege. This they knew. There was no inward voice telling them that "with God there was mercy"; no suggestion arising out of nature that their offense would be overlooked. The sentence of death is written with the transgression; and this only did they anticipate.

1.—God's gracious call.—"Adam, where art thou?" There was a double purpose in this call. It was first to judgment and then to mercy. Alas, Adam had to answer out of that terrified conscience of his, "I was naked and I was afraid!" "Who told thee that thou wast naked? Hast thou eaten of the forbidden fruit?" God must get confession before he can declare forgiveness. To this judgment every sinner must come, either as he approaches Calvary or when he is dragged before "the great white throne," where there is no mercy. God is calling to all sinners now, that he may have mercy. Happy for sinners, naked and afraid though they be, if they answer and come confessing.

2.—The shuffling confession.—"The woman thou gavest me, she gave me of the tree, and I did eat." We do not speak of the cowardly heartlessness of this reply, but only suggest that all sinners are prone to lay the blame of their sin on some one or on something else. But every man is responsible for his own sin. The woman likewise sought to excuse herself by laying the sin on the serpent, and also indirectly on God himself. So do men now. They will charge God with being the author of evil, with having put us in the way of temptation, with failing to put forth force to save and prevent us from sin. Whereas we know perfectly well that there is nothing which a sinner so bitterly resents as to be interfered with when he is set to do evil. Should God have hedged man about so that he *could* not sin, man would have cursed God for depriving him of freedom and making him a mere machine, without option or choice.

3.—God's forgiveness.—Notwithstanding the half-hearted and disingenuous character of the confessions which both the man and the woman had made to God, he at once espoused their cause, pronounced a curse upon the serpent, and at the same time gave such a glorious promise to the sinful pair, though he spoke it not directly to them, that their hearts must have burned with the hope of new-found life within them. "The seed of the woman." Of her own body, then, was the Saviour of her soul to come. First in the transgression, she should yet be the mother of "the Saviour which should be unto all people."

4.—Conflict and judgment.—Henceforth there shall be contention between Satan and the Son of God, between the followers of this dark spirit and those who take part with Christ. The choice which men shall henceforth make will be the judgment or the separation of the race. Those who take part with Christ, to them "judgment shall go forth to victory"; to them who follow in the ways of Satan and give heed to the counsels of the devil, judgment shall go forth unto everlasting punishment. (Matt. xxv, 46.)

III.

CAIN AND ABEL.—Genesis iv, 3-13.

(3) And in process of time it came to pass, that Cain brought of the fruit of the ground an offering unto the Lord. (4) And Abel, he also brought of the firstlings of his flock and of the fat thereof. And the Lord had respect unto Abel and to his offering: (5) But unto Cain and to his offering he had not respect. And Cain was very wroth, and his countenance fell. (6) And the Lord said unto Cain, Why art thou wroth? and why is thy countenance fallen? (7) If thou doest well, shalt thou not be accepted? and if thou doest not well, sin lieth at the door: and unto thee shall be his desire, and thou shalt rule over him. (8) And Cain talked with Abel his brother: and it came to pass, when they were in the field, that Cain rose up against Abel his brother, and slew him. (9) And the Lord said unto Cain, Where is Abel thy brother? And he said, I know not: Am I my brother's keeper? (10) And he said, What hast thou done? the voice of thy brother's blood crieth unto me from the ground. (11) And now art thou cursed from the earth, which hath opened her mouth to receive thy brother's blood from thy hand. (12) When thou tillest the ground, it shall not henceforth yield unto thee her strength; a fugitive and a vagabond shalt thou be in the earth. (13) And Cain said unto the Lord, My punishment is greater than I can bear.—Genesis iv, 3-13.

The object of Moses in writing the story of Genesis (under the divine guidance) was not to give us a connected and scientific account of creation, or a minute history of the world from the beginning; but to tell us the story in outline of man in his relation to God, and the development of sin, and especially of God's purpose of grace in connection with the great redemption, which seems to have been the final cause of man's creation. Therefore there is an absence of all the intermediate details of the doings of the first pair after their fall and subsequent forgiveness by God, until after the birth of these two brothers and their growth to maturity and moral responsibility before God. In Adam and Eve we have the first man, the story of his fall and recovery, and the basis of man's approach to and acceptance with God as sinner in the first sacrifice for sin, and the clothing of their nakedness with coats made from the skin of the animal slain in sacrifice for them. (iii, 21.) The next great event, as it is brought before us, shows the great division in the human race determined by the respective attitude of the believer and the unbeliever, in presence of the sacrifice which God has provided for sin, and by means of which sinners are reconciled to God (II. Cor. v, 20), and come back to him as sons of redemption through their acceptance of Christ as the second Adam, the new head of the race. We know nothing of the childhood of either Cain or Abel. We do know that in the naming of Cain (which signifies, "I have gotten a man from the Lord") Eve seems to have believed that he was the promised seed who was to bruise the serpent's head and accomplish the redemption from sin and transgression. In this she only followed the false guidance of human reason, which always looks to nature for deliverance and not to grace. We all have this lesson to learn, that it is a transcendent Son who is the Redeemer, and a supernatural birth from above (John iii, 5) which makes us sons of God. The beginning of this lesson is set before us in our present study. God's first intimation of mercy was made to Adam as it were by prophecy (iii, 15); his second intimation as to the way of life is now made to us by type. In the first intimation the promise is in the foreground, the sacrifice in the shadow; in the second intimation the sacrifice is made prominent and the promise in connection with it is implied; from which we are to learn that we are saved both by the promise and the sacrifice—that is, the promise is our warrant, while the sacrifice is the ground of our hope and salvation.

I.—THE TWO OFFERINGS.

We must suppose, though the fact is not stated, that the law of sacrifice had been clearly made known to Adam, and that he had duly instructed his two sons in the meaning and method of it. Perhaps, as in after-time, Adam himself was the priest of his own family, and that the offerings of his sons were brought to him to lay on the altar. The time of this sacrifice is not clearly stated. The expression "in process of time" may mean simply in due course of time, when Cain and Abel appeared for the first time to offer sacrifices for themselves; or it may mean, according to the marginal translation, "at the end of the days," on the Sabbath-day, the end of the days of labor, and on the day of rest and worship. Most likely the latter. The place was probably at "the east of the garden of Eden," where the cherubim were placed, "with a flaming sword which turned every way." (iii, 24.) This was where God now dwelt as the Redeemer of men, and corresponds with the Holiest of All, where God dwelt on the Mercy-seat between the cherubim (Ex. xxv, 17–22), and later on with Calvary and the place where Christ ever "liveth to make intercession for us." (Heb. vii, 25.)

1.—The offerers.—These were the two brothers—Cain the elder, and Abel the younger, of the two sons of Adam. It is quite possible that these were not even now the only children of Adam, for he begat many sons and daughters; but these two are taken because of the peculiar and tragic circumstances connected with their offerings, and because in their case the history of the division of the race into believers and unbelievers is clearly set forth. They were representative offerers, and therefore stand, so far as the principles involved in their actions are concerned, for all men. There are but two kinds of men in the world: believers and unbelievers; men accepted on account of their faith in Christ, and men rejected because of their unbelief and rejection of Christ. Or, if it suits better the thought of some, men who believe God and obey him, and men who believe him not as rightful Sovereign of their lives, and disobey him, either through pride of reason or presumptuous defiance.

2.—The offerings.—Two offerings, differing in kind as well as in motive, are here set before us. (i) The offering which Cain brought was of "the fruit of the ground, an offering unto the Lord." (ii) The offering which Abel brought was "of the first-fruits of the flock and of the fat thereof." Before entering into any examination of these sacrifices, we may venture to remark that they were both offered as acts of worship to God. In form they were both alike. The man who afterward was rejected was apparently as pious and as dutiful as the man who was accepted. To the common eye, and I may say to the judgment of reason, they were alike true worshipers; and to many an unthinking reader it seems an evidence of pure arbitrariness on the part of God that he accepted the one and rejected the other. But this thing is being repeated before our eyes every day, as it has been repeated before God in all ages. Multitudes of Jews in after-years continued to bring their offerings to God when their hearts were far from him, and worshiped him in vain with all their sacrifices, even though of the prescribed kind. Just as also we have seen in New Testament times "two men going up into the temple to pray; the one a Pharisee, and the other a publican." Yet one was accepted and the other rejected. Both were apparently true worshipers; but one in fact was a hypocrite, and the other a broken-hearted penitent. One boasting of his good works and parading his righteousness, while the other was confessing his sin and pleading the propitiated mercy of God. So to-day who can judge between the sincere worshiper, who in his faith brings Christ with him to worship in the church, and the mere empty-headed and heartless formalist, who enters the church with Bible and hymn-book, and bows both the knees and the head in the form of prayer, while Christ is furthest from his thoughts and has no place in his heart? "Behold, to obey is better than to sacrifice." The sequel of this study will show that the real difference here was not so much in the form of the sacrifice as in the spirit of it. In the one case faith, which is obedience; in the other unfaith, which is always disobedience, however plausible it may seem to human eyes or appear at the bar of human reason.

II.—THE DIVINE JUDGMENT.

The judgments of God may be either of approval or disapproval, of acceptance or rejection. God as Judge may either be the enemy of the wicked and disobedient man, or the friend and defender of the righteous and obedient man. God judged sin in Adam in respect of the transgression of the law of obedience; and now he comes to pass judgment upon these two brothers in respect of their relations to him under a dispensation of sacrifice. By the law all men are condemned, because all men have sinned. In respect of the gospel, those who accept Christ are delivered from condemnation, while those who reject Christ have the added condemnation. This principle is set forth in the two cases before us.

1.—The accepted sacrifice.—"And the Lord had respect unto Abel and to his offering." Two questions arise here. First, how did the Lord indicate his acceptance of the offering of Abel? The answer to this may be discovered by consulting the twentieth Psalm and third verse, where the Psalmist prays: "Remember all thy offerings, and turn into ashes thy burnt sacrifice" (margin). It must be remembered that God's sign of acceptance was (at the time of the inauguration of the sacrificial service of Israel) a flame leaping from the pillar of fire (the Shekinah presence) upon the altar and consuming the sacrifice which Aaron offered. (Lev. ix, 24.) This method of divine acceptance is also testified in the following passages: I. Chron. xxi, 26; II. Chron. vii, 1; I. Kings xviii, 38. At any rate, there was some outward sign of acceptance, which Cain observed, and which led him into the state of wrath leading up to his awful deed later on. The other question is, Why was Abel's sacrifice accepted rather than Cain's? We are assured by the writer of the

Hebrews (xi, 4) that Abel offered his sacrifice by faith. Now this means "in obedience to God's word," and we gather therefrom that the offerings were not left to the whim or caprice of the offerer, but that they were prescribed by God. We know that, later on, when worship was systematized and set forth in circumstantial detail, the prescribed offering was that of a lamb or a kid from the flock (and that of the best, if not always the firstling, of the flock). (Ex. xii, 5; xiii, 12; Leviticus i, *et seq;* John i, 29; Heb. ix, 12.) This law of offering for sin upon the principle that "without shedding of blood there is no remission" was undoubtedly first promulgated in Eden. Sin can only be put away by the blood of an adequate substitute. That substitute of course is Christ, but from the beginning the type of that great sufficient sacrifice was the blood of a perfect animal selected for that purpose. Abel, then, obeyed God and brought such an offering. It is not without significance that the record says that "the Lord had respect unto Abel and to his offering." If coming to God in the way appointed for our return (that is to say, by Christ), we are to understand that we are accepted as well as the sacrifice. To come to God without the sacrifice of Christ is impossible. To plead the sacrifice of Christ without personal faith is likewise useless. The true worshiper approaches God by faith, pleading the sufficiency of the sacrifice. Not *without* faith, and not *without* the sacrifice. It is vain that Christ has died for those who have not faith. And by faith we do not mean some abstract mental condition, but such a heart toward God as leads us to believe that he is, and that he is the rewarder of them that diligently seek him; to obey him in the things concerning Christ which he has revealed to us, and to surrender ourselves to him without reserve; for all these things, faith, obedience, and surrender, are implied in the action of Abel. There must be the inward condition of the penitent sinner's heart, as well as the outward condition in the sacrifice of Christ, in order to our acceptance with God.

2.—**The rejected sacrifice.**—Now, why was Cain's sacrifice not accepted? For the very opposite reasons stated in the case of Abel. First, the sacrifice was not that prescribed by God. It is not true that it does not matter how we approach God if only we come into his presence sincerely. Cain, setting aside God's command, brought of the fruit of the ground. Not only was this not sufficient, but it is such a sacrifice as was never offered to God. The very least thing that could be offered under the law of Moses was flour mingled with oil (Lev. ii, 1)—that is, something that has been broken and bruised —and this was not allowed except in the case of the man so poor that he could not afford even two turtle-doves. (Lev. v, 11-13.) Cain's offering was therefore a distinct repudiation of the principle that sin is guilty and must either be punished or expiated with an offering which has life in it, and that life laid down. Cain was a rejecter of the atonement. He did not believe that "without shedding of blood there is no remission." He was a Unitarian in his theology. His was a religion of reason and not of revelation. His doctrine was: "It does not matter what a man believes, so he is sincere, or how he comes before God, so he comes." It was the setting up of his own will in place of the will of God, and his own thoughts in the place of God's commands. He has a vast following to-day of those who seem to be worshipers of God, but who in fact are only worshipers of their own wills. Against this error Paul has distinctly warned us. (Col. ii, 18.) But then, again, as we have just hinted, Cain's attitude toward God was as far from right as his offering was. He did not come in faith as did Abel, but in pride and self-will, recognizing no sin, or need of a sacrifice for sin, and so without penitence, obedience, or surrender. His after-actions demonstrated how far his heart was from God. A man with a false creed is apt to be a man with a false heart. There is no more dangerous error among us to-day than this very error of Cain—the error of substituting reason for revelation, and self-will for the will of God.

3.—**The wrath of Cain.**—"And Cain was very wroth, and his countenance fell." No sooner did he perceive that his sacrifice was not accepted (as was Abel's), than his heart flamed up with fierce resentment against his brother, whose only offense was that he had obeyed God and won God's approval; and possibly against God also, because his own proud self-will was rejected. No sorrow for sin here; no self-inquiry, not even an outcry, as Esau made, for a blessing also. But envy and jealousy now took the place of pride and impenitence. Well, the race of Cain is a present one until this day. Ishmael hated Isaac, and the Jews crucified Christ, even as the believers in reason, who reject revelation, are ever bitter against those who insist on coming to God through a crucified Christ. "His heart was not right with God." "God was not in all his thoughts."

III.—DIVINE INQUIRY AND REMONSTRANCE.

God is a spectator of our actions and a reader of our hearts. "Thou God seest me" should be always before our minds and hearts, especially when we come into his presence to worship. Cain had not only set God's word aside, but he had insulted him by his willful defiance and contumacy. Cain was quickly brought to book for his sin, as was Adam. Now God waits upon men, but "he is not slack concerning" his judgment; and if we are not at once called to account (as we are indeed by his word at all times) we shall soon be, in the day when God shall judge the actions and the secrets of men's hearts by Jesus Christ. We, however, notice another fact, that God is patient and gentle with sinners, even contumacious sinners, for he will have even them to be saved. So we are told that God spoke to Cain, making inquiry as to the cause of his anger.

1.—The divine inquiry.—"Why art thou wroth, and why is thy countenance fallen?" God is ever ready to remonstrate with sinners. He is long-suffering, not willing that any should perish. He remonstrated with the Jews. (Isaiah i, 18.) Jesus did so with the leaders of the people in his day; he even remonstrated and patiently sought to win Judas from his evil purpose. How God spoke to Cain does not appear; but most probably from between the cherubim (as the Lord spoke to Moses out of the burning bush). The question which he asked him was asked in mercy—just as before he had called to Adam and said, "Where art thou?"—in order first to awaken his conscience and then to give time and place for repentance. All God's summonses to us are in mercy, if we will have them so. Even when Christ at the last supper intimated that one should betray him, we detect in the words our Lord's yearning desire to awaken Judas, and to give him another opportunity to withdraw his hand from the hellish work to which he had set it. "O Israel, why will ye die?" is the refrain in all the prophecies to the ancient people. So here also God would save Cain.

2.—The divine remonstrance.—But God goes further with Cain, and sets the whole matter before him in terms of remonstrance and entreaty. It is as though he had said: Come now, let us reason together; and though your sin be as scarlet and crimson, it may yet all be made whiter than snow. "If thou doest well, shalt thou not be accepted?" You are angry with Abel and with me; but you have no occasion. You are angry because his offering is accepted and yours rejected. But it is not favoritism that has led to this. If indeed you desire acceptance, then consider. First, if you had been innocent of sin, your offering of fruit as a thank-offering would have been accepted. If, confessing your sins, you had offered the prescribed offering, as did Abel, you would also have been accepted. Even now, if you will retrace your steps and come to me in penitent mood with a sin-offering, your offering shall be accepted. Second,

"If thou doest not well, sin lieth at the door." There are two interpretations of this: first, if thou art determined to stand by thy impenitent and proud spirit, then sin croucheth at the door (of thy soul) like a wild beast ready to spring upon thee and destroy thee; second, if thou hadst done well, thou wouldst have been accepted; but if thou doest not well, then a sin-offering is at hand, and thou mayst yet recover thy lost position and be accepted. It is something like the saying of Christ to the Laodiceans: "Behold, I stand at the door and knock." God is ever patient, and even very determined sinners will not be cast off by him. A sin-offering is always in reserve for them.

3.—**Salvation and human precedence.**—Cain was the elder; he was angry that Abel (the younger brother) was preferred before him; angry as the elder brother in the parable was with his younger brother who was received with such joy by the father on his return from his prodigal wanderings. This jealousy seems to have implied that God's favor to Abel was favoritism. The Lord hastens to disabuse Cain's mind of this. That Abel is accepted in respect of his person in the matter of salvation does not give him precedence over Cain as the elder brother. "His desire shall be unto thee, and thou shalt rule over him." Our relation to God does not alter the relations which exist between men naturally and socially. The saved younger brother shall not have precedence over the unsaved elder brother. The believing servant shall still serve the unbelieving master. That we are on an equality before God in spiritual things does not upset the distinctions which exist in material and natural positions. The believer must still "honor the king" and give "honor to all to whom honor is due." The law of Christ is not that of a rampant and absurd democracy which blots out all distinction of position, honor, and respect among men. Because both master and servant are Christians, it does not follow that the master must make place for his servant at his table, or invite him into his drawing-room with his guests.

IV.—THE FIRST MURDER.

We now come to the saddest part of this dreadful story. Cain, hardened and implacable, both toward God and his brother, turns away from the tender remonstrance of the Lord, still impenitent, and with his heart still full of anger and bitterness. He lures Abel out into the field, doubtless under a false pretense of talking over the matter of the offerings, and at a convenient moment for his hellish purpose he lifts up his hand and slays his brother there. Awful tragedy! The first death was a murder.

1.—"**Where is Abel thy brother?**"—God observes the impiety of men and he takes note of their crimes. Whether Cain slew his brother in defiance of God, or in the blinded ignorance that God would take account of it, I know not. Only I know this, that sin blinds men and leads them to do the maddest as well as the wickedest things. But God takes account. Cain hated his brother, but God loved him and watched over him. He indeed suffered Cain to slay him, but he now becomes his avenger and his judge. "Where is thy brother?" will be a question asked of many a man who has not actually slain his brother, but who has hated, or, it may be, only neglected to care for him.

2.—"**Am I my brother's keeper?**"—This was the desperate answer of a man who knew he could make no defense for himself, and only sought to divert the inquiry from the direct line. It has been said that in this answer Cain showed himself a liar, in saying, "I know not;" wicked and profane, in thinking he could hide his sin from God; unjust, in denying himself to be his brother's keeper; and obstinate and desperate, in not confessing his sin. (Ps. x, 11.)

3.—"**What hast thou done?**"—This was a word, not of inquiry, but of accusation. Look at thy work, thou wicked man! "The voice of thy brother's blood crieth unto me from the ground." Thou hast silenced his voice, but his blood crieth with a voice out of every drop. The earth has soaked up his blood, but it has become a mouth out of which a voice can come. This blood cried for vengeance. The writer of the Epistle to the Hebrews has seized on this tragedy to set forth the mercy of God in Christ, whose "blood speaketh [or crieth] better things than the blood of Abel." Abel's blood cried for vengeance, the blood of Christ crieth for mercy. Abel's blood cried not in vain, so neither does the blood of Christ speak in vain. As sure as the blood of Abel brought down a curse upon Cain, so sure shall the blood of Christ bring forgiveness to those who plead it.

4.—**The curse upon Cain.**—"And now thou art cursed." This was the first curse upon man. God had before cursed the serpent and the ground, but he had not cursed Adam. Cain, however, for the accumulation of his sins, for trampling the blood of sacrifice under foot, for the defiant murder of his brother, and for his insolence to the Lord, has brought a bitter curse upon himself. This curse is threefold in its character: cursed in his soul, being doomed to carry his awful guilt unforgiven with him wherever he went;

cursed in his labor, for the earth should not henceforth ⸺ her fruit; cursed in his person, for wherever he went he was h. forth a vagabond upon the earth. How far, to what extent, thes curses shall extend in the future, we do not know; but the contemplation of it is awful enough as it stands.

5.—Cain's despair.—"My punishment is greater than I can bear." There is no penitence, no sorrow, no regret, no plea for mercy; only despair. This is characteristic of the finally impenitent. "I am tormented in this flame." (Luke xvi, 24.) The wicked must finally come under an unbearable punishment, which yet they must bear throughout eternity. (Prov. i, 24-29; v, 11.)

hellish r
Awfr'

IV.

GOD'S COVENANT WITH NOAH.—Genesi ix, 8-17.

(8) And God spake unto Noah, and to his sons with him, saying, (9) And I, behold, I establish my covenant with you, and with your seed after you; (10) And with every living creature that is with you, of the fowl, of the cattle, and of every beast of the earth with you; from all that go out of the ark, to every beast of the earth. (11) And I will establish my covenant with you; neither shall all flesh be cut off any more by the waters of a flood; neither shall there any more be a flood to destroy the earth. (12) And God said, This is the token of the covenant which I make between me and you, and every living creature that is with you, for perpetual generations: (13) I do set my bow in the cloud, and it shall be for a token of a covenant between me and the earth. (14) And it shall come to pass, when I bring a cloud over the earth, that the bow shall be seen in the cloud: (15) And I will remember my covenant, which is between me and you and every living creature of all flesh; and the waters shall no more become a flood to destroy all flesh. (16) And the bow shall be in the cloud; and I will look upon it, that I may remember the everlasting covenant between God and every living creature of all flesh that is upon the earth. (17) And God said unto Noah, This is the token of the covenant, which I have established between me and all flesh that is upon the earth.—Genesis ix, 8-17.

As we have before remarked, the Bible is not a complete history of the world, nor even of the human race. It is a history of God's dealing with our race on the basis of redemption. Hence the dismissal of Cain and his family from the main stream of the history contained in Genesis, and the continuance of the line of Seth, who was the successor of slain Abel in the line of righteousness. Hence also the exceeding rapidity and brevity with which the earlier ages of the race are passed over, the historian only touching upon those facts which are necessary to his purpose. Adam, Abel, Seth, Enoch, and Noah are brought before us, because in these men faith was kept alive, and with them God continues to deal in mercy. Noah is the third man of faith introduced to us in the gallery of heroes preserved in the eleventh of Hebrews. By faith (which is also obedience) he built the ark, and when it was finished entered into it with his family, and so was saved from the overwhelming judgment which de-

stroyed the world that then was. After the subsidence of the
he emerged from the ark as the second head of the race, thus ta
the place of Adam as the father of all living men. He occupie
however, quite another position in the world, and his relation to
God was quite different from that of Adam when first created. Noah
stands now on this new earth, not so much a created man as a redeemed man, whose relations to God were regulated by faith rather
than upon the basis of literal obedience to any law. Noah, in fact,
stood in the place Adam occupied after the promised seed of the
woman had been announced and accepted. Noah's first act after
leaving the ark was to build an altar, and sacrifice unto the Lord.
(viii, 20-22.) From this account we conclude that a regular ritual
of worship had become the established order long before the Flood
—indeed, since the days of Seth, when "men first began to be called
by the name of the Lord." The use of clean animals and birds
proves that these distinctions had been in existence before the Flood.
God accepted the sacrifice offered to him, and which came up to him
as a "savor of rest." "And the Lord said in his heart, I will not
again curse the ground any more for man's sake." This is the announcement of the beginning of that dispensation of forbearance
which characterizes all God's dealings with men since the Flood
(Acts xvii, 30; Rom. iii, 25), and which merciful dispensation we
hope is still being kept good to the heathen who have not as yet
heard the gospel. Having purposed this great purpose in his heart,
God blessed Noah and his sons, and made a covenant with them,
commanding them to be fruitful and replenish the earth, and promis-
ing them that they should have dominion over all the beasts of the
field and every living thing; giving them permission to eat the flesh
of animals, as well as the green herbs; only they were not to eat
blood, which is sacred to God because of sacrifice, that being his
part. He not only promised them protection from the beasts, but
charged them to protect each other's lives, and added the first statute
in the penal code of the world. He had already given unto them,
and to their children after them, a general promise that the world
should no more be destroyed by water, as had been done, but would
bring the earth under the sway of regular seasons and continued
seedtimes and harvests so long as the world stood.

I.—THE COVENANT.

God in his condescending mercy to man represents himself as
thinking and speaking after the manner of men, and in his dealings

hellish ... he also represents himself as adopting the methods which men adopt between themselves to insure the performance of promises and agreements. So here God speaks of, and condescends to enter into, a covenant with Noah and his sons (and with their descendants) to the end of time. A covenant is an agreement which one person enters into with another by which he promises to perform certain things specified therein. Thus has God from the beginning dealt with men: voluntarily binding himself with a promise to do certain things. Such covenants are easily recognized throughout the progress of the history of redemption. He covenanted with Adam that the seed of the woman should bruise the serpent's head, and in connection with this covenant forgave our first parents their transgression; now he covenants with Noah never more to destroy the earth with water, and to extend over him and his descendants a beneficent reign of providence; he covenanted with Abraham to bless him, and in his seed all nations of the earth, and in token gave him a son when he was old; he covenanted with Moses that when he saw the blood of the slain lamb he would pass over the children of Israel in Egypt on the dreadful night of death; again he covenanted with the children of Israel at Sinai, and confirmed his promise in respect of "the good land and large" into which he would bring them. These covenants were renewed with Joshua after the people were brought into the land. He covenanted afresh with David for everlasting mercies, called the "sure mercies," the token of which was the establishment of his house and throne forever. This covenant was reaffirmed to Israel by Isaiah and others, and the token was to be the birth of the son of a Virgin, who "should be called Wonderful, Counselor, Everlasting Father, Mighty God, and Prince of Peace." Finally, all the covenants of the past are gathered up and confirmed in Jesus Christ. In these earlier covenants we see the buds of promise gradually bursting into flower, and then, later on, the fruit appears in the person of Jesus, who fulfills them all to us.

1.—The covenanter.—The covenanter is God, the Creator. It is great condescension on the part of God to enter into covenant with man; but then this is the wondrous revelation which we have of God in the Bible, that "his delights are with the sons of men." (Prov. viii, 31.) Man is his favorite creature, honored in his creation with his own image, and now, according to God's eternal purpose, redeemed with his precious blood. When we know the purpose of grace, we are not surprised at the condescension. It is good to know that it is none else than God who enters into covenant with us, for now we are sure that there is no other to let or hinder. What

THE COVENANT.

God promises to do he is able to perform, and none can pre‐
"I, behold, even I, establish my covenant with you." No on
than I, and there is none greater besides me. So rest in quietn.
and confidence, knowing who it is that promises thee.

2.—The beneficiaries of the covenant.—I say beneficiaries, because in this case all the benefits are conferred by God himself without any equivalent given by man. Who are these beneficiaries, then? Why, first of all, Noah and his sons; and then, after them, their descendants. The promise in this covenant was the same in form with the gospel covenant, of which this indeed is an adumbration, which says, "For the promise is unto you and to your children, unto them that are afar off, even as many as the Lord our God shall call." (Acts ii, 39.) Then it includes the men of our generation, even you and me. The universality of God's gracious purpose toward sinful man is a truth which even now is hard for us to comprehend, so selfish and narrow are our ideas naturally. But from the beginning God took all men into his heart, and so when Jesus came it was said by the angel, "I bring you glad tidings of great joy, which shall be unto all people."

3.—The characteristics of the covenant.—These are (i) *Grace*. It was grace that led to the first covenant of mercy with Adam. Surely it was grace which led to this covenant with Noah in favor of all men. God purposed this ratification of the original covenant of grace with Noah and his descendants, notwithstanding he saw that the heart of man "is evil from his youth." (viii, 21.) Foreseeing the future wickedness of man, even as he had just witnessed and punished it in the past by the Flood, he nevertheless brings forward the covenant made with Adam, and reëstablishes it with Noah and with his descendants. "If God should mark iniquity, who could stand?" But there is forgiveness with him, that he might be loved and that sinners may hope in him. His covenant is based on the eternal sacrifice of Christ, and not on the goodness or merit of man. (ii) *Strength*. "I establish it." That is, I cause it to stand. He had made it with Adam in the garden; he had ratified it with Noah just before the Flood came upon the earth (vi, 18); and now, in the face of the dead world which had perished under the awful stroke of his judgment, he assures Noah and us that the covenant shall stand. Grace shall still be the rule of his dealing with man. Nothing can ever happen, either by the malice of the devil or the wickedness of man, that shall change God's mind and heart of grace toward us. (iii) *The duration of it*. This covenant shall stand forever. "It is an everlasting covenant." So long as there remains a

hellish ~~~t of Noah alive on the earth, the gracious purpose of God
Awfr~~~e mercy upon man) shall stand.

4.—The beasts fellow-beneficiaries.—So far as the particular promise that the world should no more be destroyed with water, God included the beasts of the field and the fowls of the air with Noah and his descendants, and took them all under his gracious protection. No doubt this inclusive clause was for man's sake. The beasts are for food and for service. We perhaps do not know how much of our temporal prosperity depends upon the presence of the beasts upon the earth. I would fain even hope that since they were cursed for man's sake with the earth, they might somehow be brought under the blessings of redemption; and indeed we know that in the millennial period the lion and the lamb will lie down together, and the bear and the calf shall be companions, and even the serpent shall be a playfellow of the young child. At any rate, God's goodness and provident care according to this covenant extended to all his creatures. "The Lord is good to all, and his tender mercies are over all his works."

5.—The general contents of this covenant.—I have treated it as being a part of the covenant of grace, and so I believe it to be. It is true that in this particular statement of it there is no mention made of the forgiveness of sins, or any of those things which we commonly include in the gift of salvation. But that is to be accounted for on the ground that such particulars had already been given both to Adam, and to Noah before he went into the ark. God here does but add to that. In addition to salvation from sin, God also assures man that his earthly life shall be under his special care, and that he will supply all his need. The forces of nature shall not overwhelm him again as in the Flood, the beasts of the field shall not devour him, winter's cold shall not be perpetual, nor summer's heat all the year through. The night shall come to relieve man from the wear of the day, and the day shall bring in new hope after each night. The earth shall yield her increase by seed-time and harvest. It is a good thing to know that our God takes care of the body as well as the soul, and that all earthly things pertaining to us are included in the covenant of grace. To eat one's food is as sacred as going to church or reading one's Bible. There is nothing purely "secular" to the true Christian, and the commonest material thing is spiritual under the terms of this covenant.

II.—THE SIGN OF THE COVENANT.

When God made promise to Abraham, because there was greater he confirmed it with an oath. (Heb. vi, 13-18.) The oath was the token then. The token which he gives to Noah was the "bow in the cloud." This, as it were, was the seal he set to the covenant which he made, and by which he confirmed it. Much discussion has arisen as to whether the rainbow now appeared for the first time over the earth; but it seems most unlikely that such was the case. The rainbow was doubtless a familiar object; but God now calls attention to it, and converts it to a special purpose. Its overarching splendor, seen in connection with the still dripping clouds, was a fit symbol of that forbearance which God now promises to manifest toward sinful man, and a pledge that though the clouds may drop their waters upon the earth, they shall never again deluge it. Such adaptation of an already existing thing to a special use is common with God in connection with his covenant of grace. Things having their place in nature yet in grace become symbols of the covenant. Christ did not make new elements when he gave to his disciples an assurance of his redeeming love, but took a piece of bread remaining from the supper and a cup of unfinished wine and translated them into the central ordinance of Christianity. Calling attention to "the flowers of the field," "the ravens," and "the sparrows" has turned every daisy under our feet and every bird that sings above our heads into a covenant sign that he will care for us. The corn that is sown in the ground assures us that "the incorruptible seed, the word of God," is sure to bring us life. The wind that fans our cheek reminds us of "the Spirit that bloweth where it listeth" and makes us sons of God. So now every time we look upon the bow in the cloud we are reminded that God's care for us is a matter of covenant.

1.—A token of grace and forbearance.—The rainbow is conspicuous as a sign of God's grace in the prophetic and apocalyptic visions of the Scripture. In the first of Ezekiel and the fourth and tenth of Revelation, the rainbow is seen surrounding the throne of splendor and glory, the head of the Son of God enthroned in his glory and round about the head of the angel who opens the plagues upon the earth. All this goes to suggest that the very government of God, his throne of glory, and even his judgments, are spanned and overarched by his grace. The colors of the rainbow (seven in number) have been identified with God's attributes. Every time we bow in the sky we are reminded of the name and glory of the Lord, the Lord God, merciful and gracious, long-suffering and full of goodness and truth, keeping mercy for thousands, forgiving iniquity and transgression and sin, and that will by no means clear the guilty." (Ex. xxxiv, 6, 7; Ps. lxxxv, 10; Is. liv, 7-10.) From the place of the cloud whence a moment ago flashed lightning, the thunder pealed, and the floods poured down, lo! appears the bow which tells us of forbearance and mercy. We read in this bright and glorious arch the sweet word of God: "Where sin abounded, grace did much more abound: that as sin hath reigned unto death, even so might grace reign through righteousness unto eternal life by Jesus Christ." (Rom. v, 20, 21.)

2.—**A sign to look upon.**—The bow in the cloud is something to be seen. It stood there as the pillar of cloud stood in the wilderness for the children of Israel to see—the sign of God's presence and faithfulness. Moreover, it was for God himself to "look upon." "And I will look upon it." Even as he said to the children of Israel in Egypt, "When I see the blood I will pass over you." In the midst of mercy he remembers judgment. When we see it in the clouds we know that God also looks upon it, and we are at peace. Jesus Christ is our bow in the cloud for all fullness of mercy. God looks upon the face of his anointed One, and we look to Jesus, and, behold! we see righteousness and peace kissing each other where mercy and truth are there met together. (Ps. lxxxiv, 9; lxxxv, 10.)

3.—**A pledge of remembrance.**—"And I will look upon it, and remember my covenant." Not that God is in danger of forgetting, but that he wishes us to know that he will not forget. Jesus gave us the last supper that we might bring him always to our remembrance—that is, that we might never forget his love and the fact that he has redeemed us by his death and justified us by his resurrection. God would have Noah, his sons, and his sons' sons, remember that he does not forget his covenant. God is "not unrighteous to forget" any of his promises, nor slack in fulfilling them. Let us remember his word and forget not all his benefits, and upon every remembrance of him and his covenant draw closer to him, and, walking under the shadow of his presence, give thanks.

V.

BEGINNING OF THE HEBREW NATION.
Genesis xii, 1–9.

(1) Now the Lord had said unto Abram, Get thee out of thy country, and from thy kindred, and from thy father's house, unto a land that I will shew thee: (2) And I will make of thee a great nation, and I will bless thee, and make thy name great; and thou shalt be a blessing: (3) And I will bless them that bless thee, and curse him that curseth thee: and in thee shall all families of the earth be blessed. (4) So Abram departed, as the Lord had spoken unto him; and Lot went with him: and Abram was seventy and five years old when he departed out of Haran. (5) And Abram took Sarai his wife, and Lot his brother's son, and all their substance that they had gathered, and the souls that they had gotten in Haran; and they went forth to go into the land of Canaan; and into the land of Canaan they came. (6) And Abram passed through the land unto the place of Sichem, unto the plain of Moreh. And the Canaanite was then in the land. (7) And the Lord appeared unto Abram, and said, Unto thy seed will I give this land: and there builded he an altar unto the Lord, who appeared unto him. (8) And he removed from thence unto a mountain on the east of Beth-el, and pitched his tent, having Beth-el on the west, and Hai on the east: and there he builded an altar unto the Lord, and called upon the name of the Lord. (9) And Abram journeyed, going on still toward the south.—Genesis xii, 1-9.

Let us still bear in mind that we are not studying the history of the world, but the history of redemption. Centuries have passed away since God made covenant with Noah. The world was well peopled again. The great impious and defiant confederacy at Babylon had resulted in the confusion of tongues and the scattering of the people. Europe, as well as Asia and Africa, was now peopled, and national life, with all the antagonisms of race and family, had grown apace. Noah, the antediluvian patriarch, and the father of the new world, had lived to see his posterity fall away from God in an apostasy almost as great as that for which God had destroyed the world by the Flood. And yet but one link in the chain of human life had been forged. For Noah had scarcely been buried before

Abram was born. The world was sunken in idolatry and false and superstitious religions. What will God do now? His purpose of grace has not changed. His promise to Adam has not been forgotten, nor his promises to Noah. Will he destroy the world again? No; he had promised never again to do that, even though man's "heart was wicked from his youth." How will he deal with men in grace now? Will he wink at their sin and let them take their own course, and say, "After all it does not matter; if they are sincere in their idolatry and superstition, that will be an acceptable substitute for an intelligent and faithful worship of me"? No; God will never do this. Will he call out another man, as he called Noah, and send him up and down the earth preaching righteousness, and warning and persuading men to turn from their idols to serve the living God? No; God never repeats old methods. His ways are always ways of enlargement and progress. The faith of man had failed in the family of Adam; it had failed in the followers of Seth; it had failed again in the descendants of Noah. The next step is to call out a single man indeed, and separate him from all the rest of the people, and especially from all the nations of the earth, and fence him about. In a word, he will revive the faith of Jehovah in the heart of one man, and isolate him from the world, and establish through him a nation or family to whom he will give special revelation of his will, and fence them in from the outside world with ordinances and religious ceremonies, and encourage him with exceeding great and precious promises, until a conviction of the fact of one only true and living God becomes a part of his very consciousness. The rest of the world he will leave to itself, to work out its own way and demonstrate, by universal failure in religion, in art, in literature, in philosophy, and in government, that man is not sufficient for his own highest needs. He does not forget them in the meantime, but still forbears with them, and to such as through lingering traditions of the old revelation and the voice of God in the conscience worship God and work righteousness he will give acceptance. It would be an awful thought, and one altogether foreign to the teaching of Scripture, to suppose that God has utterly abandoned the heathen world through all these long centuries. We do not know how he has dealt with them. That is a mystery not revealed to us, but we may be sure that the God of all the earth will have dealt in righteousness with the heathen nations. "Judgment is his strange work" and mercy his delight, and so I, at least I, have hope for millions of heathen men and women who have groped after God amid their darkened surroundings and have dimly found him. But our business now and henceforward is particularly with the Hebrew nation, which had its rise in the call of Abram.

I.—THE CALL OF ABRAM.

The eleventh chapter gives us the genealogy of Abram, the son of Terah, and informs us that they, father and son, were residents of Ur, which was the capital of the Chaldeans. It must have been while still in Ur that God first called Abram, though the call was renewed many years after in Haran. For Stephen tells us that "the glory of God appeared unto our father Abram when he was in Mesopotamia, before he dwelt in Charran." (Acts vii, 2.) We are left somewhat, though not altogether, to conjecture as to the circumstances which surrounded Abram. We learn from archæological research that Ur of the Chaldees was their capital city; that the worship of their idol gods was most elaborate; that the rites were not only magnificent, the addresses to their fancied deities lofty in language and sentiment, but that associated with all this splendor and even grandeur of thought were all those vile and filthy practices which seem the inevitable accompaniments of idolatry, not to speak of the human sacrifices, especially in connection with the offering of the first-born as a sacrifice for sin. Joshua especially tells his brethren that their fathers (undoubtedly in reference to the family of Abram) served idols while in Mesopotamia. (Josh. xxiv, 14.)

1.—Sovereignty and grace.—"The Lord said unto Abram, Get thee out," etc. The departure of Abram from the idolatrous land and people was not of his own motion, but because God called him. And yet we are not prepared to accept the statement that Abram was chosen of God on a purely arbitrary principle; that the only reason for God's choice of him was in his own will. I do not believe that the Bible teaches us that God ever does anything out of mere sovereignty—that is, just because there is none to instruct or to control him. God does all things truly according to his own will, but the will of God is always in wisdom and righteousness. It is true that Abram was no better as to his nature than the other heathen about him, for the children of Israel are reminded that though they boasted themselves of descent from Abram, he himself was, after all, but an Amorite, and Sarah was a Hittite (Ezek. xvi, 3); yet we can scarcely escape the conclusion that there was that in and about Abram which caused the Lord to choose him. Noah was chosen because he "found grace in the eyes of the Lord." Now even grace is not found, unless it is looked for and sought after.

God says, "Seek, and ye shall find." Noah was a man in that evil generation who, like Cornelius (Acts x), "feared God and wrought righteousness." So we must believe that in the midst of those idolatrous people Abram was such a man as Noah or Cornelius—a man who was disgusted with what he saw about him, and whose conscience gave witness to the existence of one only and true God, according to tradition still faintly heard even at this long distance from the Flood; and that, so feeling and believing, he sought God, perhaps by direct prayer or by earnest meditation. It was probably at such a time as this that the "glory of God appeared to him." Whether this was an outward manifestation, as God's coming later to Moses in a burning bush, or whether it was an inward revelation, we are not sure, but most likely the former. Even though it were only the inward working of God's Spirit with the spirit of Abram, it was such a conviction, such a persuasion of the truth concerning the reality of God's being and personal presence with him, that it amounted to an actual and visible presence. There is not the least difficulty in believing, however, that it was a visible appearance. In this there was great grace. God, as a sovereign, had the right to call Abram out from his country and to make the covenant with him which he did; and in doing so he displayed also his sovereign grace, for he need not have done so. Grace is the coming to us of God's unmerited mercy, however it comes and under whatever circumstances it comes, whether while we are seeking for it, or whether we come upon it unawares, like the man who found the treasure hid in the field.

2.—**A call to separation.**—Jehovah said to Abram, "Get thee out of thy country, and from thy kindred, and from thy father's house, unto a land that I will show thee." Separation is the first practical step toward salvation. God could not save Israel in Egypt, but out of Egypt. God could not bring the children of Israel into the land until they had put away the reproach of the wilderness from them by the sign of circumcision. "Come out from among them, and be ye separate, and I will receive you, saith the Lord," is still the law. If a sinner seeks salvation he may count on hearing the call from God—this call to separation. Forsake your old ground, forsake your unbelieving kindred, even your father's house, if they will not come with you. "Whosoever he be of you that forsaketh not all that he hath, he cannot be my disciple." (Luke xiv, 33.) That is, God cannot be Father of any soul who does not hold him to be the supreme good. If anything is loved better than God, then God cannot save, for he can only save the soul that sees in him the supreme good. This is not arbitrariness nor jealousy, in our sense of that word, on God's part, but it is a law that rests on the very nature of spiritual things. Now, we must suppose that love of country and kindred, father and mother, sisters and brothers, was strong in such a man as Abram; but God called him to leave all and follow his voice. This, at the very outset, was a strong test of Abram's sincerity, the depth of his conviction, and the reality of his faith.

3.—**The faith of Abram.**—He seems at once to have obeyed the voice of God, and left the land of the Chaldeans. Moreover, his decision to go at all hazards at God's command was so strong and determined, that he drew with him his wife, his father, and his nephew Lot. Though this first move is ascribed to Terah as the father of Abram, it is evident that the call was to Abram, and that he, and not the father, was the moving spirit in this emigration. "By faith Abraham, when he was called to go out into a place which he should after receive for an inheritance, obeyed; and he went out, not knowing whither he went." (Heb. xi, 8.) The migration of Abram was characterized by that promptness and obedience which are always the signs of true faith. "Unto a land that I will show thee." Abram had never seen the land; he did not even know the place where it was situated; he did not send up some of his servants to spy it out to see if it were a good land. He simply knew, with a conviction which amounted to reality, who it was that had called him, and obeyed, "not knowing." This is the true essence of faith. The unseen land was to him a reality, though unseen. "Now faith is the substance of things hoped for, the evidence of things not seen." Abram had this faith. That which made the migration of Abram the most notable event in all ancient history was not that he left his country and kindred and father's house to found a new home in a new country. Thousands of young men have done that in the last half-dozen centuries, and gone out to the colonies "to seek their fortunes," as the saying is. That which made the migration of Abram famous, and which led to such unprecedented results, was that it was a journey undertaken at the instance of Jehovah. To have explained this to his neighbors would have been to proclaim himself a fanatic. The motive that is hidden in faith in God is the spring of all that is greatest and best in this world. Had Abram been a mere prudent colonist, his migration would never have been noticed, nor led to the stupendous results which have followed through the generations since, and are yet to follow; but he was more than that: he was a man who believed God and obeyed him, not knowing where his obedience was to lead him. Hast thou such a faith? Does it lead thee to such sacrifices? Does it bind thee to the unseen God and the unseen world, so that country, kindred, and father's house are as nothing compared to God and the other world? If thou hast such a faith, then art thou the child of Abram, and "art blessed with faithful Abraham." If thou hast not such a faith, then it would be well for thee to examine again the ground of thy hope, lest instead of being an anchor to thy soul it should turn out to be a mere delusion or a drifting buoy.

4.—**The promise of God.**—" Now, faith cometh by hearing, and hearing by the word of God." Faith is not a blind and uninstructed passion, a mere wild, unauthorized persuasion of things without warrant or intelligent apprehension. God does not call us to any such faith, and any such faith is vain. I often hear people say, "I cannot believe." They mean they cannot have a conviction by a mere effort of the will, and this is quite true. Faith is drawn out by reliable testimony, and it is moved to action by some sufficient motive. God does not ask us to leave country, kindred, and father's house without offering instead of these things something better. He does not ask us to believe for the mere sake of believing, not even to glorify him. He always sets before us inducements to faith and obedience. He set before Abram very great promises, which he renewed again and again, amplifying and increasing them as Abram followed on after him. In this single call he embraced seven promises to Abram. (i) "*I will make of thee a great nation.*" This instead of the country he forsook. (ii) "*I will bless thee.*" This in place of any loss of fellowship or property which he might sacrifice in obeying God. Blessing both temporally and spiritually. (iii) "*And make thy name great.*" It may be that in forsaking his country and kindred he subjected himself to the derision and scoff of the people of Ur, as Bunyan's Christian did when he forsook the City of Destruction to set out on a pilgrimage to the City of God. Every man who really begins a life of faith suffers reproach for his name, but God will make the name great of him who obeys at all cost. How great a name has God given to that faithful emigrant! From all antiquity there has not come down to us so great a name as that of Abram, the "friend of God." Worthy progenitor of his great Son, to whom God has given a name above every name that is named. (iv) "*And thou shalt be a blessing.*" This is even greater than having a great name. To live to be a blessing to others is the highest possible end of life in this world. This is even the greatness of Christ, that he has given to millions of men eternal life, and been the means of blessing them with himself in heavenly places. Abram was blessed in what God gave him, but he was more blessed in what he was enabled through faith to bequeath to others. (v) "*And I will bless them that bless thee.*" (vi) "*And curse them that curse thee.*" That is, God promised that he should be a man in fellowship with whom the destinies of men should be determined. Those who favored him as the friend of God should be increased, while those who opposed him because he was the friend of God would be diminished, for such is the meaning of the word "curse" here. "He that receiveth you receiveth me, and he that rejecteth you rejecteth me." This is the meaning. Every man of faith in the world, in a sense, stands for God to other men. (vii) "*And in thee shall all the families of the earth be blessed.*" What a mighty promise was this! How far-reaching! What a window is this, through which we catch a glimpse of the wide and far-reaching purpose of God's grace even to the ends of the earth, and to the uttermost nation and family of men. And this man of faith was to be the means and channel through which this divine blessing should flow. Every believer in Christ— or true child of believing Abraham—is a streamlet in this mighty channel of blessing.

II.—THE DEPARTURE OF ABRAM.

At the first call of God Abram seems to have gone only so far as Haran, and there he abode for many years. We dare not say that this was not in accordance with the will of God. Perhaps there was an unreadiness on the part of the old father to go farther. We do not know. However, he tarried there for many years, until the "old man" died, just as many another believer has had to tarry on the borders of wider promise till the "old man" dies. Here in Haran he accumulated much wealth in cattle and in servants. Now the call of God came again, and this time Abram gathered all together "and departed from Haran," as the Lord had spoken unto him—that is, in literal and prompt obedience to God's word. He was seventy and five years old. There is never a time in our life when we are too old to hear the voice of God and to undertake new enterprises for him. Abram was blessed in that he took his wife with him, and Lot also, though he after suffered from the unbelief of both wife and nephew, yet both were righteous and, up to a certain point, believing souls; and he also carried all his wealth and servants with him. Happy man who can induce all his household to go with him in departing after the command of God! There are Christians who cannot take their stuff with them—at least, they do not—and who cannot induce their wives and husbands, their servants and their kindred, to go with them to heaven. "And they went forth to go into the land of Canaan; and into the land of Canaan they came." We may be sure that God led them on their way, for they would never have chosen to sojourn in that land and in the midst of that people.

III.—ABRAM'S SOJOURN IN CANAAN.

"And Abram passed through the land unto the place of Sichem, unto the plain of Moreh. And the Canaanite was then in the land." Surely this must have been a trial to Abram's faith. God had brought him into a land already occupied, and by a people who offered little promise to the pilgrim. The Canaanites were more repulsively idolatrous than the Chaldeans, and with nothing of the culture and refinement of that learned people. What could God mean by bringing him into this land and showing this to him? How little we know the power of God! How prone we are to interpret God and his promises in the light of circumstances, instead of interpreting circumstances in the light of God and his promise! But the Lord does not leave a man of faith long in perplexity and doubt. Whilst Abram was wondering at the situation, God appeared to him and said, "Unto thy seed will I give this land." Not "to thee," but "to thy seed." It is something that by our faith we may win an inheritance for our children. This promise of God was enough for Abram. He immediately built an altar, and took possession of the land by that sign in the name of Jehovah. Again he moved onward in a southerly direction, and again he planted the flag of Jehovah in the new altar which he built there. Still onward he moved and journeyed, going on still toward the south. The life of faith is that of a pilgrimage—building altars and going forward; pitching our tents and striking them again at God's command. It may seem to the people of sight that the Christian life is often an unsettled and inconsistent one—that it tends to make men unstable and discontented with their lot in life. Well, there is something in this; for here we have no continuing city, and there is nothing in all this world that fully satisfies the soul but God. Yet the true Christian is never dissatisfied with his lot, "having learned, in whatsoever state he is, therewith to be content." He sees another country and a city beyond the skies toward which he journeys, and the sight of these makes him more or less indifferent as to what kind of fare he has down here—"till traveling days are done."

VI.

GOD'S COVENANT WITH ABRAHAM.—Genesis xvii, 1-9.

(1) And when Abram was ninety years old and nine, the Lord appeared to Abram, and said unto him, I am the Almighty God; walk before me, and be thou perfect. (2) And I will make my covenant between me and thee, and will multiply thee exceedingly. (3) And Abram fell on his face: and God talked with him, saying, (4) As for me, behold, my covenant is with thee, and thou shalt be a father of many nations. (5) Neither shall thy name any more be called Abram, but thy name shall be Abraham; for a father of many nations have I made thee. (6) And I will make thee exceeding fruitful, and I will make nations of thee, and kings shall come out of thee. (7) And I will establish my covenant between me and thee and thy seed after thee in their generations, for an everlasting covenant, to be a God unto thee and to thy seed after thee. (8) And I will give unto thee, and to thy seed after thee, the land wherein thou art a stranger, all the land of Canaan, for an everlasting possession; and I will be their God. (9) And God said unto Abraham, Thou shalt keep my covenant therefore, thou, and thy seed after thee in their generations.—Genesis xvii, 1-9.

The course of study prescribed in this series leaves large gaps in the story of Abram,* so that the student is particularly urged to make careful study of the intervening chapters (xiii, xiv, xv, xvi). We last saw Abram beginning his pilgrimage through the land of Canaan, and on his way down into Egypt, whither he went on account of the famine prevailing in Canaan. Twenty-four years have elapsed. The course of Abram's life we may suppose was in the main a quiet one, such as would naturally belong to a great nomadic pastoral prince living in tents with his family and pursuing an "even tenor," taking care of his vast flocks and herds. However, during these years not a few stirring, even thrilling and significant, events occurred to vary the monotony, and to deepen in the mind of Abram the particular importance of his pilgrim "life of faith." First of all, we note his descent into Egypt (xii, 10 *et seq.*), which was the occasion of a lapse of his faith, the fruit of which led him

* See earlier series of "Bible Studies."

into falsehood and deceit, for which the Lord rebuked him severely, at the mouth of Pharaoh, King of Egypt, while at the same time dealing gently with him. We must not be hasty in censuring too severely these lapses on the part of God's ancient saints. The way of faith is a new way; the flesh is weak and liable to break down until the spiritual life becomes confirmed. Let those among us who have no sin first cast a stone at Abram; as for me, I will rather dwell on the patient grace of God, who, while he rebukes and chastens, yet draws his arms still closer about his poor children, whom he knows to be but dust. Coming up out of Egypt with Lot, his nephew, there arose a contention between their several herdsmen on account of the pasturage, which led to their separation, in which Abram, though the elder and the chief, acted the magnanimous part, and Lot (through selfishness) made the worse choice. (xiii.) Then follows the story of the taking of Sodom by the five kings, and the capture of Lot, followed by the rescue, organized and carried out by Abram; his meeting with the mysterious priest of the most high God, Melchizedek, and the magnificent scorn of Abram as to the riches offered to him by the king of Sodom. One can well decline to be made rich by the powers of this world after meeting with Melchizedek. At the same time, God is not slow to recognize such loyalty to himself, and he promptly showed Abram the greater wealth he had reserved for him (xv), and refreshed him with a renewal of his call and the assurance of his first promises. Abram believed God, and it was counted to him for righteousness (xv, 6); and God granted him a wonderful vision in confirmation of his faith. The sixteenth chapter is taken up with an account of a further lapse of faith (if it may be called so), which led Abram through doubt of the promise to seek a fulfillment of it in his own way. In this sad business with Hagar, his wife Sarai was the temptress and bad adviser. It is a hard lesson for us to learn that it is best and safest to wait God's time for the fulfillment of his promises. If we seek to make haste, we only retard God's working. This brings us to the chapter from which we are taking our study.

I.—THE ALMIGHTY GOD.

Twenty-four years had elapsed since God called Abram to leave Haran and become a pilgrim. Fourteen years had gone by since the birth of Ishmael. They were silent years so far as any fresh communication was concerned. Not once had God spoken to Abram in all those years. Abram had undertaken to fulfill the purpose of

God, as it were, by natural means, and God was allowing him to have his own way and to see what would come of it. It was a long, lonely time of waiting, not unmixed with great anxiety. The child Ishmael had come, but he was a wild and reckless lad, who no doubt gave his father much anxiety, and did not contribute much to the peace of the household. Had God forgotten? Had he been deceived as to his convictions? Were the appearances and interviews with Jehovah, upon which he had relied, mere dreams or imaginings? How we question our past religious experiences, no matter how real and vivid they were at the time, during long periods of loss of communion with God. But why did God keep silent so long? Perhaps to teach Abram a salutary lesson of faith. If we take our lives in our own hands and run before we are sent, it often falls out that we have to learn our folly by bitter experience. Moses ran before he was sent, and for forty years he was set aside in the wilderness, until he had learned humility and trust. But God had not forgotten. He was watching over Abram and his household, as he watched over Moses in the wilderness; as he is watching over the banished and scattered natural seed of Abraham to-day; as he is watching over many a poor, wandering child of faith who has become involved in the methods of rationalism, until the time shall come for him to speak again and restore to the right way.

1.—The appearance of Jehovah to Abram.—When faith was almost gone; when he was ninety and nine years old; when Ishmael was becoming troublesome; when Sarai was becoming unbelieving and scornful of her husband's faith—for we must believe that, though sorely tried and deeply dismayed at God's long silence, Abram still held fast by the old promises and his old experience, and through them to God, who called him out of Ur and made promise to him—for a little while God had seemed to forsake, but "with everlasting mercies" he now returned to him. Suddenly the sad and heavy heart of Abram was cheered by the reappearance near his tent of the old Shekinah glory, or perhaps an angel, or, it may be, of Melchizedek again. No matter how Jehovah appeared so he had come back again. How gladly we welcome the Lord back to our consciousness when there has been a long time of broken communion, it may be of doubt and fear, mingled with our persevering faith—that desperation of faith which holds on to God as our only hope when we can no longer justify faith by reason or demonstrate it by experience. When God seems farthest off he is often near at hand. It was so now.

2.—God's new name.—"And the Lord said unto him, I am the

Almighty God." This is the great name El Shaddai. By this name Abram had never known God, and, so far as we know, this is the first time God had ever revealed himself under this name. As Elohim, the Creator and Preserver of the world, God was known. As Jehovah the Saviour he was known, though perhaps the full significance of that gracious name was not as yet comprehended. But now God comes as "El Shaddai." Our English translation scarcely gives the full meaning of this significant name. It is not an all-comprehensive name, but it stands for that almighty power of God which transcends all the forces in the universe. In a word, it means the "wonder-working or the miracle-working God." A new era is about to begin. Hitherto God has wrought no wonders in connection with his personal dealings with men. He had made a promise to Abram which was according to nature little likely of fulfillment; he is about to renew that promise, when according to nature, as hitherto observed, it was impossible of fulfillment. Abram's body was dead and Sarai's body was dead, and yet God promises to him a seed to follow him, and through whom he is to become the father of nations. Abram had reasoned that the only possible way in which he should have a son was the way he had chosen (by Hagar); but now God appears and says to Abram, "What I promise I am able to perform." I am the Almighty. I am able to fulfill my promise to you, though the order of nature seems to be against it. Nature left alone can only do what has been done before, but nature manipulated by "El Shaddai" may bring forth new wonders continually. The proclamation of this new name for the declaration of Jehovah's supremacy in his own world is a warning to rationalists in all ages to come, that God has not imprisoned himself or fettered his power by natural law; that in fact this world is a vast laboratory of forces over and in the midst of which his free and almighty will is supreme.

3.—**Abram rebuked.**—It is impossible to read this account of God's interview with Abram without recognizing a rebuke, such an one as Jesus gave to Peter at the seaside after the resurrection. It is as much as to say, "Abram, I promised thee that thou shouldst be a blessing to nations after thee, through thy seed. I meant what I said; but thou wentest thine own way to fulfill my promise, because thou thoughtest I was not able to perform what I had promised. Because I delayed longer than seemed meet to thee, thou hast made haste to take the matter out of my hand, and appeal to nature when thou shouldst have waited on me." And are not we too often guilty of such unbelief, such vain attempts to do God's work for him, such impatience with God because he does not hasten matters as rapidly as it seems to us our need demands? Let us not blame Abram, but let us correct our own faults in this respect, and learn to trust God utterly, always believing that what he has promised he is able and faithful to perform. Especially let us never resort to doubtful means of hastening on God's purpose.

4.—Abram encouraged.—If the Lord rebuked Abram by announcing to him his new name, the same name El Shaddai contains in it vast encouragement. "I am the Almighty, the wonder-working, the miracle-working God." Let us remember that we are under the guardianship of a God whose power is as transcendent as his will is gracious. The materialistic age in which we live would have us look to nothing but blind and brutal force in nature to bring things to pass. The pantheistic teaching of the age would persuade us that the highest mode of God's being is found in man himself, and that whatever man cannot accomplish cannot be brought to pass. Deists would have us believe that God is so far away that he does not care. What say they all? It cannot rain unless the clouds are propitious. A sick man cannot get well unless nature permit. No prayer can be answered unless a combination of circumstances bring it about. No promise in the Bible is worth the paper it is written upon, unless it is in the order and course of nature to bring it about. But God's answer to these infidel notions is, "I am the Almighty." And from that time, beginning with the conception of Isaac down to the incarnation and resurrection of Christ, and onward throughout the history of the Christian Church, God has demonstrated that he is able to perform what he has promised. Let us trust him, and we shall never be confounded.

5.—Abram instructed.—"Walk before me, and be thou perfect." Here we have instruction mingled with gracious promise. To walk before God is simply to live a life of faith. If we walk in the light of our own eyes, or walk before the philosophers of this world, we will walk in many crooked ways and fall into many a pit. This is but the blind appealing to the blind for leadership. To walk before God is to walk in the path which he points out, and to hearken to the voice behind us saying, "To the right, or to the left." It was because Abram did not walk before God, but before Sarai his wife, that he blundered in the matter of Hagar. Now God has assured him respecting his ability to fulfill his promise literally, he says, "Henceforth walk before me, and thou shalt be free from such mistakes;" for this seems to be the meaning of the expression, "And be thou perfect." "Walk before me, and thou shalt walk perfectly."

God is a perfect guide to us. There can be no mistakes when we are walking before God. There may seem to be from the world's point of view, but there will be absolute perfection of way to those who walk before God.

II.—THE COVENANT RENEWED.

God's patience and grace are illustrated in this, that again and again he repeats, renews, and confirms his promises. "Believe on the Lord Jesus Christ and thou shalt be saved." This would seem to be enough; but this promise is but the echo of a thousand like it which God has left on record for us; not all indeed in the same form of words, but so varied that every difficulty and state of mind and heart may be met by the promises. So God again repeats, renews, and confirms his covenant with Abram. How gracious it is that when God brings us to book for our faults and sins he invariably dismisses us from the interview with a larger promise of his love and a clearer declaration of his purpose of grace.

1.—**The grace of it.**—Humbled and ashamed when he saw his mistake and understood God's goodness and greatness better, Abram fell on his face before God. We are reminded of Peter, who fell at the feet of Jesus and said, "Lord, not my feet only, but my hands and my head." And God talked with Abram and said, "As for me, behold, my covenant is with thee." I do not withdraw it, though thou didst not trust me in the matter of my promise. Still it is with *thee*, and I am going to confirm and enlarge it both to thee and to thy seed. This indeed is grace; but no greater than is manifested toward us daily.

2.—**A father of many nations.**—With this promise God changed Abram's name. It shall henceforth be called Abraham, and no longer merely Abram. Abram means "High Father," and so he was; but God now promises him more than personal dignity— "a father of many nations have I made thee." All God's futures are present perfects. What God promises to do is potentially done, and shall be fully realized. This has already been very fully accomplished in respect of Abraham's seed. This promise has a larger reference than to the descendants of Isaac and Ishmael, though perhaps Abraham did not then see beyond these. There is an intimation (Rom. xi, 11, 12) of the yet wider extension of this promise both through and after the gathering in of Gentile nations. There is a limited way in which every real believer becomes a father of men. The influence of sanctified, loyal, Christian character is pregnant with unborn souls. Every true believer lives not for himself, but for his influence upon others. Abram is honorable, but Abraham is a father of nations. Let us seek to be the true children of such a father of faith.

3.—**The father of kings.**—"And kings shall come out of thee." See how God can exalt a man who will "walk before" him. Not only did David and Solomon, those great kings of Israel, all their descendants, and the other line of kings come out of his loins, but the "King of kings" was of Abraham's seed according to the flesh. The greatest influence a man can exert has often appeared centuries after he has lived and died. We live for the future, not only of ourselves but of others.

4.—"**Thy seed after thee.**"—This, as we have said, no doubt has an immediate reference to his natural descendants through Isaac; but the great Apostle seizes upon this word and makes it apply with tremendous force to Christ and his spiritual descendants. (Gal. iii, 16.) "If ye be Christ's, then are ye Abraham's seed, and heirs according to the promise." (Gal. iii, 29.) We then are profoundly interested in the terms of this covenant, though we find our warrant of sonship and heirship rather in Christ the promised seed than directly through this ancient gospel covenant.

5.—"**In their generations.**"—This expression seems to carry with it the thought that in every generation the covenant now made is renewed. Each generation and each single descendant, especially those who are descended through faith in Christ, is as dear to God as was Abraham. Nevertheless we must not exalt ourselves too much above poor outcast Israel, for though they rejected the great Seed through whom these promises were made, God has not utterly rejected them, and will bring them "in again" within the covenant.

6.—**An everlasting covenant.**—Surely it is needless to argue this point. The centuries have demonstrated the truth of God's Word in this respect. Has there ever been a generation since this covenant was made with Abraham in which his seed have not been to the fore in the world's history? The dispersed natural children of Abraham, without country, home, priest, king, or genealogy, are even to-day the most important, as they are the most hated, people on the earth. The nations have failed to extinguish them and always will fail, because they are under the protection of this covenant. As for the spiritual descendants of Abraham, who has ever yet been able to destroy the seed of Christ? In vain do the secularists, the philosophers, and disputers of this world declare the failure of Christianity. God's covenant stands and will stand. For is it not an everlasting covenant, and has he not said, "I will be a God unto thee and to thy seed after thee"? He might well be ashamed of us, but he will never break his covenant.

7.—**The limited promise.**—The greater includes the less. Our particular interest in this covenant lies in the fact that Christ has become the head of it and our inheritance is through him; nevertheless, God promised to Abraham that his seed should possess the land of Canaan for an everlasting possession, and he would be their God. This no doubt refers to Israel according to the flesh. God has not cast them off, nor has he forgotten his covenant with them in respect of the land. They will yet be converted to Christ, the promised Seed, in whom the promise to Abraham stands, and shall be restored to their land. (Is. xl, lxi; Zech. ix, 11 *et seq.*) So it is with all God's great covenant promises, the greater includes the less. Jesus Christ brings us salvation and eternal life, and grants us "inheritance incorruptible and that fadeth not away"; but that also secures to us earthly blessings and pleasures. Our God is a sun and a shield, and "no good thing will he withhold from them that walk uprightly."

VII.

GOD'S JUDGMENT ON SODOM.—Genesis xviii, 22-33.

(22) And the men turned their faces from thence, and went toward Sodom: but Abraham stood yet before the Lord. (23) And Abraham drew near, and said, Wilt thou also destroy the righteous with the wicked? (24) Peradventure there be fifty righteous within the city: wilt thou also destroy and not spare the place for the fifty righteous that are therein? (25) That be far from thee to do after this manner, to slay the righteous with the wicked; and that the righteous should be as the wicked, that be far from thee: Shall not the Judge of all the earth do right? (26) And the Lord said, If I find in Sodom fifty righteous within the city, then I will spare all the place for their sakes. (27) And Abraham answered and said, Behold now, I have taken upon me to speak unto the Lord, which am but dust and ashes: (28) Peradventure there shall lack five of the fifty righteous: wilt thou destroy all the city for lack of five? And he said, If I find there forty and five, I will not destroy it. (29) And he spake unto him yet again, and said, Peradventure there shall be forty found there. And he said, I will not do it for forty's sake. (30) And he said unto him, Oh let not the Lord be angry, and I will speak: Peradventure there shall thirty be found there. And he said, I will not do it, if I find thirty there. (31) And he said, Behold now, I have taken upon me to speak unto the Lord: Peradventure there shall be twenty found there. And he said, I will not destroy it for twenty's sake. (32) And he said, Oh let not the Lord be angry, and I will speak yet but this once: Peradventure ten shall be found there. And he said, I will not destroy it for ten's sake. (33) And the Lord went his way, as soon as he had left communing with Abraham: and Abraham returned unto his place.—Genesis xviii, 22-33.

After the revelation of God's new name El Shaddai to Abraham, and renewing and enlarging the covenant with him, Jehovah further told him distinctly and definitely that he should become the father of a son in his old age, and that his own wife Sarah, who was also included in the terms of the new covenant, should be the actual mother, though she was long past the age when women become mothers, as Abraham was also past the age when men become fathers. This revelation filled Abraham with joy, so that he fell on his face and laughed. Straightway he proceeded to carry out God's command as to circumcision, which was the sign and seal of the covenant made with him, both upon his own body and those of all the males of his household.

Some little time elapsed after this, when one day, while Abraham was sitting in the door of his tent in the heat of the day, the Lord came to him again. (xviii, 1.) This time we have a definite account of how the Lord appeared to him. Abraham lifted up his eyes and looked, and, "lo, three men stood by him." These are called "men," but in fact they were three heavenly beings, who were as men to the sight of Abraham. One of them was afterward discovered to be the Lord himself, that Jehovah who had hitherto appeared to Abraham amid outward surroundings which were awe-inspiring and glorious. But now Jehovah comes to Abraham, "his friend" and obedient servant, as a man. This is the first of those "theophanies" which clearly point to the coming of the Son of God to us in the form and "fashion of a man," *permanently* incarnated in our nature. This was a temporary assumption of "the fashion of a man," but in the "fullness of time" Jehovah "was made flesh and dwelt among us, and we beheld his glory, . . . full of grace and truth." After having entertained these three strangers after the abundant manner of Eastern hospitality, "they" inquired after Abraham's wife, and made the final revelation to her and to Abraham concerning the birth of Isaac, putting all possible doubt out of mind concerning the actuality and literality of this gracious promise. In the fourteenth verse, after having rebuked Sarah for laughing (in unbelief and half derision) at the promise, the Lord reminds Abraham of the truth revealed in the great name El Shaddai. "Is anything too hard for the Lord?" Here that wonderful fact is brought out, of the Lord's great grace and condescension to Abraham: "Shall I hide from Abraham the thing which I do?" Having taken Abraham into covenant with himself, and especially given his promises concerning the nations of the earth, the Lord will not proceed further in his dealings with them without revealing his purpose to Abraham, seeing that all the nations of the earth "shall be blessed in him." It would have seemed strange that so soon after ratifying this covenant God should proceed to the destruction of a multitude of people so near Abraham's tent door without ever communicating his purpose to him. God has even taken us all into his confidence concerning his purpose of grace toward all men through and in Jesus Christ the seed of Abraham, and his judgment upon those people and nations, both as individuals and *en masse*, who continue in their wickedness and go on in their sin. Abraham had no Bible, but received his information from direct interviews with Jehovah; but we have all the benefit of those interviews and revelations which have been preserved to us, and all the subsequent revelations which God has made to his people, through his prophets and apostles, and especially through Jesus Christ himself, even down to the last revelation in which he has shown us the whole course of history down to the end of time (see especially Daniel and Revelation). If we are in ignorance of these great facts, it is our own fault. Therefore it becomes us to study our Bibles closely that we may come to know what the things are "which must shortly come to pass." Especially as God has pronounced a special blessing on those who read and hear the words of his prophecy. (Rev. i, 1–3.) Having told Abraham what he intended to do with Sodom, and why (vs. 20, 21), the Lord made as though he would join the two angels who had already gone from him and Abraham, and proceeded a little way toward Sodom (vs. 22); "but Abraham stood yet before the Lord." This would indicate that Abraham had, as it were, intervened to detain the Lord when the others had left him, and even now insisted on detaining him still further. We know why Abraham stayed the Lord. The revelation of his purpose to destroy those five cities had filled the heart of that great saint with a pity as divine as it was great; and with a holy boldness and a "humble audacity" he determined to interpose and divert the Lord from his purpose of judgment. Here is the first great outstanding instance of intercessory prayer in Scripture; and it gives us a hint both of the intimate relations which Jehovah has established with his believing people and how he has granted fellowship to them and allows them to participate in the administration of the kingdom which is to be finally inaugurated by the second coming of Christ. This truth is further enlarged and illustrated in the case of Moses and Elijah, both of whom threw themselves, as it were, between Jehovah and sinners against whom the divine wrath was kindled, and they were allowed to prevail. This is great encouragement for us to pray for men who are ready to perish. (James v, 16; Jude 21–23.) This brings us directly to the main incident of our study.

I.—CHARACTERISTICS OF JEHOVAH.

The remarkable interview of Abraham with Jehovah on this solemn occasion incidentally brings out at least three of the great characteristics of Jehovah, always in active movement in connection with his dealings with men, through all ages.

1.—The judgments of Jehovah.—In his covenant with Abraham Jehovah had promised that through him all the nations of the earth should be blessed. This is a plain intimation of his purpose of grace and mercy to all men, for he is a God that "keepeth mercy for thousands, forgiving iniquity, transgression, and sin." But this did not mean *then*, nor does it mean *now*, that he will pass over, without regard to the righteous government of the world, the deliberate and determined sins of men. Merciful and forgiving, he "will yet by no means clear the guilty." God had covenanted with Noah that he would no more visit the world with universal judgment by a flood, but he did not covenant that he would not take due vengeance upon incorrigible sinners, nor that he would not " turn into hell the wicked and all the nations that forget God." (Ps. ix, 17; l, 5, 6.) Nor has God yet ceased to be a God of judgment, for "he hath appointed a day in which he will judge the world in righteousness by that man whom he hath ordained; whereof he hath given assurance unto all men, in that he hath raised him [Jesus] from the dead." (Acts xvii, 31.) The resurrection of Christ is at once the pledge and guarantee of the believer's justification for all things and his deliverance from the curse of the law, and the certain assurance that unbelievers will be judged both for their sins against the law and their contempt of the gospel.

2.—The righteousness of Jehovah.—In Abraham's prayer for Sodom he appeals to the inherent righteousness of Jehovah, saying, "Shall not the Judge of all the earth do right?" Jehovah is essentially and eternally righteous. His mercy is based on his righteousness, so that even the forgiveness and justification of sinners cannot proceed until his holy law is fully vindicated and satisfied by the offering which Jesus made of himself under the law. His punishment of the wicked is not an act of mere arbitrary power, but of righteousness. He is too righteous to suffer sin to go unpunished. God longs after sinners to save them. Mercy is his delight, but if sinners will not be saved through the mercy of God founded on the atonement of Christ, then God himself has no alternative between ceasing to be a righteous God and punishing them. Whatever happens to men in this world or the next, when he displays his acts and subjects his past dealings to review by the whole intelligence of the universe, it will be seen that God has been just. Indeed, one of the objects for which a day of judgment has been appointed is that God may vindicate himself (we say this with deep reverence) before his whole creation. Then will every mouth be stopped, and every knee shall bow, not before an arbitrary power, but before the august justice and majesty of God's eternal righteousness.

3.—The mercy of Jehovah.—There is no revelation from God in the Bible that stands out so prominently as his mercy. This is emphasized over and over again. Judgment is said to be "his strange work," while "mercy is his delight." He doth not afflict the children of men willingly; to crush under his feet all the prisoners of the earth the Lord approveth not. (Is. xxviii, 21; Lam. iii, 33–36; Micah vii, 18.) See how now he lends his ready ear to the prayer of Abraham. Though the iniquity of Sodom was very great, so that "the cry of it had come up unto heaven," yet even while on his way to inquire into their condition, and to destroy those vile cities, he is ready to stay his hand and save, if only he might find ten righteous men among them, for whose sake he could justify himself. Behold how he spared that wicked city Nineveh, even when the prophet Jonah was so angry at his tender mercy. And has he not spared us and given space for repentance when he might have justly cut us off? And what shall we say of the mercy which bears long with the most horrible iniquity of men to-day, whose sin is still like a cry heard even to heaven? Let no man say that there is not mercy with the Lord, for with him is abundance of "goodness and truth, keeping mercy for thousands."

II.—THE PRAYER OF ABRAHAM.

The sin of Sodom was very grievous. It is described by the prophet Ezekiel (xvi, 49, 50) as follows: "Behold, this was the iniquity of Sodom, pride, fullness of bread, abundance of idleness was in her and in her daughters, neither did she strengthen the hand of the poor and needy. And they were haughty, and committed abominations before me: therefore I took them away as I saw good." Thus spake Jehovah when rebuking the sins of his own people, comparing them with those of Sodom. The nineteenth chapter of Genesis sets forth in graphic lines the depth of the wickedness of the people of that city, which now Jehovah had determined to destroy, but which his mercy was ready to spare for the sake of even ten righteous men, could they be found therein. The deep, dark, turbid waters of the Dead Sea which flowed over these buried cities was a constant monument of Jehovah's wrath in the sight of his people in all the days of their residence in that land. It is one of the beacons of warning to the persistently wicked in every age of the world. God is merciful and long-suffering. He is slow to anger, and bears long with the wickedness of men, but in the end his judgments will fall swift and terrible. The purpose of Jehovah he communicated to Abraham; and this was the occasion of the intervention of this great-hearted man of faith as set forth in the passage before us.

1.—Standing before Jehovah.—"But Abraham stood before the Lord"—that is, he interposed himself between Jehovah and the doomed cities, to plead for them. It was a very bold attitude, but one warranted by God's revelation of himself. He suffers us to come and stand before him and make all our requests known to him, and especially to plead for sinners, for "he will have all men to be saved." He does not promise that all men shall be saved because we pray for them, for as a matter of fact there are sinners for whom we pray who will not be saved, will not suffer themselves to be saved; and there are those whose sins have filled up their cup to running over, so that even with God there is no place for repentance or mercy, as it is said (Jer. xv, 1): "Though Moses and Samuel should stand before me, yet my mind could not be toward this people." "Though Noah, Daniel, and Job were in it, they should deliver but their own souls by their righteousness." (Ezek. xiv, 14.) Yet Sodom's case was not as bad as these here instanced, for God was ready even for ten righteous men to spare these grievous sinners. This boldness of Abraham, however, encourages us in "coming boldly to a throne of grace that we may obtain mercy and find grace to help in time of need" either for ourselves or others.

2.—An appeal to God's character.—In his argument with Jehovah Abraham seems to have thought, or at least acted on the supposition, that if there were righteous men in Sodom it would be foreign to God's character to overthrow the righteous with the wicked. "That be far from thee. Shall not the Judge of all the earth do right?" This is like the prayer of Jeremiah for Judah: "Do not abhor us, for thy name's sake; do not disgrace the throne of thy glory: remember, break not thy covenant with us." (Jer. xiv, 21.) This is very bold pleading, but it was very honoring to God. We would do well to remember that our best plea is God's righteous character and the inviolability of his promises. This indeed is our best and only sure hope.

3.—The ingenuity of his argument.—Beginning with a proposition that God could not in righteousness destroy the righteous with the wicked, Abraham gradually veers round, and uses the supposed righteous men in Sodom as an argument for the saving of the wicked. The Scripture encourages us to the use of arguments with God, and we are led to believe that God is well pleased when we take "words in our mouths" and come before him. He himself challenges us with arguments, and graciously allows us to do the same with him.

4.—The persistency of his prayer.—Beginning with a proposition that for the sake of fifty men who were righteous God should save the whole city of wicked sinners, and having gained that point, he will still "beat God down" to better terms. Again and again he carries his point, until he wins this promise, that if there be but ten righteous men in the city God will spare it. We are not to suppose that God was unwilling in this matter, or that he yielded reluctantly to Abraham's petition. The rather it looks as though Jehovah were only too glad to accede to these requests. In fact, Abraham underrated the mercy and long-suffering of Jehovah. He might have had his last request first had he urged it; and we are not sure that had he not ceased praying he might have finally saved that city. For when he got to "ten men" he ceased to plead, as if he himself thought it were presumption to go further. We are bidden to "pray without ceasing." There is in this incident a reminder of the fact that it was only when the sons of the prophet's widow ceased to bring vessels to receive the oil that the flow of oil ceased from the cruse in her hand (II. Kings iv, 6); and of the incident in connection with that young king of Israel who was bidden to take his arrows and smite upon the ground, and he smote thrice and stayed, when he should have smitten five or six times, and so symbolized a greater victory over the Syrians (II. Kings xiii, 18, 19). If we fail in prayer it is not in that we are too bold, or ask too much, but that we lack in boldness and ask too little.

5.—Abraham's humility.—It is very touching to note how each time Abraham asks for better things in behalf of the doomed city he gets down lower and lower before God. The more bold he is in petition, the more humble he is in position. We are very apt sometimes to confound boldness with presumption, and humility with unbelieving distance from God. As Abraham drew large drafts upon God's mercy and forbearance, the sense of his own unworthiness appeared before him, and perhaps a deeper sense or conviction of the exceeding sinfulness of the Sodomites also grew upon him, and suggested that his plea must more and more stand only in utter grace. And who among us has not experienced this feeling when we have pressed our petitions with the Lord? The more we have asked, the more the deep conviction of our utter unworthiness has come upon us. It is on the same principle that the nearer we come to the light the more faults and flaws are apparent; and after all, persistence in prayer is just coming closer and closer to God. Abraham began by standing up boldly before the Lord, and ended by prostrating himself at his feet, covered, as it were, with dust and ashes. We cannot but think what might have been the outcome had he only persevered, and finally pleaded, not the presence of righteous men, but the boundless mercy of God himself. However, it is vain to speculate further.

  6.—Abraham's unselfishness.—Abraham knew those Sodomites perhaps better even than Lot did, though living among them; yet his compassion for them was great. He did indeed plead for the possible righteous men in the doomed city, but from the first his object was to save the sinners. In one sense "holy, harmless, and separate from sinners," yet his whole heart was set upon saving them. Like his great Son Jesus, he was "the friend of sinners." The nearer we are to God the more full of compassion will we be for sinful men. The Pharisee would pass them by with scorn and contempt, but the truly righteous man breaks his heart over them. Abraham had once succored them out of the hands of their enemies; he would now deliver them out of their sins. He had fought for them; now he prays for them. We cannot long be doing good to men temporally without desiring to do the greater spiritual good for them. Christian philanthropy must end in evangelical longing.

VIII.

THE TRIAL OF ABRAHAM'S FAITH.—Genesis xxii, 1-13.

(1) And it came to pass after these things, that God did tempt Abraham, and said unto him, Abraham: and he said, Behold, here I am. (2) And he said, Take now thy son, thine only son Isaac, whom thou lovest, and get thee into the land of Moriah; and offer him there for a burnt offering upon one of the mountains which I will tell thee of. (3) And Abraham rose up early in the morning, and saddled his ass, and took two of his young men with him, and Isaac his son, and clave the wood for the burnt offering, and rose up, and went unto the place of which God had told him. (4) Then on the third day Abraham lifted up his eyes, and saw the place afar off. (5) And Abraham said unto his young men, Abide ye here with the ass; and I and the lad will go yonder and worship, and come again to you. (6) And Abraham took the wood of the burnt offering, and laid it upon Isaac his son; and he took the fire in his hand, and a knife; and they went both of them together. (7) And Isaac spake unto Abraham his father, and said, My father: and he said, Here am I, my son. And he said, Behold the fire and the wood: but where is the lamb for a burnt offering? (8) And Abraham said, My son, God will provide himself a lamb for a burnt offering: so they went both of them together. (9) And they came to the place which God had told him of; and Abraham built an altar there, and laid the wood in order, and bound Isaac his son, and laid him on the altar upon the wood. (10) And Abraham stretched forth his hand, and took the knife to slay his son. (11) And the Angel of the Lord called unto him out of heaven, and said, Abraham: and he said, Here am I. (12) And he said, Lay not thine hand upon the lad, neither do thou anything unto him: for now I know that thou fearest God, seeing thou hast not withheld thy son, thine only son, from me. (13) And Abraham lifted up his eyes, and looked, and behold behind him a ram caught in a thicket by his horns: and Abraham went and took the ram, and offered him up for a burnt offering in the stead of his son.—Genesis xxii, 1-13.

The subject of our study to-day is the most tragic event in Old Testament history. There are those in the present day whose disposition to question and deny almost everything has led them, even while professing to accept the Bible as a book of revelation, to deny the historical accuracy and even the historical character of this tragic incident, classifying it with what they are pleased to call the pious allegories of the Old Testament, in which catalogue they place the story of Jacob and his dream, and especially his conflict with the Angel of Prayer and Blessing, and Elijah's great conflict with the priests of Baal on Hermon. The author of the Epistle to the Hebrews has no sympathy with these higher critical theories, for he says distinctly that "Abraham offered up Isaac; and he that received the promises offered up his only begotten son." (Heb. xi, 17.) If this is mythical or allegorical, "mere poetry for the sake of presenting a truth," we may well fear that a faith that is established on imaginations and allegories is not sufficiently firm in foundation to rest the weight of our immortal souls upon. Accepting the story as it is written as being literally true, we have a magnificent and soul-inspiring illustration of the possibilities which lie open to a man who will trust God, not sparing the dearest idol of his heart to him when called upon to make the sacrifice. The splendor of Abraham's faith in this sublime act of obedience has justly entitled him to be called "the father of all faithful" men who have lived since his day. If, indeed, ours is a day of fuller light and ampler grace, may God grant to us at least such a faith as Abraham's—

> ". . . a faith that will not shrink,
> Though pressed by every foe;
> That will not tremble on the brink
> Of any earthly woe."

I.—THE TRIAL OF ABRAHAM'S FAITH.

This is now the fourth time that Abraham has been tried by God as to his readiness to believe his word and follow it to the end. And for the fourth time his faith is victorious. It is true that there had been temporary breaks in the patriarch's faith, but mainly in little matters. Whenever he was called upon to face a mighty trial his faith seemed to rise to the height of the test. The four trials to which we allude were: the forsaking of his country, his kindred, and his father's house to go out he knew not where, at the call of God; the second was his deliberate surrender of all worldly gain rather than receive it at the hands of the king of Sodom; the third was his giving up of Ishmael, his first-born son, on whom he had set his heart and hope for an unborn son of promise, whom, according to reason, there was no possibility of his ever receiving; and now the fourth and last great trial was the surrender of this son of promise just at a time when it was most likely that the promise of God (for which he had been waiting more than forty years) was nearing fulfillment. This trial was so great, so overwhelming, that everything else in the life of the patriarch pales beside it. When it is written "that God did tempt Abraham," we are not to understand the word "tempt" in the sense of enticing him to sin, for in this sense God tempteth no man (James i, 13); but rather in the sense of James i, 3, 12; I. Pet. i, 7. That is, God did test Abraham's faith; he put it to trial to see or to demonstrate its depth and tenacity; nay, more than this, to bring it out as gold is brought out after being passed through the assayer's fire, and is seen to be more pure and precious than ever before. So was Christ, Abraham's great Son, tested in the beginning of his ministry—cast, as it were, into the very fires of hell and into the hands of Satan; and, like Abraham, he endured the trial and came out of it, "declared to be the Son of God with power." The story is so pathetic in its brief and graphic details that to comment upon them at large would be to weaken their force. But we may indicate certain features in Abraham's faith which may be helpful for us to imitate and always to keep in mind.

1.—The suddenness of the trial.—Abraham had been called upon twenty years before (for Isaac was now probably about twenty years of age) to give up and send away from him Ishmael, the son of Hagar, to whom his heart clung even after the renewed assurance that he should have a son born to him of Sarah, his own wife (xvii, 19). In the meantime Isaac had come, and grown up in his father's tent and at his knee, a gentle, affectionate, and obedient son, the perfect contrast of Ishmael in this respect, and the old father's heart was so wholly wrapped up in him that for these twenty years his life had been as quiet as a summer's day. Not a cloud had darkened it. The late evening of his life had come, and he was at peace in the thought that in Isaac the promises of God would be all fulfilled. But now, like a flash of lightning and a peal of thunder out of a clear sky, comes this dreadful summons. "Abraham." So God called. We may easily imagine that when Abraham answered so promptly, "Behold, here I am," his heart thrilled at the expectation of some fresh communication respecting the extension of the covenant, or some instructions concerning the "son of promise," in view of his advanced age and probable speedy departure; but, alas for that old father's heart, he is suddenly called upon to part with his son— the son for whom he had waited twenty-five years, and whom he had cherished and brought up for twenty years, instructing him and filling his mind and heart with all the great things that were in store for him as the head of a long line of posterity, among whom there should be kings, and from whom nations should spring and be blessed. Without a word of preliminary warning he is called to surrender that son, and under circumstances so terrible and unlikely as almost to cause him to doubt God entirely. So it is that our most serious trials come upon us unawares, and touch us in our tenderest parts. Then we are tempted, indeed, to wonder at God's ways, if not to doubt God's care and love.

2.—**The surprise of it.**—There was not only the suddenness of this trial, but the surprise of its necessity, the reason for it, and the contradiction contained in it. There had been no hint to Abraham that after the birth of Isaac things would not take a regular and natural course. Now to be called upon to surrender Isaac, and in such a way, was a surprise greater than could be imagined. But is not this the very lesson that faith has to learn, that, having begun to live a life which has for its inspiration and authority God himself, who is unseen and unknown by this world, and whose sphere is in a region beyond the ordinary boundary of nature's laws and activities ("while we look not at the things which are seen, but at the things which are unseen"), we may expect to be called upon to face situations and do things for which worldly wisdom is not prepared; and it is one of the ends of these sudden and surprising calls of God upon us, that we be reminded that we "have here no continuing city, but look for another." A well tried and trained faith is never surprised at anything which comes to pass, for it takes account of two worlds, and of God, who is over all; while the wisdom of this world knows not God, and has no apprehension of any other world than this material sphere on and in which we live; therefore anything out of the common course of things is, and must always be, a surprise, if not a disaster.

3.—**The severity of the trial.**—"Take now thy son, thine only son, whom thou lovest, and get thee into the land of Moriah; and offer him there for a burnt-offering upon one of the mountains which I will tell thee of." How dreadful! With what cruel abruptness this commandment came! The very terms of it seem to aggravate it: "Thy son;" "thine only son, whom thou lovest." Every word, every definition of the relation of that son to his father's heart, was like a sword through and through him. To have been told that his son would die and not live would have been a cruel trial; but to tell him that he must die as a burnt-offering, and by his own hand, and at the same time to remind him of the fact that he was his son, his only son, the son of his love, was most heartbreaking. Who can read the story of those three days' journey, father and son "going together," with the innocent talk of Isaac, all in ignorance of the intent of the journey, without feeling what a world and age of agony was in it all? To hear the question of Isaac: "My father, where is the lamb for the burnt-offering?" What heroism was that which enabled Abraham calmly to answer, "My son, God will provide himself a lamb for sacrifice," all the while knowing that his own hand must be lifted up against this only-begotten and well-beloved son, to slay him. That is the cold, hard, winter of criticism which would refuse to see in this a foreshadowing of that eternal love of God which spared not his only-begotten Son, but delivered him up for us all, waking the sword of justice and smiting him that we might live. This trial of Abraham's faith in the severity of it is seen in these three particulars at least: (i) In respect of his own natural affection. To have surrendered the child under any circumstances would have been a trial, but now under these circumstances the trial is aggravated an hundredfold. (ii) In respect of the commandment itself. Abraham was not unfamiliar with human sacrifice. All through the days of his youth and manhood he had seen such sacrifices in connection with the splendid and gorgeous service of the heathen temples in Ur of the Chaldees; but we must fairly believe that his conception of God and true worship must long ere this have revolted at such a rite. The question now must have come to him: "After all, is the God for whom I left my country, kindred, and father's house like unto the false gods I have left behind me? Have I been cruelly mistaken in his character?" Such questions may have arisen in Abraham's heart. We cannot certainly say. At the same time it is not for us to condemn without qualification that conviction which lies at the back of human sacrifice. After all, was it not the sorely tried and burdened human heart seeking after a sacrifice of sufficient worth with which to come before God? And in the final one all-sufficient Sacrifice on Calvary do we not see the antitype of these earlier but mistaken attempts to meet the requirements of violated moral law? (iii) A third, and perhaps more serious, trial than either of the others must have come in the form of a suggestion as to the truth of all God's previous promises. He had been rebuked in the matter of Ishmael, because he had not accepted God's promise concerning a son in whom the covenant was to stand literally; but now God himself is about to depart from his own word, and destroy the very son upon whose life the faithfulness of the promise must stand. Such we must believe were some of the thoughts, cruel and bitter, which arose in the heart of the old hero who staggered under his heavy load and yet who "staggered not at the promise of God"—his faith rising above his doubts and triumphing over his fears, hoping against hope, and believing God to be true though all the world should be proved false. He remembered El Shaddai, and said to himself, "God will show me a way out of all this, even though he should raise up my son from the dead after I have slain him." (Rom. iv, 18-21; Heb. xi, 19.)

4.—**The necessity for the trial.**—In casting about to find out the reason (if there be one for us to know) for this sore trial of Abraham's faith, these occur to my mind. (i) That the mind and heart of Abraham might be fixed on God and not on Isaac. "In Isaac shall the nations be blessed." This was the promise of God; but, after all, Isaac was not the fountain of blessing, but God. Naturally the heart and hopes of Abraham would be more and more centered in Isaac; so now God comes and takes Isaac away from this devoted and believing father, and says to him in this terrible trial: "Abraham, I am thy God: in me is the only source of hope. Look not to Isaac. Remember what I have told you before: 'Walk before me and thou shall not make mistakes.'" Something like this, it seems to me, was the lesson God sought to teach his friend. (ii) Then, again, if Abraham should say, "Truly thou art the source and fountain of blessing, but Isaac is the channel even according to thine own appointment; and if thou takest away the channel how shall the blessing flow?" The answer to this is: "My word and not the appointed instrumentality must be the foundation and warrant of your faith and hope. Let the instrumentality go; my word remains; and so long as that word remains the promise cannot fail, even though a thousand wonders have to be wrought. Am I not El Shaddai?" (iii) Beyond this the trial was intended to develop faith to the absolute point of "believing God" in spite of all apparent difficulties. Real faith will stick at nothing, sees no obstacles which may not be surmounted and no difficulties which may not be overcome—

". . . laughs at impossibilities,
And says, 'It shall be done!'"

In this connection also we see that the sacrifice of Isaac involved the absolute sacrifice of Abraham in the sense of the utter surrender of himself to God to do his will. It would have been infinitely easier for Abraham to have laid down his own life than to have obeyed God in this matter. So faith to us means this, not only believing in the integrity and power of God, but in the surrender of ourselves to God without "if," "and," or "but." Have we such a faith?

II.—THE OBEDIENCE OF FAITH.

We have often had occasion to remind our readers that faith is the soul of man in action being directed by the word of God. In other words, it is obedience to God's word, whether that obedience involves consent of mind and heart to a truth revealed, or the obedience of the whole spirit, soul, and body to the command expressed. In this Abraham displayed his faith.

1.—It was unquestioned and prompt.—"And Abraham rose up early in the morning" and prepared for the journey. Not a word of complaint or remonstrance with God, not even of inquiry. "Abraham believed God." His heart was breaking, but he obeyed God, and that at once. He did not take a day even to prepare himself for his trial. That which is done quickly is twice done. Jonah finally obeyed God, but not until after much discipline. Moses even demurred, made excuses, and begged to be let off from the task assigned to him; but Abraham obeyed unhesitatingly.

2.—It was literal.—Once before Abraham had deviated from a literal obedience to God. He had allowed human wisdom to come in and suggest another way than that of simple literal acceptance and obedience to God; but he was cured of that tendency, and now prepares to carry out God's command, not by putting Isaac away in some monastery, or consecrating him to God in some other way—he takes wood and fire and a sacrificial knife. Unless God himself interpose to stay his hand or to say, "I did not mean that you should take my command literally," then Isaac shall be slain for a burnt-offering though his heart break in the doing of it.

3.—It was unflinching.—Many of us have begun to obey God with courage who have flinched before the performance was complete. Not so Abraham. He did not flinch even when that pathetic word from Isaac well-nigh stopped his heart: "My father, here is the wood and the fire, but where is the sacrifice?" How divinely Abraham stood his trial! How nobly he demonstrated his faith!

4.—It was heroic to the end.—Who can pretend to describe the last scene in this tragedy, when at last Abraham had to tell Isaac of God's command, and then with his own hand bind his son to the altar, unsheath his sacrificial knife, and lift it high in the air over his son! Will not his heart and faith fail? Nay, his faith stands fast to the end. It is God's command. Of this he was sure. If therefore the heavens fall, he will obey and leave consequences with God. No doubt at this point he was cheered by the remembrance of "El Shaddai." "I am the Almighty God." "Is there any thing too hard for the Lord?" Whilst lifting his hand to slay, this man of faith had a resource which the world knows not of. "Accounting that God was able to raise him (Isaac) up, even from the dead." An old negro was once told of a most startling and wonderful interposition of God in bringing deliverance, but expressed no surprise, because, he said, "It is just like God."

III.—ABRAHAM'S FAITH REWARDED.

God is not unmindful of his people's faith and obedience. If he puts us to trial he is quick to manifest his approval of our trust—I may venture to say, of his gladness for our trust. Nothing honors God as does absolute faith in his integrity and in his power to perform what he has promised. Looking at the outcome of this incident, we see how God came to the rescue of Abraham at the time when he was in the direst extremity. God's help always comes at the nick of time. Not, as a rule, until we have put our feet in the brink, do the waters part; not until we have cut loose from all human help and cast ourselves on God without appeal, does his glorious help appear. The deliverance which God wrought that day was most gratifying to Abraham, not only to him as a father, but to him as "the friend of God." It was thrilling joy to be spared the deed and spared the son, and yet at the same time to know that he had not shrunk from obedience. God's voice saying, "Now I know that thou fearest God, seeing thou hast not withheld thy son, thine only son, from me"—this was a reward worth all, that he had pleased God and proved his loyalty to him. Then the end of the matter relieved the heart of the patriarch, not alone with regard to his son, but in respect of God himself, for now he saw that the promise would not fail.

IV.—THE LESSONS OF THE SACRIFICE.

I need scarcely point these out, especially as they bear upon the greater question of the great Son of Abraham. But it is certain that here we have the foreshadowing of the sacrifice of Abraham's seed as the means of blessing. In this typical sacrifice, blended as it was with the "ram caught in the thicket by his horns," we see both the *bona fide* offering of Christ and his resurrection from the dead, together with the introduction of a substitute for man doomed to die, and yet spared because another sacrifice has been provided. In Abraham we see some faint suggestion of what it cost the divine Father to give up his Son, "his only begotten Son," to die for us.

IX.

SELLING THE BIRTHRIGHT.—Genesis xxv, 27–34.

(27) And the boys grew: and Esau was a cunning hunter, a man of the field; and Jacob was a plain man, dwelling in tents. (28) And Isaac loved Esau, because he did eat of his venison: but Rebekah loved Jacob. (29) And Jacob sod pottage: and Esau came from the field, and he was faint: (30) And Esau said to Jacob, Feed me, I pray thee, with that same red pottage; for I am faint: therefore was his name called Edom. (31) And Jacob said, Sell me this day thy birthright. (32) And Esau said, Behold, I am at the point to die: and what profit shall this birthright do to me? (33) And Jacob said, Swear to me this day; and he sware unto him: and he sold his birthright unto Jacob. (34) Then Jacob gave Esau bread and pottage of lentiles; and he did eat and drink, and rose up, and went his way: thus Esau despised his birthright.—Genesis xxv, 27–34.

After his last great trial Abraham suffered the loss of Sarah his wife, the pathetic story of which is duly recorded, with the strange fact that he had to buy a piece of land for a burial-place in the very inheritance which God had promised him. The world is now in possession of the saints' inheritance, but that inheritance is sanctified and secured by the dust of the saints buried in it. Let us not weary or worry because we do not yet inherit the earth; it shall be ours in due time. Then Abraham turned his attention to the great matter of securing for Isaac, doubly dear to him now, and doubly important in the purpose of God, a wife who should be all (and, if possible, more than) Sarah had been to him. This wife was found in Rebekah, the daughter of Bethuel, the Syrian, son of Abraham's brother Nahor, so that Rebekah was Isaac's own cousin. Isaac was forty years old when he was married, so that twenty years had passed since he had been offered to God in sacrifice. He had grown into a silent, quiet, meditative man, of whom little of note is further recorded, except that he re-opened some of the wells which his father had digged, and which his enemies had filled up. He was an easy-going man, who at the last showed that he had some spirit, especially when he was fully awake to the claims of God upon him. For twenty years he lived with Rebekah, and yet no child was born to them. The story of Sarah's barrenness was repeated in the case of her son's wife, and again a cry had to be made to God for children, even though God had promised in the covenant children to Isaac. God will yet be inquired of concerning the things he has promised, and we have again and again to learn that even the things that are included in the purpose of God are not to be taken as a matter of course. There is no room for even a modified form of fatalism in the teaching of the Bible. After prayer and waiting, two children came to Isaac and Rebekah, twins as to birth, but totally unlike in every other respect,—two sons, who were destined to be the heads of two very different and distinct families of the earth, and two families who have practically monopolized the prevailing religions of the world—that is, at least so far as the great part played by them in shaping the world's destiny—Jacob, the progenitor of the Jews through whom came Jesus, the founder of Christianity; and Esau, who was the progenitor of the great Arab people, through whom came Mohammed, the founder of the religion which goes by his name. These religions, like their remote fathers, are of close kin, and yet they have been from the beginning in bitter and irreconcilable strife each with the other. Yet as Jacob was destined by God to prevail over Esau, so Christianity is destined to prevail over Mohammedanism.

I.—THE TWO BROTHERS.

Esau was the elder of the twins by the matter of a few minutes; and yet even his primogeniture was disputed by the unconscious action of Jacob, who took hold of his heel before he was born, in which there was a prophecy of the event of our study, in which he consciously and deliberately tripped up his brother, and wrested, by fraud, the birthright from him. Jacob, the younger brother, from the beginning seems to have had either some inward presentiment of his destiny, or else some resentment against the fate which deprived him of the birthright by the seeming accident of his birth, which from his youth up put him on the alert to win by subtility and craft what he could not claim by right. Esau, on the other hand, as we are told at the conclusion of this chapter, "despised his birthright." That is, it was not to him a matter in itself which represented any value, either temporally or spiritually. Thus it often is with brothers and with men. One man covets what another despises, and the order of nature or inheritance is reversed by craft, management, and persistency on the one hand, and careless indifference on the other. As this suggestive story develops, it is impossible but that certain natural sympathies go out to Esau, while certain natural indignation is indulged against Jacob. At the same time, a deeper look at matters leads us to say, "After all, Esau did not care enough for his birthright to keep it." He was ready to barter that God-given inheritance for a mess of pottage, while Jacob did care for it, and so envied it that he was ready to sacrifice everything to get it. His methods cannot be approved, but his motive certainly was a high and noble one, and marked him out as the more admirable man of the two. Perhaps, also, if we could carry ourselves back to that time, and consider the standard of moral action by which men were governed in those days, even we would judge Jacob's methods less harshly than we do by forcing upon him the higher standards of nineteenth-century Christianity. We shall see more as we go into these interesting details. In the meantime let us take notice of the characteristic differences in circumstances and character which mark these two interesting and epoch-making brothers.

1.—Different in appearance.—By a singular freak of nature, Esau (the elder of the two) was born with a red skin so thickly and roughly covered with hair that he was outwardly more allied to the animals, which he afterward hunted, than to his human kindred. His hairy skin was not simply an unusual amount of soft, downy hair, but it was a thick coating of rough hair, so that when Jacob covered his hands with the skin of a goat Isaac did not discover the difference between that false skin and the true skin of his son Esau. It may be that this unnatural deformity had something to do with the development of the reckless spirit and wild habits of the huntsman. He may have felt that he was unfitted by nature for the softer occupations and more refined associations of the home and social circles of life. It is often the case that some physical blemish or deformity sours the disposition of the unhappy possessor, and drives him into ways and moods which would have been far from him had he been as other men. The celebrated characters of Richard III. and of Lord Byron are cases in point. On the other hand, Jacob seems to have been a well-favored and handsome man. Of the two, every one who knew them would have said, "What a pity the birthright should belong to that wild, hairy man, rather than to the well-favored and handsome younger brother!" These remarks are apropos of many cases among us to-day in this land (England) where primogeniture still obtains. The birthright and the heir often seem to be ill mated, especially in view of the better gifts and graces of the portionless younger son.

2.—**Different in temperament.**—Esau was a careless, happy-go-lucky fellow; free and easy in his manners; living, as it were, by the day; rejoicing in the wild and perilous excitement of the hunt; caring more for his dinner than for his position as head of his father's house; easy-going and good-natured; jocose in temper (as note his pun on the color of Jacob's lentiles: "Red for the red; feed me, the red man, with that red pottage"). His temperament was fickle. One day he swears an oath against Jacob's life, and the next time he meets him he has forgotten his wrath, and falls on his neck, embracing him. To-day he despises his birthright, and to-morrow he weeps bitter tears because he has parted with it. Impatient of physical discomfort, he parts with his inheritance rather than postpone his supper for half an hour. Risking his life all day long with the wild beasts of the field, he yet declares he is about to die if he be not fed at once. This is the kind of man that we admire. His very inconsistencies and weaknesses make him popular, and we are apt to say superficially, "He was much the better of the two, and it was hard lines on him that Jacob should cheat him as he did." But, after all, here is this outstanding fact: there was no seriousness of purpose in his character; no proper appreciation of his position; no real disposition to honor his father or to reverence his God. The highest gift of inheritance and the unutterable blessings of the covenant-promises of God were nothing to him. On mature thought we must admit that the birthright was not safe in his hands, and the future of the chosen people would have had a poor outlook if left to him. Now, as concerning Jacob, there is much to blame and condemn in him also. We condemn his unbrotherliness in deliberately plotting against Esau to deprive him of the birthright; the unmitigated meanness of taking advantage of his brother's weakness of character, and at a moment of supreme faintness, when he was tired, hungry, out of humor with himself, and an unlucky day of hunting, cannot commend itself to us; his cold-blooded deliberateness in causing his brother to bind himself by an oath, and thus preventing him from going back on his hasty and ill-advised bargain, makes us well-nigh despise him. These traits of character were deeply ingrained (we see them in exercise later, in the affair of Laban's sheep, and other instances). But this was not all of Jacob's character. We find him a serious, thoughtful man, fully appreciating the value of that which his brother despised, both as regarded the family estate and the heavenly inheritance. We cannot but admire his steadfastness of purpose, which all through his life amounted to a dogged determination to carry his point; even when it came to wrestling with the Angel of God, he would not forego his demand. Here was a birthright of blessing that he would have, even though he contended with God himself for it. He saw the value of the future, and made provision for it. When it came to loving, he was steadfast as a rock. How he loved Rachel! For her he counted not seven years of labor, or even other seven, as anything, and wrought on patiently in the face of much wrong. Such was the man; of thoughtful nature, deep affection, steadfastness of purpose; with all his faults yet longing for God, and looking at unseen things with a more yearning eye than upon temporal things. We cannot judge a man either by his outstanding faults or virtues. We must take the man on the all-around average. And by this method Jacob was the better and truer man of the two; infinitely more fit to be the head of the chosen nation than was Esau. If the question arises, How could God condescend to use such men as Jacob to carry out his own purposes? the reply is found in the fact that all the purposes of God are planned on the understanding that all men are sinners, and it is the glory of his grace that he can use such sinners as Jacob, and you and me. It is out of such material as God found in Jacob that he makes his saints. You might as well ask how he could use such a cursing, swearing, lying, and perjured sinner as Peter, or such a blaspheming vagabond as John Bunyan. There are some critics of the Bible who are far more righteous in their own eyes than God is; that is, they object to certain acts of God because it seems to them that the divine standard of righteousness is not high enough—at least, not so high as to please them. We are content with a God of grace, who, though holy, and always hating sin, is yet gracious, and always saving and using sinners in the way of salvation to carry forward his world-wide and universal purposes of grace.

3.—**Different in manner of life.**—Esau was a hunter. Every day he was out in the fields and forests in search of sport and game. The home, the flocks, and the domestic life were irksome to him. His tastes were not in that line. He craved and sought present excitement. Harmless and good-natured if you please, he was yet a sensualist, a pleasure-seeking man. There is no evidence that he had ever given himself up to a single day of serious thoughtfulness; that he was the heir of a great inheritance did not influence him toward the training of himself for the discharge of the high and responsible duties which that great inheritance imposed, especially on its spiritual side. He was (like many another eldest son) a pleasure-seeking lover of himself, a sportsman pure and simple, self-indulgent, petulant, impatient of the least disappointment or delay in gratifying his present whims or appetites. Jacob, on the other hand, with all his grave faults of character, was a quiet, thoughtful man, fond of home, and mindful of the highest and best things of life. No doubt he often reflected on the greatness of the inheritance which belonged of right to Esau, but for which the latter cared so little, and thought within himself how much better it would be if he were the heir. This habit of mind, no doubt working together with his ambition and somewhat loose or ill-matured moral sense, led him to plot for the acquisition of the birthright. The proposition which he made later to Esau, and to which Esau in a moment of self-indulgence acceded, leads us rather to suppose that this was not the first time Jacob had made such a proposal to him. At any rate, here were the two brothers, as different in character and calling as they were in physical traits.

 4.—Different parental relation.—Esau, bright, sprightly, easy-going, and good-natured, with more of his mother's spirit than Jacob possessed, was his father's favorite, "because he did eat of his venison." This seems a strange and puerile reason, and is more suggestive of Isaac's own character than of Esau's. However, such was the case. Jacob, more quiet and reflective, home-loving and domestic, than Esau, with a greater likeness in this respect to Isaac, though he had the grit of his mother, was Rebekah's favorite. It is not unusual that these favoritisms manifest themselves on these lines. The father loves the child best who is most like the mother, while the mother loves the child best who is most like the father. Favoritism may not be easily avoided as to natural suggestion, but it is a thing to be suppressed in a parent's heart. It has bred much mischief in families, and is not always so well overruled as in the case of Isaac's twin sons.

II.—BARGAIN AND SALE.

 We come now to consider one of the most disgraceful instances of bargain and sale on record,—a younger brother taking advantage of an elder brother's weakness of character and present distress to wrest from him the birthright of the family, and the elder brother, in order to gratify a present spasm of hunger, selling a God-given inheritance, with a laugh, for a mess of pottage, thus profanely making light of that which God had given him. Esau had been out all day in the fields hunting. It had been an unlucky day for him, and he had killed nothing. From early morning to the close of the day he had been following the shy game, and tired, faint, and hungry, he comes home, out of sorts with the day's ill luck and himself, to see Jacob quietly seated at his tent door cooking a savory mess of pottage made of lentiles. The fumes from Jacob's pot assailed the nostrils of Esau, and he made a sudden demand: "Feed me, I pray thee, with that same red pottage, for I am faint." Now, it would have been brotherly in Jacob to have at once complied with the request of his tired and hungry brother, and given it to him; ninety-nine brothers out of a hundred would have done so gladly and cheerfully under the circumstances. But this did not suit the crafty purpose of Jacob, and he turned his back upon all brotherly courtesy and good feeling, in order to score the advantage he had so long been waiting for against his brother, or rather in favor of the coveted birthright.

1.—A crafty proposition.—We must believe that this matter of the birthright had often been discussed between the two brothers. Esau had probably, more in the spirit of careless, good-natured consciousness of possession, refused to discuss the question rather than resented Jacob's advances. He did not care for the birthright in itself, but, like many a good-natured man, he was tenacious enough of his rights. But now Jacob had him at a disadvantage on his own ground. His long-waited-for opportunity had arrived to achieve his purpose. "Sell me this day thy birthright," he says to Esau, faint and hungry, and ready for anything, if he only might be fed and relieved of his present pressing hunger. Now, the birthright was a mighty thing to barter away for a mess of pottage. But Esau had never really cared for it, never rightly appreciated it; but he did care for himself. His god, by a last appeal, was his belly; he minded earthly things; and so when present gratification and future promise were in the opposite sides of the scale, the carnal man easily made the lower choice. The birthright carried with it the following privileges in ordinary circumstances: (i) the official authority of the father; (ii) a double portion of the father's property; (iii) the functions of the domestic priesthood. In this case it meant even more: (1) succession to the earthly inheritance of Canaan; (2) possession of the covenant blessings transmitted through the paternal benediction. And yet all this Jacob proposed to purchase for a mess of pottage; and all this Esau sold for that. Jacob knew Esau's practical contempt for the birthright, else would he not have made such a crafty proposal. He knew well that Esau would consider *first* the mess of pottage, and only second the birthright.

2.—**The base surrender.**—If we are indignant at Jacob for thus taking advantage of his weak and careless brother, we are more disgusted and angry with Esau for his base and heartless parting with his God-given birthright. We say finally: "Well, if Esau cared so little for it that he gave it up for a single bowl of soup, it were better in the keeping of Jacob, who valued it above all things." No indignation flashed from Esau's eye at Jacob's proposal; his lips uttered no reproach for his selfishness; nor turned he sternly away from a cruel and crafty brother, saying, "Well, if that is your game, I let you know once for all, that, though I am starving, I would rather starve and die here than give up to you that which is mine by Providence and divine right. You keep your lentiles, and I'll keep my birthright." Hear him: "Behold, I am at the point to die; and what profit shall this birthright do to me?" Its blessings are in the future of this world and of the next; my hunger is present and pressing. "A bird in the hand is worth two in the bush." After all, I may never come into it. I may be killed in the field any day and miss the birthright; or if I keep it it is not to my taste to go about looking after estates and dreaming of future generations and covenant blessings. What I know now is that I am hungry, and feel as though I would die if I do not get something to eat at once. I can't wait to have my dinner cooked. "Let us eat and drink, for to-morrow we die," is my philosophy just at this moment; so take the birthright, and much good may it do you, and give me your savory soup. This is Esau. This is the worldly man to-day. The present! the present! The future is dim and misty; the present is real and pressing. The man of faith discounts the present for the future; the man of Esau's kind discounts and even parts with the future, so far as the good there is in it, altogether for the present.

3.—**The unholy oath.**—Jacob knew his brother, and feared that after he had revived a little he would repent his bargain, and repudiate it. Jacob was too thorough-going a man not to have things *fixed*. "An oath for confirmation is the end of all controversy." So an oath he exacted. Esau gave the oath as readily as he had parted with the birthright, though had he cared a rush for it the very suggestion of the oath would have aroused him to the dastardly thing he was doing. Judas betrayed his Master with a kiss, but Esau sold his birthright and confirmed the bargain with an oath. No wonder he is called in the Epistle to the Hebrews a "profane person" (Heb. xii, 16), and is alluded to by Paul as "an enemy of the cross of Christ." (Phil. iii, 18, 19.)

4.—The despised birthright.—Esau drank his soup, wiped his mouth, rose up, and went his way. Thus Esau despised his birthright. Thus are many doing to-day—trading heaven for a mess of pottage, the wealth of God's grace for a day's carnal enjoyment. They too are going their own way. But "there is a way which" etc. (Prov. xiv, 12.)

X.

JACOB AT BETHEL.—Genesis xxviii, 10–22.

(10) And Jacob went out from Beersheba, and went toward Haran. (11) And he lighted upon a certain place, and tarried there all night, because the sun was set; and he took of the stones of that place, and put them for his pillows, and lay down in that place to sleep. (12) And he dreamed, and behold a ladder set up on the earth, and the top of it reached to heaven: and behold the angels of God ascending and descending on it. (13) And, behold, the Lord stood above it, and said, I am the Lord God of Abraham thy father, and the God of Isaac: the land whereon thou liest, to thee will I give it, and to thy seed; (14) And thy seed shall be as the dust of the earth, and thou shalt spread abroad to the west, and to the east, and to the north, and to the south: and in thee and in thy seed shall all the families of the earth be blessed. (15) And, behold, I am with thee, and will keep thee in all places whither thou goest, and will bring thee again into this land; for I will not leave thee, until I have done that which I have spoken to thee of. (16) And Jacob awaked out of his sleep, and he said, Surely the Lord is in this place; and I knew it not. (17) And he was afraid, and said, How dreadful is this place! this is none other but the house of God, and this is the gate of heaven. (18) And Jacob rose up early in the morning, and took the stone that he had put for his pillows, and set it up for a pillar, and poured oil upon the top of it. (19) And he called the name of that place Beth-el: but the name of that city was called Luz at the first. (20) And Jacob vowed a vow, saying, If God will be with me, and will keep me in this way that I go, and will give me bread to eat, and raiment to put on, (21) So that I come again to my father's house in peace; then shall the Lord be my God: (22) And this stone, which I have set for a pillar, shall be God's house: and of all that thou shalt give me I will surely give the tenth unto thee.—Genesis xxviii, 10–22.

The covenant blessing promised to Abraham and confirmed in Isaac had now passed to Jacob over Esau, the firstborn, who "despised his birthright." (Gen. xxvii, 27, 28; xxviii, 1.) We cannot admire the way in which Jacob obtained this blessing, which nevertheless God had meant for him from the beginning. (Rom. ix, 12, 13.) Had he waited upon Jehovah, God would have brought it about in his own way; but (like Abraham, his grandfather) he sought to fulfill God's purpose by wrong means. It is true, God accepted the result of Jacob's trickery, but he did not approve it; and, moreover, the consequences of this fraud followed him during his whole life. Later on he himself was the victim of fraud and roguery on the part of Laban, when he caused Leah to come in to him disguised as Rachel. (Gen. xxix, 23, 25; see also xxxi, 7.) "Whatsoever a man soweth, that shall he also reap." Jacob never got rid of the bad conscience which his practice of deception and fraud brought upon him. Let us not be deceived. Should God never use or permit wickedness, and overrule it for his gracious ends, it would appear that wickedness and sin were something beyond his power and control. God was not responsible for the sin of Pharaoh, Judas, Pilate, or the "wicked hands" of the Jews who caused Jesus to be crucified, yet he used all these wicked things and wicked men to carry forward his own blessed work of grace, thus showing that he is supreme and that grace is triumphant over sin, and even brings it into subjection, and compels it to serve the holiness of God.

When Esau saw that linked with the despised birthright went his father's blessing, he "hated Jacob" his brother, and then planned to murder him. Here is the old Cain spirit. He had no faith to choose the birthright and the covenant blessing, but when he saw that which he had flung away for a mess of pottage pass to another, then he was angry. There is no hint that he was angry with himself, or sorry that he had despised God's promises, but only regret that he had lost some good thing himself. Fearing the vengeance of his brother (and justly), and yielding to his mother's advice, Jacob departed by command of his father into the country of his uncle Laban. The mother had shrewdly brought this about out of love for her favorite son.

I.—JACOB THE PILGRIM.

Evil deeds bring their recompense, in part, at least, even in this world, and that after the sin underlying them may have been forgiven. Jacob was now practically a fugitive from his own home—banished, to all intents and purposes. He had his father's blessing, it is true, but he is virtually cast out of his father's house. Had it not been for his double dealing with Esau and with Isaac, the most natural thing in the world would have been that Isaac should have sent to Laban for Rachel, as his father Abraham had sent for Rebekah. We can well imagine that this journey of Jacob's was not a very cheerful one. Sorrowful, and let us hope, penitent thoughts were in his mind. He was a man of intense domestic instincts.

He loved his home, and was loth to leave it. Perhaps he was thinking, "After all, will my father's blessing with the birthright, secured as I have secured it, be of any good to me?" Perhaps also amid these forebodings his heart may have turned to God; for Jacob was at bottom a man who truly feared God, and valued his blessing more than anything else. Had he not schemed to get it? But he was doubting now whether this Jesuitical system of his was wise, not to say *honest*. Would God forsake him and leave him to be forever a wanderer from home, perhaps the victim of other men's fraud and wickedness? Surely that was a most uncomfortable day's journey from home. That such thoughts as these were in Jacob's mind and heart is clear, because of the things which were said to him in his dream. There are few of us who have not spent similar bitter moments of cringing fear and bitter repentance, mingled with fearful wonderings and hopings as to what may be expected from God, whom we at once fear and love, and yet whom we have dishonored and wounded by our sins.

1.—"A certain place."—It was a wild, desolate spot in the mountains, with an almost perpendicular cliff rising up before him, the shelving and fractured rock looking in the gloaming much like a flight of stairs, up and over which he must climb in the morning. This probably was the physical basis of his dream. But the point in this to us is the fact that Jacob was brought into this place alone. Here, as we have intimated, his thoughts began to turn to God, much perhaps as the prodigal's thoughts turned toward his father as he considered all the miserable folly of his wayward sins. So Jacob found himself alone with God. No man can be alone, especially in some such desolate place as this, with his sin for his only companion, without having some consciousness of God's presence come to him, either to fill him with terror, or to suggest new hope. This was a part of God's discipline to bring Jacob to repentance. It is often God's way with us to bring us to repentance. One seldom thinks seriously toward God in a crowd.

2.—**A stone for a pillow.**—This was in itself not an unusual thing for a shepherd like Jacob to do. Nevertheless, a stone in a lonely place like this is a hard pillow. So, when we have to spend a night all alone with our bitter thoughts, with the remembrance of our sins, and some present affliction, such as Jacob was suffering, the pillow upon which we lay our repentant head is usually but a stone. Nevertheless, a stone for a pillow with repentance in our heart is better than down to lie upon if the heart is hard toward God. Afterward that very pillow became a pillar of memorial and gratitude to God. So our repentance becomes as a memorial stone from us to God. We bless God for the hard pillow, and we bless him that, lying on such a bed, he reveals himself to us in grace. So it was with Jacob, so it has been with us, and so it will be to every penitent soul.

II.—THE WANDERER'S DREAM.

However this dream may be explained psychologically in connection with his physical surroundings, it is certain that this was a real dream, in which God took occasion to reveal himself. That it was always considered by Israel in all after-centuries as a real event is sufficiently attested by the fact that Christ refers to it and uses it in connection with his revelation of the grace of God to Nathanael, "an Israelite indeed, in whom there was *no* guile."

1.—What Jacob saw in his dream.—As he slept, the rocky sides of the cliff, the last things his eyes had rested upon, became a mighty stairway resting indeed upon the earth, but stretching away up to the very heavens. This vision (partly natural and, we may easily believe, partly supernatural) was the means God used of showing to Jacob a great truth. The rainbow in the sky was to Noah a token of God's mercy over the whole earth; this vision was God's way of showing Jacob that heaven was open and accessible to man—at least, that heaven was not so far off that no communication could be had with it. The angels of God ascending and descending tell plainly of a divine providence administered by "guardian angels." (Heb. i, 14.) "And behold the Lord [Jehovah, the God of grace and salvation] stood above it." Here, indeed, was a revelation of unspeakable comfort to Jacob: heaven was not shut against him for his sins; he was not cast off entirely, for was not Jehovah watching over him even in his present outcast lonely condition, and were not angels coming and going in his behalf? Is this a fanciful interpretation of this dream? Turn to our Lord's use of it in his conversation with Nathanael: "Verily, verily, I say unto you, hereafter ye shall see heaven open, and the angels of God ascending and descending upon the Son of man." What Jacob saw was the adumbration of the incarnation. Jesus is the true stairway—the medium of communication between God and sinful man—and he is the way up to God from the earth, as he is the revealer of Jehovah over all our path of life, and the true means by which the angels of God take charge of us. I would have gladly had Jacob's dream, and seen what he saw and heard, but it is infinitely better to have lived in "the day of Christ."

2.—What Jacob heard.—As he looked in wonder upon this vision of the opened heaven, and the angels of God ascending and descending, with Jehovah standing above it all, he heard the voice of Jehovah speaking to him. In this communication two special things are said:

(1) The covenant made with Abraham and confirmed to Isaac is now confirmed to Jacob. (vs. 13, 14.) All the promises made to the two great ancestors are renewed to himself. (Gen. xiii, 15, 16; xxvi, 3.) In the passage, "And thou shalt spread abroad to the west and to the east, and to the north and to the south," we have another confirmation of the purpose of God in respect of the universality of the kingdom of Christ. Concerning this part of the declaration of Jehovah, what a blessing and comfort it is to know that even our sins cannot set aside his covenant faithfulness; though this is no warrant for sin. In this respect the foundation of God standeth sure.

(2) In the second part of Jehovah's communication there is abundant promise that the grace of God and his providential care is not merely national, but special, particular, and individual. (i) "Behold, I am with thee." This was balm to Jacob's sorely troubled heart. He had sinned, but God had not forsaken him, nor would he ever do so. "Having loved his own, . . . he loved them unto the end." This promise was renewed by Christ to his disciples (Matt. xxviii, 20), and is most precious. It means not only presence, but tenderest sympathy and fellowship. (ii) "And will keep thee in all places whither thou goest." How this must have allayed poor Jacob's fears! A wanderer, even an outcast from his father's house, he might be, but God had now promised to keep him and take care of him, not in this place only, but in all places whither he might go. Who can measure the value of such a promise? God is always with us to keep us. No true child of faith would for a moment think of turning such a promise as this into a license to go into places of temptation and sin. It means that in all places where we are led in our earthly pilgrimage as children of the covenant and followers of Christ, we may count on the divine presence and protection, even though it be in a den of lions, or in a furnace of fire. (iii) "And will bring thee again into this land." Jacob was going outside the land of promise. The most anxious earthly question in his heart, perhaps, at that time was, "Will I ever come again into this land of my fathers? Esau will possess it, and will never suffer me to enter it again." Jacob was a banished man. The promise of God to bring him into it again was most precious. We often lose much

present enjoyment of our spiritual inheritance because of transgression, and then fear that the joys of salvation shall never be restored again; but God is gracious and faithful. "The gifts and calling of God are without repentance." He will bring us again. Jacob is a type of the banished Israel (as Abraham was of Israel in possession). Jacob is now a wanderer over the whole earth still, but God has never forgotten, and will "bring him in again." (Rom. xi, 27, 29.) (iv) "For I will not leave thee." See how this promise has been renewed again and again. (Deut. xxxi, 6-8; Josh. i, 5; I. Chron. xxviii, 20; Is. xli. 17; Heb. xiii, 5.) (v) "Until I have done that which I have spoken to thee of." This refers not only to Jacob personally, but to his seed. The miraculous preservation of the Jews till this day, in spite of centuries of cruel treatment and fierce destructive persecution, is a striking testimony to the faithfulness of God's promise.

III.—JACOB AWAKES FROM DREAMING.

And behold, it was not all a dream! We often have most vivid dreams, but on awaking know that they were, after all, but dreams. But when Jacob awoke he was convinced that his dream was a reality, and so he expressed himself. From that moment he was a new man.

1.—His conviction.—"Surely the Lord is in this place, and I knew it not." This may be our comfort, that the Lord may be, and is, near us, even when our consciousness does not testify of his presence. There is vast blessing for us which we do not recognize. How few careless sinners know the love that God hath to them. How many believers dream of the nearness of the Lord in hours and circumstances of distress. They say, "The Lord hath forsaken me;" but, did they only know it, the very angels of God are ascending and descending from heaven on their behalf. "I am persuaded that neither death, nor life, nor angels, nor principalities, nor powers, nor things present, nor things to come, nor height, nor depth, nor any other creature, shall be able to separate us from the love of God, which is in Christ Jesus." This is the Christian's persuasion based on the revelation of God in Christ, as the former was Jacob's persuasion based on the revelation of God in this dream.

2.—His fear.—"And he was afraid." Well, so was Moses afraid when he saw and heard Jehovah in the burning bush. So was Isaiah afraid when he had a vision of God. So were the shepherds afraid when they saw the angels and heard their song of annunciation and their declaration of peace at the birth of Christ. No wonder that sinful man is afraid when God reveals himself. It is sin which makes us afraid. It is the reassuring word of grace that gives us courage and takes away our fear.

3.—The house of God.—There was a dreadful and awful solemnity attaching to the place where God had revealed himself. "The place whereon thou standest is holy ground," said Jehovah to Moses at the bush. Did we but fully realize how really God is present in all the earth, and in every place, there would come a solemn reverence for God everywhere: not only in "the house of God," but in the home and in the office, in the shop, in the field, on the train, and on board ship. "Earth is full of heaven, and every bush aflame with fire; but they only who see take off their shoes; while all the rest are content to stand around and gather blackberries." The true house of God is wherever we may meet God, in this mountain, at Jerusalem, it is true, but also in every place where a heart lifts itself up in prayer. And every house of God or meeting-place with God is a gate of heaven. We have heard of people who live as in a dream; would God we might live in such a dream as this, which is not a dream, but a real vision of God.

IV.—JACOB'S CONSECRATION.

When Jacob rose up in the morning, after lying long enough awake to take in and digest the vision, he solemnly consecrated himself anew to God. This he did, both in act, in vow, and promise.

1.—The sacred pillar.—To the stone pillow upon which he had laid his head that night, and upon which he had dreamed a dream that was not all a dream, but a vision of God, Jacob did not attribute any superstitious virtue; but he desired to commemorate the spot, and to mark it, so that at some future day he might build a more fitting memorial of this glorious revelation of God to him. So he poured oil upon the stone and thus consecrated it to God, naming the place Bethel. This habit of rearing memorial stones is a familiar one in the subsequent history of Israel. Joshua raised his "heap," and the children of Israel built their "Ebenezer." Surely there are experiences all along down our past lives of points where we should rear some memorial of God's goodness. Notably, who would not wish to commemorate the day of his conversion, when he first saw heaven opened to him, and Jesus, the way to God, standing by with words of life and promise. This was the spirit with which Jacob set up his pillar.

2.—The solemn dedication of himself.—Better still than rearing a pillar, Jacob solemnly consecrated himself to God that day. "If God will be with me and will keep me," etc. This does not mean that Jacob made a bargain with God, or proposed one. God had promised him certain great things, assuring him of his continued presence, his keeping power, the care of him in a foreign land, and his safe-conduct home. Then says Jacob: "This being so, since God has of his pure grace promised me this, then shall the Lord be my God." That is, he would erect an altar and consecrate the place where God had revealed himself to him, as a spot sacred to worship, a purpose which was afterward fulfilled. (Gen. xxxv, 1, 15.) It is a good thing to bring ourselves into covenant obligations to God, not in a legal spirit, but in the freedom of the Holy Spirit. The old nature needs to be bound sometimes by a covenant, and compelled to act according to the best impulses of the new nature.

3.—The tithe.—"And of all that thou shalt give me, I will surely give the tenth unto thee." Jacob will not be content to worship God with words and vows, but will "honour the Lord with his substance and with the first-fruits of all his increase." The tithe is older than the law; it began, so far as we are concerned, when Abraham gave tithes of all he had to Melchizedek. (xiv, 20.) It is most meet that we should, as an expression of our gratitude to God for all his temporal mercies, give a reasonable portion of all back to him for the service of his house, and the extension of his kingdom by spreading abroad the gospel. A tenth is the least that any one of us should give, and those who have much ought to be glad to add to their tenth yet another and another proportionately.

XI.

THE RESURRECTION OF CHRIST.—Mark xvi, 1-8.

(1) And when the sabbath was past, Mary Magdalene, and Mary the mother of James, and Salome, had bought sweet spices, that they might come and anoint him. (2) And very early in the morning the first day of the week, they came unto the sepulchre at the rising of the sun. (3) And they said among themselves, Who shall roll us away the stone from the door of the sepulchre? (4) And when they looked, they saw that the stone was rolled away: for it was very great. (5) And entering into the sepulchre, they saw a young man sitting on the right side, clothed in a long white garment; and they were affrighted. (6) And he saith unto them, Be not affrighted: ye seek Jesus of Nazareth, which was crucified: he is risen; he is not here: behold the place where they laid him. (7) But go your way, tell his disciples and Peter that he goeth before you into Galilee: there shall ye see him, as he said unto you. (8) And they went out quickly, and fled from the sepulchre; for they trembled and were amazed: neither said they any thing to any man; for they were afraid.—Mark xvi, 1-8.

Three hours of darkness and stillness while Christ hung on the cross; then the veil of the Temple was rent, and the centurion confessed that Jesus was the Son of God. Three days of darkness and stillness in the earth! in the which time ceased to be counted; then the grave of Jesus was burst asunder, and he was "declared to be the Son of God with power, according to the Spirit of holiness, by the resurrection from the dead." (Rom. i, 4.) Before the Jewish Sabbath began the Lord was buried. During that day we have no account of things. What a day of restlessness on the part of the disciples on that day of rest! Their hopes were dead with their crucified Lord, whom they had hoped "should have redeemed Israel." The men-disciples had gone their way in hopeless despair. John had taken the Blessed Mother to his house; Joseph and Nicodemus had done their kindly and brave offices of respect to the body of Jesus, whom they had almost accepted as the Messiah. Gloom hung over the household of faith. Fear and anxiety still filled the breasts of the rulers, for they remembered what the disciples had forgotten, namely, that Jesus had again and again said that he would rise from the dead; and especially his calm and emphatic declaration, made under oath when he was before Caiaphas, that he would rise and sit on the right hand of power, and come in glory to possess the everlasting kingdom of Messiah; therefore, before the dawn of the Sabbath, they had secured a guard of soldiers to watch the grave. These, and other particulars, are passed over by Mark in his rapid narrative, for he had purposed only to record the fact of the resurrection. The omission of details in this singular narrative—indeed, in all the accounts of the resurrection—is one of the strong proofs of the genuineness of the story and the reality of the facts related. There is no mention or attempt at conjecture of what happened to Jesus during the time of his sojourn in the under-world; no account of how he was raised from the dead; whether his soul was escorted back to his body by angels, or how the first pulses of the resurrection life acted upon the dead body, or in what way it was changed into the marvelous body of glory which it evidently was after its revival. Nobody saw him rise or leave the grave. The fact to be laid hold of is that he is risen and was certainly alive from the dead. Not another, but the same Jesus who had been crucified; not a spirit, but a man with a body of flesh and bones. Life and immortality are brought to light by his resurrection from the dead. A new life has dawned upon the world, and the whole course of history has been changed wherever his resurrection has been preached. Without discussing any of the proofs of the resurrection (which none of the immediate eye-witnesses of the fact ever thought of doing), we cannot but wonder how it would have been possible for the subsequent events to have taken place which characterized the inauguration of Christianity, have ever since marked its progress, and are its underlying and indisputable facts to-day, had it not occurred. How came these confused and despairing disciples, who lost both hope and courage when their Lord was crucified, to become possessed with a new hope that filled their whole being, and nerved with a courage that made them very lions for boldness? What was it that energized them to confront the very men and generation that crucified Jesus with all the power of Church and State at their back, and to charge them with his murder, and at the same time in his name preach to them forgiveness? If Christ be not risen, how has that early enthusiasm continued from generation to generation among those who, not having seen, have yet believed in the risen Christ? How can we account for the elevation of human morality, the sanctification of human character, the triumph of a heavenly life over the lower and even brutal instincts of man, wherever and ever since Jesus and the resurrection have been preached? Can it be that a mere myth has wrought all that has been accomplished in the name of Christ in all these ages? Can it be that a mere fitful imagination of a few hysterical women, who constructed a story of resurrection out of half-waking dreams, has done all this, and continues to do it? Can it be that a falsehood, deliberately planned and persistently pushed in the face of torture and death, has exercised for centuries the most quickening and truth-inspiring influence on all classes of men? It is impossible to account for what has been and is accomplished in the name of Christ, if the story of his resurrection is either myth, delusion, or falsehood; for be it known, that it is the resurrection of Jesus that has been the keystone in the arch of constructive Christianity. All his life, his teachings, and his death hinge on his resurrection; for if Christ be not risen, then our faith is vain: we are yet in our sins, and they who have fallen asleep in the hope of immortality are perished, and the very promulgators of those best and most blessed hopes which have ever animated the hearts and lives of men are perjured witnesses. We refuse to accept any rationalistic or mythical theory of the resurrection, for the simple reason that the mind is incapable of it without first suffering the suicide of its best powers.

I.—THE VISIT OF THE WOMEN TO THE TOMB.

Among those who had followed Jesus, and loved him best, and believed in him the most, were some noble women—noble not by any accident of birth, but in character—among whom was Mary of Magdala, who had been greatly afflicted with devils who had possessed her, and whom Jesus, during his earthly ministry, had cast out and driven forth from her. She, with another Mary and one other woman, whose name was Salome, had waited with sorrowing love, during that dreary Sabbath day, until the dawn of the first day of the week, to go to the tomb of Jesus, that they might do with more deliberation, and with better and more loving skill, what Joseph and Nicodemus had hastily done on the Friday night after the crucifixion. They did not look for resurrection. They had forgotten, if they ever had taken to heart, any of his many sayings concerning it. He might not be the Messiah, still he had been very dear to them, and they would anoint and embalm with loving hands and fragrant ointment the dear body which had been so cruelly broken by the hands of his enemies. The men might forsake the dead body, as they had their living Master, but not they. This is not in woman's nature to do. So, consulting only their love, they made this early journey to the tomb.

1.—The difficulty and triumph of love.—As they went they bethought them of the great stone which, according to custom, or which they may have observed when they followed the body to the tomb, would be lying over against the mouth of the sepulchre. They knew nothing of the guard of soldiers; neither does Mark speak of them. "Who shall roll us away the stone?" "For it was very great." Such a difficulty occurring to men, or to any one less intent on a labor of love, would have halted them, and perhaps turned them aside; but, woman-like and love-like, they kept on, counting on an issue out of their difficulties in some way or other. True love, especially when it is mixed with faith, does not stop for obstacles or difficulties, no matter how formidable. Love has a better logic than reason. So they journeyed on undismayed, and lo! when they came the stone was rolled away. We may well surmise that they were both delighted and alarmed—delighted that their chief difficulty was removed, and then instantly alarmed lest it might betoken a greater calamity, namely, that the body had been taken away—perhaps robbed in the night; perhaps removed by the authorities. They hastened in quickly, to set their anxieties at rest.

2.—The angel in the sepulchre.—Entering in haste, they were astonished to see a young man sitting on the place where the body had been. He was arrayed in a long white garment. Who was he? What did his presence signify there? They were trembling with fear and excitement. The young man, who was no other than an angel from heaven, perhaps Gabriel again, at once sought to quiet them. "Be not affrighted: ye seek Jesus of Nazareth, which was crucified: he is risen; he is not here: behold the place where they laid him." What message was this? He is risen! How that word must have thrilled through and through them! Not stolen; not carried away by friends; but risen! Did they then remember his words? The angel may have meant to remind them of what they ought not to have forgotten, and to suggest to them that, loving as was their purpose and mission, they ought not to be surprised at not finding their Lord, and that they should have come with expectation of faith rather than mere devotion of love. How closely are angels related to us! Even in nature, for they are always seen as though they were men. They are, if not kinsmen according to nature, at least closely related to us, servants of God and ministering spirits to us. Angels ministered to the saints of old.

They especially acted as messengers to us concerning Jesus Christ. They announced his incarnation to Mary; they announced his birth to the shepherds. They ministered to him in the wilderness and in the garden; they waited on him in the first moments of his resurrection, rolling away the stone before the door of the sepulchre, and tarried to communicate the fact of his rising to these loving and seeking women, and delivered to them his first message to his disciples. They came down to receive Jesus up into glory, and tarried behind to comfort the astonished disciples by telling them of his speedy return. Let us not think of angels as being far off and with whom we have nothing to do. They are doubtless close about, watching over and ministering to us in a thousand unseen ways; for that indeed seems to be their chief mission. Like goodness and mercy, they follow us all the days of our life.

3.—**The message to the disciples.**—Having, in a measure, quieted the fears of the women, the angel bade them hasten with a message from the risen Lord to his disciples. Apprised ourselves of the resurrection, it becomes our first duty to communicate it to others. The relationship which binds us to Jesus is essentially a non-selfish one. We are his to serve and obey, as well as to be saved; and the Lord's business demands haste. There was no time wasted in idle or useless questions concerning the most stupendous fact in the world's history. Another account tells us that these women were bidden to "go quickly." There was no time to be lost; the disciples must not be permitted to sink any deeper in despair than they were already plunged. The night of their distress must be dissipated by the rising joy of his resurrection; they must be arrested in their downward career of unbelief. Hence the message to them.

It is most touching and beautiful to note the special message to Peter. "Tell his disciples and Peter." Was not, then, Peter a disciple—he who had been the very foremost and chief among them? Was he now counted out of that little band of eleven? Why this specification? Surely, the reason comes quickly to us all. Peter had denied his Lord with a bitter, unbelieving, and wicked oath. He had cast himself out and off from the circle of disciples and away from his Lord. "I know not the man," he had said. True, he had bitterly repented, with tears, his fall. The Lord had broken his heart with a look as he left the palace of the high-priest. What would be the state of his feelings when he heard of the Lord's resurrection? Could he, would he dare take to himself any message that was sent to the disciples in general? Surely, he would say to himself: "The Lord will not want to see me. I have cut myself off from his love. I have forfeited all claims upon his regard." True, the other disciples had forsaken him and fled at the time of his arrest, but none had so basely denied him as Peter. But "the Lord knoweth them that are his." He knew that it was not through lack of love, but through the weakness of the flesh, that Peter had denied him, and therefore he would send him a special message, lest his deep humiliation and cruel fear would deter him from coming, with the others, to the place appointed. It is most touching and blessed to think of this: that the first thought of the risen Lord was for the erring disciple; the first care of the Good Shepherd was for the strayed sheep. Peter, more than the rest, needed a special word, so above the rest he is remembered. The Good Shepherd, who loves all, has peculiar pity and compassion toward the wounded sheep. It is worthy of note that Paul makes mention of a special and private meeting between Peter and the Lord. (I. Cor. xv, 5.) It has been beautifully suggested that this private meeting was one in which the reconciliation between the denying Peter and the forgiving Saviour was completed. But one other private interview is recorded, and that was between the Lord and his half-brother James, who, until now, was not one of his disciples, but who, after the resurrection, became one, and subsequently the first pastor of the church at Jerusalem. We should learn from this to be specially compassionate, and particularly careful to restore those of the flock who have gone astray or been overtaken in a fault.

4.—The place of meeting.—" He goeth before you into Galilee; there shall ye see him, as he said unto you." Dear Galilee! that rough hill country where his home was; where the chief part of his life and the most memorable part of his public ministry had been spent—Galilee, where he had the most friends and disciples, removed, as he was, from the direct influences of the envious and vindictive priests; in Galilee, where the meeting might be quiet, and occasion no uproar or confusion. How the news would speed, and how, at the time appointed, the disciples and friends of Jesus would come, with fear and trembling, to meet the crucified but now risen Lord! It was at that meeting that he was "seen of above five hundred brethren at once," the greater part of whom remained alive when Paul wrote his Epistle to the Corinthians. He had before spoken to them of his rising again and meeting them in Galilee. (Mark xiv, 28.) The angel reminds them of this fact. No doubt it would come back to them now, and the remainder would help the difficult faith of his slow-hearted followers. How good it is to know that the things which are most staggering to our faith are the things which before have been clearly spoken of. The greatest benefit of prophecy is in its confirming power to our faith after the events. Jesus was wont to warn his disciples of coming events, so that when they came they would not overwhelm them either with surprise or fear.

II.—THE AMAZEMENT AND FEAR OF FAITH.

The artless simplicity of this narrative must forever dispel the theory that the story of the resurrection of Jesus does not rest on a basis of solid fact, but was concocted by his disciples, in order to justify themselves and stimulate others to believe that Jesus was the true Messiah. If they knew him to be dead, and not, in fact, alive from the dead, where would be the use of believing him to be the Messiah? What motive could they have in persuading others to believe that a dead man, however good, was the long-promised Messiah, who should fulfill all the ancient promises of God to them? In itself the theory is preposterous, and more difficult of belief than the resurrection itself. The repeated appearances of Jesus himself to his disciples under so many different circumstances, must dispose of that other speculative theory, that the honest belief of the disciples was founded on the wild fancies and imaginings of a few impressionable and hysterical women. On the other hand, the hardness of heart and slowness of belief of his disciples—the slow, almost reluctant awakening of their faith to the fact of the resurrection—disposes of any theory which rests on the assumption of invention, collusion, or mere credulity.

1.—**The flight of the women.**—In his graphic language Mark tells us that "they went out quickly and fled from the sepulchre." They had come to the sepulchre that Sunday morning with heavy and sad hearts, bent on a mission of love and homage to the dead Master whom they had loved and lost, but whom they had hoped was he that should have delivered Israel. (Luke xxiv, 21.) Not hoping to find a risen Saviour and an empty sepulchre, their walk thitherward was made the more slow because of the anxious thought about the huge stone which intervened between their purpose and the dead body of Jesus. (Mark xvi, 3.) Now those same sad hearts were stirred with an astonishment which for the moment rendered them speechless, and their hitherto sluggish feet were winged with a mixture of awful fear and thrilling ecstasy at the news they had heard from the angel. "For they trembled and were amazed; neither said they anything to any man, for they were afraid." Never before was such a message communicated to any human being as that which was intrusted to these women. A world's redemption is contained in it.

2.—**Faith and fear.**—The pathetic account of the state of confused joy and ecstasy, mixed with amazement and fear, which filled the hearts of these women, and which afterward in like manner overcame the disciples, who, upon hearing their word, "mourned and wept," gives a glimpse into the workings of the human heart when it first really confronts the eternal realities of the unseen world, especially when that world is unveiled by Jesus Christ. We are told of a ruler who came to Jesus, and cried out, "Lord, I believe; help mine unbelief." Here we find faith struggling into birth out of the womb of unbelief. A strange but true paradox. It is the truth of the proverb which we sometimes hear: "It is too good to be true." The news of the resurrection, fraught with such wealth of joy and peace, seems to the hungry heart of man too good indeed to be true; and unbelief, like Esau, comes out first, but faith, like Jacob, takes hold on the heel of unbelief, and finally supplants it and becomes heir of the promise.

Our lesson ends with the eighth verse, but our hearts press us further on through the story, which tells us of Mary lingering behind, unwilling to leave the grave (perhaps less believing for the time being than the others, just because her love was the greater and profounder). Others might fly away, affrighted by the news, even though they half believed it; but she would not leave the garden till she had found her Lord and taken him away. She sought his dead body, but in the end found him alive in the power of the resurrection. Mark does not harmonize, or attempt to harmonize, the story which he tells. He does not stop to fill in all the details or explain the discrepancies. He is not writing for critics, but for those who had become confirmed in the faith, and only needed the testimony of the fact to transmit to those who should come after them. Blessed joy! blessed confusion of details! We linger not over the seeming discrepancies, but give our hearts up to the fullness of joy arising out of the main fact, that Jesus, who was crucified, is alive from the dead.

3.—**Lessons for us.**—Of these there are several. (i) Do not let us surrender to doubts and fears, however they assail our faith. Faith is never a working faith until it has had its struggle with unbelief and triumphed. (ii) Even if we fear and doubt, let us do what we are bidden, nor wait till all our confusion is cleared up and all our fears are allayed. Mark these noble women, how they fled in wildest confusion to bring news of the resurrection, which they themselves only half believed, and could not as yet at all realize. The first heralds of the resurrection were not those who had first verified all the facts by a scientific process, and met every critical objection and difficulty which might have been urged. They did not stop to ask, "How can these things be?" but went quickly and told his disciples that Jesus was alive from the dead. Let us do likewise. Abraham did not know how the awful tragedy he was sent to enact with his son Isaac would end. He went on with his heart full of doubts and misgivings, torn with an agony which no words can portray, and yet he calmly replied to Isaac's pathetic question, "My son, God will provide himself a lamb." Let us leave something for God to do in extricating our faith from the difficulties which sometimes environ it. (iii) "Neither said they anything to any man." The reason given for this is that "they were afraid." But the lesson we may draw from this is, that we are not to loiter and gossip on the way with every one we meet about the sacred mysteries of our faith. It is a great mistake to talk with everybody and anybody, especially with those not in sympathy with Christ, when our own hearts are in confusion and doubt and fear. Unburden ourselves we may to the disciples, and talk doubtful things over with them; but it would be folly to go to a man who would laugh at our faith and encourage our doubts. The best way to have a doubt resolved is to do simply and quickly the very thing we are bidden to do, taking our orders directly from the Word of God.

XII.

REVIEW.

GOLDEN TEXT: "I am the God of Abraham, and the God of Isaac, and the God of Jacob; God is not the God of the dead, but of the living."—Matt. xxii, 32.

XIII.

JACOB'S PREVAILING PRAYER.—Gen. xxxii, 9-12; 24-30.

(9) And Jacob said, O God of my father Abraham, and God of my father Isaac, the Lord which saidst unto me, Return unto thy country, and to thy kindred, and I will deal well with thee: (10) I am not worthy of the least of all the mercies, and of all the truth, which thou hast shewed unto thy servant; for with my staff I passed over this Jordan; and now I am become two bands. (11) Deliver me, I pray thee, from the hand of my brother, from the hand of Esau: for I fear him, lest he will come and smite me, and the mother with the children. (12) And thou saidst, I will surely do thee good, and make thy seed as the sand of the sea, which cannot be numbered for multitude. (24) And Jacob was left alone; and there wrestled a man with him until the breaking of the day. (25) And when he saw that he prevailed not against him, he touched the hollow of his thigh; and the hollow of Jacob's thigh was out of joint, as he wrestled with him. (26) And he said, Let me go, for the day breaketh. And he said, I will not let thee go, except thou bless me. (27) And he said unto him, What is thy name? And he said, Jacob. (28) And he said, Thy name shall be called no more Jacob, but Israel: for as a prince hast thou power with God and with men, and hast prevailed. (29) And Jacob asked him, and said, Tell me, I pray thee, thy name. And he said, Wherefore is it that thou dost ask after my name? And he blessed him there. (30) And Jacob called the name of the place Peniel: for I have seen God face to face, and my life is preserved.—Genesis xxxii, 9-12; 24-30.

More than fifteen years have passed since we saw Jacob at Bethel, rearing his pillar of memorial and consecrating himself to God. These fifteen years have been fruitful ones. Jacob has learned somewhat of the craft of others, and has been reminded more than once of his own subtle methods of dealing with his brother. But in it all, though there is no sign of any deep heart-work having been done in him, he does not forget God nor his promise, and holds fast by the birthright. In his long service with Laban he manifests deep personal love for his beautiful Rachel, and is not bitter against Leah. Laban treats him unjustly, and Jacob, using carnal methods, cleverly outwits him, and gets the better of his uncle in this play of worldly interests. The time has come, however, when Jacob feels that he cannot safely and happily live any longer with his father-in-law, and so determines to leave, and go back to his own land. Two motives were working at this time in Jacob's mind: the hopeless incompatibility existing between him and Laban, and a strong desire to return to his own inheritance and take up his birthright. In carrying out this purpose, his old craft comes to his aid. Knowing full well that Laban would not consent to his peaceable departure, and also knowing that he could not steal away without being pursued and overtaken, he determines at least to make a good start, being well assured that he could make better terms with Laban at a distance from home than under his own vine and fig tree. In this calculation he was not mistaken. Having settled matters with Laban, he moves forward toward the promised land, covering again the road he had once traversed as a fugitive from the face of his brother Esau. On the way he is met by a company of angels of God. (vs. 1.) We have no record of what passed between Jacob and the angels. It has been conjectured by some that they apprised him of the presence of Esau at no great distance from his encampment, but at the same time encouraged him to go forward. We may well imagine that Jacob had no great pleasure in thinking of the inevitable meeting with Esau. His conscience would naturally make him a coward in such an encounter. At the same time, he considered himself in the right so far as the possession of the birthright was concerned, however he may have been in the wrong as to the measures he had taken to possess himself of it from Esau. The birthright was his according to the intention of God from the beginning, and would have come to him without his unbrotherly trickery. God had confirmed it to him, not on the ground of his fraudulent possession, but on the ground of grace. Nevertheless, he had to reckon with Esau for his behavior to him. Would he turn back? Several things prevented Jacob from turning back. First, the land was his, and he had a right to go and take it. Then he was going in direct obedience to God's command. (Gen. xxxi, 3.) Again, he was no coward, and, if need be, was quite ready to face Esau and do battle with him for the land. This, too, is a part of Jacob's character: a dogged persistency in carrying his point quietly and by craft if he can, but carry it he will, at any cost. Then Jacob knew well the vacillating character of his good-natured brother, and he counted on bringing him over. At any rate, he sent forward messengers to sound Esau, and to intimate to him that he was no longer a poor fugitive, but a man of substance, with great wealth and many retainers. This was diplomatic, to say the least. The answer which came from Esau was evidently disdainful, haughty, and non-committal. This much disquieted Jacob, but it did not turn him from his purpose. Esau's answer had in it a menace. He was coming to meet his brother Jacob with four hundred armed men. Jacob, however, at once sets about putting his forces in order. He divides his company and flocks into two bands, hoping that one of them might escape in any event, and that possibly both might come off safely. This is the state of affairs at the point where our study opens.

I.—JACOB IN TROUBLE.

Now Esau was a man of war. His four hundred men were wild, reckless, dare-devil troopers, who delighted in a battle, and were regardless of all small proprieties. Jacob was a man of peace. His huge family of servants were all shepherds and herdsmen. Besides, his flocks were his whole worldly estate, the fruit of years of toil and frugal saving. More than that, his wives and women attendants and his eleven sons, all these were in peril. Discretion would have prompted delay or temporary retreat. But Jacob, sorely troubled and distressed as he was, having once set his face toward his father's country, would not yield, no, not so much as an inch. He had done what his best wisdom could suggest for the safety of his family and possessions in case Esau meant mischief, and then he betook himself to prayer. Many may think that Jacob should have done this first. Well, that was not Jacob's way. He would never call upon God so long as he had any resources of his own. He learned a different lesson later on; but at present he was still *Jacob*, and felt, in the main, quite sufficiently strong in himself to take care of himself. But apart from this characteristic in Jacob's yet unsubdued nature, it is not certain that the part of true faith is not to make all possible preparations, to do what we can ourselves, and then cast ourselves upon God. If I were on board a sinking ship I would not call upon God and then cast myself into the sea; but I would first buckle a life belt about me, then call upon God and cast myself into the sea.

1.—An appeal to God.—Having done his best, he turns to God with this pathetic appeal: "O God of my father Abraham, and God of my father Isaac." It was no wild appeal to a distant philosophical god, but a specific appeal to him who had revealed himself to Abraham and to Isaac, and who had entered into covenant with them and with their seed, and, moreover, who had confirmed the promise to him on more than one occasion, and who had but recently spoken to him and bidden him make his way back to his father's country. "The Lord which saidst unto me." Prayer is not a mere outcry into space, even into heavenly space, as one lost in the woods would cry out to any person who might by chance hear; but it is a specific cry to God, who has made himself known, and put himself into covenant relations with us. At least, that is prayer for those who have knowledge of the true God. We pray to the Father whom Jesus Christ has revealed, who indeed is the God of Abraham, of Isaac, and of Jacob.

2.—Pleading the promises.—Now, in making his prayer to God Jacob did not depend upon the general provisions of the covenant, but took up at once a definite and particular promise, first made to him at Bethel (Gen. xxviii, 15) fifteen years before, and more recently confirmed to him, coupled with a specific command to proceed now to return to his father's land (Gen. xxxi, 3). Now, when we pray, let us gather together the promises in general under which our petition may come, and then, if we can find a specific promise that bears directly on our case, "come boldly unto the throne of grace," and face God with his own word. To some this may look like presumption and a want of humility, but this is just what best pleases God. Think of that prayer of Jeremiah: "Do not disgrace the throne of thy glory!" What boldness! And yet methinks God was most honored when Jeremiah put his petition on such high ground as this. "It would be a small matter, so far as the people are concerned, if they were blotted out; but it would be no slight matter if thy promise should fail. The very throne of thy glory in that case would suffer disgrace." Few of us know how to pray thus, because few of us are so jealous of the dignity of the throne of God's glory. Jacob had the right of grace, and he did well to plead God's last immediate promise and command, and to remind God of his own word and hold him to it.

3.—Great humility in the face of great mercies.—That Jacob, though not yet an entirely subdued man, was no self-sufficient Pharisee, or altogether proud of his strength and prowess, is indicated by his very next words: "I am not worthy of the least of all the mercies, and of all the truth, which thou hast showed unto thy servant." Jacob had been greatly prospered. In a certain sense he had won his own prosperity; but Jacob had not forgotten that God was working for and with him, and that it was to his direct interposition that all his wealth was attributable—these two great bands of people and possessions. Nor was he forgetful of the exceeding great and precious promises which had been confirmed unto him, and which he here calls "the truth." God's promises are always "the truth." So we here get a glimpse of Jacob's humility before God. Proud, haughty, and self-sufficient as he may have been before men, in God's presence he was yet humble as a child.

4.—Importunate prayer.—Jacob not only prayed, but he prayed importunately. He had come to a crisis when he must be heard. It was life or death with him. How little of our praying is importunate! We pray for things daily which we nevertheless feel that we can do without. We pray for Christ's kingdom to come, and yet are not greatly distressed if not much progress is made. We pray even for the conversion of our children, and yet we are not importunate. We somehow are half-way content even though they be not converted. We hope they will be some time, and so we cease to pray importunately for their conversion *now*. Jacob was importunate because he needed and must have help *now*. Several elements entered into this prayer. (i) He was afraid. (ver. 11.) "Deliver me, I pray thee, from the hand of my brother . . . Esau." The fear of Esau was upon him. He had determined to go forward, but yet he was afraid. This is true courage indeed. Yes, he prayed because he was afraid. Some people tell us that prayer dictated by fear is ignoble, cowardly. Well, we do not think so when we send in haste for a doctor either for ourselves or our children. Why should we not send for God when in trouble? Was it ignoble in Mary and Martha to send for Jesus, saying, "He whom thou lovest is sick"? No; fear is a motive which is perfectly legitimate in approach to God. (ii) It was not altogether a personal fear, but fear dictated because of the "mother with the children." Jacob tenderly loved his family, and he feared more for their personal safety than for himself. I have heard old soldiers say, who were in the dreadful Sepoy war in India, that it was when they thought of their wives and children falling into the hands of the fiends who sought their blood that their hearts failed them for fear. (iii) Yet again Jacob looked ahead, and remembered the covenant promises, and then he spoke to God concerning them. "And thou saidst, I will surely do thee good, and make thy seed as the sand of the sea, which cannot be numbered for multitude." "How can that promise be fulfilled unless thou bringest me and my seed safely into the land which thou hast promised to give to me and to them?" Why, then, need he have prayed if God had promised? Ah, here is a great secret. We pray *because* God has promised. God's sure word of promise does not make us careless or turn us into fatalists.

II.—JACOB WRESTLING.

Jacob, having prayed, prepared to go forth to meet his brother Esau, determined to press his way into the land and leave the result with God. He prepared his bands so at least as to save one party, and then he did more besides. He sent on to Esau relays of mighty presents (vv. 13-23), hoping thus to appease his wrath, probably counting upon his superficial good-nature in this, that the lapse of years, his real indifference to the birthright, and his own already great prosperity had already mollified the fierce anger of fifteen years ago. He seems to have calculated well, for the result showed that Esau was quite ready to let bygones be bygones. Having sent on all his servants with the advanced bands and the relays of presents, Jacob tarried behind on the northern side of the brook with his wives and his children. Then some time in the night he conveyed his family across the brook, remaining behind alone. Possibly these preparations were all made and done before he uttered the prayer above recorded. At any rate, we find him alone in the night. We can imagine him some time in the small hours rising up to follow after them. Like a good general, all his preparations had been made. He had appealed to God to give him a peaceful victory over his brother and possession over the land. Still, in all this there is seen the masterful man, determined to take possession of God's gift, as it were, by sheer strength. We often find ourselves doing this very thing: asking God to give us this or that, and then going at it with all our might, as though in the long run everything depended on our own effort.

1.—Jacob and the unknown wrestler.—Jacob was alone when this, the most marked experience of his remarkable life, came to him. It most often is when we are alone that our greatest crises in spiritual life are met, for good or evil. So Jacob, moving forward with set purpose to cross the brook and take actual possession, found himself of a sudden gripped by a man (ver. 24), who apparently opposed strength to strength, as much as to say, "If you will enter into that land by strength, then I will oppose my strength to yours." This man is called "the angel" (Hos. xii, 4), and Jacob in the end found out, although at first he did not know who it was that resisted him; he only knew that some silent man had opposed him; and so fierce was the conflict, lasting through the remaining hours of the night, that Jacob, perhaps for the first time, experienced the sensation of being in the hands of his master. He did not indeed know that Jehovah was striving with him. And why did the angel oppose Jacob? Was it not his will that he should go into the land? Why? Just because he was planning to take possession of that land, the gift of God to him, as it were by his own might and strength; and he had to learn this lesson, that the gift of God is not to be had by violence, but by surrender, at least so far as human strength is concerned. How many souls have seen the gift of God in Christ, heard the promise of God concerning it, and then sought to possess themselves of the gift as it were by strength; wrestling and struggling and fighting with God for that which God desires to bestow upon them by faith *as a gift*, and not by overcoming by strength.

2.—The thigh out of joint.—"And when he [the angel] saw that he prevailed not against him [Jacob], he touched the hollow of his thigh, and it was out of joint as he wrestled with him." Now Jacob found that he had been wrestling with One who might at any time have overcome him, and against whom it was sheer folly to struggle. Perhaps before this he had begun to suspect who his adversary was. In a moment now he knew, when he felt his chief muscle of strength wither away at a touch, and his strong thigh go down like a broken straw. How often God has to touch our thigh and take away our much valued strength from us before he can bless us; and we at last learn the lesson that we cannot win gifts of grace by the energy of the flesh. Sunday-school teachers and preachers have all to learn this lesson also, that oftentimes God himself wrestles against us right in the path he would have us to go; only he will have us walk by faith, and not by might, and limp, as it were, on the broken thigh of human ability, that the strength may be of God. Unseen things are not seen with the natural eye, neither are they won by the strength of the natural man.

3.—Prevailing prayer.—Now we come to a beautiful thing in Jacob. No sooner did he find his thigh broken and his strength as a wrestler all gone, than he flung his arms about the neck of the "man" and held him fast. "Let me go," said the angel. "I will not let thee go, except thou bless me," was the prompt reply. Here we have the old Jacob in the new man—the old persistency, the old determination to carry his point; yet now how humbly and how meekly he clings, though not struggling and wrestling. He had discovered his antagonist in the touch of power which shrank away his thigh, and now he will not let him go unless he gets a blessing. He had fought hard to be allowed to go his own way. He would fain have shaken off this "man" an hour ago, but now the great fear is that the "man" will get away from him. "What is thy name?" asked the wrestler; not that he wished to know that simply, or that he did not know who was wrestling against him, but as preliminary to this glorious communication: "Thy name shall be called no more Jacob, but Israel; for as a prince thou hast power with God and with men, and hast prevailed." But how did he prevail? Not by might and strength; not by cunning and brute persistency; but when all strength was gone, he flung his arms toward Jehovah in utter surrender, and simply clung to him in his weak helplessness. "When I am weak, then am I strong." This is the true secret of strength with Jehovah—clinging surrender. "I will not let thee go, except thou bless me;" "not till I overcome thee or till I have wrested a blessing from thee."

4.—"**Tell me, I pray thee, thy name.**"—So Jacob asks in return. Who does not desire to know the name, the full meaning of God's character? But this cannot be put into a word or into a series of words. Moses desired to see the glory of God. Is one as bold who desired to know the very secret of his being? Name! "What is in a name?" "Elohim," "Jehovah," "El Shaddai!" Do these tell the story? "Wherefore is it that thou dost ask after my name?" Is it curiosity? My name cannot be put into words. It is "WONDERFUL"; "I AM THAT I AM." Thou canst not know my name, but I will bless thee. Is not this better than to be able to solve all the mysteries of God's being and nature, and of his ways? "I know not who it was that opened my eyes," said the blind man; "but I know this, that 'whereas I was blind now I see,' and that is sufficient for me." Perhaps if we were content to be blessed with God's blessing, we might the sooner find out his name, for "the secret of the Lord is with them that fear him."

5.—**Penuel.**—This was another sacred spot to Jacob. At Bethel he saw a vision of God—such a sight of him that he was led to consecrate his life to him, and there he reared a pillar and afterward built an altar. But here he had more than a vision; he had a deep personal experience of God. "I have seen God face to face." Many of us have our Bethel; but how few of us have a Penuel, the remembrance of an experience which so effectually took from us our natural strength that ever after we have walked halting on the broken thigh of the old carnal strength? Face to face with God! Our arms about him and his about us, his blessing spoken into our soul, and we declared to be "princes and prevailers." No longer Jacobs, supplanters, reaching our goal by laying hold on our brother's heel and tripping him up, but, by the blessing of God, strong in the strength of his blessing, and not trusting to anything at all in ourselves.

XIV.

DISCORD IN JACOB'S FAMILY.—Genesis xxxvii, 1–11.

(1) And Jacob dwelt in the land wherein his father was a stranger, in the land of Canaan. (2) These are the generations of Jacob. Joseph, being seventeen years old, was feeding the flock with his brethren; and the lad was with the sons of Bilhah, and with the sons of Zilpah, his father's wives: and Joseph brought unto his father their evil report. (3) Now Israel loved Joseph more than all his children, because he was the son of his old age: and he made him a coat of many colours. (4) And when his brethren saw that their father loved him more than all his brethren, they hated him, and could not speak peaceably unto him. (5) And Joseph dreamed a dream, and he told it his brethren: and they hated him yet the more. (6) And he said unto them, Hear, I pray you, this dream which I have dreamed: (7) For, behold, we were binding sheaves in the field, and, lo, my sheaf arose, and also stood upright; and, behold, your sheaves stood round about, and made obeisance to my sheaf. (8) And his brethren said to him, Shalt thou indeed reign over us? or shalt thou indeed have dominion over us? And they hated him yet the more for his dreams, and for his words. (9) And he dreamed yet another dream, and told it his brethren, and said, Behold, I have dreamed a dream more; and, behold, the sun and the moon and the eleven stars made obeisance to me. (10) And he told it to his father, and to his brethren: and his father rebuked him, and said unto him, What is this dream that thou hast dreamed? Shall I and thy mother and thy brethren indeed come to bow down ourselves to thee to the earth? (11) And his brethren envied him; but his father observed the saying.—Genesis xxxvii, 1 11.

With this chapter begins the fourth and last period of the history of the patriarchal family dispensation. Joseph rises on the horizon of the story of the covenant people, and in the course of a single chapter becomes the principal personage henceforth in the record contained in the Book of Genesis. He becomes the head of the family practically from this time. The line is then Abraham, Isaac, Jacob, Joseph. We have seen the birthright pass away from Ishmael and Esau, and now Reuben and the older sons of Jacob must give place to Joseph. Primogeniture does not pertain to the election of grace. In the course of the revelation which God made to Abraham he told him that his seed should sojourn in a land of strangers, and serve them, and be sorely afflicted by them. (Gen. xv, 13, 14.) More than two hundred years had passed since God revealed to Abraham this sojourn in the land of Egypt. In the meantime the patriarch and his seed, Isaac and Jacob and his twelve sons, had been but strangers in the land God had sworn to give them. In view of the great promises, both as to landed possession and multitudinous seed, the fulfillment seemed up to this date to be exceedingly small. Barrenness has been the lot of the chief women of this elect family, and after two centuries all the males of the family could be comfortably housed under the folds of an ordinary tent. This does not look like a fulfillment of the promise concerning a seed that should be as the "stars of heaven." Moreover, their possession in Canaan was only a very limited one, and that held on sufferance of the natives of the land, who were already looking upon them with no friendly eye and giving them trouble. Canaan was becoming a land of danger to them, mainly on account of the lawless ungodliness of Jacob's rough sons. Manifestly, at this rate, there would never be a numerous seed nor a landed possession. But God has his own way of working. The sojourn in Egypt, which was now being brought about in so remarkable a manner, at first sight would look like a misfortune and a miscarriage of all the promises; but in the end it justified the providence of God. Once in Egypt, sheltered and protected by their very isolation as a despised family of slaves, they had time to increase and multiply in a most remarkable manner. Besides, Egypt, being a country of high civilization and permanent government, was a school in which the semi-barbarous sons of Jacob and their descendants would, even though slaves, receive training which would fit them for their future great destiny. There is no reason to believe that even Jacob was an educated man. The family had no written records, but only the traditions of the wondrous beginnings and appointed destiny of their family; and yet, so far as we may judge, Joseph was the only one of the twelve sons who laid any store by these family hopes. For twenty years past the immediate, though unconscious, preparations for the sojourn in Egypt had been going forward. It remained for God to overrule the wicked conspiracy of the brethren of Joseph to bring about the housing of the family in the safe asylum of Egypt, till the time was fulfilled for them to emerge out of that prison-house a mighty company of six hundred thousand men of war, able and equipped for the conquest of the land which God had promised five hundred years before to Abraham and to his seed.

I.—JOSEPH BELOVED BY HIS FATHER.

Joseph was the eldest son of the beloved Rachel, and the youngest of all the children of Jacob save his brother Benjamin, whose birth cost his mother her life. Even in this fact, that Joseph was the son of Rachel, the beloved wife, and the son given in special answer to prayer—in a sense a kind of Isaac to Jacob—we have a sufficient reason for the tender love, if not, alas! parental partiality, in which Joseph was held by his father. His other sons, save Benjamin, were the sons of poor Leah, who was endured, but not loved, and of the handmaids of his two wives. It is hardly possible that it could have been otherwise than that Joseph should have been the best beloved. Though Benjamin was also the son of Rachel, and the youngest of all, yet I can fancy that Jacob must always have associated him with the death of his dear Rachel; and though of course no blame attached to the child, still there was the fact; and so more than ever the heart of the old patriarch went out to Joseph. Whether or not it is a sin for parents to esteem one child more highly than another, or to allow themselves to love one more than another, the fact remains, that, strive against impartiality as one will, there is often such a discrimination in the affections of a parent. Most parents are enabled to suppress any manifestation of such partiality; but some do not even try to do so. So it came to pass that among Jacob's sons there was a favorite child. But before we pass a too hasty or severe judgment upon Jacob for his evident partiality for Joseph, it is only just to consider what seems most probable, that he was a lad who especially called forth the affectionate admiration of his father. Benjamin was too young to have developed much character; we can easily imagine that the other sons were no great comfort to Jacob; the stronger characters among them were lawless, overbearing, rollicking, roystering, licentious men, who were making much trouble between Jacob and his Canaanite neighbors; they gave not the least evidence of any moral or spiritual inclinations. While they possibly fell in with the family traditions, and outwardly worshiped God and eschewed idols, they most likely regarded the covenant promises, so cherished by Jacob, as being a superstition of their father's, to which it was hardly worth while to pay much attention. They would appeal rather to the fact that after two hundred years there was yet no prospect of inheriting or conquering the land, there being but twelve of them, all told, arguing against any reasonable or serious acceptance of the covenant traditions of the family.

But turning to Joseph, we see a different character altogether. Though only a lad of about seventeen, he was certainly what might be called a "home boy," though we find him on this occasion, as most likely he was on other similar occasions, in the fields with his brothers, though not joining in their pursuits. He passed between them and home, fetching and carrying, a kind of fag to these burly brothers of his. That he was a thoughtful, serious, and even pious boy is clearly evinced, both by his habit of dreaming (which was but the nightly result of his waking thoughts) and by his subsequent career, in which piety and intellectual ability were well blended. To this boy his father no doubt poured out the story of his grandfather Isaac and his great-grandfather Abraham, and rehearsed the wonderful things out of his own life, until he was full of high hopes and aspirations to become the head of the family and the realizer of all these promises. It was in all probability his sympathy with his father in the matter of the covenant promises, the readiness with which he listened to the patriarch's rehearsal of the family traditions, the intelligent apprehension of these things, that endeared him to his heart, as well as that which has already been mentioned, the fact that he was the son of Rachel.

The coat of many colors.—Among the other marks of his special love and preference for Joseph was this, that he gave him a "coat of many colors." It is still a custom among the Hindus to bestow a garment made of variegated colors to any one of their family to whom special honor is accorded. The dress of a prince, in fact, was this coat of many colors. Whether Jacob meant to announce by this fact that he intended Joseph to be his heir, or whether it was simply of a piece with his manifest fondness for the lad that led him so to decorate him we do not know. Under ordinary circumstances this would not have signified much to his older brethren, who were well-grown men, while Joseph was but a young lad. They indeed spent all their time in the fields among the flocks and herds, while Joseph, though now and then going out with his brethren, or carrying their food to them, stayed more at home. Some of the old allegorists have found in this coat a type of the royal and kingly garments of Christ, of whom almost all commentators find Joseph to be a type in some point or points. Clothes are for covering, and not for decoration, according to the Scripture, though they are used as much for vanity as for use among men and women. As a matter of fact they are a reminder of the fact of man's sin, for the covering of the body did not come into fashion until its nakedness was discovered after the transgression. It is true that the clothing of the body is now by the Holy Spirit taken as a sign of the better covering of the soul with the righteousness of Christ, the putting on of which is likened to the putting on of Christ. But with Jacob the motive was no doubt a double one: first, to please and gratify his favorite young son; and secondly, to clothe him as became his domestic, studious, and gentle habit and turn of mind. Such clothing would be sorely out of place on his coarser brothers; but there was a fitness in so clothing one like Joseph, thoughtful and refined beyond those around him. His brothers probably would have treated the whole matter of the coat with ridicule, had it not been for the other things which excited their ire. When once we take up a grudge against or begin to be envious of another, everything about him is wrong; the most trivial thing is made the ground of complaint.

II.—JOSEPH HONORED BY GOD.

That Joseph was a person marked out by God for a high and distinguished place among men, and especially in his family, the whole of this history abundantly proves. In Joseph and the honor God chose to put on him, we see not only sovereignty, but reason. In general, if we look closely at every case of election recorded in the Bible, it will be seen that there is a wonderful coincidence of ability and fitness for the place and work to which these elect men have been chosen. Consider Noah, Abraham, Jacob, Joseph, Moses, Joshua, David, Solomon, Daniel, and Saul of Tarsus. These men were not great men because of their election, but were rather elect men because of their inherent greatness, or at least fitness for the work to which they were called.

A dreamer of dreams.—Whether we regard the dreams of Joseph as the result of the normal operation of his mind during the hours of sleep, or of a special visitation of God's Spirit, it is evident from their character that they were prophetic, and so far to be counted as direct inspirations from God, who is the author of the prophetic gift in all ages and in all men. "In a dream, in a vision of the night, when deep sleep falleth upon men, in slumberings upon the bed; then he [God] openeth the ears of men, and sealeth their instruction." (Job xxxiii, 15, 16.) The most casual reader of the Bible must have been struck with the great place dreams have had as the method of God in communicating with his servants to show them his will and acquaint them with things to come. God visited Joseph in his dreams, and showed him dimly what was in store for him. No doubt there was a natural basis for these dreams; they sprang partly out of his day-dreamings, induced by his father's constant talk about the greatness of the family according to God's promise. Giving heed to these things, and aspiring to be the head of the family and the instrument of realization, he naturally dreamed of his future greatness. At this point the Spirit of God gave direction, or used the natural dream as a means of sealing instruction upon his understanding. It is rather remarkable that this young dreamer, this thoughtful introspectionist, should have risen so early in the history of this remarkable family. Later on we find a man much like him in Daniel, as also in some respects was David. At any rate, we must see that in directing his dreams God put peculiar honor upon him, and, moreover, intimated to him his future greatness in that in one dream he showed him his brothers bowing down to him, while in a second dream he saw not only his brothers, but his father and his mother also doing obeisance to him. That the lad did not fully understand the import of these things is very evident from the simplicity with which he prattled them forth both to his brothers and to his father. To say that Joseph manifested a vain conceit of his superiority in this matter is an invention to support a theory. The most natural thing in the world is to put it down to boyish simplicity. He already had too much experience of his brothers' roughness needlessly to anger them. The brothers of David accused him of pride and naughtiness of heart because he aspired to fight Goliath, when there was not the remotest thought of pride or boasting in the mind and heart of the lad, but just the boyish innocence of one who believed in God, and thought the slaying of a blaspheming giant nothing more than the killing of a bear or a lion, both of which he himself had done, and thought nothing much about it. It is true that Jacob rebuked Joseph for presumption when he told his second dream, but at the same time "he observed the saying," as though he had gotten some inkling of what it might mean. It is very far from my thought to suggest that all dreams are matters out of which to gather forecasts of things from God; but at the same time I have no doubt that should our minds be in fuller sympathy with divine things, many hints might come to us in dreams which God would "seal for our instruction." God has things to communicate to us in the night as well as in the day. Some one has said that there is a large part of the creation which can only be explored and become acquainted with in the night, and with things that are of the night. We might know the habits of the lark by studying in the day, but how should we ever know those of the owl if we never went abroad by night? The night visions may be as important as the daytime cogitations.

III.—JOSEPH HATED BY HIS BRETHREN.

As we have before said, it was not the coat alone that aroused the hatred of his brethren, nor the father's partial love manifested in the gift of this coat. The dreams, in which his brothers recognized the prophetic quality, made them jealous, angry, and envious of Joseph. The simple truth is they both despised and hated their brother because, in the first place, he was better than they, and because he had experiences they never had, and which they could not understand. The ground of their hatred, summed up, was:

1.—**His father's partial love.**—Not that they felt any lack of love themselves, or cared for any of the petting Joseph got, only with their envious hearts they were not willing to see this stripling preferred before them. There are many people who care not for the love of certain relations, who are nevertheless wroth if it is bestowed upon any one else.

2.—**His report of their evil doings.**—Joseph has been much condemned as a meddlesome tittle-tattler in this matter. But this, it seems to me, is a hasty judgment, for he did not originate the evil reports. They did not grow out of indifferent matters. The fact is, these brothers of Joseph were notoriously bad men, and the country-side was already filled with their evil doings. The Canaanites were muttering and grumbling because of their lawlessness, and perhaps because of their rude immoralities. The honor of their father was being stained by these sons; the peace and even the safety of the family were being risked by their doings. Joseph himself loathed their ways, perhaps had remonstrated with them; he at least felt it his duty, not for the sake of tale-bearing, but because of the increasing danger of the situation and the ill report into which the whole family were falling, to tell his father what he had heard. No doubt Jacob had roundly talked to his sons about their doings, and reprimanded them, and of course Joseph got all the blame. Were those "tattlers" who brought to Paul the report of divisions and fornication in the church at Corinth? Joseph, as his after-life shows, knew pretty well how to hold his tongue when it was needful; no doubt he is rather to be praised than blamed for letting it loose on this occasion. But this did not please his brethren. Tittle-tattle for the sake of making trouble for any one is most despicable; but to be silent in the face of grave evils is to become a party to the offense. To hear men plotting murder and not to report it is to become a murderer yourself. So, had Joseph kept still he would have been giving his consent to his brethren's evil doings.

3.—His too ambitious dreams.—These dreams seemed to have angered them more than anything else. It was really that which rankled in their hearts. "Behold, this dreamer cometh. . . . We shall see what will become of his dreams." (Gen. xxxvii, 19, 20.) They had had no dreams. God had not visited them, and they were angry because Joseph had seen and heard things beyond their experience. The fact is, while they despised Joseph's gentle and quiet ways, sneered at his more thoughtful manner, and ridiculed his simpler and sterner morality, they were envious of him for this reason, that they recognized in him their moral superior. Half the reason for the hatred of the believer by the unbeliever is envy of the former's better life. Despising godliness themselves, they hate those who are godly. Then, besides, these dreams troubled them, for they amounted to a religious experience far above and beyond anything they had any knowledge of, and though they sneered at him for his dreams, there was a foreboding of fear and fact in them that went into their souls and incited them to murder. That he who had been their drudge and the butt of their coarse ridicule should rise above them, and by and by rule over them, that they should bow down to him, was intolerable to them. And yet there was that in Joseph's character, moral uprightness, force, and quietness, that made them fear that the dream was not all a dream, but a real prophecy from God; so they hated him and determined to kill him. Ah, but killing the dreamer did not by any means dispose of the dreams. They might put him in the pit, sell him to the Ishmaelites, do what they would with him, still they could not alter the course of God's providence. The Jews thought they had disposed of the words of Jesus when they crucified him; but they did not reckon on the resurrection or the power of God in the truths which he spake to them. Herein Joseph was a prototype of Christ.

XV.

JOSEPH SOLD INTO EGYPT.—Genesis xxxvii, 23-36.

(23) And it came to pass, when Joseph was come unto his brethren, that they stripped Joseph out of his coat, his coat of many colours that was on him; (24) And they took him, and cast him into a pit: and the pit was empty, there was no water in it. (25) And they sat down to eat bread: and they lifted up their eyes and looked, and, behold, a company of Ishmaelites came from Gilead with their camels bearing spicery and balm and myrrh, going to carry it down to Egypt. (26) And Judah said unto his brethren, What profit is it if we slay our brother, and conceal his blood? (27) Come, and let us sell him to the Ishmaelites, and let not our hand be upon him; for he is our brother and our flesh: and his brethren were content. (28) Then there passed by Midianites merchantmen; and they drew and lifted up Joseph out of the pit, and sold Joseph to the Ishmaelites for twenty pieces of silver: and they brought Joseph into Egypt. (29) And Reuben returned unto the pit; and, behold, Joseph was not in the pit; and he rent his clothes. (30) And he returned unto his brethren, and said, The child is not; and I, whither shall I go? (31) And they took Joseph's coat, and killed a kid of the goats, and dipped the coat in the blood; (32) And they sent the coat of many colours, and they brought it to their father; and said, This have we found: know now whether it be thy son's coat or no. (33) And he knew it, and said, It is my son's coat; an evil beast hath devoured him; Joseph is without doubt rent in pieces. (34) And Jacob rent his clothes, and put sackcloth upon his loins, and mourned for his son many days. (35) And all his sons and all his daughters rose up to comfort him; but he refused to be comforted; and he said, For I will go down into the grave unto my son mourning. Thus his father wept for him. (36) And the Midianites sold him into Egypt unto Potiphar, an officer of Pharaoh's, and captain of the guard.—Genesis xxxvii, 23-36.

The typical character of the story of Joseph has been recognized by most Bible students. Even those who are least inclined to recognize Christ in the Old Testament are constrained to admit that many incidents in the life of Joseph present striking coincidences when compared with the life of our Lord Jesus Christ. Joseph was the beloved of the father; he was sent by his father to his distant and wicked brethren, bearing, as the gift of his father's love and care, bread and wine: instead of being welcomed by his brethren, he was hated of them; they plotted against his life, and in effect took it away, having first sold him for twenty pieces of silver; but God raised him up out of the pit, and highly exalted him upon the throne of Egypt, and made him "a prince and savior" to his brethren, who would have killed him. All this is very striking, yet it might have been mere coincidence if it had stood alone; but when we recall the same striking coincidences (sic) in connection with other Old Testament characters—such as Abel, who was slain; Enoch, who was taken up alive to heaven; Noah, who provided an ark of salvation for sinners; and Abraham, who offered up his only-begotten and well-beloved son; so on through the whole book—we are constrained to say, "Surely the hand of God is in all these histories, and his providence has shaped them so as to give a living picture in type of the leading features in the life of Christ." Not that the actors or their contemporaries saw to what these things were pointing, but that, looking back, we might see how all prophecy and history were pointing to Jesus the Lord.

I.—THE DIABOLICAL CONSPIRACY.

We can call the conspiracy into which Joseph's ten brothers entered to destroy him, nothing less than diabolical. And, indeed, when we remember the word of God from the first, that there should be enmity between the woman's seed and the seed of the serpent, we are warranted in attributing this conspiracy to the devil himself. Cain slew his brother because Abel was more righteous than he; Ishmael persecuted Isaac because he was preferred before him, being the true heir; Esau hated Jacob because Jacob prized and won from him the birthright which he despised; and, finally, Judas sold his Master and delivered him up to the Jews and the Gentiles, who slew him on a tree; but God overruled all these things in order to bring about the salvation of "such as should be saved." Jacob had sent Joseph to his brethren in a distant part of the country with some home dainties, in the way of choice bread and wine. Though a stripling, and his father's favorite, he was not unacquainted with active service, and though arrayed in a coat of many colors as the mark of respect and the badge of high destiny, yet he humbled himself to be the servant of his brethren as Jesus did for us, and went to them with bread and wine. When they saw him coming, their old jealousy, which had already hatched envy, now turned into hatred, which brought forth murder in their hearts. "Behold, this dreamer cometh; . . . let us slay him, and cast him into some pit, and we will say, Some evil beast hath devoured him; and we shall see what will become of his dreams." Can any one read these things (vv. 19-22) without recalling what our Lord said of the wicked husbandman (Matt. xxi, 38), or the taunts which the Jews flung up into Christ's face when he was hanging on the cross: "Thou that destroyest the temple, and buildest it in three days, save thyself. If thou be the Son of God, come down from the cross"? (Matt. xxvii, 40-42.) How vain their taunt! They little thought that this dreamer, whom they hated for his dreams, but much more for his superior righteousness, would by their very cruelty and treachery be lifted into place and power such as would certainly bring his dreams to pass. So the Jews, in slaying Jesus from envy, only helped him to his throne of glory and power. Reuben, the eldest brother, who had perhaps least cause to love Joseph, was the only one who had any compassion for him. At his suggestion the plan to murder him outright was altered to that of slow and miserable starvation. That is, Reuben proposed a plan intending to save Joseph, while the other brothers agreed to it, supposing it would only save them from his blood. It is wonderful how strangely conscience will adjust itself. A mother who should draw a knife and murder her child would be hanged for it, but if she only neglects it until it dies, nothing is said about it; and yet, if possible, murder by neglect is more cruel than murder with a knife.

1.—Joseph seized.—If he had been a thief or a robber they could not have been more violent; and yet they seized him when his hands were full of his father's gifts to them. Even so did the Jews with Jesus when they came out with a mob to seize him. The act was as cowardly as it was devilish. Ten grown men pounce upon this lad of seventeen or eighteen years of age, or possibly now twenty. But wickedness is always cowardly. It would have been as easy for God to save Joseph out of their hands as it was to interpose to save Isaac, or to have sent twelve legions of angels to save Jesus out of the hands of the mob sent by the rulers to arrest him; but God had better things in store for Joseph, and also for these cruel brethren. Let not the righteous be cast down because God does not come immediately to their relief; neither let the wicked be too sure in their wickedness because God does not immediately strike them down. "He that sitteth in the heavens" is taking note both of the afflictions of the righteous and the wickedness of the wicked, and in due time he will reward both according to their deeds.

2.—Joseph humiliated.—Joseph's brethren strip him of his beautiful coat of many colors. This coat was the badge of his superiority over them, the first occasion of their jealousy, and they cannot help venting their hatred against even that. It was a great humiliation to Joseph to be stripped of this coat which his father had given him, badge both of his father's love and of his appointment to be head of the family. Even so the enemies of Christ stripped him of his seamless robe, and finally left him hanging naked upon the cruel tree, humiliated by this outrage and public exposure. But stripping Jesus of his clothes did not take away from his character; neither did the robbing Joseph of his coat degrade him from his moral superiority, or prevent him wearing and exercising that authority of which the coat was only the badge. Let us remember that clothes are not character, and that no outrage, even of our persons, can finally affect our personality.

3.—Joseph delivered to death.—It is true the brothers accepted the compromise proposed by Reuben; but they still meant death to Joseph. To let him starve slowly in the pit was now their intention (though of course Reuben hoped to effect his deliverance). We have already remarked on the Cain spirit awakened in the hearts of the cruel and unnatural brothers. "And wherefore slew he him? Because his own works were evil, and his brother's righteous." This is the Cain spirit. They hated him, not for any evil, but because he was more righteous than they. So it was with Jesus and the Jews. So it is to-day as between upright Christians and the unbelieving and licentious world—they cry out against Christ and Christians as being fanatics and disturbers of the peace, whereas they do not mind fanaticism or so-called disturbances of the peace, provided only the motive is not righteousness. Sin may do as it pleases and go "scot-free," but holiness may not be allowed to live on the earth if unbelievers have their way. The brutality of their act is seen in the disparity of force used, that of ten strong men against one slender stripling of a lad. It was as heartless as it was brutal, for though our present story does not give any intimation of struggle or resistance on the part of Joseph, we know from a later incident that he did cry out most piteously to be spared by his brothers. When these same brothers were in Egypt their consciences were awakened from a twenty years' sleep, "and they said one to another, We are verily guilty concerning our brother, in that we saw the anguish of his soul, when he besought us, and we would not hear." (Gen. xlii. 21.) If Joseph did not resist physically and cry out with his voice, there was an anguish in his face which told the agony of soul he was suffering. This was his Gethsemane, but it moved not their hard hearts. When we come to judgment, if we have not sooner been forgiven and justified, many an old memory will spring up to confront us with wicked and cruel and bitterly unkind things we have done. Is there not in memory and conscience a prophecy of judgment? How cold-blooded these brethren were, is seen in the fact that after they had cast Joseph into the pit they removed a certain distance (perhaps they could not quite enjoy his cries from the pit; perhaps they thought by moving away from it they could remove themselves from the deed they had done—at any rate, even cold-blooded men do not like to sit in too close company with their evil deeds), and they coolly sat down to eat the very dainties which Joseph had brought them. The soldiers who crucified Christ gambled at the foot of the cross for his clothes; these brothers regaled themselves on the bread and wine Joseph had brought them. It may be with boisterous laugh, and even drunken revel, they sought to efface the memory of their deed. This brutality is commemorated in the Scripture as being a proverb of cold-heartedness. Amos, in seeking to depict the utter recklessness of the people, utters his woes upon them "that drink wine in bowls, . . . but . . . are not grieved for the affliction of Joseph." (Amos vi, 6.)

4.—**Joseph cast into the pit.**—They carried out their purpose. Having stripped their young brother of his coat, and no doubt taunted him with his dreams, and otherwise wrought his soul into a great state of anguish, they carried him along and cast him into an empty pit. This pit was one of those huge cisterns which the Orientals excavated, sometimes out of the earth, and sometimes out of the rock, in which to catch water in the rainy season to last them through the dry months. In India they are called tanks, and are usually great artificial water ponds; but in Palestine and Arabia, where also I have seen them, they are deep pits more like wells; if excavated from the rock, they are entered by a narrow mouth. It was into such a pit as this that Jeremiah was cast (Jer. xxxviii, 9, 13), only this pit was in the court of the palace. These pits were often used as prisons and hiding-places, and not infrequently as burial-places, or, at least, dead bodies were concealed in them. They are likened to the grave, and even to hell itself. From one of these pits, whose bottom was filled with miry clay, and so most dreadful to be in, we have the figure used to describe the deliverance of the soul from death to life. "The horrible pit and the miry clay" is proverbial for an unsaved state. Into such a pit was Joseph cast—not let down easily, but cast in violently. To all intents and purposes it was to be his grave, and thus, in intention, Joseph was killed by his brothers and buried. They crucified him in their hatred, and buried him in their fear. But as God raised up Jesus from the dead, so he would rescue Joseph from this pit into which his brothers cast him. And so, indeed, will he finally deliver all the righteous and believing people from their troubles and out of their bitterest extremities.

II.—A PROVIDENTIAL INTERPOSITION.

"The angel of the Lord encampeth round about them that fear him, and delivereth them." (Ps. xxxiv, 7.) These murderous brothers were not to have it all their own way. God, indeed, did not interpose to frustrate their wishes, nor did he at last send an angel to pull Joseph out of the pit; yet all the same he sat in the heavens and watched the proceedings down on the earth. In the meantime he had his messengers on the way to deliver Joseph and carry him off to Egypt, where he should be highly exalted, and where these brothers should also be brought and have demonstrated to them that "this dreamer" was still alive, and that his dreams, in spite of their taunts, should come to pass, and that they should bow down to him. We speak of miracles, and have our doubts sometimes whether there be any miracles; yet God's workings daily in connection with his people in the providential ordering of every-day matters are more complicated and wonderful than ever ordinary or extraordinary miracle could be.

1.—The Midianites.—These were God's angels sent to encamp round about Joseph and bear him away out of the pit. As really angels as if they had descended from heaven for that very purpose, instead of being a company of traveling merchants who were ready to drive a good bargain for a well-favored lad whose brothers were ready to sell him for £2 10s. (about $12.50), which was about the ordinary price of a young slave; just thirty shekels (or a third more) was the regulation price for a grown man. How exalted we would feel if on our behalf God should send an angel to us to deliver us, or to supply our need in time of extremity. Ought we to be less grateful when he orders events so as to accomplish the same result? We are exhorted to entertain strangers, "for thereby some have entertained angels unawares." In this God teaches us that an ordinary stranger may as truly be his angel to us as the heavenly visitants whom Abraham entertained in his tent, supposing them at first to be but travelers, as also did Lot, who was afterward saved by them from Sodom.

2.—The profitlessness of sin.—When these Midianites drew nigh, Judah, one of the brothers, whose conscience had begun to be rather quick within him, made a new proposition. "Even suppose we slay our brother, as we have done in effect, and can conceal his blood" (that is, hide our crime), "what have we profited? We have gratified our spite and glutted our hatred, but have we made anything out of it?" Then followed the proposition to sell him to the Midianites, who would in turn sell him to some Egyptian, and that would be the last of him. Two arguments were advanced in favor of this change of procedure: first, selling instead of slaying their brother would dispose of him, and yet would not be so grave a sin; then in selling him they would receive at least a little benefit. The twenty shekels might be divided among them, and that would be something. We are divided between two thoughts in reading this incident. The despicable cupidity (Judas-like) exhibited in the subtle question, "What profit is it if we slay our brother?" as though even murder was not worth while, supposing it could be effectually concealed, if there is to come no profit out of it. Here cupidity rises higher than hate, and sinks a man lower than murder. Or it may be that this proposition was made somewhat in the spirit in which Reuben's plan was made, to disguise a secret purpose of saving Joseph. Was it the expedient of an awakened conscience? We would fain believe this. For the rest, they rose to the silver bait, and were quite willing to pocket the shekels and get rid of Joseph and his dreams without actually shedding his blood, though the real murder had already been committed. In this view of the case we are led to reflect on the action of these two brothers, Reuben and Judah. Here are two brothers with better impulses surrounded and overborne by eight bad ones, whose actions they did not indorse, and yet who had not the moral courage openly to protest against the wrong, but sought to shuffle out of it by a concealed expedient. They allowed themselves to be drawn into a crime which they loathed, but did not openly combat it and so save themselves and probably their victim. This thing is repeated over and over again every day in business and in society. If we will associate with the ungodly and go half-way with them, they will ultimately involve us in their ungodly deeds, which in our souls we abhor. Again, we are reminded of the timid friends of Jesus among the Sanhedrim which condemned him. Nicodemus and Joseph of Arimathea both sought to deliver Jesus, yet neither of them had the real courage to stand up boldly against the crime their senate was about to perpetrate. Would we have done better than they?

Alas! I for one fear to answer. Do we do better than they did in matters not so grave as the murder of a brother or a Saviour? Alas! I dare not throw a stone at these brothers of Joseph and timid disciples of Jesus. I only can pray God, Lead me not into temptation. Do not, O Lord, allow me to come into a place where my weakness would be too severely tried.

III.—JOSEPH BROUGHT INTO EGYPT.

And so God overruled, guided, and directed the evil passions and murderous intentions of Joseph's brethren, and brought him into Egypt, according to that plan which he had when, three centuries before, he had announced to Abraham, "Thy seed shall be a stranger in a land that is not theirs, and shall serve them." When will vain and unbelieving men learn that God's purposes cannot be frustrated, and that in carrying them out he will use even their most wicked devices to bring them to pass?

1.—Reuben's grief.—For some reason Reuben seems not to have been with his brethren when Judah made his proposal, and, not knowing that they had taken Joseph out of the pit and sold him to the Midianites, he went himself (in pursuance of his plan) to deliver him, and, finding him gone, he knew not how, his grief became frantic. "The child is not." It is true that he had done what little his weakness allowed him to do to save Joseph, but now that he is gone his grief is aggravated by the thought that he had in a sense been a party to his destruction, and by inward reproaches because he had not boldly stood out against his murder. Our grief often comes too late, and is aggravated by inward convictions of wrong-doing.

2.—The lying report.—One crime leads on to another. They must account to their father for Joseph. Their original proposal had been to concoct a story about an evil beast and lay the blame on a wild animal. It seems that with some men a scapegoat is necessary, even though it be a beast. And yet no evil beast was ever half so cruel as these brothers were. Carrying out their plan, they slay a kid, and, staining the coat of Joseph in its blood, send it by the hand of a servant to Jacob, and with an intimation put in his mouth, "Know now whether it be thy son's coat or no," they seek to turn all suspicion away from themselves. No wonder these lying hypocrites could not face their old father; and yet, afraid of him, they are brave in presence of God to heap up sin upon sin, and darken their own souls with accumulated crimes. It must have been hard for Reuben and Judah, but they had already compromised with sin, and were not strong enough to set themselves right.

3.—The mourning of Jacob.—Jacob quickly rose to the bait which his wicked sons had cast to him, and declared the coat to be Joseph's, and naturally concluded that he had been slain and devoured by some wild beast. The old patriarch's heart was fairly broken over this terrible calamity. In vain did all his sons and daughters seek to comfort him. How could those sons dare to offer comfort to their father? They had in effect slain Joseph, and now they had broken their old father's heart, and yet they are compelled either to confess their sins or to play the hypocrite. Verily, a little sin indulged in leads to a vast harvest of mischief and sorrow. The envy of Joseph was the seed which, being planted in their hearts, brought forth this hundredfold crop of mischief and sorrow. The lesson for us here is evidently to beware of indulging in any sin, both because all is wrong, and if indulged in cannot abide alone.

XVI.

JOSEPH RULER IN EGYPT.—Genesis xli, 38–48.

(38) And Pharaoh said unto his servants, Can we find such a one as this is, a man in whom the Spirit of God is? (39) And Pharaoh said unto Joseph, Forasmuch as God hath shewed thee all this, there is none so discreet and wise as thou art: (40) Thou shalt be over my house, and according unto thy word shall all my people be ruled: only in the throne will I be greater than thou. (41) And Pharaoh said unto Joseph, See, I have set thee over all the land of Egypt. (42) And Pharaoh took off his ring from his hand, and put it upon Joseph's hand, and arrayed him in vestures of fine linen, and put a gold chain about his neck; (43) And he made him to ride in the second chariot which he had; and they cried before him, Bow the knee: and he made him ruler over all the land of Egypt. (44) And Pharaoh said unto Joseph, I am Pharaoh, and without thee shall no man lift up his hand or foot in all the land of Egypt. (45) And Pharaoh called Joseph's name Zaphnath-paaneah; and he gave him to wife Asenath the daughter of Poti-pherah priest of On. And Joseph went out over all the land of Egypt. (46) And Joseph was thirty years old when he stood before Pharaoh king of Egypt. And Joseph went out from the presence of Pharaoh, and went throughout all the land of Egypt. (47) And in the seven plenteous years the earth brought forth by handfuls. (48) And he gathered up all the food of the seven years, which were in the land of Egypt, and laid up the food in the cities: the food of the field, which was round about every city, laid he up in the same.
—Genesis xli, 38-48.

It has been remarked that Joseph's own dreams got him into trouble, and the interpretation of others' dreams got him out again. But there was a long time between these experiences. For when Joseph told his brothers and his father his ambitious dreams, he was but a lad of seventeen years of age. When at last he stood before Pharaoh, delivered from prison, clothed with "fine linen," and made ruler over all Egypt, he was thirty years of age. A long time to wait for the beginning of the fulfillment of his dreams of greatness. And the way to the throne had been rough, painful, and full of darkness (at least so far as external circumstances were concerned), though we have reason to believe that Joseph's heart was full of light all through these long thirteen years. And yet other seven years must go by before his brothers and his father bowed down to him. But God had specially given him these dreams, and therefore they were true and must come to pass, in spite of the murderous intention of his brothers, the wickedness of Potiphar's wife (whose wickedness had him cast into prison after years of faithful and prosperous duty in Egypt), or the ingratitude of the king's "butler" or chamberlain. We last saw Joseph a mere lad, in anguish of soul at the pitiless treatment he was receiving at the hands of his brethren; now we see him the honored ruler of the greatest empire then on earth. But the step from the pit, into which he was cast when last we were with him, to the throne was not a sheer nor a single one. It is necessary that we gather up into a chain the links of providence by which God brought him from the pit in the wilderness to the throne of Egypt. Sold by the Midianites to Potiphar, the captain of Pharaoh's guard, he speedily commended himself to his master, for "the Lord was with him"; and this Potiphar saw, and so made him ruler over all his house, and the Egyptian prospered because of Joseph. (xxxix, 1–6.) It began to look already as if the dream was to be fulfilled and Joseph was speedily to become a great man.

Just when hope perhaps was beginning to beat high in the young man's heart, a great temptation befell him, when a wicked woman sought to ruin him. Joseph had grown a handsome and attractive man, and his manly beauty became a snare to him. But he feared God, and was superior to the blandishments of his master's wife, and the grace of God in him was stronger than all the natural weakness of human nature. The secret of Joseph's strength was his deep conviction of duty to his master on the one hand, and his reverent fear of God on the other. "How then can I do this great wickedness, and sin against God?" (Gen. xxxix, 9.) A woman scorned is a dangerous enemy, and so Joseph found, for a false and cruel report was made to Joseph's master of his conduct, and he was immediately cast into a dungeon. Now where were his dreams? A slave, a disgraced slave, a dishonored servant, in a dungeon from whose depths few ever escaped. And yet God lifted no hand to save him, but allowed this great wrong. "But the Lord was with Joseph" in the prison; and here he found favor with his keeper, and he became practically the ruler of the prison. (Gen. xxxix, 20–23.) What strikes us most in these circumstances is, first, Joseph's magnanimity in keeping silence when he was charged with so grave a sin, rather than expose his master's wife to shame. Like Jesus, "when he was reviled" he "reviled not again"; he was taken to the prison, yet "opened he not his mouth." Here is evidence of Joseph's great strength of character, of his great goodness of heart. Surely this is better evidence than all his prosperity that the Lord was with him. Then in the prison we do not find him soured or embittered, but, true to his character, he devotes himself to the prison rules, and shows such superiority that he is quickly promoted, and his training for the government of the great empire goes on in the prison walls, where he rules for the jailer. Then comes, after a long time of prison life, the incident of the butler and the baker and their dreams, with Joseph's inspired interpretation of them. (Gen. xl.) Now, what strikes us in all this prison experience, and especially in the incident of the interpretation of the chamberlain's dream, is that Joseph still had faith in God, who sent the dreams, and held fast by the prophetic destiny to which those dreams pointed. If he had not believed that his own dreams were true, he would not have given himself to the interpretation of the dreams of others. We might well have expected Joseph to have said to the chamberlain, "Take my advice, and pay no attention to dreams. I had dreams of a most remarkable kind repeated to me again and again some years ago, and they have come to nothing, except that I can trace all the misfortunes of these years past to my foolish belief in them. My brothers were quite right to resent them, and call me a 'dreamer' and sneer at me. They were cruel in the way of their resentment, but they were right in their judgment of me as a visionary." But Joseph did not speak thus. He believed in his God-sent dreams. They were an experience which he could not banish from his deepest conviction. He held them to have been from God, and this loyalty to a spiritual experience was no doubt in part the secret of his strength of character during all these years of trial. Nothing is more valuable to us than a definite spiritual experience. Nothing is more important than that we should hold on to it, and wait for the fulfillment of it, or its supplement in other and following experiences. One definite transaction with God, no matter how trivial it may be, if kept in mind and adhered to, will prove a sheet-anchor to the soul through many a storm of life. This fortieth chapter reveals other things also about Joseph. He was a tender-hearted and sympathetic man. He was a man whose heart yearned for liberty, and whose thoughts went back to his own land and his own people. Ah, those weary years of prison life! How brave must Joseph have been to have kept up faith and heart! Had God forgotten? Were his dreams mere mental vagaries? No; he will not be cast down; he will not doubt God;

he will hold true to his purpose; he will not be debased by his prison life; he will live even in that dungeon in such a way as to leave him freer and stronger when he comes out. Only faith in God can make us superior to such circumstances. There are many of God's children who need to study this history in order to learn how to trust and wait. Search thine heart and see if God hath ever spoken to thee at all. Then hold on to that, and wait patiently, and though a chief chamberlain forget thee, God will compel him to remember, and will bring thee out of all thy troubles.

I.—JOSEPH BEFORE PHARAOH.

It came to pass that Pharaoh had a dream. This was two years after Joseph had interpreted the dream of the chamberlain. His prison experience was not yet finished. Then Pharaoh dreamed, and none of the court astrologers could give an interpretation. Then the chief butler's conscience and his memory awakened together, and he told Pharaoh of his dream in the prison two years before, and how Joseph, a Hebrew slave and felon, had interpreted it for him, and one for the baker, too. Then Pharaoh sent and called Joseph, and told him what he had heard concerning him, "that thou canst understand a dream to interpret it." And Joseph said, "It is not in me. God shall give Pharaoh an answer of peace." Here is the man of faith. We see how Joseph had kept his faith in God, and also his own humility. He was not ashamed to confess God and to stand before Pharaoh as his servant, not seeking his own. "God hath showed Pharaoh what he is about to do." The God of Israel is also the God of Pharaoh, and he presides over the destinies of Egypt as well as over those of Canaan. This is not the first time we have seen the beginning of that Providence which, working with God's grace, includes all nations. It is true that "to Abraham and to his seed were the promises made," but the blessing is for all nations. The purpose of God in saving Egypt from famine is but a prophecy of that mightier purpose of God's to give to the heathen nations bread better than Joseph stored up during those seven years of plenty. Also in this divine interpretation of Pharaoh's dream we begin to see the difference between the shrewd guessing of natural philosophers (or magicians) and that spirit of prophecy which is the spirit of revelation. Only God can tell what is in the future, and he only can tell us what to do to provide against, and for, the future. The wisdom and good sense of the answer which Joseph gave to Pharaoh, as also, no doubt, his dignified yet humble bearing, so pleased him that he determined there and then to make Joseph the agent for carrying out the plan he had indicated.

1.—"A man in whom the Spirit of God is."—This is the link which binds men to God. Heaven and earth are married by the Spirit of God. Joseph was a man in whom dwelt the Spirit of God. It is something in favor of Pharaoh that he was as quick to discern this fact as to recognize the wisdom of Joseph's suggestion. Magicians were kept at the court of the Egyptian king for the purpose of solving the various riddles of life which are constantly cropping up, and these wise men of this world had given themselves to the business of unraveling and solving them. But it is not in man to do this, not even in good men. Joseph was a good man, but he said, "It is not in me." "God shall give Pharaoh an answer." This is the clew to inspiration. "Holy men of God spake as they were moved by the Holy Ghost." This inspiration reached the culminating-point in Jesus, to whom the Spirit was given without measure. Therefore we are bidden to "hear him." Though it is not given to us in our day to prophesy in the same way that Joseph prophesied, it is given us that the Holy Spirit dwells in us, and if we give place to him as Joseph did, heeding his teaching and obeying his voice, then men of the world in their extremity, when their wise men and "the prince of this world" fail them, will turn to us "in whom the Spirit of God is" for counsel and help. In this way we become even now "the light of the world" and "the salt of the earth." And no man is in so obscure a position but that, if he is faithful to God in the place where he is put, God may not bring him forth to testify for him.

2.—A discreet and wise man.—Having consulted his ministers, they agreed with the king that Joseph was the proper man to carry out the measures which he had suggested. So he said to Joseph, "Forasmuch as God hath shewed thee all this, there is none so discreet and wise as thou art." Thus Joseph, who sought no preferment, but only to be faithful to God and give the message he was sent to give, suddenly found himself recognized by Pharaoh, not only as an interpreter of dreams, but as a man to be trusted and commissioned to do a great work. Joseph honored God before Pharaoh, and God caused Pharaoh to honor *him*. It is true that the Spirit of God dwelling in a man makes him discreet and wise. In an emergency I would rather have the advice and counsel of the humblest man on earth, who walked with God and was faithful to him, than that of the most brilliant philosopher.

II.—JOSEPH HIGHLY EXALTED.

After thirteen long years, Joseph (who dreamed ambitious dreams and told them to his brethren and to his father, and got hated by the former and rebuked by the latter for his presumption and vanity) now finds himself on the eve of being exalted to a position in which his brothers, and even his father, should bow before him. Could this all have come about without that long discipline of waiting, suffering, and training? Joseph was wise and discreet because the Spirit of God was in him, but that wisdom and discretion was tested in Potiphar's house, ay, and in the prison, during which time he had "kept the faith" and endured "hardness as a good soldier." If there came a thought to Joseph concerning the sneers of his brethren when they said, "We shall see what will become of his dreams," it does not appear; but I feel sure that such thoughts did come to him, not to exalt him overmuch (he had suffered too much for that), but to fill him with devout thankfulness to God who had kept him. Suppose he had yielded to Potiphar's wife; suppose he had turned morbid and sour in the prison, and said to himself, "I have been honest and faithful, and all God has given me is slander, reproach, and degradation; I will not serve God, who thus deserts the righteous and lets the wicked go free,"—Joseph would never have been where he was now. Suppose, even, the butler had remembered him, and secured his freedom according to promise, he might only have been sold to some other master, or at best gone home to suffer and die with the rest of his family in the famine which came upon all the world. Surely it pays to wait patiently for God to move. I think we must learn that it is only necessary for us to be true to God in the place where we are, doing with our might what our hands find to do, and God, whose thoughts for us are "thoughts of peace and not of evil," will give us the expected end.

1.—**Honored and lifted up.**—"Thou shalt be over my house, and according to thy word shall all my people be ruled: only in the throne will I be greater than thou." And so, with the ring of the king upon his hand, the signet-ring of authority, with the fine linen royal robe, more precious than gold, upon his person, with the king's proclamation that the people should bow down to Joseph, and the second chariot of the kingdom for him to ride in, Joseph is made ruler over all Egypt. It is impossible for us not to see here again the analogy between Joseph and the Lord Jesus, whom "God exalted with his right hand to be a Prince and a Saviour"; sealed with the signet-ring of authority—"All power is given unto me in heaven and in earth,"—and commanded all the people to hear. "He that honoreth not Joseph honoreth not Pharaoh." Such was the purport of the proclamation; even as it is written, "He that honoreth not the Son honoreth not the Father." Now the coat of many colors was exchanged for the royal fine linen, and the slave's and prisoner's fetters for the golden chain of honor and authority. So does God bring things to pass. No wonder, in long centuries afterward, the psalmist sung of Joseph, "The king sent and loosed him; even the ruler of the people, and let him go free. He made him lord of his house, and ruler of all his substance: to bind his princes at his pleasure; and teach his senators wisdom." (Ps. cv, 20-22.) So complete was his authority that without him no man might "lift up his hand or foot in all Egypt."

2.—**The saviour of the world.**—Pharaoh changed Joseph's name to Zaphnath-paaneah, which, scholars tell us, means "saviour of the world." The angels brought "good tidings of great joy which shall be to all people" when Jesus was born. So when Joseph was delivered from the dark prison, and born, as it were, into this new place of power, he was proclaimed "saviour of the world." Highly exalted, indeed, to be "a prince and a saviour," not only to Egypt, but to all the countries round about, even unto his brethren, who had rejected him and delivered him over to death. Shall not Jesus in the end have the joy of seeing his brethren according to the flesh, the unbelieving Israel, come to him for corn, and finally recognize him as "their Brother" whom they had so bitterly wronged?

3.—**Joseph married.**—Pharaoh, having given Joseph a new name, also married him to the daughter of the priest of On. Thus did the Hebrew boy become allied to one of the great families of Egypt. This is one of these incidents, of which there are several, in connection with the "elect people" of alliances with the heathen nations and the interweaving of Gentile threads into the fabric of the chosen people. Later on we find Rahab, the Canaanitish woman, becoming incorporated with them. Still later Ruth, the Moabitess, also takes her place. These latter two became ancestresses of our Lord according to the flesh. Is there not in this the hint of God's purpose of universality in connection with the covenant of grace? Are not these the forerunners of that vast Gentile ingathering which has been going on ever since the rejection of Jesus, the Great Joseph, by his brethren according to the flesh?

III.—JOSEPH'S WISE ECONOMY.*

Joseph, having been appointed grand-vizier of Egypt and set over all the land, his domestic happiness settled and his authority fully published throughout the kingdom, went out from the presence of Pharaoh, armed with full authority to inaugurate those far-reaching and wise arrangements by which the coming years of famine were to be provided for. In this work three things were conspicuous, though the details of them are not given.

1.—Economy.—This was the principle upon which Joseph wrought. The way to provide for the future is to economize in the present, for the waste of plentiful years brings want in years of famine. It is the waste of our abundance which breeds want and poverty. When there is much we should learn to lay by in store that which is not wanted for present need. This is a very hard lesson to learn. We are all naturally extravagant and wasteful, spending that which we should save, and wasting that which should be laid up in store. Joseph demonstrated that, properly managed, the produce of the earth is sufficient to supply the needs of all men, taking years of plenty and years of scarcity together. God means us to learn how to manage our substance so that in years of plenty there shall be no waste in order that in years of famine there be no lack. These great granaries which Joseph built and filled were the first savings-banks ever constructed. All men should have a savings-bank account. Again, it is suggested that if properly administered there would be no want of substance by any in this world; for what the rich waste every year would more than feed and clothe all the poor.

2.—Joseph's industry.—It must have required a vast amount of careful industry to arrange for the housing of the surplus corn of those seven plentiful years. Houses had to be built. Contracts had to be made. Transportation had to be provided. We doubt not that much authority had to be exercised in compelling the farmers to sell their wheat and cultivate all available land. The perfect success of his plans demonstrate that every detail had been carefully thought out. During all these seven years, so fully occupied was Joseph that he had no time to think of his old home, of his beloved father, or his faithless brothers. We are sure that he did not forget them or that he belonged to them, for this fact comes out in the names of his two sons. (Gen. xli, 51, 52.) To him Egypt, though a land of prosperity, was still "the land of his affliction."

3.—Joseph's patient persistence.—Now Joseph was carrying on all these toilsome works solely upon the authority of the conviction of the truth of his interpretation of Pharaoh's dream. Seven years was a long time to hold fast by a purpose, especially when there was no outward sign of need. But Joseph had learned to wait. Had he not waited thirteen years already for his dreams to begin to be fulfilled? Surely he knew how to wait patiently for seven other years. He had learned that God is never in a hurry, and so neither was he. Patient too, I fancy, under many a scoff, though uttered not in his hearing. The people, blinded by their present prosperity, must have thought of him as a visionary dreamer. Well, he had borne that taunt before. Still, it is hard to persevere in the face of unbelief, especially when our patience is taxed for years on years. But Joseph, like Noah, lived to see his patience and faith rewarded.

XVII.

JOSEPH FORGIVING HIS BRETHREN.
Genesis xlv, 1-15.

(1) Then Joseph could not refrain himself before all them that stood by him; and he cried, Cause every man to go out from me. And there stood no man with him, while Joseph made himself known unto his brethren. (2) And he wept aloud: and the Egyptians and the house of Pharaoh heard. (3) And Joseph said unto his brethren, I am Joseph; doth my father yet live? And his brethren could not answer him; for they were troubled at his presence. (4) And Joseph said unto his brethren, Come near to me, I pray you. And they came near. And he said, I am Joseph your brother, whom ye sold into Egypt. (5) Now therefore be not grieved, nor angry with yourselves, that ye sold me hither: for God did send me before you to preserve life. (6) For these two years hath the famine been in the land: and yet there are five years, in the which there shall neither be earing nor harvest. (7) And God sent me before you to preserve you a posterity in the earth, and to save your lives by a great deliverance. (8) So now it was not you that sent me hither, but God: and he hath made me a father to Pharaoh, and lord of all his house, and a ruler throughout all the land of Egypt. (9) Haste ye, and go up to my father, and say unto him, Thus saith thy son Joseph, God hath made me lord of all Egypt: come down unto me, tarry not: (10) And thou shalt dwell in the land of Goshen, and thou shalt be near unto me, thou, and thy children, and thy children's children, and thy flocks, and thy herds, and all that thou hast: (11) And there will I nourish thee; for yet there are five years of famine; lest thou, and thy household, and all that thou hast, come to poverty. (12) And, behold, your eyes see, and the eyes of my brother Benjamin, that it is my mouth that speaketh unto you. (13) And ye shall tell my father of all my glory in Egypt, and of all that ye have seen; and ye shall haste and bring down my father hither. (14) And he fell upon his brother Benjamin's neck, and wept; and Benjamin wept upon his neck. (15) Moreover he kissed all his brethren, and wept upon them: and after that his brethren talked with him.—Genesis xlv, 1-15.

No doubt Joseph had suffered during the thirteen years between the time he was cast into the pit by his brethren and his elevation to the viceregal dignity and power of Egypt. Those long, lonely hours in the prison; the bitter disgrace of lying under false accusation; the chain and iron collar; the ingratitude of men all around him; the severe trials of his faith; God's long silence; the apparent triumph of the wicked, and his own abandonment both by men and apparently by God; hard and possibly bitter thoughts of his brethren; his longing desire for freedom; homesickness; and all the rest of it must have caused him mental and physical anguish. Who can tell what the sufferings may be of thirteen years of slavery, a large part of it spent in prison? But then, though Joseph had trial of faith he did not lose faith; nor did he suffer any deterioration of character, and came out of his trials gloriously. On the other hand, we cannot but contrast Joseph's estate during those years with that of his ten unnatural brethren. From the very first theirs was a hard and bitter time. They had indeed got rid of the dreamer, and heard no more of his dreams; but they had committed a crime which never left them a moment's peace in all those years. They had witnessed the heart-broken distress of old Jacob, who never ceased to mourn for Joseph, and perhaps to reproach them by his suspicions of foul play. Joseph sold into Egypt was always present in their consciences, and the crime of their action was a stalking presence wherever they went. The mutual reproaches which they passed upon each other show this, when they first came down to Egypt and confronted the great ruler there, who bade them go back and bring their youngest brother. The ghost of Joseph rose up before them. When they found the money in their sacks, when Benjamin was detained, whenever anything went wrong with them, their consciences at once connected it with their crime in selling their brother, attributing their misfortune and trouble to the just vengeance of Heaven. A bad conscience is a dreadful thing to carry with one, and it is remorseful. Time has much power to assuage a sorrow, but time can never obliterate a bad conscience. Years may pass, and conscience may seem to sleep; but of a sudden some trifling thing will come, suddenly wake it up, drag our sin out before us, and lo, we are smitten before it. No, upon the whole Joseph had the best of it, even before his exaltation.

Nothing could possibly be more dramatic than the facts detailed in the four preceding chapters; nothing more touching and pathetic than the events immediately antecedent to our study: the brethren of Joseph before him supplicating him for bread, not knowing that he was Joseph; Joseph suddenly leaving his brethren to relieve his pent-up feelings upon recognizing them and hearing of his father and Benjamin; then again, on their second visit, when they are brought back with the apparent evidence of a fresh crime in their hands, and Benjamin by their own word delivered to death. Behold them this third time, bowing themselves to the ground, and listen to the words out of the mouth of Judah, their spokesman: "My lord;" "O my lord," over and over again. Now where is Joseph's dream? What a contrast between this scene and that of twenty-five years before, when Joseph was lying in anguish of spirit in the pit, and his brethren withdrawn out of hearing of his cries, eating and drinking. Verily God knows how to bring matters to pass. Then we cannot but notice how the individual and personal interests and family matters are interlaced with the larger purposes of God, in connection with the covenant promises concerning the future not only of the theocratic family, but of nations.

I.—JOSEPH ALONE WITH HIS BRETHREN.

The three different occasions on which the brethren of Joseph were brought before him seem to have wrought a considerable change in Joseph's mind toward them. When they first came he spoke to them roughly. Perhaps there was yet some bitterness in his heart toward them; and what wonder? The news of his father and Benjamin softened him a little, but it looks much as if Joseph's first intention had been to avoid all dealings with these men. He schemed to get Benjamin down to him, but beyond this there is no evidence that he intended either to make himself known to his brethren or bring them to Egypt. The device of making Benjamin a prisoner on a charge of stealing his cup was successful, and his disclaimer of any intention of holding the rest of his brethren responsible for what was charged (and apparently proved) against Benjamin seems to carry out the thought that he intended to send them back to Canaan without revealing himself to them. (Gen. xliv, 17.) Then came the eloquent and pathetic plea of Judah not only for Benjamin, but for Jacob, the old father, and his voluntary offer to redeem Benjamin by surrendering himself to lifelong bondage. There is not in all history a more eloquent and pathetic speech than that of Judah. This same Judah who proposed the sale of Joseph is now ready to give himself a ransom for Benjamin, Joseph's brother. A great change has come over this rough man—now all full of tenderness and compassion for Jacob and the lad. Is there not in this fact an evidence that in Judah's heart at least a great sorrow had wrought a great repentance? He would now atone for his sin against Joseph by saving the life, as it were, of Benjamin, and sparing the already broken heart of Jacob from this fresh sorrow. It was this evidence of real repentance in Judah and possibly in the others also which finally changed Joseph's mind and determined him to alter his plan and inclose them all in his love again and become a father to them.

1.—Joseph's love for his brethren.—The pathetic plea of Judah for Benjamin, and his evident deep desire to save the lad, and his father from a final crushing sorrow, as we have said, convinced Joseph that there had come another heart to his brethren. A thousand memories crowded in upon him. The old home and his boyish days came back to him, and his heart welled up with a large and tender pity and forgiving love for them all. He felt that another moment and he would break down before his servants, and so he at once ordered the presence-chamber where they were to be cleared of all the Egyptian servants, that he might be alone with his brethren. No doubt it was God's love in his heart yearning over them, and mingling with his human love, that moved him so. It is deeply true also that there are seasons of sacred joy as well as of sorrow, when we desire no strangers present. What had these Egyptians to do with this family gathering, this reconciling interview? They did not know, could not appreciate; and so he sent them all away.

2.—Joseph makes himself known to his brethren.—Up to this moment Joseph's brethren had only known him as "Zaphnath-paaneah," the great lord of Egypt; and he had been rather rough and stern with them. True, there had been that in their experience which had brought the memory of their ill-treated brother Joseph keenly back to their consciences, but they did not dream that this great lord was he. Far from it! For had they suspected it, a thousand cart-ropes could not have dragged them into his presence. Now again we fancy they trembled when the order was given that they should stand in his presence alone. What did he mean? What further ill thing was about to happen to them? The sinner's bitterest moment of fear and trembling, of despair, is just before the revelation of Christ as a Saviour. So it was with these guilty men before their brother Joseph. Now he made himself known to them. "I am Joseph." How the words in the old Hebrew tongue must have smitten through and through them! Hitherto they had spoken through an interpreter; but now they hear him speak in their own tongue; and with the revelation of himself comes back a recognition of the family features, the lighter skin of Joseph. In a moment the whole truth comes before them, and they shrink back appalled with fear and confusion. It was perhaps to avert the confusion and dismay which he saw in their faces that Joseph, in order to assure them that his intentions were pacific, asked for the third time, "Doth my father yet live?" It is not now, "Is your father well, the old man of whom ye spake? Is he yet alive?" But in the words "my father" they might detect the voice of a brother, and his intention of resuming relations with them as a son of Jacob. But they were too much dismayed to answer him. They were terrified and perplexed at his presence, as well they might be. Adam and Eve fled at the first revelation of God after their sin, and these brothers' thoughts were of their sin and of the righteous indignation and punishment they might justly expect from Joseph. And so it is with sinners who are under conviction of sin. They are too fearful to take note of the peaceable words of God spoken to them. Not the promises of the gospel, but the denunciations of the law, overwhelm them and fill all their thoughts.

3.—Joseph entreats his brethren.—Is not this most strange? He does not wait for them to fall on their faces and beseech him, but he reaches out his hands and entreats them. He is now filled with a deep desire to reconcile his brethren. Does not this remind us of what Paul tells us of the love of God in Christ? "God was in Christ, reconciling the world unto himself, not imputing their trespasses unto them." God was in Christ beseeching us to be reconciled to him. Amazing grace is this! So now Joseph entreats: "Come near to me, I pray you." When they had cast him into the pit, they fled from him. They had been alienated and estranged from Joseph by their wicked works, and now Joseph seeks to draw them back to him. He entreats them to come near to him. My thoughts keep running out to Christ, and I remember how he entreats sinners, seeks to win them to himself, stretching out his hands "all the day long," and says in a thousand ways, "Come, come, come unto me." They still hesitated, though they came near. No doubt they thought, "What will he do to us now?" But they were quite ready to surrender, overwhelmed with a sense of their guilt, speechless and defenseless before the power of Joseph. What could they say? What could they do? Like Saul of Tarsus before Jesus, whom he had persecuted, they were at the end of defense and resistance. We can almost imagine them saying, "What wilt thou have us to do?" When they were thus drawn near to Joseph, waiting to hear what next he would say to them, Joseph said to them, "I am Joseph." Ah, it was a terrible revelation! They could have filled out the sentence very well: "Whom ye cast into a pit; whom ye sold into slavery; whom ye mocked and jeered; from whose anguish ye turned without pity or compassion." But this is not what they heard. "I am Joseph your brother." This was the first word he wanted them to get into their hearts. "Your brother." There was no word of enmity in this, but affection. "Whom ye sold into Egypt." This indeed he had to say, but this he said not in terms of reproach, but rather to explain his presence there in Egypt. He did not say, "Whom ye would have slain," though he might have reminded them of the worst of their crime, their intention to murder him. But the emphasis is laid on the term "brother." He did not say, "I am Joseph, the real ruler of Egypt, who has you in his power as you once had him in yours," but, "I am Joseph, your brother; I own you, I still claim kin with you, though ye denied me. I am not ashamed to call you brethren." Here is the grace of it. What a picture of the gospel there is in all this, and how our hearts and minds keep going out to our Great Brother, who says to us indeed, "I am Jesus, whom thou persecutest," but only that he may further say, "But I forgive you freely, and only long for you to be reconciled to me. High and exalted as I am, low down and in deep distress and dependence as you are, I am not ashamed of you, but desire to confess you before God and all men and angels."

4.—Joseph forgives his brethren.—We are first of all struck with Joseph's generosity. He utters not one word of reproach against them. He does not first gratify himself with a triumph over them before forgiving them; but, on the other hand, seeks to put them at ease concerning the past. "Now therefore be not grieved, nor angry with yourselves." He saw the bitterness of their repentance in their faces, in their downcast looks, in the fearful convulsions of remorse working in their persons. He was more than content with their repentance, and would now have them cease from their self-condemnation and enter into his love. God will indeed have us repent of our sins, but he will not have us forever doing this, and casting discredit on his forgiveness by mourning over that which he has cast out of his heart and behind his back and remembers no more. (Isa. xxxviii, 17; Jer. xxxi, 34.) He would have us accept his forgiveness frankly and enter into the joy of reconciliation. When the father prepared the feast for the prodigal son he did not wish that son to spend all the night in rehearsing to him how bitterly he repented his past folly. He would have said, "True, my son, all that is made plain to me by your coming home. Now let us forget all about that bad time and enter into the joy of the present and the future."

5.—The theocratic explanation.—Joseph, besides, explained to them that there was now another side to the whole matter. True, they had sinned grievously, but God had a purpose in it all which he secured by overruling their sin. It was needful that Joseph should come into Egypt in order that he might be placed in a position of power and authority, so that he might not only save life in general, but "preserve you a posterity in the earth, and to save your lives by a great deliverance." (vv. 5, 7.) They indeed had wrought sin against Joseph, but God had sent him to Egypt for a great and high purpose. It is not that we may excuse sin that we point out the fact that in and through sin God works out most noble, high, and divine ends. It is no justification of sin that it has become the occasion for the great deliverance which God has wrought by Jesus Christ. We do not excuse the Jews that they "by wicked hands" "crucified the Lord of glory," because we know that his death was "by the determinate counsel and foreknowledge of God." But having been saved from our sin, we may the rather rejoice that "where sin abounded, there grace did much more abound." And so Joseph would have his brethren to rejoice in the manifest goodness of God to them and to their father, and to their posterity, through whom the blessings of God upon other nations must come.

6.—**Joseph's brethren reconciled.**—After all this had been explained to them, Joseph "fell upon his brother Benjamin's neck and wept; and Benjamin wept upon his neck. Moreover he kissed all his brethren, and wept upon them; and after that his brethren talked with him." (vv. 14, 15.) This was the completion of the reconciliation. That kiss of Joseph sent away all the offense against his brethren, and was the pledge to them that there was henceforth nothing but love in his heart for them. That they returned the kiss was on their part their acceptance of Joseph's forgiveness. Their subsequent talking together was the communion of the reconciled brothers. Before the forgiveness and reconciliation there could be no communion; but after these then talk, blessed talk. How sweet to know that being forgiven and reconciled to God we have perpetual access and communion. Rightly apprehended, prayer is not simply asking and thanking God for gifts, but it is also communion, sweet fellowship, the bathing of our souls in the joy of his love. Forgiveness without reconciliation would be but a mockery; and reconciliation which is not followed by communion is but a delusion. If forgiven, then I am reconciled to God; and if truly reconciled, then I "talk" with God, or have communion.

II.—JOSEPH PROVIDES FOR HIS FAMILY.

Whether Joseph originally intended to bring down all his family to Egypt does not appear. There is much to suggest that he did not. That he intended to secure Benjamin (his mother's son and his full brother) and make him a sharer with him of his honor and power, is certainly clear; but when Judah's tender plea and evidently changed heart was made manifest and lead up to the final and complete reconciliation of the brethren, then a large and legitimate purpose followed naturally.

1.—Glad tidings of good news.—Now they must hasten home and break the double or triple good news to Jacob. First, Joseph is alive, and not only alive, but exalted to power and great glory in Egypt. Besides that, they must tell of the reconciliation to the brethren. This, indeed, is the first duty of converted men, of forgiven sinners, to go home to their families and "tell them how great things the Lord hath done for" them in saving their souls, and of the exaltation of Jesus to power and glory. It was not vanity that led Joseph to send this message of his exalted place and power, but to assure Jacob that he had power to save him and do for him all that he promised, and thus to induce him to come quickly down to Egypt. They were appealed to by their own experience, that there was no delusion in all this. They could go back to their father with no hearsay report, but with a testimony based on their own experience. This is the kind of testimony we need to give to others if we are to induce them to come to Jesus. We must tell them about Jesus and also what he has done for us, then will men believe the testimony, especially if we bring with it sacks of corn and wagons to bring them down. It is a great thing to be able to show to "Jacob" corn and wagons and changes of raiment received at the hands of "Joseph."

2.—Joseph the keeper of his brethren.—Not only did God through Joseph work a great deliverance from past sin and temporary want, but by bringing his father and all the family to Egypt he provided for them during the remaining five years of famine, and also settled them near him in the land, where he could watch over them for good. Is it not so with us? Jesus first forgives our sins, then reconciles us to God, and establishes communion between us; then he keeps us from falling and "supplies all our need," keeping us near to him. (Jude 24, Phil. iv, 19.) Salvation is begun in forgiveness, but it is carried forward in and by the keeping power of God. There remain yet five years of famine, and what would we do if Joseph, our brother, did not provide for us, and put all the resources of his power and authority at our disposal?

XVIII.

JOSEPH'S LAST DAYS.—Genesis l, 14-26.

(14) And Joseph returned into Egypt, he, and his brethren, and all that went up with him to bury his father, after he had buried his father. (15) And when Joseph's brethren saw that their father was dead, they said, Joseph will peradventure hate us, and will certainly requite us all the evil which we did unto him. (16) And they sent a messenger unto Joseph, saying, Thy father did command before he died, saying, (17) So shall ye say unto Joseph, Forgive, I pray thee now, the trespass of thy brethren, and their sin; for they did unto thee evil: and now, we pray thee, forgive the trespass of the servants of the God of thy father. And Joseph wept when they spake unto him. (18) And his brethren also went and fell down before his face; and they said, Behold, we be thy servants. (19) And Joseph said unto them, Fear not: for am I in the place of God? (20) But as for you, ye thought evil against me; but God meant it unto good, to bring to pass, as it is this day, to save much people alive. (21) Now therefore fear ye not: I will nourish you, and your little ones. And he comforted them, and spake kindly unto them. (22) And Joseph dwelt in Egypt, he, and his father's house: and Joseph lived an hundred and ten years. (23) And Joseph saw Ephraim's children of the third generation: the children also of Machir the son of Manasseh were brought up upon Joseph's knees. (24) And Joseph said unto his brethren, I die: and God will surely visit you, and bring you out of this land unto the land which he sware to Abraham, to Isaac, and to Jacob. (25) And Joseph took an oath of the children of Israel, saying, God will surely visit you, and ye shall carry up my bones from hence. (26) So Joseph died, being an hundred and ten years old: and they embalmed him, and he was put in a coffin in Egypt.—Genesis l, 14-26.

The first impressions received of Joseph, introduced to us in this record as a petted, favorite, and it may be partly spoiled child, with his coat of many colors, walking about day-dreaming and telling his dreams to his brothers, is not very favorable to the expectation of a great character. He seems to us rather an effeminate boy, as children of a man's old age are apt to be. We pity him as we see him cast into the pit and finally sold by his brethren into Egypt. We begin to admire him as we see him in Potiphar's house, the capable ruler of his master's affairs, trusted, honored, and prospered. Our admiration increases as we observe his stern and sterling virtue, fearing God and regarding the rights of his master above every blandishment of a seductive, crafty, and persistent woman. We still more wonder at his generosity in accepting his dungeon life without opening his mouth in defense lest he should work grievous mischief in his master's house. We admire him in the prison; not becoming soured or surly under false imprisonment, but active, and energetic as of yore, again winning esteem and trust by faithfulness, and rising into place and power even as a prisoner. Most of all we are charmed and delighted to find that he has not lost sympathy for his fellow-sufferers, though no one seems greatly to have sympathized with him. He is grieved at the distress of the butler and the baker who had been cast into prison for some court offense and were distressed by dreams. We rejoice that these thirteen years have not shaken his faith in God, nor his confidence in the divine source of his own boyish dreams. Emerging from prison at thirty years of age, we wonder at his calm, self-possessed, yet humble confidence before Pharaoh. Disclaiming any powers of his own, but asserting the presence and possession of the prophetic Spirit of God, he boldly and confidently interprets Pharaoh's double dream. We are delighted that after long and faithful waiting the lad who has made himself conspicuously useful in every place where his lot was cast, is now called upon to take the very highest place in the greatest kingdom on the earth. We are not now altogether surprised at the sagacity and strength which he displays in the administration of the affairs of Egypt in those years of successive plenty and famine. In his exaltation and boundless power he does not forget his home, nor the covenant of God with his fathers. When his brothers come to him, whatever his first impulses were, he quickly puts everything aside, and receives those into his heart who had put him out of theirs. He is not ashamed of his shepherd origin, though it makes him despised in Egypt. Bringing his family about him, he is forward to identify himself with them (as Moses also was later on), and to use his wisdom and power so well that he secured for them the very best part of Egypt for their dwelling-place, where he nourished them for seventeen years, till Jacob's death. Truly here is a great man. We discern the secret of his greatness in his unshaken faith in God, in that he exalted his heavenly dreams above all his earthly vicissitudes, and clung to his Heaven-appointed destiny in the face of all adverse circumstances. For down to his last moment he was careful to order his last will and testament in accordance with the promise of God made to Abraham, to Isaac, and to Jacob, concerning the land of promise, where he stipulated that his bones should be finally buried.

I.—THE HAUNTING GHOST OF AN OLD CRIME.

Jacob lived in Egypt for seventeen years. Before he died he adopted the two sons of Joseph, and by the spirit of prophecy that was in him, set aside the younger of the two and made him to be as the firstborn, even as he had taken precedence of his elder brother. He then blessed them and all the rest of his sons, and charged them to carry his dead body up into the land of Canaan and lay it beside the bodies of his fathers, Abraham and Isaac, in the cave of Machpelah. (Gen. xlviii, 5, 14–22.) His last wish was carried out by Joseph, and at the command of Pharaoh with great pomp and ceremony, Joseph going up out of Egypt into Canaan at the head of a mighty and royal escort. After the days of lamentation were over, all the sons of Jacob returned again to Egypt: Joseph to his high dignity and duties as grand-vizier of Egypt, and the sons of Jacob to their possessions in the land of Goshen. This brings us to the last chapter in the life of Joseph.

1.—The fear of Joseph's brethren.—No sooner had the brothers gotten back from Canaan, where they had buried their father, than their old crime against Joseph rose up to haunt them again. Now that Jacob was dead they feared that Joseph would (when unrestrained by the father he so much revered) turn upon them and wreak a vengeance which they felt they richly deserved. True, Joseph had freely forgiven them seventeen years ago, and since then he had nourished them, and caused them to prosper beyond the Egyptians. But they could not understand forgiveness for such an offense, and they thought and said among themselves, "Joseph was only restrained for our father's sake; he never could have meant what he said to us." And, conscious of the fact of their former treachery against him, they could not believe his kiss upon their cheeks was not a false one. Truly, it is hard to lay a bad conscience. Do we wonder that these brothers should have so misjudged Joseph and doubted his word and the sincerity of all his subsequent dealings with them? Then let us still more wonder that as these brethren doubted Joseph, so have we doubted our heavenly Father and our divine Redeemer. Have not our old sins often risen up to plague us? And we have said within ourselves, "It cannot be that God has forgiven them." We look back to the hour when we were at his feet in contrition and confession, and where we received his gracious word of forgiveness; we remember all the spiritual mercies, all the temporal blessings since then received from God's good hand, and yet we doubt whether, after all, our sins were forgiven. These brethren, haunted by this fear, sent a messenger to Joseph—most likely Benjamin, as being the one brother not involved in their crime, and being tenderly loved by Joseph—representing to them that it was the will and wish of their father that Joseph should forgive their trespass and their sin which they had done against him.

2.—The grief of Joseph.—This message from his brethren greatly grieved and distressed Joseph. "And Joseph wept when they spake unto him." We can well understand how and why Joseph was so grieved and distressed, for he had fully and frankly forgiven his brethren. He had tried in every way to demonstrate the fullness of his love for them. He had loaded them with benefits, he had often come down to see them, and thus shown that he had no intention even of withdrawing fellowship from them; and yet after these years of kindness he was still misunderstood and distrusted. His generous heart was bowed down with sorrow. He could and did bear, years ago, without a word, the doubt and distrust of Potiphar, who believed the evil report against him, though that must have been a sore trial to him. He had bitterly suffered at the remembrance of his brothers' unnatural treatment of him; but it is doubtful if this blow was not the hardest he had received of all the evil happenings of his life. Nothing is so severely trying to a generous nature as to be persistently misunderstood, and to have the generous kindness of its heart misinterpreted and set down to the score of insincerity. But may we not carry this thought higher than even the throne where Joseph sat? May we not say that there is no grief greater to God than that we doubt his love and distrust all his promises? True, our sins and our trespasses have been great, beyond measure; true also, that, left to ourselves, we could never forgive such offenses against ourselves; but when God has assured us over and over again that he has forgiven our sins, and "will remember their sin no more," and when we consider Jesus, the suffering and dying Redeemer who gave his life for us that we might be forgiven and justified from every offense, is it not the very height of ingratitude to doubt the truth of God's word and the divine sincerity of his grace? We sometimes hear people say that to have assurance of forgiveness is presumption; but to our mind, to go on doubting God's grace and the absolute sincerity of his word of forgiveness, though our sins had been as scarlet and crimson, is greater presumption, and base ingratitude besides.

It may be that we can never forgive ourselves for our horrible sins against God, but we *may* not, we *must* not, doubt God's forgiveness, for this is to deny the very glory of his nature. "Have I been so long time with you, and yet hast thou not known me?" This, I fancy, might be the word of Jesus to us in those hours when we come back to him with old sins long since forgiven. Do not let us doubt him more.

3.—Joseph's generous love.—Following quickly their messenger, the brethren came into Joseph's presence, and, casting themselves down at his feet, said, "Behold, we be thy servants." Had this been a grateful act of consecration in recognition of all the grace and goodness which they had received from their brother, it might have been a graceful thing for them to do; but it was the action of abject fear and cringing submission. Joseph recoiled from this, and said to them at once, "Fear not: for am I in the place of God?" That is, do you suppose for a moment that I would take vengeance upon you to punish you for your transgression? God has forgiven your sin; I have forgiven it; now, therefore, do not grovel before me as though my business were to search out your sin and punish it. (Rom. xii, 19, 20.) Or it may mean: "Fear not. Am I not in the place of God?" That is, have I not already, in God's name, forgiven you your sins, and shall I then take back that forgiveness? When God forgives he also forgets. Therefore, as in his place, I have forgiven and have forgotten your sin and trespass against me. Thus did Joseph; nor did he once allude to the fact that kneeling there before his face they might behold the fulfillment of his dream for which they had hated him and sold him into Egypt. This was not the first time opportunity had presented itself for Joseph to call their attention to the fulfillment of his dream. But his love was like the love of God, that "giveth to all men liberally and upbraideth not." It is true that when the Spirit of Christ is in a man it will lead him to do and act as Christ would do in the same circumstances. This is why in some sort so many of the Old Testament worthies, in whom the Spirit of Christ dwelt, seem to us to be types of Christ, because they did so many things which remind us of Christ.

4.—Joseph's larger view of the matter.—It was a part of Joseph's generosity that he was always ready to sink his own personal wrongs in the larger purposes which he saw were involved in his sufferings. It is true that they meant him evil when they sold him into Egypt, but Joseph had come to see clearly that God had been all the time working out a great and beneficent purpose toward his family and other people, and therefore he was ready to forget his wrongs, while rejoicing in the great deliverance brought through him, and especially that his sufferings were the means of preserving a posterity to his father, and so serving the purpose of God in blessings to many nations. This is a real and a grand faith. It is a wider view of things which we, too, should learn to take. We are all apt to make ourselves, and what affects *us*, the center and even the circumference of God's providence. "All things work together for good to them that love God." But the good is often seen in the general good of the people of God, and not always in the immediate profit or pleasure of the individual. The good often is seen in the ultimate result, even though the intermediate experiences of individuals are full of pain and suffering. "Ye thought evil against me (and it did work evil—thirteen years of bitter suffering and sorrow to me), but God meant it unto good, to bring to pass, as it is this day, to save much people alive." So said Joseph, and he might have added in words (as in effect he said), "I am quite ready to forget all the personal evil I suffered at your hands, that I may rejoice in the great good to you, to my father, and to much people, that has been the final outcome of it all." So ought we to take large views of things. Small men brood over their personal things; large men, generous men, men in whom the Spirit of God is, think on the large and wide things of God, that are bounded by the whole universe and inclosed in the cycles of the ages.

5.—Joseph's comforting words.—Having assured them again of his and of God's forgiveness, and pointed out to them that there were greater things to think of than their trespasses against him and his personal sufferings, he bade them to dismiss all fear so far as any resentment of his might concern them; assured them that he would still be their patron and protector, as he had said, and as he had already been, and that their children should also share in his care. Thus "he comforted them, and spake kindly unto them." Surely Joseph was a great-hearted man. The effeminate youth grew into the strong and tender man. His little coat of many colors covered the heart of the great-minded ruler and generous-souled brother. So may we learn to bear with patience our wrongs and suffering, looking for God to work out a larger good for many people, to surrender our resentments in a generous forgiveness of injury, and take a godlike revenge upon those who mean and work us harm, by returning to them good for their evil.

II.—THE DEATH OF JOSEPH.

For sixty years after this last interview with his brethren nothing is further recorded of Joseph. That he lived to the age of one hundred and ten years, ruling in Egypt wisely and well, being kind and generous to his brethren (such as survived) and their children, we may infer. Nothing necessary to the history of redemption occurred until the time came for Joseph to die. He saw his children's grandchildren about him; took them on his knees and adopted them as his own, and so reached a peaceful and vigorous old age. Though he did not live as long as his father, his grandfather, or his great-grandfather did, yet his life was more eventful than theirs. It is not the number of years we live, but what is crowded into or left out of them, that makes age important.

1.—"I believe God."—Joseph did not say these words, but he lived them. From a youth we must believe that Jacob had instructed Joseph in the covenant promises made first to Abraham, confirmed to Isaac, and repeated to him. It was probably Joseph's readiness to hear these words that made him so dear to his father. It was his profound conviction of the truth of these covenant promises that filled his mind and heart with dreams. It was this faith that kept him steadfast in all the years of his suffering and obscure humiliation. This faith did not desert him in his exalted prosperity. The fine linen, the signet-ring of Pharaoh, the gold necklace and all the royal appurtenances of Egypt did not obscure his spiritual vision. God's covenant was more to him than the throne of Egypt. Canaan was more to him than the land of Egypt. He was no near-sighted saint, but saw things afar off, as did Abraham. He felt that his hour to die had come, so he called his brethren about him, and said to them, "I die." But what of that? God's promises are for eternity as well as time; they are for others as well as for me. We may die, but God's promise shall still hold good to the elect family. A hundred, two hundred, or three hundred years may pass; but "God will surely visit you, and bring you out of this land unto the land which he sware to Abraham, to Isaac, and to Jacob." God had not appeared to Joseph, as he had done to his ancestors, by angels or adumbrating fires, but it was enough. The promise had been sufficiently attested, and Joseph believed it, not because it had been given to him personally, but to his fathers. So we may and should believe the promises of God, though not made to us personally.

2.—Concerning Joseph's bones.—Having reminded the brethren of God's covenant with them, and declared his own unwavering faith, he now asked them to take a solemn oath that when the time came for them to go up out of that land they should carry his bones with them and bury them in Canaan. This act of Joseph is reckoned the greatest act of faith which he ever did. "By faith Joseph, when he died, made mention of the departing of the children of Israel; and gave commandment concerning his bones." (Heb. xi, 22.) Egypt was a foreign land to him, Canaan was the "home land." He did not count himself "annihilated" when he died. When his brethren went up he would go up with them—that is, he would have his bones transferred to the land which God had given to them. In this it is not too extravagant to suggest that there is a hint of resurrection, though Joseph may not have been conscious of it. "Precious in the sight of the Lord is the death" and the dust "of his saints." The question arises: "Why did not Joseph give commandment that his body be taken up and buried in Canaan at once, as Jacob's was? Surely there would be no opposition to this by Pharaoh." It is possible that it was love for his brethren that led him to choose to lie embalmed in Egypt till God sent them all out of that land together. They would feel terribly lonely, those Hebrew strangers, in Egypt when their great brother died. They would possibly be less lonely if their brother's bones were in Egypt with them. Perhaps Joseph thought that if he left his body in Egypt it would be a kind of guarantee to them of the kindness of succeeding Pharaohs. His body in Egypt would be a perpetual reminder to the Egyptian kings of the great services he had done their country, not only in saving the people alive from the famine, but in consolidating the land and giving it as a vast possession to the crown. But still more I think he chose to remain in Egypt and exact an oath from his brethren to carry up his bones, because this oath, constantly renewed, and passed on from father to son, would keep alive in their hearts the truth of the covenant, and prevent them in the possible long flight of years from forgetting that there was something for them to look forward to. For he reminded them of God's promise in connection with the oath he required of them "concerning his bones." We know of no monument erected to Joseph in Egypt; no temple built to commemorate his great reign; though these may easily have been done, as it was done to the memory of many other great rulers and captains of Egypt. We must think that it was at Joseph's request that no such state memorials were raised. He did not regard himself as belonging to Egypt. He would have no tomb built for him, because he was expecting all the time that his bones would be carried to Canaan. Monuments of granite and marble are intended to be permanent, but those who have hope in the resurrection of the body do not care to have their dead bodies perpetually guarded by perishable tombs and monuments. Joseph's true monument was his life and work, and truly it has survived, and the inscriptions written thereon are familiar to men of many generations, whilst his great contemporaries have been forgotten, and are even now only remembered because of their relation to Joseph. The good man has a double immortality: one in the memory of this life, and the other in the resurrection life conferred by Christ. And so Joseph died, and laid his bones down in hope of God's great future deliverance, "being an hundred and ten years old."

XIX.

ISRAEL IN EGYPT.—Exodus i, 1-14.

(1) Now these are the names of the children of Israel, which came into Egypt; every man and his household came with Jacob. (2) Reuben, Simeon, Levi, and Judah, (3) Issachar, Zebulun, and Benjamin, (4) Dan, and Naphtali, Gad, and Asher. (5) And all the souls that came out of the loins of Jacob were seventy souls: for Joseph was in Egypt already. (6) And Joseph died, and all his brethren, and all that generation. (7) And the children of Israel were fruitful, and increased abundantly, and multiplied, and waxed exceeding mighty; and the land was filled with them. (8) Now there arose up a new king over Egypt, which knew not Joseph. (9) And he said unto his people, Behold, the people of the children of Israel are more and mightier than we: (10) Come on, let us deal wisely with them; lest they multiply, and it come to pass, that, when there falleth out any war, they join also unto our enemies, and fight against us, and so get them up out of the land. (11) Therefore they did set over them taskmasters to afflict them with their burdens. And they built for Pharaoh treasure cities, Pithom and Raamses. (12) But the more they afflicted them, the more they multiplied and grew. And they were grieved because of the children of Israel. (13) And the Egyptians made the children of Israel to serve with rigour: (14) And they made their lives bitter with hard bondage, in mortar, and in brick, and in all manner of service in the field: all their service, wherein they made them serve, was with rigour.—Exodus i, 1-14.

Genesis is the book of Creation; Exodus is the book of Redemption. That prince of commentators, Matthew Henry, remarks that "some allude to the names of this and the foregoing book, and observe: that immediately after Genesis, which signifies the beginning or original, follows Exodus, which signifies a departure; for a time to be born is immediately succeeded by a time to die. No sooner have we made our entrance into the world, but we must think of making our exit and going to another world. When we begin to live we begin to die." I quote this quaint bit of comment just to bring to remembrance the wonderfully suggestive line of thought which the careful student may observe in the study of the Bible in connection with the allegorical sense or spiritual teaching to be observed running parallel with the lines of historical detail.

The first thing to be observed in opening this book is the astonishingly long period of time, reckoned by some to be 430 years, and by others 315 years, since the last event in the history of Israel was recorded in the last chapter of Genesis. The explanation of this great hiatus in historical record is to be found in what we have before noted. The Bible records only that portion of the history of the chosen family that is essential as a medium of revelation to us of God's purposes of grace. The several hundreds of years between the death of Joseph and the time of the Exodus was a time during which nothing necessary to a further communication of God's will occurred. During this time Israel was quietly but steadily increasing and multiplying up to that point when they should be numerically strong and capable of going back to Canaan and taking possession of it, according to the promise which God had made to Abraham. (Gen. xv, 13–16.) According to one method of reckoning, the four hundred years began at this time. According to another, it began from the time Jacob entered Egypt, 215 years after the promise God gave to Abraham. The weight of testimony seems to me to be in favor of the later computation. It is, however, not very essential, as it is certain that a new era had begun for Israel. Up to the time Jacob with his sons and their descendants (seventy in all) entered into Egypt, the history had been only a family one. Now we have the beginning of a national history, and so on throughout the Bible record it continues. The Jewish seed lay, as it were, long in the ground. Nearly three hundred years passed away before the shoots (which were afterward to bear the mighty harvest of souls gathered out of Egypt) gave place to the full corn in the ear. God works slowly but he works surely.

Another purpose in keeping Israel so long in Egypt was, that they might be trained in that land of prosperity and also of cruel bondage for their future national career. While the children and grandchildren of Abraham were not altogether unacquainted with the arts of agriculture, they were for the most part but herdsmen and shepherds: a nomadic people, living in tents, and migrating from place to place according to the exigencies of their flocks and herds. But here in Egypt they gradually became the leading agriculturists of the land in the most fertile part of Egypt, the "land of Goshen." (Deut. xi, 10.) That they understood the arts of fishing and gardening is also clear. (Num. xi, 5.) They also lived in houses and cities, even in royal cities. (Ex. xii, 37.) From I. Chron. iv,

14, 21, 23, we learn that there were at least in the family of Judah craftsmen (housebuilders or carpenters), weavers, and potters who were regularly employed in the king's work. This is borne out also in the fact that while in the desert there were men and women who were skilled in all the finest arts of civilization, workers in brass and iron, in silver and gold, and finest manufactures, weaving tapestry and embroidery, all kinds of fine needlework, and even dyeing, all of which were used in the rearing and decoration of the tabernacle in the wilderness. It is quite true that some of them, especially the tribes of Reuben, Gad, and part of the half tribe of Manasseh, continued to be herdsmen to the end. (Num. xxxii, 1–4, 33.) And we know that when they went out of Egypt they had acquired great substance besides that of which they despoiled the Egyptians, and vast herds and flocks, of which Pharaoh vainly hoped to become possessed at the time of their departure. (Ex. x, 24, 26.) From all this, as well as from the fact that the children of Israel were scattered all over the land of Egypt as well as dwelling in Goshen, and employed, under the cruel edict of Pharaoh, in making bricks and building treasure cities (Ex. i, 11), we know that they were well acquainted with the general arts of civilization. Had they continued a rude company of herdsmen during all these years, it would have been difficult to reduce them to the work which the king imposed upon them. No doubt this process of civilization in the most advanced nation of the earth had been carefully inaugurated and fostered under the hand of Joseph. He was at once too firm a believer in the ultimately great destiny of his people, and too wise and skillful a statesman to suffer them to abide as they were, for he must probably from the beginning have trained them for a national and civilized occupancy of the land of promise.

As to their spiritual history while in Egypt during these long centuries, we have not much data on which to form an opinion, except a few stray hints gathered from the several books of Moses. That they carried with them the family traditions handed down from Abraham is certain; that Jacob reminded them of their covenant God at the time of his death and burial is sure; that Joseph at the time of his death (when he made them swear to take up his bones with them into the land of Canaan whenever they should be sent up by God) strongly impressed upon them the necessity of training and preparing themselves for their future career seems almost certain; that his injunctions were handed down from generation to generation is equally true. No doubt some of them contracted idolatrous habits while in Egypt, and came to be more or less mixed up with Egyptian ways;

but the great bulk of the people remained separate in religion from the Egyptians, as they did from family alliances with them. In the genealogical table in I. Chron. iv, verse 18 we read of a case in which one of the daughters of Pharaoh married a man of the tribe of Judah, but changed her Egyptian name to the Hebrew name Bithiah, which would indicate that coming into relation thus with a Hebrew family she renounced both her nationality and her religion. She was, in fact, a kind of prototype of Ruth, who took Israel's God to be her God, and Israel's people to be her people. This in itself is a remarkable testimony to the fact that the Hebrews maintained their theocratic faith as a whole, and did not become apostate in Egypt. The great essential features in connection with their religious life and faith are seen in connection with: (i) *Circumcision.* This sign of the covenant which God made with Abraham, which seems to have been kept up regularly through these centuries, must have constantly reminded them of it, as baptism and the Lord's Supper remind us of our Lord's death and resurrection, of his second coming, and of our union with and life in Him. (ii) *Sacrifice.* We know that they were used to this form and expression of worship and faith, both from the instructions given in connection with the passover night (Ex. xii), and also from the declaration of Moses (Ex. x, 25). (iii) *The Sabbath.* This we know was observed by the Hebrews in Egypt, and that fact is especially indicated in the terms of the law afterward published. "Remember the Sabbath day to keep it holy." This indicated that it was an already existing institution among them. Here, then, are the three great essential points of their religion: they believed in one only true God who had revealed himself to them and made a covenant with them; they believed that sin was guilty and must be expiated, and that that expiation was to be found in sacrifice; they believed in a promised rest typified by the Sabbath. Here all the essential doctrines of Christianity are prototyped. Observing this will enable us the better to appreciate the history, which the sacred writer now resumes.

I.—GOD'S KINDNESS TO ISRAEL.

The names of the sons of Jacob are frequently mentioned in these records, not because they were personally very good men, such as Joseph, but because they were the sons of Jacob, and through them the people of God had their being. Besides, it was most necessary that a careful genealogy should be kept, that Israel might always be surely differentiated from other families and nations. After the captivity, when Nehemiah brought up the people from Babylon, he required them all and each to declare their genealogy, so that none but the covenant people might enter into the new inheritance. We who are God's people now do not have to declare our descent from this or that son of Jacob, but "ye are all the children" of Abraham "by faith in Jesus Christ," the great Son and Seed who has become the head of the new redemption race. Before we can go up into the heavenly Canaan we must declare our genealogy and trace our descent by the Holy Spirit from Jesus Christ.

1.—**In preserving the descendants of Jacob.**—Through all these years and generations (whether we count 430 or 215 years in Egypt) God had preserved and watched over these Hebrews. He had kept them from mixing by marriage with the Egyptians; he had preserved them, in the main, true to the faith of the patriarchs; he had prospered them in the land, and given them a long time in quiet and peace to develop their resources and to educate them in the necessary arts of civilization, which they would need when they went up to their own land to possess and subdue it. There is no greater kindness than to suffer us to live in peace with our neighbors and possess our souls and our substance in quietness and safety. "A nation that has little history to record is a happy nation," for then are there no wars and contentions and complications, either internecine or with other nations. It was this long period of peace and quietness that made it unnecessary for Moses to make any record. Their history might all be summed up in a sentence like this: "God was with them and they prospered greatly."

2.—**"And Joseph died."**—"And all his brethren, and all that generation." One might possibly say: "Is this a part of the kindness of God, that his people die?" For "it is appointed unto men once to die." It would be a woeful affliction if we were doomed to live forever on this earth, contending with sin, suffering, and sorrow, and carrying on a continual warfare with the god of this world. God has some better thing in reserve for us—a better inheritance, as well as a better life. "To depart, and to be with Christ . . . is far better." And especially as God has in reserve a glorious "restitution of all things" (Acts iii, 19-21; Rom. viii, 19-23), when Christ and all his redeemed people in glorious resurrection immortality shall again inherit the redeemed and regenerated earth. So all the patriarchs died, and their successors in the life of faith—that is, in that life which they lived in this world looking for a better country, even an heavenly, not having received the promises, "God having provided some better thing for us, that they without us should not be made perfect." (Heb. xi, 40.) To die without God and Christ is indeed hopeless loss; but if we live knowing and loving the Lord, then "to die is gain."

3.—In the marvelous increase which God gave them.—"And the children of Israel were fruitful, and increased abundantly, and multiplied, and waxed exceeding mighty; and the land was filled with them." They not only fully occupied the land of Goshen, but overflowed its borders, and ran like the waters of the Nile all over the land, yea, and "watered it" with their industry and labor. They came down into that land seventy souls; they went out of it six hundred thousand men of war—that is, men beyond twenty years of age. The whole population of Israel is estimated at over two million souls at the time of the Exodus. For two hundred and fifteen years, from the call of Abraham to the entry into Egypt in the days of Joseph, the chosen family contended with barrenness, which seems to have been a family affliction. This in the first three patriarchs was overcome by faith, as faith can overcome the obstacles of nature, and now the promise of God to Jacob was abundantly fulfilled. "And he said [to Jacob] I am God, the God of thy father: fear not to go down into Egypt; for I will there make of thee a great nation: I will go down with thee into Egypt; and I will also surely bring thee up again." (Gen. xlvi, 3, 4.) It is not likely that the vast multitude sprang alone from the children of Jacob, but also from the several hundreds of servants and retainers, who were already incorporated into the covenant by circumcision, from the days of Abraham, and who after the settlement in Egypt intermarried with the Hebrews and became a part of them. It will be noticed that this great increase began to take place after the death of Joseph; just as the great increase in the number of the believers began to increase and multiply exceedingly after the death of Jesus, our great Joseph, when the Gentiles also were incorporated with the children of Abraham, and became part of that great commonwealth. Here we see again a hint of that universality of grace which God from the first destined for all nations of the earth through the promised Seed. There is no record of any supernatural communication with the children of Israel during all these centuries when they were in Egypt, but nevertheless God was with them, and the effect of his unseen presence was seen in their rapid increase. There are those among us to-day who sometimes doubt God's presence with the Church because there are no longer miracles, and because the tongues of fire are no more seen resting upon the heads of believers; but in the rapid increase of believers all over the world we see that God is with us. The millions of electric lights, some of them small incandescent burners and some great arc lights, testify the presence somewhere of the mighty dynamos from whose wonderful power these lights are generated. The gospel is the dynamo of God through which his presence and power in the world are made manifest.

II.—THE UNKINDNESS OF PHARAOH.

In the beginning of their sojourn in Egypt, God made the king of Egypt to be as a father and "nursing mother" to the Hebrews, but now this "world-power" became a persecuting tyrant. Egypt began by holding the Hebrews in contempt, for the Egyptians despised these shepherd people, and were only kind to them for Joseph's sake; but they ended by hating and fearing them. This is both in accordance with the nature of things, that the world or the seed of the serpent shall hate the seed of the woman (Gen. iii, 15; Ps. ii, 2, 3); and it also accords with God's plan for his people. He did not mean them to be at home in Egypt, which was a strange land to them and not their rest; so "as an eagle stirreth up her nest, fluttereth over her young . . . beareth them on her wings," he sent them forth out of that land. (Deut. xxxii, 11.)

1.—The new king.—God brought about this exodus of the people at the hands of a new Pharaoh, who was of a different dynasty from the Pharaoh of Joseph. This Pharaoh was Seti I. The Pharaoh who actually drove them out was his grandson, Rameses II. These "knew not Joseph." When kings reign who "know not" Jesus, then the people of God suffer persecution. But the affliction of God's people is sure to work for good to them, especially when it comes through a persecuting enemy. Let us, then, "count it all joy" when divers trials befall us, and remember that God watches over us also for good.

2.—The king's wisdom.—The king of Egypt at last began to observe the mighty increase of these strange people, whose manners and customs were so different from those of the Egyptians. Not only did their vast and increasing numbers alarm him, but he probably observed their strong religious habits, their Sabbath-keeping, and their sacrifices without idolatry. In the same manner, in the first and second centuries of the Christian Church the Roman emperors began to observe with alarm the spread of that sect, and that through them the temples of their gods were being deserted, and the new and heavenly morality was condemning their pagan civilization and social habits. They, like Pharaoh, began to "deal wisely with them."

That is, the wisdom of the enemies of God is always wickedness, and their wisdom God turns into folly as he did the wisdom of this tyrannical Pharaoh.

3.—The fear of the king.—At first, as we have already observed, the Egyptians despised the Hebrews, but now they have come also to fear them. This also is a true manifestation of the "world-spirit." The world which rejects Jesus affects contempt for the people of God; then they hate them for their witnessing, both in doctrine and testimony; and whenever they have the power they end by persecuting them. Contempt, hate, fear, persecution—this is the world's program. Look how the heathen world manifested itself against Jesus, and observe how in the early days of Christianity and the later days of Papal supremacy it dealt with Protestant believers. The same is seen and felt in the present day in social life. The worldly social and the agnostic scientific world would "deal wisely" with us again if they had the power.

4.—The persecutions of the king.—The result of this "wise" counsel was suddenly to come down upon the Hebrews, and by the power of the strong arm of the state reduce the whole nation to a condition of national serfdom. Taskmasters, or Egyptian superintendents, were appointed, the people were drafted off and made to work in bands and sections under overseers selected from their own number, but made subject to and responsible to the taskmasters. We do not know exactly the process, but only that it was effectual and rigorous. The object was to break their spirit, bring to an end their temporal prosperity, and, if possible, to kill them with work, perhaps to drive them into rebellion and so gain a pretext to fall upon them and slay them with the sword. They set them to all manner of service, and drove them to it with relentless vigor. "They built for Pharaoh treasure cities," or great depots or barns for the storing of the grain; they set them to the cultivation of the land, not for themselves, as heretofore, but for the king. This involved the confiscation of their land. Now behold the prosperous Hebrews, robbed of their land, and then compelled to cultivate it under Egyptian masters, and then to build storehouses in which to stow the fruit of their hard toil for the use and profit of their tormentors. This Pharaoh, who "knew not Joseph," took a leaf out of Joseph's plans, and turned it against his poor brethren. The recent discovery of the store city of Pithom absolutely confirms this bit of ancient sacred history.

5.—The frustration of the king's wisdom.—"But the more they afflicted them, the more they multiplied and grew." It is impossible to destroy God's people by persecution. They would have died *spiritually* under the continued favor of the king, but now under his persecutions they throve more and more. It is not the enmity but the favor of the world that the Church has most to fear. (John xv, 18, 19; James iv, 4.)

6.—The perplexity of the king.—"And they were grieved because of the children of Israel." That is, the king and his counselors were vexed, perplexed, and angered because all their plans for suppressing the children of Israel and for preventing their increase, came to naught, but, on the contrary, seemed even to help them on. "The blood of the martyrs is the seed of the Church." The "wisdom of this world" takes no account of God, and so they of the world cannot understand why their plans fail. But God knows, and has told us in his Word. (Ps. ii, 4, 5, 9.) Praise be to God.

XX.

THE CHILDHOOD OF MOSES.—Exodus ii, 1-10.

(1) And there went a man of the house of Levi, and took to wife a daughter of Levi. (2) And the woman conceived, and bare a son: and when she saw him that he was a goodly child, she hid him three months. (3) And when she could not longer hide him, she took for him an ark of bulrushes, and daubed it with slime and with pitch, and put the child therein; and she laid it in the flags by the river's brink. (4) And his sister stood afar off, to wit what would be done to him. (5) And the daughter of Pharaoh came down to wash herself at the river; and her maidens walked along by the river's side: and when she saw the ark among the flags, she sent her maid to fetch it. (6) And when she had opened it, she saw the child: and, behold, the babe wept. And she had compassion on him, and said, This is one of the Hebrews' children. (7) Then said his sister to Pharaoh's daughter, Shall I go and call to thee a nurse of the Hebrew women, that she may nurse the child for thee? (8) And Pharaoh's daughter said to her, Go. And the maid went and called the child's mother. (9) And Pharaoh's daughter said unto her, Take this child away, and nurse it for me, and I will give thee thy wages. And the woman took the child, and nursed it. (10) And the child grew, and she brought him unto Pharaoh's daughter, and he became her son. And she called his name Moses: and she said, Because I drew him out of the water.—Exodus ii, 1-10.

The cruel and oppressive measures taken by Pharaoh to break the Israelites' spirit and reduce them to a condition of utter bondage, perhaps destroying them altogether, had signally failed, in that the more they were oppressed the more they increased. The king next decided on what he hoped and confidently expected would be a master-stroke. The brutality of it exceeded that of Herod, who ordered all the male children from two years old and under found in Bethlehem to be slaughtered. Herod was inspired by his fear of the Christ, and the cruelty was limited to a small community; but Pharaoh decreed the death of all the male infants of the Hebrews, and, moreover, ordered them to be strangled at the time of their birth by the midwives. These women, fearing God, refused to obey the king's commandment (I wonder why they are not mentioned in the eleventh chapter of the Epistles to the Hebrews? They certainly deserve to have been), and they saved them alive as well as the female children. Enraged at this frustration of his plan, the king next ordered the parents themselves to destroy their male offspring. This was the height of cruelty, and could only have been carried out by setting watchmen and spies, house-searchers and examiners, to work. So rigidly was this brutal decree forced on them that it was almost impossible to escape its execution. We have reason to believe that it was not long in force, perhaps only a few months. In the first place, its extreme barbarity would presently have defeated it; and secondly, no doubt the rescue of Moses had something to do with putting a stop to it, though as to details the record is silent.

We come now to the birth of the most remarkable man of Old Testament times, if not of all antiquity, who did more to mold all future ages than any other man who ever lived. On the further side of Christ stands Moses, as on the nearer side stands Paul. The one we may say inaugurated the religion of revelation, and the other established it. The one prophesied of Christ both by his character and by his words and works, while the other interpreted Christ in his preaching and writings, and illustrated Christ in his life and death.

It is the fashion nowadays to account for every movement that is marked and striking by referring to what is called the "time spirit" or the "spirit of the age," which is nothing more than a stream of tendency, emanating not from any individual man, but from the general mass of humanity. Christ himself is asserted to have been nothing more than the outcome of this "time spirit," a kind of large bubble thrown up on the surface of the stream of history. But no one can read history, much less the Bible, without noting the fact that it is the individual who makes or directs the age rather than the age that gives birth to the individual. The truth is God rules this world by means of individual men. What was there in the "time spirit" or tendency of Egyptian or Hebrew life to produce a Moses, or of the more ancient Chaldean life to produce an Abraham? Was it the "time spirit" of apostate Israel that produced Elijah and Jeremiah? Was it the tendency in the cold-hearted and pharisaical Jews that brought forth a Jesus of Nazareth? Was it the spirit of Rome and mediæval Europe that produced Luther, or was there a tendency in the corrupt condition of the Church of England that gave birth to Wesley? No; the truth is that in great crises of the world's history, and more especially of the Church's need, God raises up some man who, by force of personality and character, takes the helm of affairs in his hand and gives them new direction. God has ever used men of strong character and personality to bring about his purposes, and restore the lost balance of things, or to start new impulses into motion. Moses was preëminently such a man. How interesting to study his birth and the circumstances connected with his first tender years!

I.—THE FAITH OF MOSES' MOTHER.

"By faith Moses, when he was born, was hid three months of his parents, . . . and they were not afraid of the king's commandment." (Heb. xi, 23.) It is no doubt true that the father of Moses was fully in sympathy with his mother in all the plans devised for the saving of their babe, but the detail of the narrative, as well as what we all know of mother-love, makes it certain that the mother was the moving spirit in this whole matter. "Show me the mother, and I will tell you what will be the character and end of the son;" so says some one, and it is more than less true to experience. There can be no greater blessing in this world than to have a mother who believes God and is not afraid of the "king's commandment." For faith in God takes away the fear of men, and these two great motives, faith and fear, satisfied, the way is clear for the best actions of men.

1.—**The birth of Moses.**—Amid all the trouble and sorrow which had fallen upon the Hebrew people, that saving passion in human nature was not crushed out of the people. And so it came to pass that a man of the family of Levi loved and married a cousin of his, and there were born to them children. Already Miriam, the sister of Moses, had been born, perhaps about eight years before; then, after five years, came Aaron, the elder brother of Moses by three years. These children had been born before the cruel and brutal edict for the casting of the male children into the Nile had been promulgated. That decree came a little while before Moses' birth. There must have been sore anxiety in that mother's and father's hearts before the child was born, for if it should be a son then it would mean that they must lose him, either becoming the murderers, or standing by while some hard-hearted Egyptian tore the child out of their arms and cast him into the river; or else there must be defiance of the king's commandment, which might be both fruitless and fatal. Such are some of the dilemmas which are presented to us with our children. Will their coming be the precursor of joy or sorrow? Will the end of the child justify its beginning? Will the joy that comes when a man is born into the world be more than counterbalanced by the sorrow that accompanies his development and end? Who can tell? And yet amid all these conflicting fears and hopes we must believe that when little Moses came there was a throb of joy in the mother's heart, even though it was half smothered by the terror of knowing that her darling son was already under sentence of cruel death.

2.—Moses concealed.—The child was born, and was a son. Did his mother's heart fail or falter for a single moment as to the course she would pursue? Would she tamely surrender and deliver her son up to the murderers? Not for a moment did such a thought enter into her mind. No doubt she had long before the birth of her boy schemed out her plan of concealing its birth, in case it were indeed a son. But when she saw that he was "a goodly child" (ver. 2), "exceeding fair" (Acts vii, 20), and "a proper child" (Heb. xi, 23), she determined at once, and at all hazards, so much the more to save this babe from the cruel fate which was befalling the other Hebrew men-children around her. We are told in Hebrews xi, 23, that this act of Moses' mother was an act of faith. We know, then, certainly that here was a Jewish mother, though in Egypt, who had not become apostate in that unholy land. She believed in God. But the question arises, How was her faith manifested in this particular act? It was awakened by what she saw about the child. Her mother's heart doubtless had already dictated a purpose to save the child, but there was something about his fair countenance, his wise and wistful look, as his little eyes sought hers, as though God had spoken to her by that look, and the "properness" of his countenance that seemed to say to her, "This is God's child; he must be saved at all hazards." Certain it is that she was moved to act as in obedience to God in this respect, as Abel was, and Noah, and Abraham. Moses was already, not only her son, but God's chosen servant. Her mother-love, strengthened and deepened by her faith in God and consecration to him, now conspired with her faith to defy the king's commandment and conceal the child. So the child was hidden in his father's house for three months, from the evil which threatened it. Is it pressing this lesson too far to say that we may see in all our children those goodly marks, those fair traces of beauty, and that promise which speaks to us and says, "I am your son, but I am also God's; therefore shelter me and save me from the evil that threatens me"? Especially when we as an act of faith bring our children in consecration to God, have we not a right henceforth, in a double sense, to expect divine interposition for their salvation, and should not our natural affection from that moment be put under the direction of faith? There will come a time when our children must be cast out into the place of danger, but in the meantime we must shield, conceal, hide, and shelter them from it as long as we may or can.

3.—Moses exposed.—For three months these God-fearing parents had succeeded in concealing their child. The searchers for hidden children were on their rounds again. Perhaps their secret had leaked out, and they knew what would befall the babe if the searcher for male children should find him. Therefore a heroic device was speedily executed. A little basket cradle-boat was prepared, carefully made water-tight with bitumen or pitch. How tenderly and carefully the mother lined it! Then, with shrewd mother-wit, and, let us add, guided by the Spirit of God, she directed it to be placed among the rushes near to the place where the royal daughter of Pharaoh was in the habit of going daily to bathe. Little Miriam was placed near by to watch events, and we may be sure the mother was not far off. In thus planning, the mother no doubt was moved by an instinctive feeling that the daughter of Pharaoh, being a woman, would be moved with compassion at so pathetic a sight; and though the daughter of a cruel king, her woman's heart might yet be stirred with sympathy for the poor Hebrew woman, whose heart's story could be easily read. A more romantic, pathetic, and thrilling situation could not well be conceived. Of course the mother could not know certainly what the daughter of Pharaoh would do; but she acted in faith, doing what seemed best as in the sight of God, making every earthly provision that human love and foresight could suggest. She was like a general going into battle, with a mighty host of evil against her, but, relying upon God, she disposed of her forces, and then left the issue of the battle to him. Faith has not to do with events, but only with actions. That she put her child in the river, the very place where Pharaoh had commanded the children to be cast, seems strange. But sometimes the place of danger is the place of safety. The searchers would look everywhere else than in the river to find her child. Again, I cannot but think that, like Abraham, she offered up her child in faith as it were to death, accounting that God could raise him up. There is yet another lesson which we may learn from this incident. As long as she could, this mother hid her child from evil—kept him back, as it were, from exposure to the world. Then, when she could no longer hide him she flung him forth into the very stream of danger, committing him to God, and standing by to be of service in a crisis if need came. So must we do with our children. We would fain hide them in our own houses, safely within the shelter of home; but we cannot always keep our boys there, in the home nest. Time comes when we must send them forth, to school, to business, to far-away situations, in places where we know danger is; but then we must do it in faith and stand by to see what God will do. And it is a comfort to know that God is as able to keep a boy safely near the very jaws of death, as he can while safely dwelling in the home.

II.—THE KINDNESS OF PHARAOH'S DAUGHTER.

"Fact is stranger than fiction," and the romances of history more wonderful and beautiful than those of art. Here we have a number of incidents which are worthy of attention. First, Pharaoh was exercising all his wicked might to decimate the Hebrews by destroying their male children. But God (as his wont is) was using man's wrath to praise him and to work out his gracious purpose of grace toward his chosen. We need to be patient before despairing or complaining under strange trials, until we see what God will do. Then, was it not strange that the very daughter of the king should be the instrument for saving one of the doomed children, who should be brought up in the house of Pharaoh and trained to be the leader to deliver the Hebrews out of the hands of the king? Human actions weave the woof, but God's providence puts in all the delicate embroidery that belongs to the fabric of our lives. Again we are struck with the strange mixing up of the Gentiles with the history of the chosen people. Hereby is illustrated the great truth which may be traced throughout their history, that somehow the salvation of Israel was always connected with the instrumentality of the Gentiles. It was so in the story of Joseph, and even before, and certainly after, this time; and it will continue so to the last, till through "their mercy" Israel shall obtain mercy. "Is he the God of the Jews only? . . . Yes, of the Gentiles also."

1.—Her curiosity.—Walking by the riverside, the daughter of the king saw the little ark in the rushes, and, curious as to what it might be or contain, she directed her maid to fetch it; and when it was brought to her she opened it and discovered the babe. Here we see how a mother's wise plans and a woman's careless or at least passing curiosity work together, under the direction of God's providence, to bring to pass one of the most momentous events in the world's history. Let us for a moment suppose that Pharaoh's daughter had not seen the little floating basket, or, seeing it, had been too languid to care anything about it—what then? According to the old mythology, when Pandora's box was opened a host of furies were let loose upon the world—that is the echo of what happened as a result of the curiosity of Eve; but when this royal lady through curiosity opened that little basket of rushes, there came out of it the world's greatest statesman, soldier, lawgiver, and the saviour of the Hebrew race.

2.—**Her compassion.**—No sooner has the basket been opened, than there rings out the pathetic cry of that little three-months-old baby boy. How long he has been there is not told, but perhaps only at most an hour or two, for the mother has timed her action to the well-known habits of the royal bather. What woman's heart can resist the pathetic cry of a baby? The mother instinct in her (though she was no mother) awakes at that cry. Perhaps the beautiful, fair, comely, and possibly shining face of the child also has to do with her decision. (Moses' face shone when he was an old man; perhaps it had some remarkable aspect when he was a babe.) Her awakened compassion and her quick wit, which suggest to her that "this is one of the Hebrews' children," determines her to save the infant. We can easily believe that this gracious princess was not in sympathy with the cruel edict of her father, and that she was glad of an opportunity of entering a practical kind of protest against it. Would her father persevere in destroying the children of the Hebrews after she had adopted one of them as "her son"? So Moses began to be a saviour of his people even while he was yet a babe. What a world of possibilities, both for evil and for good, there is in a sudden impulse. Here we find a woman obeying a humane impulse and doing a thing which she would never have done of deliberate purpose. Shall we then despise impulses and set down all impulsive people as untrustworthy? I wonder what would have become of this world had it been delivered over to the cold reason of the philosophers and the masterful wisdom of men who are always crying down the impulsiveness and "illogical intuitions" of women. Thank God for this gracious and tender-hearted princess. Shall we not also meet her in God's kingdom as one of those who "did it unto" Christ, though she knew it not? Where the Spirit of Christ is, there also is Christ; and where Christ is, there is salvation.

3.—**Her care.**—Wheels within wheels are also God's providences. Perhaps that gracious impulse of Pharaoh's daughter would not have been strong enough for the whole emergency if left to herself alone. A mother's love had left a little girl on watch, to report what became of the child, and she, all quivering with excitement, with wits sharpened by the strain put upon the family love and care, and with a presence of mind that indicated the presence of the prophetic spirit, promptly came out of hiding and boldly suggested to the princess the propriety of calling a "nurse of the Hebrew women, that she may nurse the child for thee." Here was a seed dropped into the soil of compassion. "Nurse the child for thee." This perhaps suggested the thought of adoption to the princess. Blessed little girl! Was it not also a captive "little maid" who suggested to Naaman's wife that there was a prophet in Israel who had power to heal even a leper? The revelations of God to "babes and sucklings" are wiser than all the schemes of the prudent of this world. I wonder how much we lose by hushing the prattle of children with the hasty and impatient words so often on our lips: "Run away, my child; don't bother now." Suppose Pharaoh's daughter had impatiently sent this little girl away—what then? But happily the princess heeded the child's advice and suggestion, so away she went to call "a nurse of the Hebrew women." And who so good a nurse as the child's own mother? The little advice was too thinly veiled to deceive the princess; but it was to her mind, and she employed that happy mother to be her son's nurse. It did not require the wisdom of a Solomon to tell the royal lady that the nurse's beaming face, filled with a thrilling joy, told of the rescued child's mother. And the royal lady's heart beat in sympathy with the slave mother's. "One touch of nature makes the whole world kin." The princess said, "Take the child and nurse it, and I will give thee wages." What wages but the joy of pressing her boy to her mother's breast did she want? But she undertook the charge, well pleased, and with strengthened faith that God had been guiding her in all that she did.

4.—**Moses is adopted.**—"And the child grew, and she brought him unto Pharaoh's daughter, and he became her son." No doubt Moses' mother, as the nurse of the pet of Pharaoh's daughter, was put under special protection from that day, enabling her to care for her child without fear. No man-slayer would touch him now. When the child was weaned (at three years, perhaps) he was brought to Pharaoh's daughter, "and he became her son." Stephen tells us (Acts vii, 21, 22) that "Pharaoh's daughter took him up, and nourished him for her own son. And Moses was learned in all the wisdom of the Egyptians, and was mighty in words and deeds." Here he got his training as philosopher, as statesman, and as soldier. If it is a matter of surprise to any one that the daughter of the king could do so strange a thing as this, we need only to remind our readers that as an Egyptian princess and as a daughter she had a double power. A daughter may do what a statesman could not compass, and as a princess and, as is supposed, the direct heir to the throne, her wish was also a kind of law in the house of her father. Thus did God work out his plan and purpose for Israel. Verily it is a good thing to be one of the chosen people, and as such it is safe to commit all our ways to him. The grand lesson of it all is to keep our faith in God; watch opportunities for faith, fearing God rather than man; do the thing that is right at the present moment, leaving results to God, who "will bring to pass" our best desires, "as may be most expedient for" us.

XXI.

MOSES SENT AS A DELIVERER.—Exodus iii, 10-20.

(10) Come now therefore, and I will send thee unto Pharaoh, that thou mayest bring forth my people the children of Israel out of Egypt. (11) And Moses said unto God, Who am I, that I should go unto Pharaoh, and that I should bring forth the children of Israel out of Egypt? (12) And he said, Certainly I will be with thee; and this shall be a token unto thee, that I have sent thee: When thou hast brought forth the people out of Egypt, ye shall serve God upon this mountain. (13) And Moses said unto God, Behold, when I come unto the children of Israel, and shall say unto them, The God of your fathers hath sent me unto you; and they shall say to me, What is his name? what shall I say unto them? (14) And God said unto Moses, I AM THAT I AM: and he said, Thus shalt thou say unto the children of Israel, I AM hath sent me unto you. (15) And God said moreover unto Moses, Thus shalt thou say unto the children of Israel, The Lord God of your fathers, the God of Abraham, the God of Isaac, and the God of Jacob, hath sent me unto you: this is my name for ever, and this is my memorial unto all generations. (16) Go, and gather the elders of Israel together, and say unto them, The Lord God of your fathers, the God of Abraham, of Isaac, and of Jacob, appeared unto me, saying, I have surely visited you, and seen that which is done to you in Egypt: (17) And I have said, I will bring you up out of the affliction of Egypt unto the land of the Canaanites, and the Hittites, and the Amorites, and the Perizzites, and the Hivites, and the Jebusites, unto a land flowing with milk and honey. (18) And they shall hearken to thy voice: and thou shalt come, thou and the elders of Israel, unto the king of Egypt, and ye shall say unto him, The Lord God of the Hebrews hath met with us: and now let us go, we beseech thee, three days' journey into the wilderness, that we may sacrifice to the Lord our God. (19) And I am sure that the king of Egypt will not let you go, no, not by a mighty hand. (20) And I will stretch out my hand, and smite Egypt with all my wonders which I will do in the midst thereof: and after that he will let you go.—Exodus iii, 10-20.

It is with extreme reluctance that we must pass over the interesting, instructive, and thrilling details of the life of Moses from the time of his adoption till God called him and sent him forth to be the deliverer of his people from the cruel bondage of Egypt, and to bring them up to the land which he had promised to Abraham so many hundred years before; but the incidents may be easily studied and mastered by the earnest student. We left Moses a little child in the house of Pharaoh, the adopted son of the king's daughter. We know that his education was early begun and carefully completed, and for thirty years or more he remained in that proud court, being "learned in all the wisdom of the Egyptians" and, history tells us, trained to deeds of arms as well. All this time it is possible that his mother continued to have intimate access to her son, instructing him, meanwhile, in the faith of Abraham, Isaac, and Jacob; so that his sympathy and love for his own people were never allowed by that pious mother to die out of his heart. Indeed, the instructions and training of his mother were more powerful in determining his character and future career than the instruction he had received from his Egyptian masters. At the age of forty a great crisis came in his life. He made his choice, and "by faith Moses . . . refused to be called the son of Pharaoh's daughter"; by which statement we suppose some definite offer of political preferment was offered to him. It is not improbable that some legal and royal right was his to claim, perhaps even to become the regent of Egypt. The call of God was in his soul, love for his people began to burn hot in his eager heart, and he determined to cast in his lot with them, and, if possible, at any cost, to deliver them from the cruel tyranny under which they were groaning. "Choosing rather to suffer affliction with the people of God, than to enjoy the pleasures of sin for a season; esteeming the reproach of Christ greater riches than the treasures in Egypt: for he had respect unto the recompense of the reward. By faith he forsook Egypt [that is, left the palace, and went to dwell with the Hebrews], not fearing the wrath of the king: for he endured, as seeing him who is invisible." (Heb. xi, 25–27.) This tremendous energy of faith grew up within his soul purely through hearing the story of God's dealings with Abraham, Isaac, and Jacob, and all the subsequent history which had befallen them from the days of Joseph until that day. All this goes to show us how faith can survive and be developed even without miraculous communication; for there is no hint of any further revelation from God to Moses at this time, except that old revelation given to his fathers kept alive through the word of tradition.

Clearly perceiving that God meant to deliver his people and to send them out of Egypt, Moses formed some heroic plan of becoming their leader. An opportunity soon offered in the cruel blows laid upon "one of his brethren" by an Egyptian taskmaster, which fired his soul, and he smote the Egyptian and killed him. Then came that other incident of his unsuccessful interference between two Hebrews who were quarreling, which suddenly opened his eyes to the fact that his generosity and self-sacrifice were not appreciated, and that he was liable to be arrested for murder. This led him to perceive that his efforts were premature; that the people themselves were not ready for revolt, and that they were ungrateful besides. (Ex. ii, 11-15.) Moses was chagrined and hurt, and being, as we know, of a quick and passionate temperament, he abandoned his purpose; and his former courage gave place to an immediate fear for his own safety, with the result that he fled from Egypt.

For forty years he dwelt in Midian, giving himself up to the quiet inaction of a shepherd's life. It is impossible to tell how his faith fared in these long years, or whether he had utterly abandoned all hope for his people. In the meantime the enslaved Hebrews were coming to a better mind themselves. Nearly a hundred years of bondage under cruel taskmasters had reduced them to the point of despair. They could not deliver themselves, neither could they bear any longer their sufferings. The king who had inaugurated their slavery was dead, but his oppressive policy was continued by his son and grandson. The cruelty of the work laid upon them was increased, and their last refuge was in crying and sighing out their troubles into God's ear. (Ex. ii, 23-25.) "Man's extremity is God's opportunity," and their sighs and cries came up to God, and he hearkened and heard, remembered his covenant with their fathers, and came down to deliver them.

So it came to pass that one day the "great sight" of the burning bush was noticed by Moses. As he drew near to see it, God spoke to him as it were face to face; telling him all he had seen, and what he was now about to do. (Ex. iii, 1-9.) This brings us to the point where the text for our study to-day begins.

I.—GOD COMMISSIONS MOSES.

For four hundred years God had now been silent, but not unmindful or unwatchful over Israel. He was as really their loving and covenant-keeping God during those four centuries as when he was talking and revealing himself from time to time to Abraham, Isaac, and Jacob. He now renews his revelation to Moses, and unfolds to him fully his purpose as well as his love and sympathy. "I have surely seen the affliction of my people which are in Egypt, and have heard their cry, . . . for I know their sorrows; and I am come down to deliver them." (vv. 7-9.) How precious this long remembrance, this faithful love and care! What encouragement this is for us to endure hardness and bear with patience our afflictions! In due time God will come to our relief.

1.—**A call to arms.**—"Come now therefore, and I will send thee unto Pharaoh, that thou mayest bring forth my people." This was the trumpet call which God sounded in the desert to his chosen servant. God announced his intention of delivering his people. "And I am come down to deliver them." But how was he to deliver them? Why, by taking into partnership with himself this man. God never came to man but to save him, but he very seldom saves a sinner but by means of some human agency. Indeed, in the incarnation of Christ we learn that before God could save sinners (we speak it reverently) he had to become a man himself. And then after Jesus Christ had wrought out redemption he committed to men the charge of delivering them: "to turn them from darkness to light, and from the power of Satan unto God." (Acts xxvi, 18.) Men become the "ambassadors for Christ," and "workers together with him." Therefore it was that Jesus said to his disciples, "Go ye into all the world, and preach the gospel." This commission was here in effect first delivered to Moses. It now is a commission to every believer in the world; for while some are chosen to be leaders in this work of bringing God's people up out of the bondage of Egypt, all are charged with the business of aiding and helping in every possible way. Let no Christian man or woman, therefore, think for a moment of excusing himself.

2.—**The reluctance of Moses.**—"And Moses said unto God, Who am I, that I should go unto Pharaoh, and that I should bring forth the children of Israel out of Egypt?" What a change do we discover in this man Moses! Forty years ago, without a commission he had essayed this task. Then he was full of self-confidence, enthusiasm, and courage. He felt able for the work, and threw himself into it with all his heart; but he ran without having been sent, and so he failed. It was a case of well-meant zeal, without authority or knowledge. "The king's business required haste," but we may not make haste *before* the King commands. Now God commands Moses to go down and bring up the people, and he is reluctant to undertake the task. His self-appointed task, which resulted in failure, had both discouraged and humiliated him. In a kind of noble pride he undertook his self-appointed mission forty years ago, and failed; now, moved by a proud kind of humility, he declines to go when God sends him. "He once would when he ought not, now will no longer when he ought." There was no doubt some real humility in Moses' answer, but there was dejection and apathy as well. Humility is no reason why a man should not undertake a great work for God. Indeed, it is the prime condition. "Who is sufficient for these things?" is a question which all God's servants have had to ask. But if, when his time comes, God calls us to do any work for him, he knows best what our fitness is, and what are the conditions under which the work is possible. That time had come now, and Moses, however humble and self-distrustful, is no longer warranted in declining the commission. All Christian work, no matter how trivial it may seem, is too great for us to undertake in our own strength or without divine commission; but no Christian work is too great even for the least able or fit, when God commands.

3.—**God encourages Moses.**—God was not angry with Moses; indeed, we detect in the answer given to Moses' reluctant spirit and humble protest, a divine compassion and sympathy most tender and touching. "Certainly I will be with thee." Ah, this makes all the difference in the world! What a hopeless task was that imposed by Christ upon his fisherman and publican disciples when he bade them "go into all the world" and make disciples. But how great was the encouragement to undertake this herculean task when he declared "all power is given unto me in heaven and earth," and added, "Lo, I am with you alway." So God says to Moses now, and so he says to every one of us whom he sends forth to win a soul out of Egyptian bondage. What preacher would dare to preach without being sent, and without this encouraging word? What Sunday-school teacher would dare to teach? What missionary would dare go forth to the heathen world without this assurance? Nay, what one of us would dare undertake a single day's ordinary work of life for God without his word, "Certainly I will be with thee." On the other hand, who would not dare anything or all things when God sends us and says this? In addition to this, God appoints a sign for Moses' further encouragement. "And this shall be a token unto thee that I have sent thee: When thou hast brought forth the people out of Egypt, ye shall serve God upon this mountain." That may seem a token far in the future, and not practical. But when God gives us success in our service, that success is the token that he has sent us. When we win a soul for Christ how sure we are that God has sent us, and what a comfort that is! The grandest and best proof, after all, of the divinity of our cause is the success God has given us in the work. I used, in India, fairly to laugh and cry with gladness when I saw the Hindus bowing to Christ and rejoicing in new-found life in him. This was the token that God had sent forth his servants into that dark land.

II.—"I AM THAT I AM."

Moses could answer nothing to God on the score of his unfitness after the assurance of his presence with him, and so without another word he surrenders his humility, his self-distrust, and dejection; but having done so much, new difficulties arise before his mind, and not unwarrantable ones, either. If he went down to Egypt he must go in some name, and by some authority. Both the people and the king would demand his authority and some assurance that he was not undertaking a second time a self-appointed task. The people must arise at his word and themselves support his demand upon Pharaoh. They must be inspired. He did not ask for armies and weapons of war, but only for an authoritative message. Moses was a man of trained mind. His past experience had made him both more thoughtful and wary. He anticipated a difficulty. "When I come unto the children of Israel, and shall say unto them, The God of your fathers hath sent me unto you; and they shall say to me, What is his name? what shall I say unto them?" They once asked him, "Who made thee a prince and a judge over us?" and he had no answer, and so had to flee. He would not fall into the same pit again, but would be well furnished with an answer which would absolutely satisfy them. Matthew Henry remarks well that "they who go forth in God's name must be prepared to answer all reasonable questions." And whoever would know how to answer questions must go to God for information. The appeal he was to make to them was religious rather than patriotic or addressed to their immediate temporal distress. God only is sufficient to awaken that high and holy purpose which will inspire men to do and dare anything for freedom and the right. It would not be sufficient to say, "God hath sent me," nor even "the God of your fathers." God is only a very general designation of the Deity, for "there be gods many, and lords many." The deist, the pantheist, and we might almost say the atheist, strange as it may appear, will say, "Oh yes, I believe in God." But the question is, What God? What is his name? Tell us about him. We wish to know what his nature is; what his relations to us are; what our obligations to him are. What particular interest has he in us, that he should answer our cry any more than respond to the appeal of Pharaoh? In appealing to the world, and especially to the individual sinner, we must be specific in defining to them who God is.

Not a mere god of nature, such as all heathen believe in; not a mere philosophical god, such as the seekers after God in all times have constructed out of their own brains; and I may say not even a theological god, such as has been constructed out of the Scriptures by men who have more of the logical faculty than of the Spirit of God; but God who makes himself known to us by revelation and opens up all his heart to us and tells us of his purpose to save. The name we proclaim to sinners in our day is that name above every name, "Jesus" who "is in the bosom of the Father," the only begotten Son, who has revealed God to us in all fullness. (John i, 14, 18.) Indeed, the name which God gave to Moses is just that name. For the "I AM" of Exodus is none other than the Jesus of the New Testament, who has proclaimed himself in many ways. "I AM the way, the truth, and the life." "I AM the light of the world." "I AM the Good Shepherd." "I AM the door." "I AM the true vine." "I AM the resurrection and the life." "Before Abraham was I AM." It is not difficult to recognize in the I AM of the burning bush the Incarnate Word of the New Testament. No other being on earth has ever dared to take this name and proclaim it as being his but Jesus. That burning bush, therefore (whatever else it may mean in the language of symbol), is certainly the most wonderful type of the incarnation we meet with in the Old Testament. The eternal flame of the Godhead coming down to dwell in the bush human nature, and yet not consuming it, but out of it speaking forth the gracious purpose of God to come down and save, and sending forth the apostolic message to deliver, commissioning his messengers with power, and assuring them of his certain presence with them in their mission.

1.—**The name unfolded.**—"I AM THAT I AM." It is a large promise to unfold that wonderful name in a few sentences, which has taxed the best learning and the most pious study of many generations to explain to us. But the difficulties are less than at first appears. My purpose here is simply to give the results of the inquiry so far as the most important points are concerned. (i) Essentially it is the name "Jehovah," that greatest of all the names of God, the sacred name by which he was most feared and revered amongst his ancient people. This is not the first time he was so named, but it is the first time that it was so distinctly interpreted; just as Jesus first really revealed God as the Father of his people, though the name was in use in the olden time, but not fully understood and appreciated. (ii) It points to the eternity of his being. "I am that I am,"—existing both in all the past as in all the future.

(iii) It points to the absoluteness of his being, apart from all creation, all circumstances, and conditions of time. (iv) It points to the unchangeableness of his nature. "This is my name forever, and this is my memorial unto all generations." "The same yesterday, to-day, and forever."

2.—His relation to the Hebrews.—"The Lord God of your fathers, the God of Abraham, of Isaac, and of Jacob." This is the especial declaration of his active, ever-present, and gracious relation to them. He is not a God afar off, dwelling in his infinite perfections, taking no note of men, and indifferent to their need; but the God who had come to their fathers, and declared himself in promises renewed and repeated over and over again, who had guided and guarded them in all their history, and who had now visited them to bring them up out of their bondage and to give them the land promised to Abraham, Isaac, and Jacob; who (though he had not lately spoken to them) knew all their sufferings, having seen and noted all that Pharaoh had done unto them, who had heard their sighing and crying. As though he said, "I have said, I will bring you up out of the afflictions of Egypt, and now I will perform my promise." Thus was Moses to speak to the people.

III.—INSTRUCTIONS AND ENCOURAGEMENT.

God does not send us forth without encouragement, as we have already seen, nor does he leave us to our own devices as to how we are to do his work.

1.—Summoning the elders.—"Go and gather the elders of Israel together." The first thing is to get the ear and confidence of the leaders of the people. We can deal with the masses better when we have won their natural leaders. God work is not haphazard work. It is folly to hope to win the "masses" until we have won the "classes." The masses are, after all, set in families, ranks, and orders, and must be reached with the gospel on natural lines.

2.—"They shall hearken to thy voice."—"Thy people shall be willing in the day of thy power." This was the day of God's power, and the people would hear. It is not by the might of our arguments or eloquence that we gain men to God, but only by the presence and power of his Spirit. "Not of blood, nor of the will of the flesh, nor of the will of man," but by a new birth are men saved.

3.—The courteous demand made upon Pharaoh.—God knew that Pharaoh would not hearken, yet Moses was commanded to go before him and in God's name prefer a request for the people to go and sacrifice to him in the wilderness. The whole of God's purpose was not unfolded to Pharaoh, but a declaration of God's right in this people of Israel and their right to worship and serve him. There would be time enough to unfold the whole purpose as Pharaoh developed his opposition, and to speak of judgment after he had determinedly hardened his heart. In dealing with the enemies of Christ we must first be courteous, then authoritative, and then with power, not of the flesh but of the Spirit, lifting up without qualification the standard of Jehovah and making no compromise. "If," said God, "you oppose a mighty hand to the king he will crush you with his power at the very beginning, for he 'will not let you go, no, not by a mighty hand.' Leave me to break his pride and power, but go you and preach the gospel of your deliverance as I bid you." The mighty hand has always failed in the propagation of the gospel. "They that take the sword shall perish with the sword."

4.—God will deliver.—"I will stretch out my hand, and smite Egypt with all my wonders : . . . and after that he will let you go." The New Testament comment on this is found in that wonderful prayer of the apostles : "And now, Lord, behold their threatenings : and grant unto thy servants, that with all boldness they may speak thy word, by stretching forth thine hand to heal; and that signs and wonders may be done by the name of thy holy child Jesus." (Acts iv, 24–31 ; Ps. ii.)

XXII.

THE PASSOVER INSTITUTED.—Exodus xii, 1-14.

(1) And the Lord spake unto Moses and Aaron in the land of Egypt, saying, (2) This month shall be unto you the beginning of months: it shall be the first month of the year to you. (3) Speak ye unto all the congregation of Israel, saying, In the tenth day of this month they shall take to them every man a lamb, according to the house of their fathers, a lamb for an house: (4) And if the household be too little for the lamb, let him and his neighbour next unto his house take it according to the number of the souls; every man according to his eating shall make your count for the lamb. (5) Your lamb shall be without blemish, a male of the first year: ye shall take it out from the sheep, or from the goats: (6) And ye shall keep it up until the fourteenth day of the same month: and the whole assembly of the congregation of Israel shall kill it in the evening. (7) And they shall take of the blood, and strike it on the two side posts and on the upper door post of the houses, wherein they shall eat it. (8) And they shall eat the flesh in that night, roast with fire, and unleavened bread; and with bitter herbs they shall eat it. (9) Eat not of it raw, nor sodden at all with water, but roast with fire; his head with his legs, and with the purtenance thereof. (10) And ye shall let nothing of it remain until the morning; and that which remaineth of it until the morning ye shall burn with fire. (11) And thus shall ye eat it; with your loins girded, your shoes on your feet, and your staff in your hand; and ye shall eat it in haste: it is the Lord's passover. (12) For I will pass through the land of Egypt this night, and will smite all the firstborn in the land of Egypt, both man and beast; and against all the gods of Egypt I will execute judgment: I am the Lord. (13) And the blood shall be to you for a token upon the houses where ye are: and when I see the blood, I will pass over you, and the plague shall not be upon you to destroy you, when I smite the land of Egypt. (14) And this day shall be unto you for a memorial; and ye shall keep it a feast to the Lord throughout your generations; ye shall keep it a feast by an ordinance for ever.—Exodus xii, 1-14.

Of the final commission and departure of Moses down to Egypt, and the tragic conflict with Pharaoh, the intervening chapters since our last study furnish us with the graphic details. The nine plagues which God sent upon Pharaoh and Egypt at the command of Moses were in the nature of admonitions to the proud king, and to demonstrate to him, and to all Egypt, and to all ages, that Jehovah is the Almighty God, and that all the power of man and the gods of Egypt were vanity. Not by one stroke, but by a series of ascending and cumulative acts of power, did God make this demonstration. Had God delivered his people by one single act of power it might have been attributed to mere natural phenomena; but the successive strokes could not be accounted for, except on the ground that God was directly dealing with this proud and self-sufficient world power. It will be noticed that these acts of God's power were distributed over all the various elements of creation—over the water, the air, the earth; the cattle of the field, and the people; and over the growing herbs and trees of the field. Moreover, in these plagues God separated between the Egyptians and his people, so that no plague came upon the Hebrews, their cattle, or their fields. Thus he taught Pharaoh that he was not only God, but that the Hebrews were his people. The last interview between Moses and Pharaoh closed dramatically. Enraged with the steadfastness of Moses in demanding the unconditional release of the people of God, Pharaoh drove Moses forth from his presence, ordering him, "See my face no more." Moses was equally stern in his reply, only more dignified: "Thou hast spoken well, I will see thy face again no more." (Ex. x, 29.) After that came the proclamation of the last plague, and the final deliverance. (Ex. xi.) If there remained any doubt in the mind of Pharaoh as to the special relation in which the children of Israel stood toward God as his elect people, this last plague, or rather judgment, in which all the firstborn of Egypt should die, would demonstrate that. "That ye may know how that the Lord doth put a difference between the Egyptians and Israel." (xi, 7.)

The twelfth chapter of this book is largely taken up with an account of the slaying of the paschal lamb; the sprinkling of the blood; the final judgment upon Pharaoh and all the land of Egypt; and the starting forth of the children of Israel from the land.

I.—THE LAMB THAT WAS SLAIN.*

We are happily not in the least doubt as to the signification of this lamb or the meaning of the sprinkled blood. In I. Cor. v, 7,

---

* Instead of writing a new lesson on this interesting chapter, I have ventured to transfer the substance of a chapter out of my book entitled "*Out of Egypt*," in which this whole story is more minutely detailed, which I would recommend to the readers of these Studies to peruse.

we have the clear declaration that the passover lamb of Egypt is the type of "the Lamb of God, which taketh away the sin of the world," and which was slain for us. Indeed, the whole subsequent history of Israel, and the entire history of the Church of Christ, go to show that this Egyptian history, now culminating in a final act, is a divine parable of the greater work of God in delivering sinners from the slavery of Satan, sin, and hell. As we see the power of Pharaoh broken almost simultaneously with the slaying of the lamb, so are we reminded of the declaration of our Lord just before he went to the cross whereon he was slain. It is as if by anticipation he saw his great enemy and ours cast down. "Now is the judgment of this world: now shall the prince of this world be cast out. And I, if I be lifted up from the earth, will draw all men unto me. This he said, signifying what death he should die." "And he said unto them, I beheld Satan as lightning fall from heaven." (John xii, 31-33; Luke x, 18.) This anticipated and predicted triumph was accomplished on the cross when he cried, "It is finished." By his voluntary death he judged both Satan and the world which took part with Satan in his crucifixion. This will be made manifest to all the universe when he finally casts the devil into hell forever, with the nations that forget God, and all unbelievers who have heretofore, and who will hereafter, take their part with them "that obey not the gospel of our Lord Jesus Christ."

Several important things are to be noticed in connection with the choosing out and slaying the lamb; the study of which will, I am sure, greatly help us to understand more fully the preciousness of the death of Christ.

1.—**The lamb was of God's appointment.**—"And the Lord spake unto Moses and Aaron, . . . Speak ye unto all the congregation of Israel, saying, In the tenth day of this month they shall take to them every man a lamb." (vv. 1-4.) The thought of bringing the people up out of the land of Egypt by means of slaying a lamb was probably a new one to Moses. Certainly it was not of his devising. Left to himself, there was no reason why he should not have supposed that it would have been enough for God to have slain all the firstborn, without putting the children of Israel in peril. Why should not God separate between them and the Egyptians, as he did in the case of the previous plagues?

God did, indeed, tell Moses that he and the Egyptians should see that "the Lord doth put a difference between the Egyptians and Israel." But he did not tell him at that time that the difference was one that stood in the fact that Israel should be protected by the blood of the lamb that was sprinkled over them. And this truly is the main difference between saved and unsaved people. It is not that there is by nature any difference; nor practically is there any difference in the quality of the good works done by believers and unbelievers. "For," saith the Scripture, "there is no difference: for all have sinned, and come short of the glory of God." The Israelites were as bad as the Egyptians, perhaps worse, seeing that with them there was the knowledge of God, as he had been known to Jacob their father and to Joseph their elder brother. The only difference, therefore, was a difference which the Lord put between them. That difference was that Israel was under the blood, and Egypt was not.

Now if we apply this fact to our present purpose, we should say that redemption was, and is, wholly a matter of grace, both as to the divine purpose and also as to the righteous condition. Man's idea of getting out of Egypt, or escaping the bondage of sin, is by his own works, or at least only by the power of God. It never yet occurred to man that the way of escape was by blood. This is God's thought, and his only. From before the foundation of the world Christ is a lamb slain. (I. Pet. i, 20.) Indeed, it is a part of the characteristic enmity of the human heart to reject the salvation God has provided through faith in the blood of atonement. (Heb. xi, 28.) When God ordered sacrifice in the beginning, Abel, the man of *faith*, brought the animal sacrifice, for the offering of blood or life to God; but Cain, the man of *nature* and reason, brought of the fruit of the field. He did not see the need of a sacrifice of blood. So it is now; human wisdom does not suggest deliverance through blood. But being once revealed to faith, reason justified the wisdom of God in appointing that we are to be saved through blood. For "without shedding of blood is no remission." (Heb. ix, 22.)

2.—**The lamb is of God's providing.**—It is true that in the text immediately before us this truth does not come out so clearly; but as we go forward in the history of this lamb slain for sinners, it becomes evident that we are to understand that the lamb was understood as of God's providing. In a later ordinance, enacted that this sacrifice might be a perpetual one, it was ordained that the firstborn of both man and beast should be redeemed, on the ground that these were the Lord's. "And it shall be when the Lord shall bring thee into the land of the Canaanites, . . . that thou shalt set apart [cause to pass over] unto the Lord all that openeth the matrix, and every firstling that cometh of a beast which thou hast; the males shall be the Lord's." (Ex. xiii, 11, 12.) That is also a beautiful reminder of this great truth, which we have in that pathetic but mighty saying of faith, when Abraham made answer to Isaac, who was going up Mount Moriah to be offered: "My son, God will provide himself a lamb." (Gen. xxii, 8.)

In the fullness of time, when the shadows were fleeing away and the true substance was about to appear, we read: "Wherefore when he cometh into the world, he saith, Sacrifice and offering thou wouldest not, but a body hast thou prepared me: in burnt offerings and sacrifices for sin thou hast had no pleasure. Then said I, Lo, I come . . . to do thy will, O God. . . . He taketh away the first, that he may establish the second. By the which will we are sanctified through the offering of the body of Jesus Christ once for all." (Heb. x, 5–10.) From this we learn that the true sacrifice which does take away sin once for all, and delivers us from its power and bondage, is a sacrifice provided by God himself: that this lamb slain in Egypt, and which continued to be slain through all the intervening centuries by the high-priest of Israel, was but a shadow of the eternal purpose which God had for sinners. In the light of this, the saying of Peter, "Forasmuch as ye know that ye were not redeemed with corruptible things, . . . but with the precious blood of Christ, as of a lamb without blemish and without spot: who verily was foreordained before the foundation of the world, but was manifest in these last times for you" (I. Pet. i, 18, 19), is very significant and suggestive. So, too, the public introduction of Jesus by John the Baptist—"Behold the Lamb of God, which taketh away the sin of the world."

As we come into the clear light of the New Testament, we learn, in the face of Christ, that the Redemption Lamb was not only of God's appointment, but also of his providing. This sets forth the grace of God to us sinners most wonderfully. Why should he accept any redemption at all? Why should he not let us perish altogether from his presence and the glory of his power, as he has done with the angels who kept not their first estate? Surely, having sinned, we had no claim upon him, even as these Israelites had no claim upon him. But more than this, is it not amazing grace that he not only has thoughts and purposes of grace for us, but that he himself provides, in so wonderful a way, a Lamb—and such a Lamb!—for our redemption? For when there was no eye to pity, and no arm to save, his eye pitied us, and his arm brought us salvation. (Is. lix, 16; lxiii, 5.)

These most rich and precious declarations of Scripture concerning the great salvation make this whole story of Egypt beautiful and clear. The coming of Jesus Christ into the world, his dying for us on Calvary, was only making true to our sense, and in time, what was eternally true in the purpose of God. Moreover, his coming and his redemption were only the fulfillment—to the called of God, everywhere and in every age—of that promise made in Egypt. We cannot but rejoice in anticipation of that time when, with the redeemed in heaven, we shall sing the song of redemption, as the children of Israel did on the other side of the Red Sea. "Thou art worthy to take the book, and to open the seals thereof: for thou wast slain, and hast redeemed us to God by thy blood out of every kindred, and tongue, and people, and nation; and hast made us unto our God kings and priests." (Rev. v, 9, 10.)

3.—**The lamb must be without blemish.**—"Your lamb shall be without blemish, a male of the first year." (ver. 5.) This corresponds with that to which we have already called attention in the first epistle of Peter, where he says we were redeemed "with the precious blood of Christ, as of a lamb without blemish and without spot." Why the lamb should be without spot or blemish is most apparent. If it was to be a type of Christ, as we have seen it to be, then it must be a spotless lamb. Christ was "holy, harmless, undefiled, separate from sinners." It must needs have been so. If he is to redeem sinners he himself must be without sin. And that this might be more manifest: before he was slain, his human nature was subject to every temptation that has beset man. He did not offer himself up as an untried or unproved substitute. For God sent him forth into the world, born of a woman indeed, without the taint of Adam's sin on him, but with Adam's nature in him; and in that nature he was put under the law, and driven into the wilderness to be tempted of the devil, that he might be proved able as well as willing to undertake for us.

If God had offered his Son before his human nature had been tried, the devil might have said that Christ's nature was not a real human nature; or else that God did not dare to subject him to the same trial as that under which Adam fell. So God gave him up to be tried. He was made subject to law, as well as to all the temptations arising from the enticements of the world, the flesh, and the devil; so that in coming days we might appeal to One who "was in *all points* tempted like as we are, yet without sin"; and who can the better be "touched with the feeling of our infirmity." (Heb. ii, 18; iv, 15.) When he hung on yonder tree for us, the Enemy could not impeach the value of his redemptive work on our behalf, by charging that he himself had sins that needed to be put away. What a blessed assurance is this!—that our Lamb was without spot or blemish, and after trial and temptation was without fault before God.

4.—A costly sacrifice.—"A male of the first year." This speaks not only of beauty and perfection, but of worth. Our Lamb must be worthy. These sacrifices of beasts continually offered could not take away sin. But when the eternal Son of God came into the world, in a body which God prepared for him in the womb of the Virgin without the knowledge of sinful man, then we had the most worthy sacrifice that God could provide. As man, he was the most worthy, for there was none ever like him; he was the only sinless and perfect man that ever lived. But besides that, "in him dwelleth all the fullness of the Godhead bodily." He was "God manifest in the flesh." Oh, who can tell the rest there is to a believing soul in the thought that he has been redeemed with the blood of such a sacrifice? We should not dare say some things which we do, were it not that they are written in the inspired Word: for instance, Paul exhorts the Ephesian elders, "Take heed therefore unto yourselves, and to all the flock, over the which the Holy Ghost hath made you overseers, to feed the Church of God, which HE HATH PURCHASED WITH HIS OWN BLOOD." (Acts xx, 28.)

Here we have in most unmistakable language the fact that the sacrifice which Christ made for us is so costly that if we were ten thousand sinners rolled into one, there is worth enough in him who has given his life for us to put our redemption beyond doubt. That for thee, O believer! Can you doubt your salvation if the blood of the Lamb of God is between you and condemnation? I sometimes hear people say that it is presumption for believers to say that they know they are saved. Why, if saved at all, we ought to know it beyond a doubt. If we are resting on that Sacrifice which has all the worth of God in it, and which God has accepted, how can we not be saved? It is presumption to fear, if you have made him the ground of your hope. If you are hoping for salvation on any other ground, you may well be in doubt; but if you are resting here, then there is no place for doubt.

5.—A willing sacrifice.—Some people seem to think that God had no right to send his Son to die for sinners; that there is an element of injustice in "making" Christ die for the guilty. But this is an objection founded on a misapprehension of the truth. If God had sent his Son into the world *against* his will, and had caused him to die under protest, the objection might lie; but Christ was a willing sacrifice. It is well known that a lamb is the most ready of all creatures to submit to death. It makes no resistance, but looks upon the knife which is to slay it without effort to escape. This same truth is wonderfully foreshadowed in Isaac, who, after he was on the mount, seems without remonstrance to have allowed himself to be bound to the altar whereon his father placed him.

But in the life of our Lord, who was brought "as a lamb to the slaughter," and who "as a sheep before her shearers is dumb, so he opened not his mouth" (Is. liii, 7), we see not submission merely, but willing acquiescence in all the work. Indeed, we hear him crying, "Lo, I come; . . . I delight to do thy will, O my God." (Ps. xl, 7, 8; Heb. x, 7.) Never in all the record of his life is there one murmur of complaint. "For this cause came" he "into the world." His delight was in our salvation. "Who for the joy that was set before him endured the cross, despising the shame." (Heb. xii, 2.) It is certain that one of the most important elements in the atoning work of Jesus Christ is that he willingly offered himself. His sacrifice was not compulsory, but voluntary. "Therefore," saith he, "doth my Father love me, because I lay down my life, that I might take it again. No man taketh it from me, but I lay it down of myself. I have power to lay it down, and I have power to take it again." (John x, 17, 18.) Truly he is the Good Shepherd; and "the Good Shepherd giveth his life for the sheep." (John x, 11.)

6.—"**Ye shall take it out from the sheep.**"—It is to be noted that God everywhere compares his people to a flock of sheep. "Give ear, O Shepherd of Israel, thou that leadest Joseph like a flock." (Ps. lxxx, 1.) We have already seen that Jesus, who was the true Lamb, was none other than the eternal Son of God, who came to be a sacrifice for us; and we have seen also how God prepared a body for him. We learn now that in order to save us he must be identified with us in real nature and kinship. The sacrifice offered up to God for man's sin must be a sacrifice in human nature. An angel could not be an acceptable sacrifice for man, because he belongs to a different order of beings.

So when we see Jesus dying for us, we see a Lamb that was taken from the flock, "one from among the brethren." This is in part the significance of the Incarnation. We read in the second of Hebrews that "he took not on him the nature of angels; but he took on him the seed of Abraham." (Heb. ii, 16.) "Forasmuch then as the children are partakers of flesh and blood, he also himself likewise took part of the same; that through death he might destroy him that had the power of death, that is, the devil; and deliver them who through fear of death were all their lifetime subject to bondage. . . . Wherefore in all things it behooved him to be made like unto his brethren, that he might be a merciful and faithful high priest in things pertaining to God, to make reconciliation for the sins of the people." (Heb. ii, 14, 15, 17.)

Paul tells us that he "made himself of no reputation, and took upon him the form of a servant, and was made in the likeness of men: and being found in fashion as a man, he humbled himself, and became obedient unto death, even the death of the cross." (Phil. ii, 7, 8.) Also, in Romans i, 3, where he speaks of the gospel of God "concerning his Son Jesus Christ our Lord, which was made of the seed of David according to the flesh; and declared to be the Son of God with power . . . by the resurrection from the dead." These and other passages show that in becoming our Sacrifice, or our Lamb, he was made in all points like as we are, except sin. He took our nature. He was not only made flesh, but he was also made man—intensely, really human; that he might stand before God *as* man and *for* man, as really as he came forth from God, the "express image" of his Father's person, and the very "brightness of his glory." (Heb. i, 3.) This is the significance of choosing the lamb "from the sheep." Let us not forget it. Though Jesus was God's Lamb in the sense that God appointed and sent him into the world, he is our Lamb in the sense that he is of us and from among us, as he is our representative before God.

7.—**The lamb must be slain.**—"And ye shall keep it up until the fourteenth day of the same month: and the whole assembly of the congregation of Israel shall kill it in the evening." (ver. 6.) It was not enough to choose out a lamb: *the lamb must be slain*. This introduces us into the very center of the mystery of our redemption. "Forasmuch as ye know that ye were . . . redeemed . . . with the precious blood of Christ, as of a lamb" slain. (I. Pet. i, 18, 19.) It is not the *teaching* Christ, or the *miracle-working* Christ, or the holy and faithful Son of God, *living out* a loyal human life before God as an example to and for us, that saves us; or stands between us and the avenging judgment of God upon sin: but it is the death of Christ, the *slain Lamb*.

Suppose that some tender-hearted Israelite had said, "I do not see the use of slaying the lamb at all. I think such a command unnecessary and cruel. But I quite agree that we ought to make the sweet spirit of a lamb our example. So I have decided to take a lamb into the house with me to-night; and I will fold it in my arms and fondle it. When the destroying angel sees how really I admire and love the lamb he will pass me by, as he will know that though I did not slay the lamb, I was not wholly indifferent to the necessity of having some relation to it." Or suppose he had just taken the living lamb and tied it to the door-latch, so that the death-angel might see that the lamb was there. Would either of these courses have been sufficient? Not so! The command was, ye "shall kill it."

Now, there are many who profess to have great respect for God's command and for his Word, but still they say, "I do not see the need of salvation through blood." Indeed, they declare that such a plan of salvation is revolting to them, and not according to their reason or taste. But they say, "We admire and greatly respect Jesus Christ. We believe in taking him as our example. We will adopt that beautiful life as a pattern and model. We will strive to catch his spirit and reproduce his life in ours." Others simply place Christ outside the door of their houses in a kind of formal assent to the truth of Christianity. But all this will not do. "He was wounded for our transgressions, he was bruised for our iniquities, . . . and with his stripes we are healed." It was the *slain lamb*, and not a *living lamb*, that availed the Israelites in that dread crisis; even so it is Christ, and *him crucified*, that will avail us to turn aside the stroke of divine judgment on account of sin.

It is quite the fashion nowadays for not a few preachers and people, who even call themselves "evangelical," to make light of salvation through or on account of the blood of Christ, and to speak of it as the "doctrine of the shambles," and a "bloody religion." Well, my friends, we need not be alarmed at such talk; it is very old. Cain did not like it; for when God commanded him and his brother to offer a sacrifice of blood or life, he offered the fruit of the ground. But when he saw that his brother Abel's bloody sacrifice was accepted and his rejected, he was angry. He would not offer a life to God in death, because that would be a bloody religion; but he did not hesitate to slay his brother in anger. That old Cain spirit is still rife. The Jews would not have Christ as an atonement; and so they murdered him: and the Crucified One is rejected to-day. When Moses offered a sacrifice of blood to God his heathen wife was offended, and called him a "bloody husband."

It is well to be reminded that the whole Bible, which is a revelation of God's will and the way of salvation through Jesus Christ, *is crimson with the story of the blood*. From the offering of Abel, recorded in Genesis, to the song of the redeemed, recorded in the Revelation, the blood is conspicuously present. If you were to take a brush and dip it in red ink, and then go carefully through the Bible, painting over those passages that refer to the blood, and all those promises that are associated with and rest on the blood, you would be surprised to find how red your Bible would be; and then if you should take your penknife and carefully cut out all the passages that you had before marked with red, you would be still more surprised to find how ragged your Bible would be. Indeed, there would be no intelligibility left in it. The historical portion would be meaningless; the ethical teaching would be powerless. No "forgiveness," no "justification," no "regeneration," no "peace," no "joy," no "sanctification," no "rest," no "hope," no "resurrection," no "heaven," no "robes washed and made white and clean," no "song"; nothing but sin, and blackness, and darkness, forever.

Blessed be God for these two sayings concerning the blood—one in the beginning and one at the end of the Bible! "When I see the blood I will pass over you" (ver. 13); and, "Unto him that loved us, and washed us from our sins in his own blood." "And they sung a new song, saying, Thou art worthy, . . . for thou wast slain, and hast redeemed us to God by thy blood out of every kindred, and tongue, and people, and nation." (Rev. i, 5; v, 9.) I often wonder what those people would do in heaven—if they could get there without the blood—when the redeemed began to sing of, or to worship, the Lamb that was slain. They would certainly feel greatly out of place. But they will never be there. He who denies the blood on earth shall never sing of it in heaven.

8.—The blood must be sprinkled in God's sight.—"And they shall take of the blood, and strike it on the two side posts and on the upper door post of the houses, wherein they shall eat it." (ver. 7.) In this passage we have a most important truth: the striking of the blood on the outside of the house, and not on the inside. It is also to be observed that this blood was not an offering to Pharaoh. The offering of Jesus Christ is not made to the devil. Satan has no rights in us, or over us. His power is an usurped power, and it is broken, not by blood, but by the power of God. Neither is the offering of blood made to sinners. It is *for* them, but not *to* them. But the offering was made directly to God. When the high-priest in later times made atonement for the sins of the people, he bore the blood into the Most Holy Place, and there sprinkled it on the Mercy Seat under the eye of God alone. Jesus, at once our High-Priest and our Sacrifice, "by a greater and more perfect tabernacle, not made with hands, that is to say, not of this building; neither by the blood of goats and calves, but by his own blood he entered in once into the Holy Place, having obtained eternal redemption for us"; having "through the eternal Spirit offered himself without spot to God." (Heb. ix, 11, 12, 14.)

Much more Scripture might be quoted to show that the blood or sacrifice—by, or on account of, which we are saved—was offered to God, and had to do with some necessity in the divine nature in regard to sin, which had to be met and satisfied before the judgment against sinners could be averted, but which, being met by the blood of Christ, enabled even justice herself to take the sinner's part against death. In other words, we learn from this that sin is essentially sinful and guilty; and that a holy and just God must meet and will punish it. The offering up of Jesus Christ has entirely met the claims and demands of the divine nature and government against sin; and the blood, which is the sign of this satisfactory expiation, is brought before the eye of God. It is God who sees the blood and is satisfied, not the sinner. The sinner is at peace because God has declared himself satisfied with the one Offering which has been made. It is of considerable importance to keep this truth before your mind, if you are to have peace as well as salvation.

9.—The sinner must pass under the blood.—It was not enough that the Hebrews had the blood sprinkled on the door-posts of their houses. They must take refuge under that blood. For we are assured that danger and death awaited any one who went out of their houses till the morning. "And ye shall take a bunch of hyssop, and dip it in the blood that is in the bason, and strike the lintel and the two side posts with the blood that is in the bason; and none of you shall go out at the door of his house until the morning." (Ex. xii, 22.) Now it would not have availed to save any of the firstborn of the children of the Israelites, even though the blood were shed and duly sprinkled on the door-posts, if they had not passed under it into their houses. So it is of no avail to sinners that Christ has been slain on the cross, and his blood presented to God as a sufficient atonement for sin, if sinners do not avail themselves of it by a cordial and hearty acceptance of God's mercy built and established thereon. Christ, by the grace of God, tasted death for every man, and God hath set him forth "a ransom for all" (I. Tim. ii, 6; Heb. ii, 9); but if men do not humbly acknowledge their sin and helplessness, and take refuge under the blood as their only hope, it will avail them nothing. The cross of Christ is the door into life. On that cross Jesus shed his precious blood. They are saved who bow their hearts in confession before him as he hangs on that tree, and pass by faith into the household of God.

I can fancy that many of the people who had known Jesus from childhood, and who had followed him through his entire ministry even to the hour and moment of his death, of which they were eye-witnesses, nevertheless never said to him or in their own hearts: "He is my Saviour; I *believe* in and *trust* him; I *accept* the offering which he has made, and which God has accepted, as the only and sufficient ground of my salvation." And so it is with some of you. Christ has died. You say you do not doubt it. The Blood has been sprinkled, and God, by raising him up, hath declared that it is sufficient, and that he is satisfied with it as a settlement of the question of sin. And yet you have not accepted it as the ground of your hope: you have never passed in under that Blood. The Hebrew had to go into his house through and under that blood-sprinkled way. We enter the door of salvation by confession. "If thou shalt confess with thy mouth the Lord Jesus, and shalt believe in thine heart that God hath raised him from the dead, thou shalt be saved." (Rom. x, 9.) Why not do so now?

I remember distinctly when this crisis came to me. I knew that I was a sinner. God's Word told me that I was a guilty, lost, and helpless one. This I believed. Nevertheless, he told me in that same Word that he had given his Son to die for me, and that he was satisfied with what Christ had done, as a ground of acceptance and settlement of my sins. The gospel further put this question to me: "If God is satisfied with the shed blood of Jesus, can you not be satisfied and reconciled to him, accepting the full and free forgiveness of your sins, and the entire justification of your soul before God on that basis?" My reply was instantly made upon seeing that this was the gospel offer: "If God is satisfied, I *ought* to be, *and am;* and do from this moment yield and surrender myself to God both for salvation and service." From that moment I have been a saved sinner; and that took place more than twenty years ago. My friends, will you accept that sacrifice as the ground of your salvation, and, confessing your sin and helplessness, will you pass in under that Blood? You may do so this moment—by the choice and decision of your heart.

10.—The ground of peace.—God says, "When I see the blood, I will pass over you, and the plague shall not be upon you to destroy you, when I smite the land of Egypt." (ver. 13.) Notice here, in the first place, that they had the sure word and promise of God, that, having taken refuge under the blood, he would pass over them. So we have the Word of God, that, having fled for refuge to lay hold upon the hope of eternal life in Christ Jesus, we shall never be confounded. (Heb vi, 17-20.) The blood was the *ground of safety;* the word was the *guaranteeing promise.* Again, we ought to take notice that he does not say, "When *you* see the blood." The blood is for his eye, and not for ours. We deal with God through his *Word,* and he deals with us on the basis of *Blood.* While God looks at the Blood, we ought to be taking heed to his Word. Very many, however, are not content to deal with God on the basis of his Word, but want to take God's place and view the Blood. Our peace is not determined by our feelings, but by the sufficiency of the ground of salvation (the Blood), and the value of God's word of promise. Many persons are always complaining because they have not peace. They are afraid they are not saved. In a word, they do not *feel* that they are saved. We are not told to feel. We are told to believe, or take refuge in the blood of Christ; and then we have the absolute and oath-bound word of God that we are and shall be saved.

There is among the Hebrews a legend of two sisters who that night had, with the rest of their household, gone into their dwellings. One of them stood all ready to depart, and began quietly eating her portion of the roast body of the lamb (a type of the soul feeding on Christ), her mind at perfect peace and rest. The other was walking about the dwelling, full of terrible fear lest the destroying angel should penetrate therein. This one reproached her sister for being so careless and confident, and finally asked her how it was that she could be so full of assurance when the angel of death and judgment was abroad in the land. The reply was, "Why, sister, the blood has been sprinkled, and we have God's word that when he sees the blood he will pass over us. Now I have no right to doubt God's word. I believe he will keep his word. If I were in doubt about the blood having been shed, or if I doubted either the integrity or ability of God in connection with his word, I should be uneasy. But as I do not question the fact that the blood has been shed, and as I believe that God will be true to his word, I cannot but be at peace."

They were both equally safe, but one was at peace while the other was not—or, as we should say now, one had assurance and the other was full of doubts. But if the doubting one had believed what God said, she could not have been in distress. It is even so now. Those believers who make the finished work of Christ the ground of their hope, and are resting simply and sincerely on his Word, are at peace; while those who are trying to find peace in themselves, in their frames and feelings, are never at rest. It is the BLOOD OF JESUS CHRIST that makes us *safe;* it is the WORD OF GOD concerning that Blood that makes us *sure.*

II.—"YE SHALL GO OUT IN HASTE."

Since we have spent so much space on the principal lesson of our text, we must pass over, with a word or two, the directions for eating the lamb and leaving Egypt. The lessons, however, are obvious (vv. 8–11), and are these: (i) The feeding upon the lamb, no doubt, signifies communion. (ii) The unleavened bread, the purpose and necessity of a pure and holy life. (iii) The bitter herbs signify the sorrowful remembrance (repentance) of the bitter bondage (sin) out of which we have been delivered. (iv) The loins girded, the staff in hand, the shoes on the feet, the standing posture—all suggest emergency and haste. When the Lord went to bring Lot out of Sodom, the angel laid his hand on him and "hastened him." There is no time to linger in this Egyptian world. We must break with it and come out with haste, for it is a doomed world. We do not want to be entangled again in its sin and bondage or lost in its certain doom. We have no "to-morrows" at our disposal. If we are to be saved we must be saved *now;* for now, and now only, "is the accepted time."

Thus we see how God delivered Israel out of the hands of Pharaoh, and how at the same time he delivered them from the common doom that hung alike over Israel and Egypt on account of sin. In the gospel we see the same thing: how Jesus delivers us out of the hands of the god of this world and all his spiritual powers, as well as from the wrath of God against sin. No one can read with attention this vivid story without being struck with wonder and amazement at the grace parabled therein. May God make it profitable to our souls and helpful to our lives. (See "*Out of Egypt,*" Chapter VI.)

XXIII.

PASSAGE OF THE RED SEA.—Exodus xiv, 19-29.

(19) And the Angel of God, which went before the camp of Israel, removed and went behind them; and the pillar of the cloud went from before their face, and stood behind them: (20) And it came between the camp of the Egyptians and the camp of Israel; and it was a cloud and darkness to them, but it gave light by night to these: so that the one came not near the other all the night. (21) And Moses stretched out his hand over the sea; and the Lord caused the sea to go back by a strong east wind all that night, and made the sea dry land, and the waters were divided. (22) And the children of Israel went into the midst of the sea upon the dry ground: and the waters were a wall unto them on their right hand, and on their left. (23) And the Egyptians pursued, and went in after them to the midst of the sea, even all Pharaoh's horses, his chariots, and his horsemen. (24) And it came to pass, that in the morning watch the Lord looked unto the host of the Egyptians through the pillar of fire and of the cloud, and troubled the host of the Egyptians, (25) And took off their chariot wheels, that they drave them heavily: so that the Egyptians said, Let us flee from the face of Israel; for the Lord fighteth for them against the Egyptians. (26) And the Lord said unto Moses, Stretch out thine hand over the sea, that the waters may come again upon the Egyptians, upon their chariots, and upon their horsemen. (27) And Moses stretched forth his hand over the sea, and the sea returned to his strength when the morning appeared; and the Egyptians fled against it; and the Lord overthrew the Egyptians in the midst of the sea. (28) And the waters returned, and covered the chariots, and the horsemen, and all the host of Pharaoh that came into the sea after them; there remained not so much as one of them. (29) But the children of Israel walked upon dry land in the midst of the sea; and the waters were a wall unto them on their right hand, and on their left.—Exodus xiv, 19-29.

The awful and blessed night of the passover was past. The cry of Egypt over the death of all the firstborn in the land went up, if not to heaven, throughout all the land. The king's son and the son of the lowest and meanest slave in the land died that night. The firstborn of all the beasts died also, and so of course all the "gods of Egypt," for they were the choice firstborn of the cattle, and other sacred animals that were kept and pampered in the temples. Thus did God show to the Egyptians the vanity of their gods and the impotence of their own worldly power. Yet not even a dog barked against one of the children of Israel, so safely were they housed and protected by the blood in the land of Goshen. This is the picture of the beginning of that judgment which will yet come upon all the earth, when God shall judge and condemn an unrighteous world.

The next morning, with loins girded, with household goods on their backs, laden with the spoil of Egypt, in gold, jewels, and precious stones (the wages which God now gave them for the long years of unrequited toil exacted of them by the Egyptians), the children of Israel, with their wives and little ones, their flocks and their herds—a mighty company of about two millions of people, with probably as many head of cattle, sheep, and goats—started out of Egypt to make the first stage of their journey toward the land which God had promised them. The way marked out for them to go out of Egypt was not the shortest or easiest, lest they should encounter the Philistines and, without weapons of war, and unaccustomed to fight, should be discouraged, and, through fear, turn back and fall again into the hands of the Egyptians. A young convert's dangers are many at the beginning of his march toward Canaan. But God led the people by "way of the wilderness of the Red Sea," himself accompanying them by the visible sign of his presence, a pillar of cloud by day, and a pillar of fire by night. This is the symbol of the Holy Spirit, who, from the moment a sinner gives himself to God by passing under the blood, becomes his companion and guide by day and by night. The second day's journey was by a most peculiar route: down the west side of the borders of the sea, where they were hemmed in on the one side by the rocks and on the other by the water. Two things were in God's purpose: one was to spread a trap for Pharaoh, and the other to give himself the opportunity of doing a great wonder for his people, which through all ages should be a memorial to them of his power to deliver them from any possible extremity. When Pharaoh heard of the position in which the Israelites were, he roused himself from the stunning blow of the night of death, and, mad with rage and defiance, gathered the choice chariots and captains, and called out all his army, and pursued after Israel, probably concluding that if Moses had made such a tactical blunder as to lead Israel into such a trap, God, who was guiding him, was only a local god of circumstances, and not universally wise and omnipotent—a kind of god of the hills but not of the valleys (1 Kings xx, 28); a god of Goshen but not of the wilderness. The mad rage of Pharaoh is typical of the last desperate effort of Satan to overcome the saints. (Rev. xvii, 13, 14.) When the people saw the armies of Pharaoh coming, and that there was no human possibility of escape, they cried out in unbelieving fear, upbraiding Moses for bringing them out of Egypt. It was a wild, unbelieving cry, showing how quickly and easily faith is obscured by sight. It seems hardly possible that after all God had wrought they should doubt him; but I doubt if we now are much better. We are prone to cry out and complain when any trouble comes to us, if we do not see our way out of it immediately. This very difficulty was for their instruction as well as for the overthrow of their enemy. Moses quieted them with the assurance, "The Lord shall fight for you," and then betook himself to prayer, not a little anxious himself. The Lord told him that it was not a time to pray but to act, and instructed him what to do, telling him at the same time that he would open a pathway of salvation through the Red Sea, which should also prove the grave of the hosts of Pharaoh.

I.—THE SALVATION OF ISRAEL.

The life of Moses in Egypt is in four great chapters of faith: by faith he was preserved from death as a babe; by faith he voluntarily forsook the court of Pharaoh and identified himself with Israel; by faith he kept the passover; by faith he led the people through the Red Sea. We have come now to this final act of faith so far as Egypt was concerned.

1.—The Angel of the Lord.—This was the "I AM" of the burning bush, now present with Israel in the cloudy and fiery pillar. Encamped and trembling, with the seashore on one side and impassable rocks on the other, and the advancing hosts of Pharaoh behind them, it was drawing toward the close of the second day. Hitherto the Angel of the Cloud had moved on before them; but now, instead of going before, he moves and takes up his position between them and Pharaoh's army. "A cloud and darkness" to the Egyptians, but it flooded the whole camp of Israel all that night with a refulgence of light which made the night as the day to them. How safe they were with that bright cloud between them and Pharaoh! Not until the proud king could charge that cloud, and burst through it, could he come near to harm the people of God. So does God stand between every trusting believer and all the powers of sin. The revelation of God in Christ is darkness to the determined and disobedient unbeliever, but it is light even in the night of natural human ignorance to those who "walk before the Lord." "I am the light of the world," said Jesus: "he that followeth me shall not walk in darkness, but shall have the light of life." (John viii, 12.)

2.—**A pathway through the sea.**—When all was quiet and restful in the camp, the people becoming reassured again, Moses stretched out his rod over the sea, and the Lord caused the sea to go back by a strong east wind, leaving the "dry land." To say that the writer of this account of Israel's deliverance did not intend us to understand that God wrought here a stupendous miracle is to charge upon these writers utter nonsense. Here is the plain account of a wonder that was celebrated in Israel through all generations. Whether this account be true or false is one question; but that we are to read it as history is certain, or else we must fling away the whole thing. God here performs a miracle, "not suspending the forces of nature, but wielding them in a fashion impossible to man." That he utilized the wind does not mitigate the tremendous interposition of power beyond any natural force of the wind. The wind was but the attendant upon his power. Why should not God hold back the waters of the sea, and what is there in his doing so that should shock the sensitive reason of those men who are so jealous of God that they would, if they could, reduce him to be a man like to themselves, or even lower, and make him nothing more than "a tendency" in matter and force? A man can take a piece of steel wire and roll it up into a coil until it is filled with power to move the wheels of a watch or of a mighty engine. Left to itself, the steel wire would lie flat on the ground and accomplish nothing; but manipulated by the will and power of man, it works what nature itself could never do. No violation of law is seen in the working of a steel spring; but natural law is so manipulated that the forces of nature put forth their utmost power. So is it in the working of miracles—God manipulates the forces of nature so that wonders are wrought. That is all. But it is enough.

3.—**The passage through the sea.**—We need not indulge our fancy here, nor let loose our imagination in describing this wonderful journey. The psalmist has set it forth beautifully: "Thy way is in the sea, and thy path in the great waters, and thy footsteps are not known." How wide the pathway was, or how many abreast the people marched, we do not know; but it is likely that the way was vastly wide and the people marched in battalions of hundreds, for there were two millions of them, and they crossed in one night. Sprinkled by the flying spray torn from the waters by the strong wind, but dry shod as if on dry land, they went over, a triumphant host of believers, almost literally baptized into death by passing through what became death to Pharaoh and his host. "The waters were a wall unto them on their right hand and on their left." How God can make the very things which, without him would be our destruction, a protection and a safety! He is "head over all things to the church." If we are walking by faith—that is, according to his Word—we need not fear either anything on earth or of hell.

II.—THE DESTRUCTION OF PHARAOH AND HIS HOST.

All night long the children of Israel passed on, and the Angel of God kept the great procession safe by the blackness of darkness which enveloped the Egyptians and by which he hid his people from their sight. Early in the morning, when the last of the children of Israel were reaching the farther shore, the Angel of God suddenly revealed to Pharaoh the wonderful way in which his prey had escaped. Still blinded by his rage and fury, he ordered his host forward after them, nor did he stop to consider the stupendous danger.

1.—"Which the Egyptians essaying to do, were drowned."
—So we are told by the author of the Epistle to the Hebrews. Pharoah's hatred and fury were intensified by the sight of the escaped Hebrews, and he did not stop to consider what this mighty miracle might portend, nor to remember how he had lately fared in all his controversy with Moses. The Egyptians essayed to travel in the same path by which the Israelites had crossed the sea. It is not wise for the enemies of God to attempt what only the people of God can do by faith. Many self-righteous sinners essay to follow Christ, but their righteousness is spurious. The presumptuous guest at the marriage feast essayed to clothe himself, and was cast out. Many modern Egyptians are essaying to organize new churches on rationalistic and materialistic principles, thinking they can do for man even better than the Church of God can do; but one by one they perish, and always will.

2.—The host of the Egyptians troubled.—Now the morning was fully come. The Hebrews were safely over the sea; the Egyptians had all followed them into the mighty trough through which Israel had passed. The watery wall still stood up. All seemed well to the Egyptians, and that they would soon overtake the fugitives. But "the Lord looked unto the host of the Egyptians through the pillar of fire and of the cloud, and troubled the host of the Egyptians." Just what this means it is difficult to tell. Most likely the cloud, which had been black all night through, now began to have an angry and fiery appearance, shooting out forks of flame threatening the Egyptians. At any rate, it awakened their fears and shook their nerves; just as the fears of the soldiers were aroused when in Gethsemane they "went backward and fell to the ground," when Jesus said, "I am he." Oh, there is something terrible in the face of the Lord, even in "the face of him that sitteth on the throne," when his wrath is about to blaze forth. One look of the Lord against our enemies is mightier for our defense than all earth's armies. (Ps. ii, 12; Rev. vi, 16.)

3.—The panic-stricken Egyptians.—Now a new danger threatened them, increased their fear, and led up to the final panic. The hard dry sand of the sea upon which the children of Israel had walked over, and which so far had served the Egyptians well, suddenly began to soften under the chariot wheels, so that "they drave them heavily," and the horses, plunging, wrenched the wheels off as they sank into the sand. The floor of the sea, like a pavement of stone to Israel, became a bed of quicksand to Egypt. "The Lord knoweth how to deliver the godly," and how to overthrow the wicked. Let us mind this lesson. Their fear now wholly possessed them. The iron discipline of the army is torn to shreds: wild fear breaks out among them; some one raises the cry: "Let us flee from the face of Israel; for the Lord fighteth for them against the Egyptians." No sooner did this cry sound (interpreting the thought in the hearts of all) than the panic became general, and, regardless of all order, the whole host broke and fled. Charioteers forsook their sluggish wagons of war and took to their feet. The softening sand sucked them down and held them as in fetters. We can see in our mind's eye the whole host falling upon each other and fighting like demons to get away, each man regardless of all the rest and fighting for himself alone. Men band themselves together to fight against God and his people; but when judgment comes all will fail, and wild confusion will fill every man's breast as he flees from "the face of . . . the Lamb."

4.—Final destruction.—In the midst of this wild panic, and before a single man had regained the Egyptian side of the sea, Moses, standing on the far shore with all Israel safely over, at the command of God stretched out his hand, and the water, which had been standing like glassy walls, began to sway and break here and there, until finally the whole vast mass was released from the grip of Jehovah's hand and came tumbling and thundering down like a thousand Niagaras upon the miserable Egyptians, and drowned

THE DESTRUCTION OF PHARAOH AND HIS HOST.

the entire host in the sea. "The sea returned to his strength," "and the waters returned, and covered the chariots and the horsemen, and all the host of Pharaoh that came into the sea after them; there remained not so much as one of them." Awful judgment! Like another flood it stands as a warning beacon to admonish all sinners that whosoever fights against God must perish. Those who pursued after Israel now fled from before him and perished because of him. Pharaoh had said defiantly to Moses (Ex. v, 2): "Who is the Lord that I should obey his voice? I know not the Lord, neither will I let Israel go." How now, proud Pharaoh? "Behold, ye despisers, and wonder, and perish: for I work a work in your days, a work which ye shall in no wise believe, though a man declare it unto you." (Acts xiii, 41.)

5.—A happy echo.—The twenty-ninth verse is an echo of the twenty-second. "But the children of Israel walked upon dry land in the midst of the sea; and the waters were a wall unto them on their right hand, and on their left. Thus the Lord saved Israel that day out of the hand of the Egyptians; and Israel saw the Egyptians dead upon the seashore. And Israel saw that great work which the Lord did upon the Egyptians: and the people feared the Lord, and believed the Lord, and his servant Moses." * (vv. 29-31.)

* The recent discovery of the mummy of the Pharaoh of the Exodus, Menephtah II., has caused some to declare that the record here does not say that Pharaoh himself was drowned, but only his hosts or the "Egyptians." This king of Egypt was known to be a weak and vacillating man, and, moreover, all the inscriptions recently discovered indicate that he was personally a coward. He would ride out to battle with his warriors, but never went into the conflict himself. It is most likely that he with a small body-guard stood on the African shore and witnessed the destruction of his army, and then returned to Egypt to repent at leisure his rashness in fighting against Jehovah.

XXIV.

THE WOES OF THE DRUNKARD.—Proverbs xxiii, 29-35.

(29) Who hath woe? who hath sorrow? who hath contentions? who hath babbling? who hath wounds without cause? who hath redness of eyes? (30) They that tarry long at the wine; they that go to seek mixed wine. (31) Look not thou upon the wine when it is red, when it giveth his colour in the cup, when it moveth itself aright. (32) At the last it biteth like a serpent, and stingeth like an adder. (33) Thine eyes shall behold strange women, and thine heart shall utter perverse things. (34) Yea, thou shalt be as he that lieth down in the midst of the sea, or as he that lieth upon the top of a mast. (35) They have stricken me, shalt thou say, and I was not sick; they have beaten me, and I felt it not: when shall I awake? I will seek it yet again.—Proverbs xxiii, 29-35.

The temperance lesson for this quarter is the same as that assigned for the second quarter of last year. I can add nothing of sufficient importance to warrant a rewriting of that lesson. I content myself, therefore, with repeating the lesson as the committee has done. It may be profitably studied again. There is no evil in this life to which drunkenness does not lead up, and the end of it is eternal death; for no "drunkards . . . shall inherit the kingdom of God." (I. Cor. vi, 10.) It is not only a physical evil destroying the body; it is also a mental and moral evil destroying the soul. Drunkenness is classed with stealing, covetousness, reviling, extortion, and adultery. It is said to have its seat in the heart of the natural man, and is not therefore merely a physical vice. (Matt. xv, 19; Mark vii, 21; Gal. v, 19, 21.) One has only to look at the sins associated with drunkenness to see what a frightful source of evil it is, and how properly to classify it; and to see what the dreadful end of the drunkard will be. It is a singular fact that the devil has so deceived the world on this point, that drunkenness is treated as a misfortune and not as a sin, and that the drunkard is regarded rather as weak than a bad man. A thief or an extortioner or a murderer is regarded as a criminal; but the drunkard is looked upon simply as one of unfortunately weak habit of mind, who cannot avoid getting into an excess of appetite. A man convicted of theft is forever a disgraced man in the eyes of the community in which he lives, whereas a drunkard is forgiven his drunkenness whenever he chances to be sober. Hosea draws a graphic picture of the misery to which Israel had been reduced by sin and transgression, and for which, finally, she as a nation suffered the judgment of God and was made drunk with the wine of the wrath of Almighty God. (Is. li, 17, 22.) "By swearing, and lying, and killing, and stealing, and committing adultery," the land was filled with violence and sin. (Hos. iv, 2.) All of these sins are in other places in the Bible ascribed to the habit of strong drink. It is not claimed that none of these sins are committed except by drunkards, but that all these sins are induced and led up to by that fearful habit.

Drunkenness is one of the oldest sins spoken of in the Bible. It must have been the common sin of that fearful age of violence and lawlessness before the Flood, and have so spread among all classes that even so good a man as Noah was overtaken by it. (Gen. ix, 21.) We know also that Lot, the one righteous man that dwelt in Sodom, was not without fault in this matter; for if he had not been in the habit of drinking, and that to excess, it is certain that his wicked daughters could not have plied him with drink to such an extent as to lead him into the awful sin of incest. (Gen. xix, 32.) It is supposed that the sin of Nadab and Abihu, for which they were stricken dead before the tabernacle, was the result of drunkenness; for immediately afterward the ordinance was enacted forbidding a priest to drink wine and strong drink when ministering about the house of God. (Lev. x, 1, 9.) It had become a common practice even among the priests in the days of Eli, so that he was not surprised to see Hannah in the tabernacle, as he supposed, drunk. (I. Sam. i, 13.) And certainly it had gone so far that the sons of Samuel were but sons of Belial, even in their drunkenness and debauchery going so far as to bring lewd women into the very courts of the tabernacle to commit sin with them. But to follow the subject in its general history would be to cite passages from the history of Israel out of every book in the Bible. So common and notorious was the sin of drunkenness that in the days of Joel he addressed the whole nation as a nation of drunkards and "drinkers of wine." (Joel i, 5.) That it was a prevalent sin in the days of our Lord and the apostles is abundantly testified by the many exhortations and warnings against it. "Take heed to yourselves, lest at any time your hearts be overcharged with surfeiting, and drunkenness, . . . and so that day come upon you unawares." (Luke xxi, 34.) "Let us walk honestly, as in the day; and not in rioting and drunkenness." (Rom. xiii, 13.) "Excess of wine" was one of the marks of an unconverted state, and is spoken against as inconsistent with the Christian life, just as lasciviousness, lust, and abominable idolatries are. (I. Pet. iv, 3.) But we need not follow these general teachings further. He who runs may read the language of God's Word on this subject. To see how true those considerations are, one only has to look around him in every walk and condition of life. Not until the Church and even the world wake up to the fact that drunkenness is a sin against God and a crime against society, and begin to deal with it and treat the drunkard as they treat the thief, the robber, the libertine, and the murderer, may we hope to check, not to say subdue, this terrible evil, which is a growing one, especially under the fostering care of governments and municipalities who are accessories to the evil by a league with the liquor-sellers for the sake of revenue.

It is a fact which must be acknowledged, that the teaching of the Bible is not that of total abstinence from the use of wine, but from the too great use of it, even to the point of drunkenness. In the discussion of this subject nothing is to be gained by trying to force teachings out of the Bible which are not in it. The priest during the period of his service, and the Nazarite while his vow was upon him, were absolutely forbidden the use of wine or strong drink; but there was no such prohibition laid upon the people at large. The charge is against drunkenness and not against the legitimate use of wine, just as the charge is against gluttony (ver. 20) and not against the use of food. Whether or not it is wise and expedient for Christian men and women to become total abstainers as a matter of liberty and expediency for the purpose of checking the horrible evil of drunkenness is another question, and will be discussed in a study later on in this series. There is no doubt, however, that all men who indulge in wine-drinking are in the first instance exposed to the danger of the sin of drunkenness. Every man must urge for himself whether his strength is sufficient to drink temperately of the wine, without the danger of wakening an appetite for it which will lead to drunkenness. And so every one must judge for himself whether in all circumstances it is his duty for the sake of others totally to abstain from the use of all wine and strong drink.

I.—A QUESTION AND AN ANSWER.

The question raised in the passage of Scripture which we have immediately under discussion is a further commentary on the exhortation of Solomon found in the twentieth verse of this chapter: "Be not among wine-bibbers; among riotous eaters of flesh." His purpose is to dissuade from the excessive use of strong drink, and to this end he draws a vivid picture of the general consequences of the habit. The questions which he puts are sarcastic as well as affirmative. The picture which he draws is true to life.

1.—"**Who hath woe?**"—The woe here spoken of is descriptive of direful distress, in which is implied both the condemnation of God for a sin committed and a certain awful condition of suffering. "Woe unto them that rise up early in the morning, that they may follow strong drink; that continue until night, till wine inflame them!" "Woe unto them that are mighty to drink wine, and men of strength to mingle strong drink." (Is. v, 11, 22.) There is a threat contained in these two "woes" pronounced by the prophet, and there is a subtle touch of meaning in the word "inflame." Until wine inflame them—that is, until wine "pursue them." Drunkenness which is first indulged in as a pleasure becomes a master and a pursuing avenger. Sin of all kinds brings its own punishment, but there is no sin which so speedily and relentlessly pursues its victim as the sin of drunkenness.

2.—"**Who hath sorrow?**"—Everybody has more or less sorrow, but all sorrows are not the sorrows of sin: some are those of affliction from the good hand of God for our nurture, such as Job suffered; and some are they which come on account of the sins of others, as the sorrow of a father over a prodigal son; and some are the sorrows that come in the course of nature, as the sorrow that comes because of the death of those whom we love. These are the sorrows which cannot be hindered or helped; but the drunkard has sorrow of his own making: he deliberately brings it upon himself. There is in the early stages of the drunkard's career an agony of sorrow and remorse which is sometimes very distressing and bitter to behold, and much more to bear; this sorrow wears away after the drunkard has become sottish. I have seen a drunkard, long after he has ceased to care for the evils which he has brought on himself, bitterly lament and curse his folly because of the sorrow he had brought upon his wife, children, and friends. The drunkard sows a crop of sorrow that springs up all around him; all the more so because it is most apt to be perpetual so long as he lives, for drunkenness, once it gets a man in its grip, seldom relaxes that grip until it has laid the drunkard's body in the grave and sent his soul to hell.

3.—"Who hath contentions?"—It is a well-known fact that drunkenness more than any other habit or vice leads to strife and contentions. Nine tenths of all the brawls and fights, quarrels and misunderstandings in the world are traceable directly to this vice. It filled the world with violence before the Flood, and it has filled the world with strife ever since. There is that in strong drink which not only inflames the passions, but clouds the understanding and so weakens the will that small offenses which would otherwise be passed by are magnified into grievous wrongs, which call for resentment; nay, it causes men to take offense where none is intended, and leads to quarrels without a cause. If we could dismiss drunkenness from the land, we might be sure that nine tenths of the family quarrels, legal quarrels, and violent conflicts that lead to assault and murder would cease out of the land.

4.—"Who hath babbling?"—Drunkenness so beclouds the intellect that a man under the power of strong drink loses control both of his senses and of his tongue. The consequence is that a drunkard is a "babbler" of foolish things, makes himself a laughing-stock to the bystanders; it induces small quarrelings about nothing, and leads to coarse, vulgar, and profane speech. It opens the floodgates of the heart, which is full of evil and foolish thoughts, and they rush out of the drunkard's lips like a brood of silly and vicious demons, to spread folly and misery around. Who has not seen with both pity and contempt the drunkard with thickened tongue and senseless thought babbling forth his folly, until for very shame of humankind he has turned away with more disgust than pity? The drunkard usually knows he is making a fool of himself, and yet has not the power to check his speech.

5.—"Who hath wounds without cause?"—A bruised body and a battered face is the usual accompaniment of a drunkard's debauch. There are wounds which a man may carry with honor to himself and pride to his neighbors and friends: such as he may have received in defense of his country, or in the protection of the innocent, or the vindication of that which is right; but the wounds and bruises of the drunkard are without a justifying cause. They are the badges of his shame, the proofs of his sin.

6.—"Who hath redness of eyes?"—The wounds which a drunkard receives are not all given by the hands of others. Drunkenness itself inflicts wounds on the body of the drunkard. It poisons the blood, disorders the vital fluids of the body, corrupts the functions, and finally brings about a watery blear-eyed deformity which at once disfigures the face and makes the whole countenance contemptible and revolting, and at the same time stamps the brand of the drunkard's sin upon him. We sometimes see a blind man going about with a placard around his neck proclaiming his affliction, "I am blind"; but the drunkard needs no placard. His eyes and his face tell their own story and make this proclamation to all the world: "I am a drunkard; a man given up to a deadly sin; one who has woe self-imposed; who has ruined his family, brought his children to poverty and shame, broken his wife's heart, forfeited the respect and esteem of all good men, and is on the broad road to hell." Thus does the drunkard advertise himself. The very devils must laugh at the wretched spectacle which a drunkard makes of himself.

The answer to this series of pertinent and sarcastic questions is found in the thirtieth verse.

1.—"They that tarry long at the wine."—Wine, if used at all, should only be taken as a relish and in small quantities, and never to the extent of firing the brain or inflaming the blood. The drunkard is the man who tarries long over his cups, spending hours, and whole days and nights sometimes, drinking from place to place. Oh, the wasted time, the misspent hours, which the habit of drinking induces! If all the time spent over wine and strong drink were spent in useful labor or refreshing sleep, which fits for business and work, there would be little poverty in the world and comparatively small suffering; for with the spending of time over wine goes the spending of money and the waste of energy and strength, and even the disposition to industry and labor. "Woe unto them that rise up early in the morning, that they may follow strong drink; that continue until night, till wine inflame them!" This is the drunkard, who begins the day (and even takes pains to begin it early) with drink, and follows after it all day and into the night, and then is followed by drink the rest of his life until he is chased through the grave into the drunkard's hell.

2.—"They that go to seek mixed wine."—There was in use a plain simple wine that hardly intoxicated, and then there was a mixture of wines with other ingredients which was stronger and more intoxicating. The drunkard's taste becomes dulled by drink and the desire for something stronger, and so he rises up and goes in search of all kinds of strongest drink, that he may add fuel to the fire he has already kindled in his blood. These mixed wines were probably the strong drink of the Scriptures.

II.—DISSUASION AND WARNING.

The wise king now speaks a word of earnest advice to avoid temptation, and a solemn warning as to the final consequences of drunkenness.

1.—"**Look not thou upon the wine when it is red, when it giveth his colour in the cup, when it moveth itself aright.**"— This is probably a mark of distinction between the harmless wines of the country, the pure juice of the grape, and those highly combined and deeply fermented wines which were manufactured with special reference to delighting the taste of the wine-bibber. Strong wines were red and fiery in appearance, perhaps by reason of high fermentation, or by reason of certain juices and herbs which were used in combination with the juice of the grape to add to its strength. The giving of its color in the cup probably refers to the sparkling bubbling of the strong wines, the sparkle of the fermentation, which causes quick intoxication. The expression "moveth itself aright" may refer either to those movements of the fermented cup which satisfies the strong drinker that the wine is of strong and rich quality, or to the delight with which the drunkard allows the wine to flow sweetly and deliciously from the cup down his throat, like "the best wine . . . that goeth down sweetly, causing the lips of those that are asleep to speak." (Song of Solomon vii, 9.) Whenever wine becomes such a delight as this to the drinker, it is a sure sign that he is in danger of falling into the habit of drunkenness.

2.—"**At the last it biteth like a serpent and stingeth like an adder.**"—"Wine is a mocker, strong drink is raging: and whosoever is deceived thereby is not wise." (Prov. xx, 1.) The wine-cup promises pleasure, but it is a deceiving mocker. That is, it first deceives and then mocks its victims. It allures with the promise of pleasure, and then laughs when the calamity comes. It is a poison like that of the serpent and the adder. The frightful antithesis to the habit of drinking strong and mixed drinks until drunkenness becomes the habit and state of a man's soul and body, is seen in the terrible words of the Psalmist: "For in the hand of the Lord there is a cup, and the wine is red; it is full of mixture; and he poureth out of the same: but the dregs thereof, all the wicked of the earth shall wring them out and drink them." (Ps. lxxv, 8.) The harvest of the drunkard is sown in red and mixed wine, and is reaped in wrath, the last bitter dregs of which he must wring out of the cup and drink, as he washed out the dregs of the wine-cup and drank them that he might lose nothing of the sweet poison contained therein.

III.—MORAL EFFECTS OF DRUNKENNESS.

Drunkenness does not travel in single harness. It yokes itself up with other sins.

1.—"Thine eyes shall behold strange women."—Wine fires the blood and inflames the passions of a man, and leads him to look lustfully after the strange women, whose "house is the way to hell." In a drunken or half-drunken state the moral sense is so blunted that the drunkard will give way to the lower lusts of his nature, which would shock him to think of if he were sober.

2.—"Thine heart shall utter perverse things."—In drunkenness perverse and wicked things out of the heart are framed into words which bind men to sin or involve them in most dreadful consequences. Many a drunken promise or speech has led to entanglements which a whole lifetime has not been long enough to unravel or disentangle.

IV.—TEMPORAL CONSEQUENCES OF DRUNKENNESS.

The drunken man is a man devoid of good judgment, and is constantly running into senseless dangers both physically and socially.

1.—"Thou shalt be as he that lieth down in the midst of the sea."—To make one's bed on the waves of the sea, or in the trough of the sea, would be to be swallowed up in death. So is the drunken man. Or he is as a pilot who has gone to sleep when his ship is in the trough of the sea, allowing the tiller to slip out of his hand and his ship to be swamped with the waves which he might else have outridden.

2.—"Or as he that lieth upon the top of a mast."—The mast of a ship (especially in a storm) is a place of danger where the sailor needs all the alertness of a steady head to keep his footing. What folly for one to allow himself to fall asleep in such a place! Yet so will the drunkard fall asleep anywhere, on a railway track, in a burning house, or out in a winter's blast where death by freezing will overtake him. A drunkard loses all sense of danger.

3.—Insensibility to all shame, and pain, and danger.—"They have stricken me . . . and I was not sick, they have beaten me and I felt it not." He is imprisoned or beaten as a common vagrant, but is insensible to it. It makes no difference to him. He is neither ashamed nor corrected by punishment or suffering.

"Though thou shouldest bray a fool in a mortar among wheat with a pestle, yet will not his foolishness depart from him." (Prov. xxvii, 22.) So it is with a drunkard under suffering and punishment.

4.—"When shall I awake? I will seek it yet again."—Every other thought is swallowed up and lost in the absorbing thirst for drink. Out of prison or drunken sleep or perilous danger he will (without thought of the perils which he has escaped or the sufferings and punishments which he has endured) rush straight for the dramshop again, and go still deeper into his degradation. Drunkenness, being first pursued, becomes the relentless pursuer, and there is no escape except by the almighty grace of God.

XXV.

REVIEW.

GOLDEN TEXT: "The Lord's portion is his people."—Deut. xxxii. 9.

XXVI.

THE BIRTH OF JESUS.—Luke ii, 1–20.

(1) And it came to pass in those days, that there went out a decree from Cesar Augustus, that all the world should be taxed. (2) (And this taxing was first made when Cyrenius was governor of Syria.) (3) And all went to be taxed, every one into his own city. (4) And Joseph also went up from Galilee, out of the city of Nazareth, into Judea, unto the city of David, which is called Bethlehem; (because he was of the house and lineage of David:) (5) To be taxed with Mary his espoused wife, being great with child. (6) And so it was, that, while they were there, the days were accomplished that she should be delivered. (7) And she brought forth her firstborn son, and wrapped him in swaddling clothes, and laid him in a manger; because there was no room for them in the inn. (8) And there were in the same country shepherds abiding in the field, keeping watch over their flock by night. (9) And, lo, the angel of the Lord came upon them, and the glory of the Lord shone round about them: and they were sore afraid. (10) And the angel said unto them, Fear not: for, behold, I bring you good tidings of great joy, which shall be to all people. (11) For unto you is born this day in the city of David a Saviour, which is Christ the Lord. (12) And this shall be a sign unto you; Ye shall find the babe wrapped in swaddling clothes, lying in a manger. (13) And suddenly there was with the angel a multitude of the heavenly host praising God, and saying, (14) Glory to God in the highest, and on earth peace, good will toward men. (15) And it came to pass, as the angels were gone away from them into heaven, the shepherds said one to another, Let us now go even unto Bethlehem, and see this thing which is come to pass, which the Lord hath made known unto us. (16) And they came with haste, and found Mary, and Joseph, and the babe lying in a manger. (17) And when they had seen it, they made known abroad the saying which was told them concerning this child. (18) And all they that heard it wondered at those things which were told them by the shepherds. (19) But Mary kept all these things, and pondered them in her heart. (20) And the shepherds returned, glorifying and praising God for all the things that they had heard and seen, as it was told unto them.—Luke ii, 1-20.

It is a fact of no little importance that we have here the account of the birth of Jesus, showing how his coming into the world was mixed up with the affairs of the Roman Empire. Jesus is not only the Saviour of the Gentiles, who were used of God in the pursuit of a new legal edict to bring Joseph and Mary to Bethlehem, according to the prophecy of Micah (v, 2), just in time for the birth of Jesus; but this is also wonderfully suggestive of the fact that our Lord came into the world to sanctify and touch with his own heavenly glory all the commonest affairs of life. Here we find him born, amid the bustle of the village preparations for the taking of the census, amidst the crowd of people who had come up according to the decree of Augustus. How few knew it, how few cared! And yet he came to sanctify all these earthly and temporal details of daily life. As Jesus was born in the midst of these circumstances, so we may be assured that in those which surround us to-day he is "not far from every one of us." Again, we notice that the birth of Jesus is a part of the history of this world. If we would only bear this fact in mind, that the life of our Lord, as recorded by the four evangelists, is not only a sacred record but the most important chapter in this world's history, it would help us to grasp more easily the unseen and eternal realities associated with him. There is no difficulty in believing that Augustus Cæsar was on the throne at Rome at this time, because it is a matter of history. Neither can we doubt that Jesus was born in the days of Augustus Cæsar. The one fact does not affect my spiritual and eternal interest in the least, while upon the other all my hopes are founded. The one fact has nothing to do with my salvation, but the other has everything to do with it, and makes it sure; not because I believe that Augustus Cæsar was Emperor of Rome at the time, with one kind of faith, and that Jesus was born at Bethlehem, with another kind of faith; but just because Jesus is a saving object of faith, while Augustus is simply a historical object of faith without any saving power.

I.—THE PARENTAGE AND BIRTH OF JESUS.

We have remarked already that Jesus was born in the time of the Roman supremacy. As to his parentage, on his mother's side he was a son of David (Rom. i, 3); but according to the political condition of the world he was born a subject of the Roman Empire. That empire, at the time of his birth, was at the very extreme height of its power and glory. Jesus belonged to it, as he did to the whole family of mankind, in virtue of his remoter descent from our common ancestor Adam. Thus we see him linked to the whole world of mankind. This was most necessary, in order that when the time came for publishing his gospel to all nations he might claim kin with all the world and thus come to them as no alien or stranger.

THE BIRTH OF JESUS.

Compelled by the decree of an earthly king to be brought to the ancient town of Bethlehem, the birthplace and home of his great prototype David, Jesus was destined to fill the Roman world with the new and essentially spiritual principles of his kingdom; and thus in a large measure by his followers (and the new life communicated by him to them) to overthrow the idolatrous systems with which the whole world had been deluded, and therefore in no small degree to contribute to the overthrow of the empire itself, that it might give place to his reign of righteousness. Bethlehem was a little village in an obscure Roman province, but there lay that night, in the meanest part of it (the stable of its inn), One greater than the great Cæsar who sat on the throne in the imperial city of Rome. How little the world knows what great things God is working amid all the bustle and confusion of the kingdoms of this earth.

1.—Of Joseph and Mary.—Joseph was the foster-father of Jesus; nay, more, he was his legal father, since God expressly bade him take Mary to be his wife (notwithstanding she was "with child of the Holy Ghost," Matt. i, 18–25), and to treat and care for the Child as though he were his own. We can well understand that Joseph received this holy Child with an affection infinitely beyond the love he would have had had the child been his own offspring. Jesus was known all through the days of his childhood, and even after he had reached man's estate, as the "son of the carpenter," though the Scripture is careful to give us the full details of his divine generation. The world may sneer at Jesus as the "low-born son of a carpenter," but we know that he is the Son of the Highest, even the Eternal Word, which "was made flesh and dwelt among us." (John i, 1–5, 14–18.) Mary, the lineal but far-off daughter of royal David, was but the daughter of an impoverished family, and had no standing beyond that of a peasant maiden, the espoused wife of the poor carpenter of Nazareth. Noble by descent from David, she became divinely royal by the honor conferred upon her by God the Holy Ghost, who chose her to be the mother of the Eternal Son. So the humblest man or woman in this world, though he cannot trace his genealogy back to any noble ancestor, may yet become more than noble by receiving Jesus Christ the Son of God into his soul. The miracle of the incarnation of Jesus is repeated in substance every time a sinner opens his heart to Jesus. All ages have since then exalted Mary above all other women in the world; but God shall exalt all sinners to a state and place in glory not only with Mary, the mother of Jesus, but with Jesus himself, by whom Mary was ennobled and glorified.

2.—The birthplace of Jesus.

—This was in the stable of the "khan" or *inn*, which is common to every Oriental town. It was an inclosure built of stone, covering perhaps half or quarter of an acre of ground. Within these walls was first the inn proper, in which travelers were lodged, and the rest of the inclosure was used for the beasts of burden and travel, asses, oxen, and camels. I have seen many of these "khans" in the East, not only in ordinary times, but on special occasions on which they have been crowded just as at the time of Jesus' birth, the rich and well-to-do travelers filling all the available room provided for the accommodation of men and women, and the poorer wayfarers lying down on their mats among the cattle, or perhaps a little sheltered in some corner where the favored beasts were stalled. Had Joseph and Mary been noble or rich people, room would have been found for them; but being but poor peasants, no one in the inn proper would make place for them, notwithstanding the delicate condition in which Mary was at the time; and so she had to find a resting-place in the stable. Here the Saviour of the world was born, and in this humble place he was "wrapped in swaddling clothes," as any other poor child might have been. "Jesus Christ, . . . though he was rich, yet for your sakes he became poor, that ye through his poverty might be rich." How poor he became let these few graphic lines tell! No wonder that Jesus has been the trusted friend of the poor and humble in all ages. In after-years a costly and magnificent church was built on the spot where that manger stood; and if we give room to Jesus in our hearts, we shall, by his Spirit abiding within us, erect a splendid and beautiful life, by which we may honor him before the world.

II.—THE ANGELS AND THE SHEPHERDS.

The ministry of angels is one of the most interesting subjects of study in the Bible. Far too little is thought of these holy servants whom God sends forth "to minister to them who shall be heirs of salvation." (Heb. i, 14.) There is a beautiful and well-known painting by Albert Dürer, the subject of which is "The Holy Family in Egypt." Joseph is at work in a carpenter's shop, and in the same room Mary is busy with some kind of handiwork, while the Babe is asleep in a little cradle beside her. The singular thing about the picture is, that down on the floor, apparently picking up the chips and shavings falling from Joseph's tools, are several little angels. The lesson of the picture seems to be, that where work is being done quietly and faithfully for Jesus, no matter though in humblest circumstances, God sends the angels to minister to those who are ministering to Jesus. This is a sweet and comforting truth. So came the angels to the shepherds by night, as they were watching their flocks. If ever angels appear to men on earth, or minister to them unseen, it will be in such circumstances, while they are faithfully and loyally doing with their hands the work which their hands find to do.

1.—The announcement made to shepherds.—Just as at a later time Jesus was made known to an obscure man in Jerusalem (Simeon) when he was presented in the Temple, so now his birth is intimated to some obscure and unknown shepherds. The temple-tending priests had so entirely turned away from God in their hearts, that he could hold no communion with them at this time. We may hope that these shepherds were true worshipers, even as Zacharias and Elizabeth were, as also Simeon and Anna, not to speak of Mary and Joseph, who were all "waiting for the consolation of Israel"; as of old Moses, Gideon, and David were, to whom the Lord made revelation of his gracious purposes concerning the coming of Christ. Besides, it is most suggestive that the birth of our Lord was announced to the poor and unlearned, rather than to the rich and cultured priests and doctors of the law. It would have been far more difficult for the poor people of Israel to have accepted as theirs a Saviour who came first to the great ones of the earth, than for the great ones of the earth to accept a Saviour born of a poor maiden and announced to humble shepherds. Of course it is one of the stumbling-blocks to the "wise and prudent" and the mighty of the earth, that Jesus has as his disciples so many of the poor of earth's inhabitants. Yet this is God's plan. Therefore, also, when our Lord chose his apostles he did not select such men as Nicodemus and Joseph of Arimathea, however true and worthy they were, but Peter, James, and John, and such-like humble fishermen. One end of the gospel is to humble the proud and the rich, and to exalt the poor and the oppressed. "He hath put down the mighty from their seats, and exalted them of low degree. He hath filled the hungry with good things; and the rich he hath sent empty away." (Luke i, 52, 53.)

2.—The fear of the shepherds.—It is a marvelous fact that every announcement which God has made to man of his gracious purpose of salvation has at first filled with fear those to whom the revelation came. When he came walking in the garden seeking after Adam and Eve, after the Fall, they fled from him, because they were afraid; a "horror of great darkness came upon" Abraham when God came to him; Moses was afraid to look upon God in the burning bush; Jacob, Manoah, and Isaiah were all afraid when they saw the Angel of the Lord; Zacharias came trembling from the interview with the angel; and Mary was "troubled" at his sayings; now the shepherds were filled with fear when the angels came to them with the great and good news. Why should the appearance of these supernatural beings fill us with fear? There are many reasons. First of all, there is an element of fear of the supernatural in man because of his ignorance; and then there is a natural superstition in man that makes him afraid; but besides there is a consciousness of sin in us, that fills us with fear at the thought of God's coming to us, lest he consume us for our disobedience. It is the same cause that makes us fear to die, until our fears are quieted by the assurance of God's love and grace. It is right that we should fear God, and it is blessed that God has quieted our fears by assurance of mercy.

III.—THE GLAD TIDINGS.

When an earthly prince is born, his birth is announced by the boom of cannon. The birth of kings of the earth usually means the continuation of oppression and war; but when the Saviour of the world is born, the angels' song praises God and proclaims "on earth peace." The first note of the song is "Fear not." The giving of the law wrought fear, but the coming of the Saviour allays that fear.

1.—**A Saviour.**—What glad tidings of great joy is here! "Unto you is born this day, in the city of David, a SAVIOUR." (i) *Who is this Saviour?* It is Christ the Lord, that mighty one of whom Isaiah prophesied (Is. ix, 6, 7): "For unto us a child is born, unto us a son is given: and the government shall be upon his shoulder: and his name shall be called Wonderful, Counselor, The mighty God, The everlasting Father, The Prince of Peace." (ii) *Where is he born?* Here in Bethlehem, in Judea, on the earth, among men; within reach of sinners; born of woman, thus becoming kin to us, and so our Redeemer; whose name is called JESUS, because he shall save his people from their sins. (iii) *For whom is he born?* For the Jews; yes, and for the Gentiles; for he is a Saviour whose coming shall be "tidings of great joy which shall be to all people." For God "will have all men to be saved." (I. Tim. ii, 4-6.)

2.—**A sign.**—Where shall they find him among all the children? Will he be in the guest-chamber in the inn, in the best room in the town? Will he be wrapped in softest and finest array? Will he be lying in a little downy cradle around which the great and mighty ones of earth shall gather? No, no. "This shall be a sign unto you; Ye shall find the babe wrapped in swaddling clothes, lying in a manger." A child of poverty. No place for him in the inn; born in a stable, with none to watch over him but his peasant mother and his hard-working carpenter foster-father. So it has ever been. Jesus is too often looked for in vain among the rich and the mighty. Usually he is found among the poor and the lowly. When the world loses sight of Jesus, as it does every now and again, then he is found again in some manger. Revivals and reformations always begin down among the poor. This a most important lesson. Let us not fail to learn it.

3.—**A song.**—No sooner was the announcement completed, than of a sudden the herald angel was joined by a heavenly host, who broke forth into a glorious chorus of praise. "Glory to God in the highest." Surely this is God's greatest glory. Not in the heavens above, but in the face of Jesus Christ. "Good will toward men." What better evidence of God's good will could come to us than in this: "God so loved the world, that he gave his only begotten Son, that whosoever believeth on him should not perish, but have everlasting life." "On earth peace, good will." There is no permanent peace in this world except it come with reconciliation to God through Jesus Christ. Two men who are reconciled to God cannot surely be otherwise than at peace with each other.

IV.—THE SHEPHERDS' FAITH.

How will these shepherds receive this astonishing and glorious bit of good news? Will they believe it, or will they consider it a phenomenon which passes belief, or some mystery that is too high for them, and simply let it pass as a wonder? Let us see.

1.—**A present faith.**—The thing "*is* come to pass." They did not say among themselves, "We wonder if this can be true," but they said, "Let us now go . . . and see this thing which *is* come to pass." This is faith, to accept the things as *done* which God declares *to be done;* not because we either see it or understand it, but because God has said it.

2.—**An immediate faith.**—They did not wait till the morning and talk the matter over. Had they done so, likely enough by morning they would have come to the conclusion that they had dreamed a dream, or seen a vision, or had been deceived by a shower of meteors, or something of the kind. So they said, "Let us *now* go." At once. This is faith, to obey at once. Many souls to whom the

Lord has spoken by the Holy Spirit have failed to find Jesus just because they have not obeyed the first conviction that has come to them. They have waited, and postponed till the conviction has faded away, and they have never gone at all.

3.—An active faith.—Their faith did not spend itself in professing, and assenting, and saying over and over again, "We believe." Their faith started them into action toward Jesus. "Let us now *go*." No faith is worth the having that does not bring men to Christ. He cannot be found by speculation, but by going to him, or coming to him, as the case may be. Faith is the soul in action toward God.

4.—An urgent faith.—They were no laggards in this matter, but "they came with haste." If there is anything in this world that demands haste, it is the call of God to Jesus Christ. Every moment's delay involves the soul in more sin, gives Satan a further opportunity of destroying us, and makes it possible for intervening obstacles to arise. That convenient season that so many souls have waited for seldom comes. When Bunyan's pilgrim set out from the City of Destruction to the City of the Great King, "he put his fingers in his ears and ran with all his might." So ought we to do in coming to Christ.

5.—A rewarded faith.—And they "found Mary, and Joseph, and the babe lying in a manger." So shall all find who believe the Word of God and immediately go in haste to Jesus. They shall find it even as it is told unto them. Sight follows faith, finding follows seeking. God is faithful, and will not disappoint any who are prompt to obey the heavenly vision which he gives us through his Word and by his Spirit.

6.—Faith turned into testimony.—"And when they had seen it, they made known abroad the saying which was told them concerning this child." So will all true believers do. The good news of salvation is not something to be locked up in our own breasts. He is for all people, and all people should be informed of Jesus. God has made us his witnesses of these things. A believer who is not a testifying Christian is not one that can set much store by his salvation, or have much of the Spirit of Christ in his heart; for who can really believe that in Christ there is life and immortality, and not make it known to others who are living in sin and death?

XXVII.

PRESENTATION IN THE TEMPLE.—Luke ii, 25-38.

(25) And, behold, there was a man in Jerusalem, whose name was Simeon; and the same man was just and devout, waiting for the consolation of Israel: and the Holy Ghost was upon him. (26) And it was revealed unto him by the Holy Ghost, that he should not see death, before he had seen the Lord's Christ. (27) And he came by the Spirit into the temple: and when the parents brought in the child Jesus, to do for him after the custom of the law, (28) Then took he him up in his arms, and blessed God, and said, (29) Lord, now lettest thou thy servant depart in peace, according to thy word: (30) For mine eyes have seen thy salvation, (31) Which thou hast prepared before the face of all people; (32) A light to lighten the Gentiles, and the glory of thy people Israel. (33) And Joseph and his mother marvelled at those things which were spoken of him. (34) And Simeon blessed them, and said unto Mary his mother, Behold, this child is set for the fall and rising again of many in Israel; and for a sign which shall be spoken against; (35) (Yea, a sword shall pierce through thy own soul also,) that the thoughts of many hearts may be revealed. (36) And there was one Anna, a prophetess, the daughter of Phanuel, of the tribe of Aser: she was of a great age, and had lived with a husband seven years from her virginity; (37) And she was a widow of about fourscore and four years, which departed not from the temple, but served God with fastings and prayers night and day. (38) And she coming in that instant gave thanks likewise unto the Lord, and spake of him to all them that looked for redemption in Jerusalem.—Luke ii, 25-38.

In all ages, even the darkest, God has had his saints and witnesses: Abel, immediately after the Fall; Seth, after the apostasy of Cain; Enoch, in the dark and violent antediluvian age; Noah, in the time of the judgment that closed that dispensation. Then came Abraham, who in his day found Melchizedek, the priest of the Most High God; then Joseph in Egypt, and Moses later on, both in Egypt and in the wilderness. During Israel's apostasy in the desert, Caleb and Joshua shine forth in splendor of faith, men in whom there was "another spirit." Joshua made his age brilliant; Samuel stood forth like a saviour when even good old Eli had suffered his dissolute sons to lead Israel into sin. Then came the other judges. Following David were some good kings, amidst almost universal apostasy in Israel and Judah. Then came Elijah and the seven thousand unknown saints in his day who had not bowed the knee to Baal. Then the Hebrew children, Daniel, Ezra, and Nehemiah, in the time of the long captivity. In the time of Christ we find a few names who still worshiped God and kept his commandments, among whom were Zacharias and Elizabeth, Simeon and Anna. In this lesson we are introduced to Simeon, who was a simple-hearted old man who loved God's Word, and had not been carried away with the almost universal formalism and rationalism under the leadership of Pharisees and Sadducees. Let us never despair of religion so long as there are such men living in the land, though they be but obscure believers like good old Simeon.

I.—SIMEON AND HIS CHARACTER.

In the previous lesson we have the story of the birth of Christ and the joy which his advent occasioned; in this lesson we have the touching record of the joy of this good old man. It is more with Simeon than with the child Jesus that we have to do at present. Of course he is only introduced to us in connection with the presentation of Jesus, so that, after all, Jesus was the well-spring of his holy character and the fountain-head of his joy. Simeon was one of the last believers under the Old Covenant, and has been styled a good example to those under the New Covenant. The Spirit of God, no longer dwelling with the temple-tending priests (who minded earthly things while they pretended to be engaged about heavenly matters), had taken final refuge in the hearts of a few unofficial believers like Simeon.

1.—He was just and devout.—In this respect he did not differ from Zacharias and his good wife Elizabeth. These two words probably set forth his character both in respect to God and to man. He was just and upright in all his dealings with man because he was a devout and true child of God. All acceptable character hinges on these two relations. Righteousness toward man without devoutness toward God is not a characteristic that will bear the test of God's searching eye, even were it possible; and devoutness toward God that does not bear fruit of righteousness toward man is mere hypocrisy. The grace of God under both dispensations taught men "that, denying ungodliness and worldly lusts, we should live soberly, righteously, and godly, in this present world; looking for that blessed hope, and the glorious appearing of the great God and our Saviour Jesus Christ; who gave himself for us, that he might redeem us from all iniquity, and purify unto himself a peculiar people, zealous of good works." (Titus ii, 11-14.) These two characteristics "must always go together and support each other, for neither, found alone, will atone for the defection of the other." Simeon fulfills this description of a righteous man.

2.—**Full of faith.**—A true child of God always has something yet to look forward to and expect. So Simeon was looking for and expecting the coming of the Messiah. Faith traffics with God on the basis of his promises and lays hold of unseen things, which, however, are substantial realities to the soul. Simeon had been promised that he should not see death until his eyes had rested on the world's Redeemer. He was living in daily expectation of this event. *He* looked for the Saviour in his first advent; *we* are bidden now to look for and hasten the coming of Christ in his second advent. (II. Pet. iii, 12.) We, indeed, have not a promise that we shall see him before we die, but are told that he may come at any time, and are so bidden to watch, wait, and expect. If these promises lay hold of us, they will cause us to live with uplifted eyes and to hold to this world but loosely and lightly.

3.—**Filled with the Holy Ghost.**—The Old Testament saints did not have the Holy Ghost in the same way or measure as is vouchsafed to those under the New Covenant, and yet here and there was found a man on whom the Holy Ghost rested with power. Simeon was such an one. "The Holy Ghost was upon him." Only such men as Simeon are thus honored, whether under one dispensation or the other. If we would be filled with the Holy Ghost, we are to be so blessed only as we are just and devout. Many of God's people are seeking for the Holy Ghost "in power" to rest upon them. They expect or seek for him by praying or waiting simply; but we are persuaded that there must be righteousness and real devoutness before the Holy Ghost will abide in power with any one. Simply to lust after the Spirit for the purpose of spiritual joy and personal power is to invite a defeat of our desires. Men may work themselves into frenzies of excitement and develop strange and mystical experiences by long prayers, fastings, and high mental tension; but the Holy Ghost rests only upon those who, like Simeon, cultivate justice and devoutness, and, like Barnabas, are "good men"; or, like Cornelius, who was another "devout man," who "feared God . . . and gave much alms to the people" from love to God.

4.—Possessed of confidence.—There were no particular signs of Christ's coming at this time. The nation was spiritually dead. But Simeon had received of the Lord word that his eyes should see the Christ. "The secret of the Lord is with them that fear him." Simeon feared the Lord, and the Lord had revealed to him this secret of the near approach of his Christ. This was enough for Simeon. He did not *feel* that Christ was near, nor was he able to prove it by demonstration or sign. He believed. He was persuaded. He was confident. The word of God was the basis of his trust. It must be the ground of ours too. "Sirs, . . . I believe God." This is Christian assurance.

II.—WHAT THE HOLY GHOST DID FOR SIMEON.

It is suggestive to note what the Holy Ghost did for Simeon, and thereby we may learn a lesson in spiritual life for ourselves, for his general work is the same in all ages.

1.—He revealed Christ to him.—We do not suppose that it was a miraculous revelation; but that, as he studied the Scriptures concerning the coming of Christ, those promises were energized in his heart and soul, and a deep persuasion of their truth was wrought in his mind. Others read the word and had a literal knowledge of Christ; but Simeon gained a spiritual knowledge of him. Along with this came to him a profound and confident persuasion that he would live to see him. It is the office of the Spirit to take of the things of Christ and show them to us. (John xvi, 8-15.) If we will wait on God, we may have just such revelations out of the written Word.

2.—He led him to Christ.—We do not know just how, but suppose that by a strong sudden impulse he was led up to the Temple at the very time that the parents of Jesus brought the young child to the Temple. The leading of the Spirit is not always a conscious one, but it is always a sure one. If our life is given up to God, we may be sure that he will lead us "in a plain path." We can scarcely imagine that Simeon felt, at the time of his going into the Temple, that he would see the Lord's Christ, much less that he would recognize him in the person of a tender babe lying in the arms of a young peasant mother.

3.—He moved him to embrace Christ.—It is one thing to be led to where Christ is and to have our eyes opened to see him; but it is another thing to be led to embrace him. We do not know how Simeon recognized the child Jesus as his Lord, but somehow he evidently did, and at once he reached out his arms and embraced him. This, also, is the work of the Spirit. They are blessed who, seeing or being persuaded that Jesus is the Lord, believe on him. Jesus came to all the nation as well as to Simeon, but they received him not. "But as many as received him, to them gave he power to become the sons of God, even to them that believed on his name." There are many even now who believe that Jesus is the Christ of God, who do not embrace or receive him.

4.—He filled his mouth with a testimony.—It has been truly said, "When the Saviour is seen by faith the spirit of testimony is aroused." No sooner had Simeon seen and embraced Jesus as the Redeemer than his mouth began to speak forth his praise. There is no surer sign of conversion than that which is seen in frank and happy confession of Christ. And where there is a lack of readiness to testify of him, there is always a doubt as to whether Jesus has been really received. Many persons refuse to testify of Jesus with their lips, on the ground that they prefer to do it in their lives. No doubt that lip-testimony without life-testimony is to be doubted; but, on the other hand, little confidence is to be placed on the testimony of the life if that testimony does not sometimes rise out of the heart and fall from the lips. "Out of the abundance of the heart the mouth speaketh," says God. It is written that "they that feared the Lord spake often one to another." Look what a variety of testimonies Christ had in the early days of his coming. Angels brought the news of his advent. The aged Elizabeth and her unborn babe, the virgin mother, and the long-speechless Zacharias; the shepherds from the hills; the wise men from the East; and Simeon and Anna, one from the people and the other from the seclusion of a cloistered life in the Temple—all these bore their testimony. Shall we only be behindhand in this blessed matter? If all of us who profess to have received him would join in this glad testimony to him, we would soon see the mighty effect of it on the unbelieving world.

III.—SIMEON'S TESTIMONY TO CHRIST.

In the testimony of Simeon, brief as it is, we have a great body of important truth touching Jesus and the salvation of God through him.

1.—Jesus is God's salvation.—"Mine eyes have seen thy salvation." We learn from this and other important Scriptures that Jesus and "God's salvation" are identical. That is to say, salvation is not something apart from God and Christ. "He that hath the

Son hath life; and he that hath not the Son of God hath not life." (1 John v, 12.) "Behold, God is my salvation." (Is. xii, 2.) "How shall we escape, if we neglect so great salvation?" (Heb. ii, 3.) In these and other passages God and Jesus are set forth as being not simply the authors of salvation, but the very substance of it. Many persons, in seeking salvation, come short because they want not Christ, but only some gift of his—some work of the Spirit. Forgiveness is not salvation; justification, regeneration, sanctification, the peace of God, or any other blessed grace is not salvation. Jesus is salvation. He "of God is made unto us wisdom, and righteousness, and sanctification, and redemption"; "in whom we have redemption through his blood, the forgiveness of sins." (I. Cor. i, 30; Eph. i, 7.) This is a most important truth. Do not come short of it.

2.—**A light to the Gentiles.**—It is most remarkable that Simeon, a devout Jew, should, in his song of praise, first speak of Jesus as being a blessing to the Gentiles. As a rule, the Jews, especially those who were most strict, would scarcely think of any benefits of Messiah's kingdom being bestowed upon the outside world. Those without were dogs, not worthy to "eat of the crumbs which fall" from the Master's table, in their estimation. Yet here is a devout Jew seeing in Christ, from the first moment, a "light to lighten the Gentiles." Did he foresee at that moment that the Jews would reject him, and that this salvation would first flow out to others as a stream of life, giving light to the nations of the earth? Or was he so truly and deeply versed in a spiritual understanding of the Scriptures that he anticipated this order of things? This was, indeed, clearly indicated by prophetic teaching. (Is. xliii, 6; xlix, 6; lxi, 1.) But this was not according to Judaism. It is Christianity. Christ, indeed, was first offered to the Jews, but he was first believed on by the Gentiles. This is a part of that "mystery of godliness" as set forth by Paul. (I. Tim. iii, 16.)

3.—**"The glory of thy people Israel."**—Here is also a great truth, and one that we Christians too often overlook. They were seeking a national and temporal glory, and so rejected the Saviour King, as they always did—as, indeed, we are all inclined to do, choosing the shadow rather than the substance. To-day the Jews are suffering still under the dread curse they brought upon themselves by the rejection of Christ—a scattered and despised people. And yet they are not an abandoned or a forsaken people. They are still God's people, preserved through all the ages so wonderfully, and they will yet be gathered again when the Lord comes a second time. They will then see him, believe on him, and be converted, and Jesus whom they crucified will be their glory forevermore. God hath not cast them off forever. Let us not despise them or cease to follow them with our prayers; especially do not let us boast ourselves against them. We are living in the benefits which they rejected, but which came to us through them. Do not let us treat them as they treated him. We commend a careful reading of the ninth and eleventh chapters of Romans on this point.

IV.—HAPPY DYING.

"Now lettest thou thy servant depart in peace, for mine eyes have seen thy salvation." Only they who have seen God's salvation can depart in peace. Men have died without Christ and without God bravely, even serenely, but not in peace. How could they? What ground of peace has any sinful man who has not known the Saviour? The wicked have "no bands in their death," said the Psalmist, but this is not peace. There is as much difference between the oftentimes quiet death of the wicked and the peaceful death of the righteous as there is between the dead conscience of the wicked and the purged conscience of the believer. Let us look at this anticipated death of Simeon.

1.—**A departure.**—Death to the believer is a departure, to be with Christ (Phil. i, 23); the passing from communion with God in this world to closer communion with God in another one. An old Scotch clergyman said on his deathbed: "It is all one whether I get well or whether I depart to be with Christ. If I get well he will still be with me; if I die I shall still be with him."

2.—**The ground of peace.**—Old Simeon uttered this beautiful prayer whilst holding Christ in his arms. Jeremy Taylor says that holy living makes happy dying. No doubt; but this is not the ground of confidence in dying. It is only as we have Christ in our hearts, as Simeon had him in his arms, that we may or can look forward in peace to our departure into the unseen world.

3.—**The joy of his departure.**—With Christ in his arms, this good old man had a song in his heart, which song was also a triumphant and blessed testimony to God's faithfulness to his word, a song full of prophetic hope for all nations. It is worth dying when we may die singing and testifying. During a recent storm in which a ship was wrecked and many lives were lost, one boat's crew, searching for possible survivors in the water, was directed in the darkness by the sound of singing. Following the strangely sweet tones that mingled with the roar of wind and sea, they came upon a woman clinging to a floating spar—not expecting rescue—singing in a sweet and strong voice:

> "Jesus, lover of my soul, let me to thy bosom fly,
> While the nearer waters roll, while the tempest still is high;
> Hide me, O my Saviour, hide till the storm of life is past;
> Safe into the haven guide, oh, receive my soul at last."

"Do not pray with me," said another dying saint to his minister, who came to his dying bed, "but praise God with me." Such is a Christian's death—Christ in his arms, a song of joy in his heart, a testimony on his lips, and heaven in his eye. Who would not wish to die so?

V.—SIMEON'S PROPHECY.

Turning to Mary and Joseph, old Simeon blessed them, and prophesied to Mary of her divine Child, and of her sufferings because of him.

1.—Jesus "set for the fall and rising again of many."—This undoubtedly referred primarily to the effect of his coming upon the Jews themselves, but it is equally true of all men. The Jews first stumbled over him, and so fell from the favor of God—a fall from which they have not yet recovered. But, as has been said already, Jesus shall yet be their glory. When he comes again, they shall see him "whom they pierced and . . . mourn." He will receive them, and then will they rise again. But, in yet another sense, Jesus is "set for the fall and rising again of many." They that believe him not and reject him, as the bulk of the Jewish nation did, will fall into lower depths of sin, and wholly and finally out of God's favor forever. "He that believeth not shall be damned." Damned, not because God would have it so, but because, rejecting Christ, there is no salvation. God himself cannot save a man who rejects Christ, for Christ is salvation. Yet though many reject him, there are those who receive him, and so are enabled to rise up and stand before God in the full glory of forgiveness, life, and salvation. He that despiseth Jesus, however high, shall fall, and he that layeth hold on him, however low down, shall rise again. He is for death or life according as men reject or accept him. (Luke xx, 18; Acts xiii, 38–40.)

2.—A sign spoken against.—Lasting neutrality with respect to the Lord is impossible. "He that is not with me is against me." (Luke xi, 23.) He draws all men to him, either in adoring gratitude or in bitter hatred. What a strange power there is in Jesus! Meet him all men must, in mercy or in wrath. There is no escape. Other religious teachers, if they are not believed, or if their teachings are not accepted, are simply allowed to rest; but it seems impossible for any man to reject Christ without speaking against him. His presence in the world reveals the thoughts of many hearts. It is easy to ascertain the attitude of any man toward God by putting him to the test as to his relation to Jesus. "A stumbling-stone and rock of offense." His good is evil spoken against, and those who are his friends indeed are hated for his name's sake. "Blessed is he whosoever shall not be offended in me," said our Lord, as though he knew what an offense he would be to many.

3.—**Fellowship with his sufferings.**—In a parenthesis, old Simeon said to Mary, "Yea, a sword shall pierce through thine own soul also." Whoever loves Jesus will suffer with him and for his sake. Jesus was Mary's son, but Jesus says that whosoever believeth on him is as mother, brother, and sister to him. It must have cut through her soul when she saw her Son despised, rejected, maligned, and crucified. Well, it is so now. What pain and sorrow to see him rejected by the world, hated and despised by men! What worse sorrow it is to see his worthy name blasphemed by faithless friends, who scandalize him and his gospel by evil and disobedient living; but especially, what suffering it causes those who love him to know that many who even call themselves his ministers yet crucify him by the false gospel which they preach in his name—even denying his Godhead, rejecting and pouring contempt on his atoning death, and explaining away his resurrection; reducing him to a level with all the false teachers, who have but led men into the ditch with themselves. It is appointed that we shall bring up that which remains of the sufferings of Christ, some in one way, and some in another. But "if we suffer, we shall also reign with him."

VI.—ANNA THE PROPHETESS.

The prophetic words and the glad joy of old Simeon were presently confirmed by the coming in of Anna, another saintly witness whom God had had in waiting for this event; and she also was suddenly filled with the Holy Ghost, and spake forth her testimony and joy in a prophetic address to all them in Jerusalem who were looking for the redemption of Israel. Those who fast and pray before the Lord in the spirit are they who have spiritual discernment and are fitted to be the testifiers of Jesus to the people.

XXVIII.

VISIT OF THE WISE MEN.—Matthew ii, 1-12.

(1) Now when Jesus was born in Bethlehem of Judea in the days of Herod the king, behold, there came wise men from the east to Jerusalem, (2) Saying, Where is he that is born King of the Jews? for we have seen his star in the east, and are come to worship him. (3) When Herod the king had heard these things, he was troubled, and all Jerusalem with him. (4) And when he had gathered all the chief priests and scribes of the people together, he demanded of them where Christ should be born. (5) And they said unto him, In Bethlehem of Judea: for thus it is written by the prophet, (6) And thou Bethlehem, in the land of Juda, art not the least among the princes of Juda: for out of thee shall come a Governor, that shall rule my people Israel. (7) Then Herod, when he had privily called the wise men, inquired of them diligently what time the star appeared. (8) And he sent them to Bethlehem, and said, Go and search diligently for the young child; and when ye have found him, bring me word again, that I may come and worship him also. (9) When they had heard the king, they departed; and, lo, the star, which they saw in the east, went before them, till it came and stood over where the young child was. (10) When they saw the star, they rejoiced with exceeding great joy. (11) And when they were come into the house, they saw the young child with Mary his mother, and fell down, and worshipped him: and when they had opened their treasures, they presented unto him gifts; gold, and frankincense, and myrrh. (12) And being warned of God in a dream that they should not return to Herod, they departed into their own country another way.—Matthew ii, 1-12.

The birth of Jesus Christ seemed to set heaven and earth in motion around him. Angels from the skies came to announce his birth, and filled the earth with a new song. Stars moved in their courses to guide wise men from the East to his feet. Shepherds and astrologers, holy men of Judea of lowly birth, and wise men from the East of exalted position, alike led by a Providence working from within and from without, came to worship him. The worldly old Idumean king was moved with fear, and all Jerusalem, instead of rejoicing with the men from the East, was stricken with fear like the tyrannical king. Faith was represented by a small company of Gentiles, while orthodox Judea was asleep in its unbelief, and awakened in terror at the news that their long-expected king was born amongst them. The wily old king who sat on David's throne sought to murder the new-born King of the Jews, but holy angels interposed to defeat his purpose. All through this chapter we have the beginning of that divine tragedy which culminated on the cross and was glorified by the resurrection of Jesus Christ from the dead. Our Christmastide, full of festivity and joy throughout the world, is, after nearly twenty centuries, the echo of the angels' song, and the memory of the gifts of the wise men; for when we give our gifts to our children, is it not that we lay at the feet of Jesus a grateful tribute of gratitude for the joy which his coming into the world brought to us all?

I.—CIRCUMSTANCES CONNECTED WITH HIS BIRTH.

It is somewhat remarkable that in this Gospel, which was written by a Jew especially to demonstrate that Jesus was the true Messiah, the long-expected theocratic King of the Jews, his birth is announced to the nation by wise men from the East—that is, by Gentiles; while the third Gospel, written to show that Jesus was the Saviour of the whole world, the Son of Adam rather than the Son of Abraham, was written by a Gentile, and we see Jesus introduced by holy but humble men of the Jewish nation, the shepherds of Bethlehem. This is only another proof of that grace of God which is no respecter of persons. The Gentiles shall be ministers of grace to the Jews, and the Jews shall share with the Gentiles that salvation which has been prepared from of old.

1.—**The place of our Lord's birth.**—The little town or hamlet of Bethlehem-Judah was scarce worth a place among the cities of the land, yet out of this small and insignificant town of less than six hundred inhabitants at the time of our Lord's birth, came the world's Redeemer. If Nathanael asked Philip, "Can there any good thing come out of Nazareth?" some might ask, "Can there any great thing come out of Bethlehem?" Long centuries ago the prophet Micah had indicated to the ancient people that this little village should be the birthplace of their Messiah, as it had been the birthplace and home of their great king David. The passage in Micah (v, 2) reads as follows: "But thou, Beth-lehem Ephratah, though thou be little among the thousands of Judah, yet out of thee shall he come forth unto me that is to be ruler in Israel; whose goings forth have been from of old, from everlasting." Matthew gives us a free translation of it at the sixth verse of our portion: "And thou Bethlehem, in the land of Juda, art not the least among the princes of Juda: for out of thee shall come a Governor, that shall rule my people Israel." This little village was not mentioned in the hundreds of towns at the time of the partition of the land; it was the least among the thousands—that is, among the villages or cities where dwelt the heads of the thousands, into which number the children of Israel had been divided for the purpose of government, Bethlehem was the very least, and yet it was not too small for God to honor by making it the birthplace of the world's Redeemer. It had before been the birthplace of David. The worth, dignity, and greatness of a place do not depend on the greatness of its population or the vastness or size of its buildings. The small town of Stratford-on-Avon is more famous as being the birthplace of Shakespeare than Manchester is for being the greatest manufacturing city in the world. Bethany, the home of Mary, Martha, and Lazarus, is better known than many an ancient city in which kings have lived and had their palaces. True greatness does not depend on worldly importance. David, the shepherd-lad of Bethlehem, was the youngest and least of the sons of Jesse, and not thought worthy even to be brought into Samuel's presence with his brothers; yet God had chosen him. The manger in the caravansary was a mean place for one to find lodging in, and yet here the Son of God found a birthplace. This world is almost the least among the planets, and yet God has selected it to be the theater on which he has displayed the wonders of his love, and where he has wrought out the mystery of the ages. We should learn not to despise a man either because he is small or mean in outward appearance, or poor in worldly goods, nor to look for the true greatness of anything in the mere externals. Bethlehem and Nazareth, the one a small town and the other a village of vile reputation, are really the two towns which have received more honor from God than Jerusalem itself.

2.—**The visit of the wise men.**—"Behold, there came wise men from the east to Jerusalem." Who these wise men were, and from whence they came, has been the occasion of endless speculation. Tradition has determined that there were three of them, and has even assigned names to them: Gaspar, Melchior, and Balthasar. It has assigned to them the title and dignity of kings, and has determined that they came from Arabia, Mesopotamia, Persia, India, Egypt, or even Greece. Of these particulars we can know nothing certainly. That they were "magi," or "astrologers," or "magicians," we know. They belonged to a sacred caste of scholars and priests of the East who made the study of the heavens their chief occupation, and because of their real or supposed knowledge of the stars, and what their movements portended to the inhabitants of the earth, they were held in high repute by the people, and were made the instructors and advisers of kings. Every court had a company of these men about it, to whom the dreams of the kings and all difficult questions were referred. (Dan. ii, 48; iv, 9; v, 7, 11.) While many of these magi or wise men were but charlatans trading on the superstitions of the people, as were Jannes and Jambres who contended with Moses in Egypt, as was Simon Magus (or the magician) who pretended conversion at Samaria, there were yet among them devout souls who, looking up into the heavens, had come to believe in and fear God, whom they perceived to be beyond the stars. We may confidently believe that these wise men who came seeking for Jesus were men in whom the Spirit of Christ dwelt, though they were ignorant of it; men who, though uninstructed in the mysteries of God's revelation, had yet received a revelation of God from himself, even though it may have come through a star, which in due time led them to the feet of Christ. In every nation there are those who have feared God and wrought righteousness, and have been accepted with him. I have met in this strange country (India), during the past year, wandering fakirs nominally belonging to both the Hindu and the Mohammedan religions, who also were real seekers after God; whose spirits were chaste and humble; who had long since eschewed idolatry and the harsh tenets of Islam, and were striving through nature to reach up to nature's God. These wise men from the East had been led of God by his inward and outward cords to come from their distant home to Jerusalem in search of the new-born King.

3.—**The new-born King of the Jews.**—The wise men came to Jerusalem asking of those whom they met here and there, "Where is he that is born King of the Jews?" It must have been a great surprise and shock to them when they reached Jerusalem to find the entire population ignorant of the birth of their King; and not only ignorant, but quite asleep and non-expectant, while they, who were but Gentiles and strangers, had for months been journeying toward his birthplace, led by a star. We oftentimes find the grossest unbelief where we naturally look for faith. Jesus found more unbelief in his home-town of Nazareth than he did in the cities of semi-pagan Samaria. The people of Jerusalem, even the very high-priest and other rulers, murdered him, while publicans and harlots received him. A blind beggar recognized in him the Son of God, while the Pharisees saw in him only an impostor and blasphemer. We often find the worst infidelity in a Christian home, while faith springs up in the most unpromising places. There was at that time reigning over Jerusalem a foreign king, Herod, surnamed the Great, an Idumean by birth, though he was externally a Jew. He did not come of the stock or lineage of David, and was on the throne only by the power of Rome, the hated Gentile oppressor of the Jews. But now, in accordance with a long line of prophecies, there had come one who was the born King of the Jews, the long-expected Messiah. Jesus is that Shepherd whom God has sent into the world to be the Ruler and Governor of his people. We love to think of him as the Saviour of sinners, who, by his voluntary death, hath redeemed us from sin and the curse of the law; but he is also the royally born King of his people, with all power in heaven and in earth, not only to rule and reign over them, but with them also. He was rejected both as Saviour and king by the Jews, and he is rejected by the many to-day; but he is nevertheless the born King of the Jews, and he will yet appear in power and great glory and rule over this earth—over his enemies with a rod of iron; over his friends and followers with the mild scepter of righteousness and peace. In the meantime he gives us salvation.

4.—"**We have seen his star.**"—Here again we have a puzzle which has given rise to endless speculation. What was this star, and how could it guide them? Or how, in the first place, could they know that it pointed to the birth of Jesus the King of the Jews? How could they follow it to Jerusalem and afterward to Bethlehem? The nearest star is so remote from the earth that it could not possibly be a guide to any one to any particular locality on the earth. Stars indeed may guide the mariner by showing him which way is north, south, east, or west, but he could not sail by a star to any particular spot except by taking a general direction. Eminent astronomers from the days of Kepler have tried to identify this star with some phenomena in the heavens which appeared about that time. That there were several remarkable astronomical wonders in the sky about that time is fully ascertained, but that any one of them can be identified with the star of the wise men (the star of Bethlehem) is more than doubtful. Why must it have been a star at all, in the ordinary sense? Why may it not have been a miraculous point of light, hanging low in the heavens, first appearing to these devout men in the east, and then moving forward toward the west, steadily guiding them, first to Judea and Jerusalem, and then to Bethlehem? Must we reject as absurd or even improbable such a miracle? When the Holy Spirit fell upon the people, God gave an accompanying sign in the "tongues like as of fire," just as there was a strange appearance "like a dove" resting on the head of Jesus when he was baptized in Jordan. Why may not God have set a point of light low in the heavens, first to arrest the attention of these wise men and then lead them forward? Did not God give to the children of Israel a cloud by day and a pillar of fire by night to guide them? Did he not manifest himself to Moses in the burning bush? Why should he not do another wonder? The whole sphere of the divine activity at this particular time was pregnant with supernatural wonders. Why may this star not have been the guiding angel, or of the same order as he who appeared to the shepherds, and in the night, as he moved forward, seemed to these astronomers of old to be a star? We think this is the more reasonable solution. But how came these wise men to know anything of the coming of Jesus Christ into the world, and how did they come to associate the appearance of the star with that expectation? It must be remembered that God has had in all the ages of the world men in all nations who have dimly known and truly worshiped him: Gentiles, into whose hearts the Light of the world has shined; men like Job, Jethro, Naaman, and even Nebuchadnezzar and Cyrus. Nor must it be forgotten that during the captivity of the Jews in Babylon, and through the earlier dispersion of the ten tribes throughout the East, there had gone forth among those distant nations much knowledge concerning the expectation of the coming of the Messiah. Even here in far-away India I have come across many things which point indubitably to the fact that prophetic knowledge of Christ has been in this land for many centuries, and not only so, but here we find unmistakable evidences even of the impact of Jewish customs. Together with this knowledge of the expected birth of a heaven-sent king in Judea, there was a longing among many of the ancient wise men for a deliverer. God used all these circumstances, and by his Spirit led these men, in connection with the star, to conclude that it was his sign, and so they followed it. Our star is the Holy Scriptures, which are always shining as in the heavens above us, and which, if we follow them, will lead us to Jesus. God's Holy Spirit works with his Word in those who are devoutly looking and longing for salvation.

5.—"**And are come to worship him.**"—There are many who make inquiry concerning Jesus, but their inquiry is curiosity only. These men inquired concerning Jesus because they had come to worship him. The Jews made many inquiries of the prophets, and had much knowledge of him—more than these wise men had; but they never found Jesus, because they had no purpose or desire to worship him. Jesus is revealed not to "the wise and prudent," who merely desire knowledge, but to those simple-hearted babes among men who long for salvation and are ready to worship at his feet.

II.—HEROD AND JERUSALEM.

The advent of the wise men into Jerusalem, their persistent inquiries on every hand for the new-born King, taken together with their probably large and imposing train of camels, set the city talking and the people wondering. The news of the arrival of these Eastern princes, and the object of their visit, quickly penetrated to the palace, and smote Herod with fear.

1.—Herod and Jerusalem troubled.—This usurping king was yet so much a Jew that he knew well the prophecies concerning the coming of Christ. He knew well also that he was not a king according to the strict letter of the Jewish law. He did not belong to the royal line. He knew also that the Pharisees particularly hated him and would seize on any pretext to dethrone him. The news of the birth of Christ was a menace to him, and he was troubled, and, for other reasons, all Jerusalem with him. There was something fearful and portentous to them in the fact that the Messiah had come. Why were they troubled? Were not all the theocratic hopes of the nation centered in him? Then why should they not rejoice? Because they were spiritually out of sympathy with the holy reign of righteousness that they knew he came to usher in. Jesus is coming again, according to many promises made by himself, his prophets, and apostles, and his coming again is the hope of the Church. Is it not likely that if "the sign of the Son of man" should appear in the heavens to-night a multitude of Christians would be filled with fear, even many among those who are loudest in declaring their faith in the second advent? The promised King of the Jews was to be none other than God himself in the form and likeness of a man; but the cold and wicked hearts of these people were not prepared to receive and welcome God in their midst. This is why they feared.

2.—Herod plans the death of Christ.—The wily old tyrant recognized all the danger there was to his throne in the appearance of the "born King" of the Jews. He was not a "born king," and he knew full well that if the Son of David appeared he would have to abdicate. Perhaps skeptical of the real appearance of the new-born King, he yet felt that there would be danger to his throne if the belief should get abroad that Christ had come. Under a wily pretense of giving the desired information to the wise men, and of desiring himself to see and worship the Messiah (if indeed he had come), (i) Herod sent out and gathered together all the chief priests and scribes of the people, and demanded of them "where Christ should be born." Here was a strange appeal to the Scriptures even while murder was hatching in his heart. It is not seldom that we find this outward deference to God's Word while there is inward rebellion against his divine purposes. (ii) The testimony of the scribes and priests agreed that Bethlehem was the place where Christ should be born. Here was a greater marvel: that the very priests and doctors of the law should be compelled to testify to the coming of Christ and yet be destitute of any spiritual desire for it. This is an illustration of that dead orthodoxy which in all ages has been a curse in the Church of God. Of what good to us is it that we know the Scriptures if they do not lead us to Christ? What a contrast we have here between the faith of Gentiles coming from afar to find and worship Christ, and the unbelief of the Jews and even their teachers, who, when Christ has come to them, know him not, neither do they go to worship him but only plot to destroy him! Again and again we see this thing. Many people who represent themselves to be Christians, who are indignant if the fact is questioned, who point to their church and to the fact that they are punctilious in the ceremonial performance of their duties, yet are the very worst enemies we have to contend with in the prosecution of our evangelistic work. Jesus in the church, Jesus in the Bible, Jesus in the prayer-book, they know all about; but Jesus in Bethlehem they will have none of. (iii) When Herod had gotten the information he sought from the scribes, he turned to the wise men and made inquiry as to when the star first appeared. Though Christ had but just been born, the star announcing his birth had probably appeared months, even a year or two, before to these men, who had been following it till now; God having planned its appearance and suited it to the time which would be necessary for them to make the journey and to find the new-born King. It was probably the statement of the wise men concerning the appearance of the star many months previously which led Herod to order all the children "from two years old and under" to be massacred. He would be sure to include the new-born King in this way in either case: whether the birth had taken place at the time of the first appearance of the star, or had but just now occurred. (iv) Then the wily king sent them away with the command to "search diligently" till they had found him, and to come again and bring him word, that he also might go and worship. Thus did the hypocrisy of Herod show itself. Hypocrisy is the dark shadow which follows faith. If there had not been true and simple faith in the wise men, the hypocrisy of Herod would not have been aroused. If there had not been a superstitious faith in Herod's wicked heart (like unto that which the devils have), he would not have plotted the destruction of Jesus. Superstition makes men tremble at the presence of God, but it does not convert them to any spiritual faith in him.

III.—THE WISE MEN WORSHIPING.

After their interview with Herod, the wise men departed toward Bethlehem to find the Child-King whom they had been seeking, and whose star had thus far led them to Jerusalem.

1.—The reappearance of the star.—Whether they had lost sight of it of late, or whether it ceased to shine in and about Jerusalem, where there was no faith but only dead orthodoxy concerning Christ, is not clear; but certain it is, as these simple-hearted wise men took up their journey toward Bethlehem, their guiding star reappeared in the heavens and moved on before them. Those who follow on to know the Lord he will never leave without a guide in the darkness. Perhaps this star was invisible to other eyes than theirs; just as many who read the Scriptures fail to see the divine light in them, while others, reading the same portion at the same time, see the light and are guided by it. Paul saw Jesus, but the soldiers who were with him saw him not; he heard the voice, but the soldiers heard it not. It is even so with men to-day: some have eyes and see not, ears and hear not, while others are filled with rejoicing and gladness at what their eyes see and their ears hear. The wise men rejoiced when they again saw the star which they had seen in the east going before them. It led them not only to Bethlehem, but to the very house where Joseph had taken Mary and the young Child after his birth in the khan. What an exceeding great joy there is in knowing that we are being led of God, and in being brought to the very object of our search and desire.

2.—Steps in the journey of faith.—We are told that these wise men came, they saw, and then they worshiped. Thus must we, being led by the Word and Spirit, come to Jesus; and so coming, we shall see. "Come and see," said Philip to Nathanael. He came, and he saw for himself. But it is not enough to see even; we must worship—that is, cordially accept the Son of God as our

Saviour, and surrender ourselves to him. When Nathanael came to Jesus and saw him, he worshiped in a good confession, saying, "Rabbi, thou art the Son of God."

3.—**The gifts of the wise men.**—So soon as they were in the house and saw the Child, they recognized and accepted him as the new-born King for whom they had been searching. Then they opened their boxes or bags and laid down before him their gifts. These gifts consisted of gold, frankincense, and myrrh. It is the custom of all Easterns thus to present gifts to those whom they desire to honor. These wise men were honoring Jesus with better things than even these costly gifts. They worshiped him. They poured out before him their hearts' faith and devotion. Innumerable ingenious guesses have been made as to what may have been the symbolic meaning of this threefold gift which was presented to Christ. Some have seen in it the symbol of the Trinity; some, the threefold nature of man; some, the three great graces of faith, hope, and charity. These speculations are as idle as they are ingenious. Just let them stand for the desire on their part and ours to give to Jesus our best, yea, and all that we have. Let us first present ourselves living sacrifices, holy, acceptable to God, which is our reasonable service (Rom. xii, 1)—our whole spirits, souls, and bodies, which are rightfully his, because he has both created and redeemed us.

> "Here I give my all to thee—
> Talents, time, and earthly store,
> Soul and body—thine to be,
> Wholly thine, forevermore."

XXIX.

FLIGHT INTO EGYPT.—Matthew ii, 13-23.

(13) And when they were departed, behold, the angel of the Lord appeareth to Joseph in a dream, saying, Arise, and take the young child and his mother, and flee into Egypt, and be thou there until I bring thee word: for Herod will seek the young child to destroy him. (14) When he arose, he took the young child and his mother by night, and departed into Egypt: (15) And was there until the death of Herod: that it might be fulfilled which was spoken of the Lord by the prophet, saying, Out of Eygyt have I called my son. (16) Then Herod, when he saw that he was mocked of the wise men, was exceeding wroth, and sent forth, and slew all the children that were in Bethlehem, and in all the coasts thereof, from two years old and under, according to the time which he had diligently inquired of the wise men. (17) Then was fulfilled that which was spoken by Jeremy the prophet, saying, (18) In Rama was there a voice heard, lamentation, and weeping, and great mourning, Rachel weeping for her children, and would not be comforted, because they are not. (19) But when Herod was dead, behold, an angel of the Lord appeareth in a dream to Joseph in Egypt, (20) Saying, Arise, and take the young child and his mother, and go into the land of Israel: for they are dead which sought the young child's life. (21) And he arose, and took the young child and his mother, and came into the land of Israel. (22) But when he heard that Archelaus did reign in Judea in the room of his father Herod, he was afraid to go thither: notwithstanding, being warned of God in a dream, he turned aside into the parts of Galilee: (23) And he came and dwelt in a city called Nazareth: that it might be fulfilled which was spoken by the prophets, He shall be called a Nazarene.—Matthew ii, 13-23.

How busy are the angels in these times! First we find Gabriel visiting Zacharias, the father of John the Baptist; then he visits the Virgin Mary and announces to her the distinguished honor God was about to confer upon her; then, to pacify Joseph's fears, the angel visits him in a dream and assures him that his suspicions concerning Mary were unfounded, and that he might not only take her to wife, but in the meantime, till the child Jesus was born, he was to be the guardian of her who was appointed to be the mother of the Lord.

Then we find the angels in hosts announcing the birth of Jesus to the shepherds. After the wise men had been "warned of God in a dream" not to return to Herod, the angel of the Lord, presumably Gabriel again, warns Joseph in a dream to "arise . . . and flee into Egypt." Again, after the death of Herod, Joseph is visited a second time by the angel, and instructed to return to the land of Israel. How happy must have been the service of these angels, Gabriel and the others, in connection with the coming of our Lord into the world; and how honored are we that these same heavenly ministers are appointed about our business and keep constant watch and ward over us, though we may not be conscious of their presence.

Those were momentous days to Joseph and Mary after the birth of the holy Child. We can well imagine that with such a charge they were in need of special instructions. But God was watching over his Eternal Son, and knew how to deliver him out of the hands of his enemies. Even so he knows how to deliver the godly out of temptation (II. Pet. ii, 9), for every godly man and woman is identified with Christ and enters into all the benefits of his Sonship. Moreover, it is a comfort for us to know that when God commits any great work or charge to us, putting responsibility upon us, he does not leave us to our own devices for the necessary wisdom to discharge our trust. This is fully demonstrated by the way in which Joseph was guided and led in the matter of the care of Jesus and his mother during the critical time of Herod's bitter hatred.

I.—JOSEPH'S MARCHING ORDERS.

No sooner was Jesus born into the world than trouble began to encompass him. The world offered him nothing but a manger for a birthplace, and now an earthly king was trying to compass his death ere he could come to his own kingdom. Not only was Jesus compassed about with danger, but they who were identified with him were involved in trouble. Here again we find the suggestion of a truth which some fail to understand. No sooner is Christ the hope of glory, born in us, than some world power or devil power seeks to destroy him. The young convert is always the object of Satanic attack and worldly machinations; and all who are intimately connected with Jesus may count on trouble and inconvenience (if it may be thus adjudged) for Jesus' sake.

1.—**Sent down into Egypt.**—Joseph was a poor man, dependent upon his daily work for his daily bread. He had come up to Bethlehem in obedience to the Roman decree to be enrolled, and now without a moment's warning he is ordered to flee into Egypt. But when we get orders straight from heaven we can afford to abandon home and business without fear, and go far hence across the wilderness, even down into Egypt.

2.—**How he received his orders.**—The angel of the Lord appeared to him in a dream. Joseph was a dreamer of dreams, as that other Joseph was who was carried down into Egypt for the sake of paving the way for bringing Israel out of it in the olden times. Dreams are common occurrences. They are like the multitudinous blossoms on a tree: not all of them bring forth fruit, but now and again a dream is used of the Spirit of God or by an angel to communicate God's will to us. I would not counsel any one to pay too much heed to dreams, yet I am persuaded that many a time we might profitably think over our dreams in the morning and reverently turn our hearts with inquiry toward God if perchance there might be a message for us in them. Certainly God of old used to communicate with his people in dreams, or by means of their dreams.

3.—**The contents of Joseph's orders.**—In this dream the angel bade Joseph to arise and flee into Egypt and take with him the young Child and his mother. There was need of haste. He was not to return to his home in Galilee to arrange his business, but with all possible haste "flee" into Egypt. What a picture is this—Jesus a fugitive from the hand of man almost as soon as he is born. Jesus, the Eternal Son of God, the Creator of the world, in the custody and keeping of a poor carpenter. How high are the honors which God confers upon humble men! If the person of Jesus is not now committed to our keeping, his honor is; and sometimes we have to flee in order to protect it. There is a time to face danger and a time to flee from it, and it oftentimes takes more courage to flee than to stand. In any case, when we are under God's orders we must flee or stand as we get the order from Heaven. He was to remain in Egypt indefinitely, until he got word again from the angel. Sometimes it is easier to obey definite than indefinite orders. "Until I bring thee word." How long might this be? What will become of my business in the meantime? What matter, so that all is in God's hands? "Wilt thou at this time restore again the kingdom?" That is not for us to know. We must just go on serving God and wait till we get word. Patient waiting is often the hardest part of obedience, just as inactivity is harder than activity. Such, however, were Joseph's orders.

4.—**Joseph instructed.**—He was so far let into the secret of the necessity for this hasty flight that the angel told him that Herod would seek to destroy the young Child. This indeed, no doubt, was calculated to arouse all Joseph's love and tenderness, and made him doubly willing to obey the command which he had just received, no matter at what inconvenience to himself. God does not always open up his reasons to us, or explain every matter, but we may be sure that there is no command laid upon us, either to do, to suffer, or to wait, except there be a good and weighty reason for it.

5.—Prompt obedience.—Joseph did not hesitate, but immediately, even that very night, took the young Child and his mother by night, and departed into Egypt. Here was a hasty journey, and a journey by night, and down into Egypt. If it is true that our Lord was made "like unto his brethren" in all respects, there must be something in all this full of meaning to us. Many a hasty journey must the people of God make, and not infrequently by night, and ofttimes down into Egypt. Abraham went down into Egypt; Joseph was sold into Egypt; the sons of Jacob with their father went down into Egypt. Egypt is a type of the world under "the god of this world" which knows not Jehovah. Yet into such a land the people of old had to go; into such a land Jesus had to go; and into such a land we must needs go. Egypt was a place of affliction and bitter trial and hard discipline for God's people, but it was at the same time a place of refuge and education under trial. Moreover, it was a place where God left a mighty testimony. A night journey, in haste, down into Egypt must be suggestive of sudden trials to be endured and a testimony for God left. Is not this true of our trials? Afflictions, hard as they are to bear, are always a way of escape from some worse thing which threatens us. Some Herod is bent on taking our life, and God saves us by sending us into Egypt, only to bring us out again chastened and prepared for a better ministry.

6.—Patient waiting.—We do not know where Joseph stayed in Egypt or how he lived, but we are sure he found some safe refuge, even as God gave to Israel a land of Goshen, where he hid them and nourished them. We know not exactly how long he stayed there as to time; but it was "until the death of Herod." "The death of Herod." How vainly do the enemies of God and his Christ fight against them! Herod sought the young Child's life, but God hid him away until Herod himself died. So shall all the schemes of God's enemies fail. Death shall overtake them, but Christ and his people shall survive. It is the old prophetic story: "He that sitteth in the heavens shall laugh," and will yet set his King upon his holy hill, though "the heathen rage" and "the kings of the earth . . . take counsel together." (Ps. ii, 4, 6, 1, 2.)

7.—The fulfillment of Scripture.—"That it might be fulfilled which was spoken of the Lord by the prophet, saying, Out of Egypt have I called my Son." (Compare Hos. xi, 1.) Matthew (more than the other evangelists) connects the life of Jesus with the words of the prophets, because it was his task to show to Israel that Jesus was none other than the Messiah of whom the prophets prophesied. Indeed, if we separate Jesus from the prophetic foretelling of him, he cannot be understood; but associating him with these Scriptures it is easy to understand all that about him which so entirely differentiates him from all other men that ever lived. This particular prophecy refers primarily to Israel, whom God brought out of Egypt by the hand of Moses in the infancy of the nation; but ultimately it had reference to Jesus; and yet again it refers to every son of God who is called into life through faith in Jesus; for out of Egypt every sinner is called who hears the voice of God spoken by Jesus, and comes forth out of the state of nature (the land of Egypt) into the state of grace—"the good land and large" which the Lord God hath given us in his dear Son.

II.—THE WRATH OF HEROD.

From the time Herod heard of the birth of Jesus through the visit of the wise men, he determined upon his murder. Dissembling with the wise men, he instructed them to bring him word when they found him, that he might go and worship him. He said "worship," but he meant "murder." The wise men could not know this, but God knoweth the thoughts of men. Therefore the wise men were warned of God to depart to their homes by another way. Herod waited in vain for their return, and when he found that they were gone, took it for granted that they had intentionally put contempt upon him, and was furiously angry, both because he thought his kingly dignity was insulted, and because he saw that his murderous intention was frustrated. God meant only to save his Son, not to insult the king, and the wise men wisely obeyed God rather than man. But vain men when intrusted with power never recognize any authority but their own fierce will, and when that is crossed they buckle on their swords and go forth to slay and kill, as though they were the owners of men, body, soul, and spirit.

1.—His bloodthirsty decree.—Here is a wholesale slaughter of innocents ordered. In order to make sure that the Child-King might not escape this bloody-minded monarch's orders, all children throughout all the region of Bethlehem, "from two years old and under," according to the time indicated by the wise men, were to be slain. Why, in the first place, he should wish to slay Jesus, even though he had come as a temporal king, is not clear. He was an old man past seventy at the time, and must in the course of nature give up his throne long before Jesus could reign as an earthly sovereign. It could not be that he was jealous for his sons, for he had already slain two of them, and after this slew another. It was pure rage—the rage of a proud, willful, godless man, who would not be brooked in his way, and who would make a display of his power though a thousand innocent children should have to be slain, and a thousand mothers' hearts be broken. What cared he for children's lives or mothers' hearts? Here is an illustration of that supreme selfishness which will have its way even though that way be reached by wickedness overmuch. This is only an exaggeration of that selfishness which most of the kings of the earth have manifested even at the cost of thousands and millions of lives which they have sacrificed in war; and of that selfishness which many a private person also manifests at the expense of others. That same lust of will and way is seen in business oppressions, which take the life-blood of thousands of patient toilers that they may be rich. That selfishness which, for instance, women of fashion manifest when they gratify their pride of dress even though all the forests of earth be cleared of the bright-plumaged birds. These are other innocents slain by millions to gratify the queens of society and their innumerable retinue of imitators.

    2.—Lamentations in Rama.—Here we find that our infant Saviour still walks forth toward his cross and throne in the steps of prophecy, for long before this time the prophet had foretold this slaughter of the innocents. Some would even charge this bloody deed upon our Lord, on whose account it was committed. True, God permitted it, but he did not bring it about. It was the deed of Herod. So far as the little ones are concerned, they were safely taken to heaven, and became the first rank in that "noble army of martyrs" which in after-years sealed their testimony with their blood. Because God overrules the wickedness of men, wicked men shall not go free of their crimes. These innocents were baptized in their own blood into the death of Christ; and though they may have lost something in earth, surely we must all agree that what they got in glory was more than a compensation for it. Marching in procession before Jesus in death, they were the vanguard of millions of children whom Jesus delivered by his gospel from things a thousand times worse than the quick death which came to these by Herod's sword. As for the poor mothers, whose voices of woe, lamentations, and weepings were heard on that fearful day in Bethlehem, and "would not be comforted, because" their little ones "are not," what shall we say? Jesus has given that word to all mothers which comforts them concerning their children who die in infancy. He has taught us that "they are," and has comforted us with the knowledge that "of such is the kingdom of heaven." And though mothers weep now, and fathers too, over their little ones lost awhile, their weeping is not without comfort and hope, for they know full well that they are with Jesus, who loved them on earth and takes them again in his arms in heaven. Rachel would not be comforted for her children because they were not, and mothers to-day still weep for their children, but are comforted because Jesus has brought sure salvation to them, taking them under his special care, both in this world and the next.

III.—JOSEPH'S RETURN TO ISRAEL.

Herod would have killed Jesus, but now he is dead, and Jesus comes forth out of his temporary refuge.

1.—Joseph's countermarch.—More dreams; more angels. How blessed to know that heaven, after all, is not far away, and that God can, if need be, speak to us and guide us by our dreams or his angels! So Joseph and Mary and the child Jesus are ordered back again into the land from which they had so hastily fled. Egypt had been their refuge, as it had been the refuge of Israel of old; and though Egypt has never been friendly with God, sure I am that God must have some good purpose in store for Egypt, which has been the sanctuary of Israel of old, and of Jesus our Saviour. "Arise, and take the young child and his mother, and go into the land of Israel." Arise and go—plain orders. Perhaps Joseph had gotten comfortably settled in Egypt, and was doing well again in that land. It might have cost him almost as much inconvenience to remove from Egypt as it had cost him to go there. Nevertheless, those who follow Jesus or have his cause in charge must be prepared always to arise and go when the word of God comes.

2.—Dead enemies.—What a significant announcement is this: "For they are dead which sought the young child's life." So shall all the enemies of Jesus perish. How vain the puny might of men who raise their hands to destroy him who is the Eternal Life! How often have they sought to destroy him and that which stands for him! They are dead who crucified him, but he is alive from the dead. They are dead who sought to stamp out his Church on earth by cruel persecutions, but the Church lives in more power and vigor to-day than ever. They are dead and their books are dead who have sought to destroy the Word of God by discrediting criticism. Behold the ignoble army of enemies! They are all dead, rank upon rank. Behold the dusty and discredited books which were printed with such flourish of trumpet, and which were to make an end of the Bible and Jesus. They are dead! And all such enemies and books now are marked for death. Let the Church of Christ rise up and go, fearless of those who seek its life; for as their ancestors who sought the young Child's life are dead, so shall these also die.

3.—**A dangerous succession.**—Joseph came into the coasts of Israel again in obedience to the word of the angel; but when he found that Archelaus was on the throne, he was afraid, for he was no man to inspire trust. Obedience to God's Word is not always rendered without fear, and fear that hath good reason in it. But God warned him again in a dream (what a dreamer Joseph was!), and directed his pathway into the hill country of Galilee and into the despised town of Nazareth. "That it might be fulfilled which was spoken by the prophets, He shall be called a Nazarene." It is not possible to identify this prophecy. Perhaps it is to be found only in some lost book, or it may be in allusion to the prophecy which calls him the "Branch" (Is. xi, 1; Jer. xxiii, 5; Zech. iii, 8; vi, 12); or it may allude to the spirit of many prophecies concerning him. At any rate, we know that henceforth Jesus is known better by the name of "the Nazarene" than by any other. He was called "the Nazarene" in derision; and also Julian the Apostate cried out, "O Nazarene, thou hast conquered!" At any rate, this Nazareth became for nearly thirty years the home of the Son of God, where in quietness and obedience he grew up to manhood, being taught by his pious mother the things concerning himself out of the Scriptures. Nazareth, this last home and refuge of Jesus, has been the sign and symbol by which all the poor, lowly, and mean of the earth have taken heart of hope to come to God by him. A town poor and mean in one way became a capital of the world because Jesus lived there so long and hallowed it together with Bethlehem, his birthplace. It was in Nazareth that Jesus first unfolded his great commission to preach the gospel to the poor, and declared himself to be the beloved of God, on whom the Spirit of God rested for the fulfillment of all the precious promises of the holy Scriptures. (Luke iv, 17-21.)

XXX.

THE YOUTH OF JESUS.—Luke ii, 40-52.

(40) And the child grew, and waxed strong in spirit, filled with wisdom: and the grace of God was upon him. (41) Now his parents went to Jerusalem every year at the feast of the passover. (42) And when he was twelve years old, they went up to Jerusalem after the custom of the feast. (43) And when they had fulfilled the days, as they returned, the child Jesus tarried behind in Jerusalem; and Joseph and his mother knew not of it. (44) But they, supposing him to have been in the company, went a day's journey; and they sought him among their kinsfolk and acquaintance. (45) And when they found him not, they turned back again to Jerusalem, seeking him. (46) And it came to pass, that after three days they found him in the temple, sitting in the midst of the doctors, both hearing them, and asking them questions. (47) And all that heard him were astonished at his understanding and answers. (48) And when they saw him, they were amazed: and his mother said unto him, Son, why hast thou thus dealt with us? behold, thy father and I have sought thee sorrowing. (49) And he said unto them, How is it that ye sought me? wist ye not that I must be about my Father's business? (50) And they understood not the saying which he spake unto them. (51) And he went down with them, and came to Nazareth, and was subject unto them: but his mother kept all these sayings in her heart. (52) And Jesus increased in wisdom and stature, and in favour with God and man.—Luke ii, 40-52.

We are indebted to Luke for this beautiful glimpse into the childhood of Jesus. It is most natural, and charming, and far removed, both as to what it tells and what it does not record, from the absurd traditions invented in the later centuries by the spurious gospel writers. It would be hard to believe that any one writing a spurious life of Jesus would content himself with these few graphic lines, giving us a single glimpse into the childhood of one whose after-life plays so important a part in the world's history as that of Jesus; for, with the exception of the moment of time in which we saw him in the Temple, in the arms of his mother and Simeon, this is the only sight or word we have of the Lord between infancy and manhood. After this he disappears from our view for eighteen years. Yet, little as we have here, we find in it the roots of his life, character, and work laid bare. The boy Jesus, in this case, is emphatically the father of the man Jesus Christ.

I.—THE FIRST JOURNEY FROM HOME.

So far as we know, Jesus had never been out of the little village home at Nazareth since his return from Egypt. Joseph and Mary had doubtless been up to Jerusalem regularly, to attend the passover feast. Jesus had now reached his twelfth year, when, according to Jewish custom, he was taken to Jerusalem and inducted into the privileges and responsibilities of a "child of the law," by taking a personal part in the celebration of the feast. We can well imagine what keen delight a lad (such as Jesus must then have been) would feel in anticipation of this great privilege—it was perhaps his first journey from home—to go to Jerusalem and see the Temple and take part in the feast, into the significance of which, without doubt, he had been so well instructed by his mother. Who can tell what swelling thoughts were already arising in the heart of this wonderful Child, of whom it is said that he "grew, and waxed strong in spirit, filled with wisdom: and the grace of God was upon him." (Luke ii, 40.) Was there already a dawning, if yet only a dim consciousness, of his divine origin and Sonship? Certainly that came upon him after he reached the Holy City, as we shall see by his reply to his mother when he was found after the parents had lost him for three days.

1.—Losing Jesus.—The holy family remained at Jerusalem during the entire feast, and then, with friends and townsmen, started on their return home. It is said that "the child Jesus tarried behind in Jerusalem, and Joseph and his mother knew not of it." Nor did they discover his absence from them until the evening of the first day on the return journey. We do not know the minute circumstances of the loss of Jesus. Certainly we cannot conceive of Mary being careless of her boy, nor of Jesus being disobedient. The probability is that, going to the Temple for the last time, on the day of their return, Jesus became interested, as was most natural, either in the ceremonies, in the building itself, or in conversation with some of the rabbis, and voluntarily lingered behind, perhaps not intending to remain alone. An irresistible impulse probably came upon him to stay, and he stayed. On the other hand, in the throng of visitors, Jesus, for a moment out of their sight, was yet supposed to be with some of the party of which they formed a part. They, "supposing him to have been in the company, went a day's journey." Is not this the way we often lose Jesus from our lives, by simply taking it for granted that he is with us, without making sure of it? There is a sense in which we may always take it for granted that he is with us; for has he not promised thee, "I will never leave neither forsake thee"? On the other hand, there is a presence of Jesus that believers often lose, and the loss is very distressing to bear. We should never take a journey or go on in the way of life a single day without making sure that Jesus is with us. It will not do to take it for granted. Day by day, morning by morning, we should be sure that he is present, and during the day, also, we should have such communion with him that there can be no doubt of his presence. It is a serious matter to lose communion with him, even for a single day. Yet how often do we allow the cares of this world, the love of pleasure, the deceitfulness of riches, or the lust of other things to come between us and Jesus. It is even possible that we may be so engaged in religious talk about the Lord that we lose sight of the Lord himself. We can suppose, without any great stretch of the imagination, that all that day Joseph and Mary were full of talk about the feast and its attending incidents; so much so that they did not miss Jesus, still supposing him to be in the company.

2.—Seeking Jesus.—At the end of the day, when preparations were being made for the night, they suddenly became aware of his absence. It is often so with us, that at the end of the day we miss Jesus. Now they became anxious and made inquiry among their kinsfolk and acquaintances, but found him not. We often fail to find Jesus among those with whom we think he is abiding. If a diligent inquiry were made throughout the Church and among all our acquaintances after this manner, "Is Jesus abiding with you?" how many would be able to say, "Yes, thank God, he has been with me all the day"? Now they were thoroughly alarmed, and it was well. It is well for us to be alarmed when we miss him, especially when on first inquiry we do not find him. They were not willing to go another step on the way home until he was found. This also was good. They no longer took it for granted that he would turn up. Alas! how many of us do this. Missing Jesus, not finding him on first inquiry, we go on supposing that he will find his way back to us. We see them now oppressed with sorrow, thoroughly distressed, turning back on their way, perhaps after a weary and painful night; nor did they cease their search until they found him. When we lose Jesus we ought to turn back with sorrow, like the spouse in the Song of Solomon seeking after her lost beloved, until we find him.

3.—Finding Jesus.—It was not until after the third day, or at the end of the third day, that they found Jesus. To lose company with Jesus for one day often involves a three days' search to find him, and sometimes longer. We are not told the details of the search, but we may naturally suppose that they went to the place of their temporary abode in Jerusalem, and among such friends as they had there, and at last, toward the end of the day, to the Temple. This was the most natural place to look for him—in God's house. Besides, it is worth while to notice that they found him just where they had left him. Is not this the most likely place for us to look for Jesus if we have lost him? Where was he in our company last? Perhaps we parted company with him when we left off the habit of secret prayer; or began to neglect his Word; or gave up some particular service for him, just because we were weary, or were led away by some temptation to pleasure; or yielded to some questionable method in business; or took up with some unholy companionship. The way to find Jesus is to search for him with all our hearts, to go back upon any evil way we may have fallen into; and the place to look for Jesus is where we last were in his company. Was it in the closet, or in the Bible, or in service? Look for him there. It is a comfort that we do not have to go either to Jerusalem or to any sacred mountain to find him now, but may search for him where we are, in the spirit of humble inquiry. (John iv, 21-24.)

II.—JESUS IN THE TEMPLE.

They found him in the Temple. This was the most natural place to have looked for him. What was that Temple, with all its appointments and services, its ritual and its sacrifices, its priests and its altars, its Holy Place and its Most Holy Place, but a great type of himself? Was there a mysterious consciousness stirring in his breast that he was spiritually connected with that building and service? Did he find himself powerfully identified with it? Certainly he was the true glory of it, and yet was finally to do away with it. He was there first as a babe, now as a boy; by and by he would come back as a man and purge it, and still later he would look upon it, weeping over it and the fair city which had rejected him, the true Lord and Temple of his people.

1.—"In the midst of the doctors."—He was not out of place amid these learned men. It was customary among the Jews for boys at that age to put themselves in the way of instruction from the rabbis. Jesus was eager to learn all he could, stimulated, doubtless, by the increasing double consciousness that was waking up in him. It is a great mistake for us to send children away from the place of highest instruction. They are much more keenly alive to religious instruction than we give them credit for. To them often the Father reveals his great truths even when hidden "from the wise and prudent."

2.—**Hearing and asking questions.**—We are not to think of Jesus as a forward boy thrusting himself in any unseemly way upon these doctors of the law, but reverently listening to their questions, and answering them with such wonderful intelligence as to attract their attention to him beyond any of the other boys in the company. He asked questions, too, for a child may ask a question as well as answer one. This is the way to learn, both by hearing, answering, and asking questions. Surely if we hear others we have a right to ask others to hear us. If we listen to the thoughts of others, we may venture to express our own. It is a great mistake either to exclude children from the presence of older people during conversation or to require that they should always be silent. They may often teach and even puzzle us, and we may oftentimes learn even from a child.

3.—**His astonishing wisdom.**—This wisdom of Jesus may have been of a twofold character: partly arising out of his unusually careful training and teaching at home, but especially because of the divine consciousness now gradually unfolding itself within this holy Child. "And all that heard him were astonished at his understanding and answers." How the fresh young wisdom of this divine Son of man cut right and left through their vain traditional and speculative teaching, going straight to the root of all matters discussed. They were getting a foretaste of what, by and by, they were to learn more. "How knoweth this boy wisdom?" They will presently ask the same of the man. "Having never learned." Ah, he learned at a different school from theirs, though he used the same text-book; he studied under a different Master, even the Holy Spirit of God. If we will have the true wisdom we must study in the same school, use the same book, and have the same Master.

4.—**About his Father's business.**—When the sorrowing parents found him, they gently chid him for what was their own fault. In answer to his mother's rebuke, "Behold, thy father and I have sought thee sorrowing," he replied also in some amazement, "Wist ye not that I must be about my Father's business?" Did he oppose the term "my Father" to Mary's "thy father"? Was it just now borne in upon him that Joseph was not his father, but God, and was this answer meant also to arouse in Mary's mind a fresh remembrance of his divine origin? which indeed she could never forget, but the importance of which she may have lost sight of. At any rate, we have in Jesus' answer the keynote to his whole after-life. "Where did you expect to find me, and what did you expect to find me doing? Have you forgotten that I came into the world to do his will who sent me?" (John iii, 34; viii, 29; ix, 4; xvii, 4.) Good were it for us all to learn to the full this lesson. "As my Father hath sent me, even so send I you." (John xx, 21.)

5.—Some important lessons.—In this interview with Jesus in the Temple we have several lessons. (i) *To parents.* If your children are inclined to God in their earliest years, suffer them to go to him. Never hinder or reproach them, or think them too young, but encourage them to go early to God's house, listen patiently to their questions, and begin as early as possible to teach them the things of God. You will find their minds receptive amazingly soon. (ii) *To teachers.* Do not underrate the powers of a child's mind. Do not stuff them with foolish twaddle when they are ready to comprehend the deepest religious truths. We do not give children credit for the capacity for spiritual things which they really possess. And do not overrate your own understanding, and despise the words of children. They often have thoughts given them of the Holy Ghost, which we may well listen to. (iii) *To children.* If God inclines you to think of him and go to his house, obey the drawings of his Spirit. Be diligent to learn of God, respectful to hear what is said to you, and not afraid to ask or answer any question which may come to you concerning God and spiritual things.

III.—JESUS RETURNS TO NAZARETH.

How beautiful is the transition! From the Temple, where he was about his Father's business, back to the mean little Nazareth village, there to wait in quietness till the time had come to present himself publicly to Israel. This, too, was his Father's business. His heart had drawn him to the Temple; now his obedient spirit bids him return and be subject to his parents. What a beautiful picture is here also: faithful to his heavenly Father and obedient to his earthly parents. He was already learned in the art and manner of obedience, for there is an art, or, we might say, "a manner" of obedience. Firm in the doing and defending that which he saw to be right toward God, yet yielding and humble in conforming to every wish of his mother and Joseph. There is nothing bold or forward in anything recorded of him. A heavenly child, whose life has since sanctified and consecrated childhood down all the ages.

1.—Jesus at home.—For eighteen years he lived after this in the humble town of his childhood. We hear nothing of it, except incidentally. We know that he was brought up there; that he was well known as "the carpenter" and "the carpenter's son"; that he lived with his brothers and sisters. We are left to infer how he lived, but no doubt as a quiet, loving, gentle boy, and then a young man of serious and reverent spirit, who had been in the habit in his young manhood, perhaps from twenty or twenty-five, of conducting the worship in the village synagogue.

2.—Increasing in wisdom and stature.—His was a healthy physical growth, accompanied by high intellectual and spiritual development. It is a sad thing for any child whose higher nature does not keep pace in its growth with physical stature and with years. What were the means of his spiritual development we do not know. He was never at the schools. He "never learned." Yet he was, no doubt, carefully taught at home by his mother out of the Scriptures. Nature was his schoolroom, and constant communion with his Father enlarged his mind and heart. No doubt there was an ever-increasing development of the divine nature dwelling in mysterious union with his human nature. Altogether, what a man was he! He never received any knowledge from man, nor wisdom from the wise, yet he has taught the world, and his wisdom has never yet been sounded to its depths.

3.—"In favor with God and man."—No wonder. If only we live so as to grow in God's favor, we will, sooner or later, win the favor of man, even though for a time we may be unnoticed or even despised. The natural disposition leads us to seek the favor of man, but though all praise us and we are without God's favor, we are poor indeed. If men favor us because they see that God is with us, then it shall be well with us, just as on the other hand it is a "woe" to us when all men speak well of us without the favor of God. Let us seek first the favor of God, then, whether we have the favor or the enmity of men, it shall be well with us.

XXXI.

THE BAPTISM OF JESUS.—Mark i, 1-11.

(1) The beginning of the gospel of Jesus Christ, the Son of God; (2) As it is written in the prophets, Behold, I send my messenger before thy face, which shall prepare thy way before thee. (3) The voice of one crying in the wilderness, Prepare ye the way of the Lord, make his paths straight. (4) John did baptize in the wilderness, and preach the baptism of repentance for the remission of sins. (5) And there went out unto him all the land of Judea, and they of Jerusalem, and were all baptized of him in the river of Jordan, confessing their sins. (6) And John was clothed with camel's hair, and with a girdle of a skin about his loins; and he did eat locusts and wild honey; (7) And preached, saying, There cometh one mightier than I after me, the latchet of whose shoes I am not worthy to stoop down and unloose. (8) I indeed have baptized you with water: but he shall baptize you with the Holy Ghost. (9) And it came to pass in those days, that Jesus came from Nazareth of Galilee, and was baptized of John in Jordan. (10) And straightway coming up out of the water, he saw the heavens opened, and the Spirit like a dove descending upon him: (11) And there came a voice from heaven, saying, Thou art my beloved Son, in whom I am well pleased.
—Mark i, 1-11.

Mark was not one of the apostles, but he was the companion of the apostles, and was well informed of (and perhaps personally conversant with) most of the things he wrote of. Matthew and Luke give us detailed genealogies of Jesus according to his human descent; John gives us his divine genealogy; but Mark does neither. He gives us a brief account of the events immediately preceding his appearance, and then plunges at once into the midst of the Lord's active ministry.

I.—"THE BEGINNING OF THE GOSPEL."

Some have thought that this expression, "The beginning of the gospel," was meant as a kind of title to the Book of Mark, but it seems hardly probable that this rapid writer would have stopped to think of a title. It was not the title but the contents of the book he had set about writing, that occupied Mark; besides, he writes more than a beginning—he goes through to the end of the earthly life of Jesus.

1.—"**The beginning.**"—This is the first sentence in Mark's memoirs. He does not mean that what he writes, or the events which he proceeds to record, constitute the beginning of the gospel literally, but the beginning of the earthly ministry of Jesus and the events which preceded it in time. Had he been writing of the beginning of the being and work of Jesus Christ, like John he must have gone back into eternity, where he was "with God"; had he desired to write from the beginning of the gospel as declared to man, he must have gone back to the Garden of Eden, where Christ's coming was first announced to Adam and Eve. His "beginning" referred only to the events immediately preceding the public life of Jesus. What a wonderful beginning of things is here! The gospel! Had he recorded the beginning of the work of justice and wrath to make an end of sinners, we should not have been surprised, after reading the story of sin and ingratitude, of unbelief and rebellion, recorded in the Old Testament; but instead, we have the beginning of the dispensation of love and mercy to sinners—a beginning which was the end of the old dispensation of law, types, and shadows, and the bringing in of the substance of all that God had promised man in grace from the foundation of the world. What a humble beginning it was! One man, one voice—and both man and voice in the wilderness. Not a mighty prince, but a prophet-man, clad in camel's hair, with a leathern girdle about him. How differently from the coming of an earthly prince did Jesus appear to take up his ministry! Yet as we get on in our study we shall see the reason for this strange and simple "beginning of the gospel." It was because it was the beginning of the gospel, and not the beginning of the kingdom; because it was the beginning of the grace of God, and not the beginning of the ceremonial pomp of a formal worship; because it was the beginning of a dispensation which was to reign in the hearts of men, and not in external paraphernalia of worship.

2.—"**The gospel.**"—The record here is of the events antecedent to the appearing of the gospel. What gospel? "The gospel of . . . the Son of God." This may be taken in two ways, both of them, however, converging into one great and blessed truth. The gospel is not primarily the contents of the gospel, but Jesus Christ himself; and then of the communications made by him, based upon who he is, what he has done and is evermore doing. Jesus himself is the gospel. Paul begins his great epistle to the Romans in much the same way. He speaks of "the gospel of God, . . . concerning his Son Jesus Christ our Lord, which was made of the seed of David according to the flesh, and declared to be the Son of God with power . . . by the resurrection from the dead." Then "the gospel" is also the contents of the gospel, or the things communicated to us by and in Jesus Christ. This is what Paul calls the gospel "of his Son," *i.e.*, the Son of God, of which he declared that he was "not ashamed, . . . for it is the power of God unto salvation." (Rom. i, 3, 9, 16.) In this gospel we have "God . . . manifest in the flesh," "God in Christ"; that is, God uniting himself with our nature and setting up again his image in man, giving to us in this "second Adam" a new head of the race, in whom we may take our stand for life, and from whom flows to us the abundant grace which is to take away our sin and restore us to God. (II. Cor. v, 19, 21; I. Tim. iii, 16; Heb. i, 2, 3.) In this gospel, of which Jesus Christ, the Son of God, is the entire substance, we have the declaration of sins forgiven and expiated, justification and regeneration, reconciliation to God and final transformation into his image. (John iii, 3, 5, 16; Acts xiii, 38, 39; II. Cor. iii, 18; v, 20; Titus iii, 4–7; Heb. i, 3.) No wonder the angels sang when Jesus was born: "Behold, I bring you good tidings of great joy, which shall be to all people." (Luke ii, 10.)

3.—"**Jesus Christ, the Son of God.**"—This title is very full and significant. "Jesus" is his human name, which was given to him by the angel of God. "Thou shalt call his name JESUS: for he shall save his people from their sins." (Matt. i, 21.) He was called "CHRIST" because he is the divinely anointed Messiah, "because he filled the office of *Saviour* by sovereign and divine appointment." "THE SON OF GOD" because he was of higher nature than that of man; because he was, in fact, one with God as to his nature. We cannot stop to expound all the significance of this. It is enough to recall to your attention the fact that from the beginning this was affirmed *of* him, insisted on *by* him, and because of this he was condemned and put to death by the Jewish Sanhedrim. (Matt. xxvi, 63–66; Mark xiv, 61–64.) This declaration corresponds with that wonderfully full and comprehensive confession of faith by Peter: "Thou art the Christ, the Son of the living God." (Matt. xvi, 16.)

II.—THE MINISTRY OF JOHN THE BAPTIST.

The event preliminary to the appearance of Jesus Christ, the Son of God (who is the substance of the gospel, concerning which this book is written), was the appearance of John the Baptist in the wilderness of Judea. This incident forms the second section of our study.

1.—"**As it is written.**"—It is a point much insisted on by all the New Testament writers that Jesus and his gospel were not new in respect of their coming into the world. That is, in Jesus and his gospel there was no new device or doctrine; they were the coming of that which had been the subject of all the prophetic utterances since the world began. Thus Paul and Peter declare the gospel to have been "according to the Scriptures." (Rom. i, 2; I. Cor. xv, 3; I. Pet. i, 11; II. Pet. iii, 2.) Jesus himself insists that he was the subject of all Scripture prophecy. (Luke xxiv, 27, 46; John v, 39.) Not only was Jesus thus prophesied of, but also his forerunner—the manner of his appearing and the method of his announcement were specifically foretold by the same inspired promises. Mark refers especially to two prophecies concerning John the Baptist. (Mal. iii, 1; Is. xl, 3.) John, then, was not only a prophet, he was a child of prophecy. These facts tend greatly to strengthen our faith in Jesus as the Son of God.

2.—**Concerning John himself.**—He was a man of austere and prophetic appearance and manner. Living apart from men, in separation from the corrupt church and from fellowship with the Pharisaical formalists and rationalizing Sadducees, he was in himself the embodiment of the protest he made. The greatness of his character and the force of his ministry testified that real religion was a matter of inward disposition and personal character, and not of outward forms and ceremonials, especially when they gave the lie to the profession of which they were the sign. He was a "voice" as well as a man. And what a voice he was! One that called a whole city to his wilderness pulpit and compelled them to hear his stern rebukes. But he was also a "messenger." He preached not himself nor any doctrines of his own, but heralded the coming of One who was greater than he, to whom all his preaching led up, and who was the only justification and reason for his mission.

3.—**The wilderness.**—John appeared not in Jerusalem, either in the Temple or in the crowded streets. His voice sounded forth from the wilderness, calling the people away from the city and the

Temple, wherein, because of their sins and hypocrisies, God no longer dwelt. The wilderness had in it lessons of separation as well as the teaching of John. To turn from Jerusalem and its burdensome, meaningless forms of worship to the wilderness, where the lusts of the flesh were denied, and to Jesus Christ the Son of God, was in itself repentance. Sooner or later all who receive Jesus must turn from the city to the wilderness. The gospel unmistakably calls us from the place and things of man to the wilderness, where the voice of the prophets is heard and where Jesus dwells. Christianity involves separation and self-denial in fellowship with Jesus Christ.

4.—The preaching of John.—John's preaching was very comprehensive. An examination of all the evangelists on this point will show that he declared every fundamental doctrine of the gospel; but if we confine ourselves to Mark's testimony, we shall find abundant evidence of the wideness of his range. (i) "Prepare ye the way of the Lord, make his paths straight." In this expression John calls on the people to make a straight way in which the Lord may travel. John prepared the way in part for the coming of the Son of God, by calling upon the people to prepare the way for him—a straight path through their thoughts into their hearts. God can only come by Jesus Christ into our hearts as we prepare the way and make the paths straight. No self-preparation, no self-straightening of the crooked ways of our lives will result in our salvation. It is only as the Son of God comes into our lives that we can be saved; but we are called upon to answer to his call, to unbar the door at which he stands and knocks. It is true that the preparation of the heart is from the Lord, but it is in response to our desire and willingness to be made whole. Here John teaches the great doctrine of human responsibility in presence of the gospel, and human ability when exercised in response to the summons of God to make a pathway for him in our lives. The making of his way straight refers to the necessity of straightening our thoughts and ways. That is, we must be straightforward and honest before the Lord, and sincerely accept him, being ready to correct our evil courses in accordance with his will. A readiness to have Jesus Christ come into our lives and straighten them is the preparation of heart that is needed to receive him. (ii) By an involution of the verses we come to the next great point. "There cometh One mightier than I after me." John was no egotist. He would not have his hearers for a moment think of himself. He was but a messenger, a voice. The real object of their interest and trust was another than himself. He, indeed, could give them some initial help and instruction, but ultimately they must deal with the Son of God, who would baptize them with the Holy Ghost and with fire. We must remember that the greatest of the servants of Jesus Christ cannot save us, or even render any substantial help. They can only point to "One mightier than" any man. (iii) John urges upon his hearers three things—remission, repentance, and confession. The most important of these is remission. "The remission of sins." This is the great truth announced by the coming of Jesus into the world. God declared by him, first, the gracious disposition which is in his heart toward sinners, viz., the forgiveness of sins. (Acts xiii, 38.) This is the putting out of his heart personal offense on account of our sins, and the declaration of his longing desire to have us reconciled to him. It has its highest expression in II. Cor. v, 19. This is the first thing to be declared in the gospel of God by Jesus Christ. But remission also refers to the putting away of penalties. Christ's appearing in our nature is God's proclamation of forgiveness. Christ's appearance as the Lamb of God, that taketh away the sin of the world, is the proclamation of remission of penalties by expiation, the blessing of which is conditioned on our faith. (Acts xiii, 39.) Forgiveness is universal and unconditioned; but justification is conditioned on our repentance and faith in Jesus Christ. Forgiveness is universal in its provision, but limited in its application to believers. "Repentance." The expression "repentance unto remission" has the force of "because of remission." In view of the fact that God, by Jesus Christ his Son, has declared his gracious forgiveness and provided in him for the remission of all penalties due to or attaching to sin, we should "repent." Repentance unto remission is the response of the sinner to the grace of God in Jesus Christ. To repent is to change one's mind in respect to God, and so in respect to sin, which is seen as guilt, and which only Jesus, by his blood, can expiate. When a man sees this grace and understands that through it his sins are forgiven and remitted, he turns to God in grateful acceptance and waits for the heart purification, which will come; and so shall he be made "a new creature" in the likeness of Jesus Christ. It is the gospel, therefore, and not the law, that leads men to repentance. Few understand this, and therefore there is great confusion in Christian experience. The third great point in John's preaching was the duty of "confession." When the people heard of the grace of God, they repented, and gladly confessed their sins. That is, they not only with their lips acknowledged their inherent sinfulness and their sinful actions, but with their hearts they practically conveyed them over to Jesus, as the sinners of old did when, through the high-priest, they laid their sins on the head of the sin-offering. (Lev. iv, 4; xxvi, 40, 42; Ps. xxxii, 5.) Confession involves both acknowledgment of sin and appropriation of Christ.

5.—The two baptisms.—John baptized his converts with water unto repentance, and promised them, at the hands of the mightier One, a baptism of the Holy Ghost. The baptism of John in water was the formal act of confession and declaration of faith or appropriation of Jesus Christ. This was but outward, and might not be significant of anything at all, unless the subject did really repent and confess sins; but when the Lord came he would send into their hearts a mighty testimony of the Holy Ghost, who would not only make himself known in a saving and purifying work within them, but would endue them "with power from on high" to overcome sin and serve God.

III.—THE BAPTISM OF JESUS.

After a while—some days, weeks, or months—Jesus, of whom John had preached, came from Nazareth and sought, even demanded, baptism at the hands of John. The fullest account of this is given by Matthew (iii, 13 *et seq.*) and Luke (iii, 21, 22).

1.—The baptism of Jesus by John.—What did it signify? Not that Jesus was a sinner, repenting and confessing sin. John saw incongruity in the baptism of Jesus as he understood the meaning and significance of the rite; but Jesus put aside his objection, saying, "Suffer it to be so now: for thus it becometh us to fulfill all righteousness." (Matt. iii, 15.) Jesus, when he came into this world, came not only in behalf of sinners, but so identified himself with them that he judicially took their place under the law and assumed their condition because of sin. Therefore he stood forth as the representative of and substitute for sinners, and walked before them in the way of confession and appropriation. In the act of baptism there was also a significant type of his own death and resurrection. In fact, it typifies two things: first, the way in which he was to fulfill all righteousness, viz., by dying and being raised again; and second, the way in which we come into righteousness, viz., by union with him in spiritual death and resurrection, signified by our own baptism.

2.—The descent of the Spirit upon Jesus.—This occurred as he was coming up out of the waters of baptism. The descent of the Spirit in the form of a dove suggests that to and on Jesus came the Spirit in all fullness. In a smaller measure that same Spirit fell on the disciples at Pentecost, in the form of tongues of fire. It was meet that on Jesus the Spirit should come without measure. This was his formal anointing and inauguration for the great work before him. If Jesus had to be so anointed by the Spirit of God for his work, how much more do we need to be! He sends *us* forth as the Father sent him forth, and gives us the Spirit as the Father gave him the Spirit. (John xx, 21, 22; Acts ii, 3.)

3.—**The voice from heaven.**—"And there came a voice from heaven, saying, Thou art my beloved Son, in whom I am well pleased." This was said to Jesus, though, possibly, John and others who were standing by may have heard it. It was said for his own comfort and assurance. He knew that he was beloved of his Father and always had been; but now, under these different circumstances, with his human consciousness uppermost, it was an assurance which he needed much to have, and was both a comfort and strength to him when it came. If we walk in his holy footsteps we shall have the heavens cleft above us, the anointing Spirit will fall upon us also, and the comforting assurance of God's good pleasure will be given us.

XXXII.

THE TEMPTATION OF JESUS.—Matthew iv, 1-11.

(1) Then was Jesus led up of the Spirit into the wilderness to be tempted of the devil. (2) And when he had fasted forty days and forty nights, he was afterward a hungred. (3) And when the tempter came to him, he said, If thou be the Son of God, command that these stones be made bread. (4) But he answered and said, It is written, Man shall not live by bread alone, but by every word that proceedeth out of the mouth of God. (5) Then the devil taketh him up into the holy city, and setteth him on a pinnacle of the temple, (6) And saith unto him, If thou be the Son of God, cast thyself down: for it is written, He shall give his angels charge concerning thee: and in their hands they shall bear thee up, lest at any time thou dash thy foot against a stone. (7) Jesus said unto him, It is written again, Thou shalt not tempt the Lord thy God. (8) Again, the devil taketh him up into an exceeding high mountain, and sheweth him all the kingdoms of the world, and the glory of them; (9) And saith unto him, All these things will I give thee, if thou wilt fall down and worship me. (10) Then saith Jesus unto him, Get thee hence, Satan: for it is written, Thou shalt worship the Lord thy God, and him only shalt thou serve. (11) Then the devil leaveth him, and, behold, angels came and ministered unto him.—Matthew iv, 1-11.

Three accounts are given us of the temptation of our Lord in the wilderness. Mark merely mentions the fact, adding a single incident not mentioned by the other two evangelists, viz., that in the wilderness, where it took place, there were wild beasts. Matthew and Luke give the fullest details (Luke's account being rather fuller than Matthew's). The order of the three temptations in Matthew's account differs from that of Luke. It is not within our purpose to seek any reason for this change, as it is not material to the case. As a matter of judgment it would seem that Matthew's order might be the most likely, as it is the most natural. This begins the second stage in the life of Jesus, and is most graphically told. Hitherto the life of Jesus had been quiet and retired, amid the scenes of his country home among the Galilean hills; but no sooner does the Lord appear in public and receive the open recognition from Heaven of his true character, than the great battle and ministry of his life begin. How sudden the change from his glorification on the banks of the Jordan to the temptation in the wilderness; from the approving voice of his Father to the lying and deceiving voice of Satan. First his consecration and then his trial! This is also the order in development of the life of many a child of God. It is in accordance with the manner of Satan that Jesus should thus be assaulted at the very outset. That dark spirit appears at the opening of every new dispensation. He first entered the Garden of Eden and there wrecked the fair creation of God. He appeared in Egypt, embodying himself in Pharaoh, and resisting God's purpose to bring out his chosen people. In the idolatrous priests of Baal and Ashtaroth he fought unceasingly to destroy the people of God, so far succeeding that he utterly corrupted them. It was not to be supposed that he would stand idly by and see the Son of God undertake and carry forward the work of redemption without desperate efforts to mar it. Nor did he admit this first defeat, for he renewed his attacks continually upon our Lord, working both through Judas (that "son of perdition"), and even through the brave and devoted Peter, over whom he obtained at least two temporary advantages. In the Garden of Gethsemane he, with all the combined powers of darkness, did his best to frustrate the sacrificial death of Christ by bringing him to death there. (Luke xxii, 53.) That he was active in bringing about his death on the cross (not knowing the purpose of God in that), there is no doubt. Nor has he ceased yet to resist God's grace. If possible, he will prevent every soul from winning Christ, through his temptations to apostasy and sin. Yet, once more, we shall see his last desperate effort, when he shall appear as the "Antichrist," wearing out the saints with frightful persecutions. But, thanks be to God, this successful battle of our Lord's in the wilderness is but the prelude to Satan's complete and final overthrow. Our Lord was alone in this temptation in the wilderness: so must we fight our battles alone in the truest sense of the word. Human friends may be near, but the real battle is solitary! Yet not alone, for as Jesus had the Holy Spirit to help him, so also have we, with this added, that he himself is near and full of tender sympathy, having been "in all points tempted like as we are," being "touched with the feelings of our infirmities." We are struck with the fact that all accounts agree that he was "led" or "driven" up into the wilderness, there to be tempted. Does God lead and drive us into temptation? "God cannot be tempted, neither tempteth he any man" to sin, or send him into temptation. Against temptation we are taught to pray by our

Lord himself. But in his case it was very different. For this purpose came he into the world, that he might meet our great enemy, overthrow him, and win back for us the life we had lost; just as his sacrificial death was appointed, and so he must go to it. This "driving" of Jesus to temptation was much like his other passion, concerning which he said he was "straitened" till it should be accomplished. Yet are we not to understand that he went reluctantly or unwillingly. The leading of God's Spirit is always with the full consent of those who are led, though oftentimes, as in this case, with an irresistible energy. Then it is that we go under the compulsion of a divinely free "must." Just as, when a boy, he "must" be about his Father's business; he "must" needs go through Samaria; he "must" be lifted up; he "must" be delivered into the hands of sinful men and be killed: so he "must" meet Satan. Thanks be to God for these "musts." So is the covenant of our salvation "ordered in all things, and sure."

I.—THE BATTLE SET.

It is almost impossible not to think of this temptation as a pitched battle between the god of this world and the Redeemer of men. So, at least, we will look at it. If Jesus will establish his new kingdom upon the earth, with redeemed men for his subjects, he must grapple with Satan, and come off victorious in the fight. Not only once for all, vicariously, but he "must" do it again and again in the person of each one of his saints, for Satan must be bruised under our feet also (Rom. xvi, 20); but he has made this victory ultimately sure to us, though in the meantime we must be wary of our great adversary and resist him "steadfast in the faith," each one for himself.

1.—The scene of conflict.—We know not exactly where this wilderness was, whether in some wild mountainous district near Jericho, or farther off in the howling wilderness through which Moses led the children of Israel. It does not matter. Jesus chose the ground on which he would meet his foe, and there challenged him to battle. We have already noted that he must meet Satan alone, save that the Holy Ghost was his comforter and ally. Whether the devil met him at once and beset him all through these forty days of fasting, or whether he appeared at the close, it is difficult to determine; but we lean to the latter conclusion, supposing that Jesus spent those forty days in meditation and prayer, extending his now fully aroused consciousness over the whole field of his ministry, and

THE BATTLE SET.

by close communion with his Father, settling and fixing all the great moral problems and issues involved in his divine work. This he did during a period of absolute fasting, while the flesh was in complete subjection to the spirit. When that prolonged interview between God and his own soul was over, being "an hungred," Satan came to the attack.

2.—**The parties to this terrible conflict.**—(i) There is Jesus himself, first, because he is principal and challenger. This was no battle of Satan's choosing, though he must accept the challenge; not to have done so would have been to give up his mastery over man without a struggle; yet we are not to suppose that he was unwilling. His malicious hatred of God and Jesus (and for their sakes of man also) would have led him gladly to any effort against them all: especially against Jesus, the Son of man and the Son of God, Jesus as man's kinsman and champion, and God's representative in this tremendous conflict between moral evil and moral good. (ii) The Holy Spirit is there, the ever-abiding Spirit of God, strengthening and helping the God-man in his conflict with the devil. It is most interesting to note how the Holy Spirit is present, working with Jesus through all his human life and ministry. "By the Holy Ghost" was he conceived in the Virgin's womb. "By the Holy Spirit" was he baptized at the Jordan. "By the Holy Spirit" was he led into the wilderness. "By the Holy Spirit" was he anointed to preach the gospel. "By the Holy Spirit" was he enabled to do all his mighty works. "By the Holy Spirit" did he offer up himself to God a sacrifice for our sins. "By the Holy Spirit" was he raised again from the dead. How blessed that this same Holy Spirit is vouchsafed to us from the moment of our acceptance of Christ, to abide with us, to teach, guide, and strengthen us to the end. (iii) The devil. It is needless for us to discuss the question as to the personality of this mighty evil spirit. We abandon the Word of God entirely if we reject the fact of a personal devil. He is as present in the entire compass of revelation as man is. The ever-active enemy of God and man, he will so remain, in some one of his many capacities, until he is finally cast out. The "god of this world," the "prince of the power of the air," "a liar, and the father of it," the "accuser of our brethren," a "roaring lion," "that old serpent, called the devil," "Satan," "Beelzebub." Enough of God's description of him. These are the parties to this conflict.

3.—**The subject of conflict.**—What was the necessity of this battle, after all? Why must Christ be tempted of the devil? Why must he humble himself to contend with this cast-out and lost spirit?

Why, in the exercise of his omnipotence, does he not destroy him out of hand? It is not difficult for those who study the whole plan of man's salvation to know the reason. The thing contended for was man himself. Satan had destroyed him morally, taking him captive at the beginning, holding him captive till now. Jesus must redeem his lost ones out of his cruel hand by opposing moral strength and purity to his moral evil. Jesus, as man, fought to deliver man out of Satan's hand, and to reëstablish human righteousness through obedience to God, contending against hard temptation to evil and disobedience. Jesus is man's champion. As man, he took up the cause just where man had failed and lost himself. To this very end he voluntarily became man, taking our nature, with all its limitations, placing himself under the law, and voluntarily subjecting himself to the same trials under which man failed and fell, being "in all points tempted like as we are." If he, thus thoroughly tried, vindicated human righteousness (and God's righteousness at the same time in exposing man to such trial), then has he destroyed "the works of the devil" so far, recovered a standing for man with God, and delivered man out of Satan's hand. On Satan's part this was set before him. He had already dragged man down to sin and death, through temptation. If he can succeed in overthrowing man's champion by tempting Jesus to sin, then is man hopelessly and forever lost; for if Jesus fail, who else will or can undertake for sinners? But more, if Jesus fail, then is the devil's triumph over God himself complete, and he who first rebelled against God would become master in the moral universe. Evil is henceforth victorious over good, and the earth is turned into hell! So that in this conflict both the salvation of man and the glory of God are at stake.

II.—THE TEMPTATION.

We come now to consider the temptation itself. Several preliminary thoughts suggest themselves before proceeding to examine the threefold attack upon Jesus. (i) What was the nature of this temptation? Was it physical, or was it wholly moral? The answer, we believe, is that it was wholly moral and spiritual. It is true that the first temptation was made through the physical sense of hunger, yet the temptation was in fact a moral one—a temptation to live after the flesh. (ii) What was the manner of the temptation? Did Satan appear before him in bodily shape? It is almost needless to answer this; yet there are so many speculations concerning this point that it may be as well to note some of them. We have no reason to believe that Satan himself has any body properly his own. He is a disembodied spirit. It has been supposed by some that he assumed a body (as in the Garden of Eden), appearing to Christ in the form of some wild beast; by others, that he possessed himself of some man, and through him tempted Christ. Some think that one of the Lord's brethren, after searching for him, found him in the wilderness in a starving condition, and tempted him, by challenging him to use his vast power (if he were the Son of God) to relieve his hunger; or that an emissary from the Sanhedrim had followed him to the wilderness and tempted him. We know that it is possible for Satan to take possession of a human soul and use it for his own ends, as in the case of Judas (and even temporarily of Peter), as at last he will do when he openly manifests himself to the world as "Antichrist," but to my mind these theories seem utterly improbable. The temptations of the mountain and of the Temple pinnacle are inconsistent with such a theory. If, then, it was purely spiritual, how was it accomplished? There are two theories. One is, that these thoughts arose out of Jesus' own heart, that he was assailed by temptations from within (instigated by the devil, it is true), and that it was a stirring up of sin in the Lord's own nature. This we abandon as being utterly abhorrent to everything known concerning Christ, and wholly inconsistent with his absolute sinlessness. We can only imagine that the temptations were suggestions made to him by the tempter himself,—"fiery darts hurled against his imagination, and pressed with all the subtle power and spiritual force of which Satan is possessed." (iii) The reality of the temptation. We must not suppose, because Jesus was sinless in his nature, that it was not possible for him to have yielded to temptation, else it would have been no temptation. But he "was in all points tempted like as we are, yet without sin." He was "touched with the feeling of our infirmities." Every temptation made a powerful appeal to him. He was human, and his hunger was real! There was that in him which could respond to both the later temptations —to his ambition and to his pride. Had he been so incased in divinity that, without effort of will, the shafts of Satan would have broken and fallen down at his feet, there would have been no virtue or victory in his triumph. He *could* not sin because he *would* not sin. He triumphed by means of a holy character, but the essence of that triumph was a voluntary choice, and a determined resistance to his enemy; by vigorous and believing use of the Scriptures. By holy will and holy weapons he prevailed, not otherwise. So may we in this wise resist the devil, and see him flee from us. (iv) The point of attack. It is interesting to note that, in two of the temptations, probably the first two in order (ver. 6), Satan challenged him on the point of his divine Sonship. "If thou be the Son of God." This was both a denial and an appeal, as though he had said, "You claim to be the Son of God. I doubt it, and challenge the claim. If you be so, prove it by doing what I suggest." How easy it would have been for Jesus to have made that demonstration! But it was just because he was the Son of God that he would not make that display. That was what he came for, to demonstrate his Godhead. (Phil. ii, 6-9.) That demonstration would be perfect when he had finished his work and God had raised him from the dead. (Rom. i, 3, 4.)

XXXIII.

FIRST DISCIPLES OF JESUS.—John i, 34-49.

(34) And I saw, and bare record that this is the Son of God. (35) Again the next day after, John stood, and two of his disciples; (36) And looking upon Jesus as he walked, he saith, Behold the Lamb of God! (37) And the two disciples heard him speak, and they followed Jesus. (38) Then Jesus turned, and saw them following, and saith unto them, What seek ye? They said unto him, Rabbi, (which is to say, being interpreted, Master,) where dwellest thou? (39) He saith unto them, Come and see. They came and saw where he dwelt, and abode with him that day: for it was about the tenth hour. (40) One of the two which heard John speak, and followed him, was Andrew, Simon Peter's brother. (41) He first findeth his own brother Simon, and saith unto him, We have found the Messias, which is, being interpreted, the Christ. (42) And he brought him to Jesus. And when Jesus beheld him, he said, Thou art Simon the son of Jona: thou shalt be called Cephas, which is by interpretation, A stone. (43) The day following Jesus would go forth into Galilee, and findeth Philip, and saith unto him, Follow me. (44) Now Philip was of Bethsaida, the city of Andrew and Peter. (45) Philip findeth Nathanael, and saith unto him, We have found him, of whom Moses in the law, and the prophets, did write, Jesus of Nazareth, the son of Joseph. (46) And Nathanael said unto him, Can there any good thing come out of Nazareth? Philip saith unto him, Come and see. (47) Jesus saw Nathanael coming to him, and saith of him, Behold an Israelite indeed, in whom is no guile! (48) Nathanael saith unto him, Whence knowest thou me? Jesus answered and said unto him, Before that Philip called thee, when thou wast under the fig tree, I saw thee. (49) Nathanael answered and saith unto him, Rabbi, thou art the Son of God; thou art the King of Israel.—John i, 34-49.

On the day previous to that on which our study opens, John the Baptist had been interviewed by an official committee sent from the Jewish Sanhedrim. Up to this time the Jewish rulers had paid little attention to John's preaching; but now the matter was becoming so notorious, and the intense and all but universal interest of the people so great, that they were constrained to inquire into it. They asked of John who he was. He frankly told them that he laid no personal claims to being "the Christ" (of which there evidently were rumors). Nor was he a prophet come again to life. Yet he declared plainly that he was the one of whom the prophet Isaiah had spoken: "The voice of one crying in the wilderness, Make straight the way of the Lord." In answer to the question as to why he baptized, he told them that he was but the forerunner of One, already in their midst, whose office it was to baptize with the Holy Ghost, as it was his own work to baptize with water. With this answer the deputation went back. Why they took no notice of John's startling announcement that the Messiah was already in their midst, is not stated. Perhaps because they did not care to recognize the fact; or because they esteemed the statement preposterous. They, no doubt, came to the conclusion that John was simply a misguided fanatic.

I.—"THE LAMB OF GOD."

The inquiry of the deputation and John's answers to them were made in public, and his replies were made so that the people standing about could hear. They constituted a kind of formal announcement to them of the advent of Messiah. Jesus had disappeared into the wilderness after his baptism, and had not as yet reappeared. But now, the very day after that first announcement, an event occurred which brought to a crisis the ministry of John.

1.—"Behold the Lamb of God."—John, the evangelist, has already introduced to us Jesus as the Eternal Word, and declared the fact of his incarnation and the purposes for which he "was made flesh and dwelt among us." Now the Lord takes advantage of the Baptist's ministry to introduce himself to us in his character of "the Lamb of God." The eternal "Word" becomes the "only begotten Son," and now he is revealed as the divine "Lamb." John the Baptist's announcement is abrupt, and was brought about by the sudden approach of Jesus toward him from among the crowd. John undoubtedly at once knew that this was for the purpose of being recognized and introduced to the people by him. What astonishes us is that John should have introduced Jesus as "the Lamb of God" rather than as "the Messiah." It shows a wonderful and advanced insight into the mission of Jesus. This at once placed the moral and spiritual importance of the mission of the Son of God above that of his temporal relation to them as Messiah or king, and indicated that the Messiah's kingdom, when founded, would rest not so much upon national as spiritual foundations; and that the members of that kingdom would not be those whose only claim was that they were the children of Abraham, but those who were attached to the

Messiah as "the Lamb of God." (i) The significance of this term. Much has been written on the question as to what John meant by designating Jesus as the Lamb of God. We will not follow these speculations. No doubt his main thought was not that of the innocent, meek, and sinless character of Jesus, but that he was the world's sin-bearer. That he borrowed his imagery from the Old Testament is perfectly certain, and every one of those present would understand the reference. The paschal lamb of Egypt would no doubt at once suggest itself to them. The daily offering of the lamb for the trespass-offerings would also occur to them. The magnificent prophecy of Isaiah would be in the minds of all the intelligent persons present, in which, as sheep and lamb, Jesus is prophetically described as bearing the sins of many, and making intercession for the transgressors. (Is. liii, 5-12.) Whether John recited these and other Scriptures to the people is not clear, but most likely he did so. It is certain that this was from the beginning understood to be the meaning of the Baptist, if we may judge of the after-teachings of the apostles and the faith of the early Christians, and, indeed, of the Church in all subsequent ages. That John the Baptist here went straight to the central doctrine of the Atonement, there can be no doubt. Like Paul afterward, he was determined to know nothing among the people save Jesus and him crucified; for without this all his other teachings would be vain. What good to be baptized unto repentance unless there be a way of forgiveness and remission; and how can there be remission where there is no shedding of blood? And whose blood is sufficient to cleanse from all sin unless it be the blood of the Son of God? (Acts iii, 19; xiii, 38, 39; Heb. ix, 12, 22; Matt. xxvi, 28.) Jesus is the lamb whom God hath provided for sinners, and his work is to bear away their sins, not by example or by "moral influence," but in being wounded for their transgressions, bruised for their iniquities, suffering the chastisement of their peace, and healing them with his stripes (Is. liii): in fact, by being "made . . . to be sin for us." (II. Cor. v, 20, 21.) (ii) "Which taketh away the sin of the world." Jesus is said here not to bear the sins, but the *sin*, of the world. This does not refer to original sin, as some have supposed, by which he freed the world from the guilt of inherited sin, but it refers to the fact of the unity of sin in respect of the unity of the race. He deals with sin as such, seen in the whole race, making a sufficient expiation to cover sin and to redeem the whole race. So John says in his first Epistle: "And he is the propitiation for our sins: and not for ours only, but also for the sins of the whole world." (I. John ii, 2.) He may be the exclusive Messiah for the Jew, but he is the sin-bearer for the whole world. That is the truest preacher who grasps this great fact and makes it the central theme of his ministry among men. All other truth is only won in the light of this great truth.

2.—How John knew Jesus to be the world's sin-bearer.
—Having made this grand announcement, he proceeds to explain himself by telling the people that Jesus, who had now for a moment appeared in their midst, was the one of whom he had spoken yesterday. When Jesus had first come to him for baptism, he declared that he "knew him not" (that is, that he did not have a perfect knowledge of him). He only knew that he was sent to announce the Messiah, but did not know the full significance of this mission. He was made known to him in this respect by a sign which he had been previously taught to expect, the descent of the Holy Spirit visibly upon him. (ver. 33.) This was the sign that he was the Son of God. It is not improbable that, when Jesus presented himself for baptism, on which occasion John had shown such hesitation, Jesus had taken him apart and explained to him the whole mystery of his relation to the world as the Lamb of God as well as the Messiah of the Jews, and why and how he must "fulfill all righteousness," of which baptism was the most expressive symbol, namely, that of death and resurrection. Until this explanation, John truly did not know him, but now he knows him, and proclaims him in his central character of the world's Redeemer.

3.—"The Son of God."—He had formerly testified that Jesus was the Son of God; he now repeats that testimony. Nothing is more important to us than to know *who* Jesus is, as well as *what* he is. To be introduced to him as "the Lamb of God which taketh away the sin of the world," would be to leave faith in need of a sure foundation, unless besides his character of "the Lamb" there was the sure fact of his divine personality. For if it is not "possible that the blood of bulls and of goats should take away sins" (Heb. x, 4), it is equally impossible that the blood of any creature, especially of a man (no matter how exalted), could do that for us. "For all have sinned, and come short of the glory of God." And besides, "every man shall bear his own burden" of sin, and so one, who was bound to the penalty of his own, could not stand as substitute for another's sin, much less for that of the world. Nothing, therefore, short of the Son of God incarnate in human nature, and yet without sin, could do this for us. So we are taught to "behold the Lamb of God." (Read Heb. x.)

II.—THE FIRST DISCIPLES.

Until now, Jesus had not drawn to himself a single follower. He had taken upon himself the task for which he had come into the world by his formal presentation of himself to John for baptism. He had subjected himself to the first and grand ordeal of temptation by submitting himself to be tried of the devil in the wilderness. He had been formally introduced to men as the "Lamb of God which taketh away the sin of the world." Now, again, the next day he appears on the scene, not approaching John the Baptist, as on the former occasion, but quietly walking by. The narrative of the calling of the first disciples is a very touching and beautiful one.

1.—The model preacher.—In the Baptist we surely have the model preacher. (i) He is not afraid, first of all, to repeat his former discourse. Yesterday he had taken for his text "Jesus, the Lamb of God." It is good enough for him to take again, even on the very next day. Some preachers are afraid of "repeating themselves," and so they give a great variety of discourses called original, but it is simply a repetition of themselves every time. Whereas, a man who preaches Christ as the Lamb of God never repeats himself, for he does not preach himself, but Christ Jesus the Lord, and himself the servant of the people for Jesus' sake. (II. Cor. iv, 5.) (ii) He is not mindful either to make or retain disciples for himself. John had gathered many disciples about him. Among them stood two—Andrew and, without doubt, John, the author of this Gospel. They were choice young men, and had been enthusiastically attached to John. But John had taught them that he was not the Christ; indeed, nothing but a herald. He had told them of Jesus, the Lamb of God. Yesterday he had formally proclaimed him in their sight and hearing, telling them that he was the true object of their faith. Now Jesus appears again, and John, pointing him out a second time, seems to say, "There he is: follow him. Having pointed him out to you, you have no further need of me; and he having come, or passing by in your sight, it is not for you to stay with me, but go to him. He is your Lord as well as your Lamb." It is one of the sure signs of nobleness and consecration in a preacher when he seeks not disciples for himself, but for his Master. John ever declared of himself and Jesus, "He must increase, but I must decrease." What a grand example of this disinterestedness is seen in Paul, who could even wish himself accursed from Christ, if thereby he might win his brethren to Christ. (Rom. ix, 3.)

2.—Two model disciples.—The two disciples heard him speak, and they followed Jesus. Why others did not do so does not appear; but there are still many who profess interest in divine things, who, though they hear and see, do not follow Jesus. They are content to be the disciples of their minister, and stop there. Not so these two. They, no doubt, greatly admired John, and were sincerely attached to him; but they had heard him preaching Jesus to some purpose, and now they were ready to follow him. Note these characteristics of these model disciples. (i) They came to the knowledge of Jesus by faith; for when they heard John's testimony, they believed it concerning Jesus. "Faith cometh by hearing, and hearing by the Word of God." Though, indeed, they saw Jesus with their outward eyes, it was the inward eye of faith which saw in that outward man the Son of God and "Lamb of God." Just as men now, who hear the Word of God, see in Jesus him of whom the Word speaks. (ii) They followed him. It is not enough to hear and come to a speculative faith concerning Jesus, but, having heard, a real disciple at once seeks after or follows Jesus. "If any man will come after me, let him deny himself, and take up his cross, and follow me." (iii) They inquired of him, "Where dwellest thou?" This was their courteous way of intimating their wish to go with him, and to attach themselves to him. A dumb following of Jesus is not sufficient. The true disciple at once opens up personal communication, and seeks after personal relations with the Lord. They had heard from John the Baptist concerning him; now they wished for themselves *personally* to know him. Is not this the true discipleship? Listening to the testimony concerning Jesus, then turning to follow him; and then, by prayer, making personal acquaintance with him. (iv) They "abode with him." It is not only to believe on Jesus and to follow him, but to abide with him, that makes the best disciple. God has always taken those whom he has specially used apart to dwell with himself. Moses abode with God in the wilderness, Elijah abode with him in Horeb, Paul abode with him in Arabia, as John the Baptist did in the Jordan wilderness, Luther in the old Wartburg Castle, John Bunyan in Bedford jail, Madame Guyon in her prison, John Wesley (ostracized from the English University), and also scores of others. No doubt a man will learn more of "the secret of the Lord" by dwelling with him one day than he could gain by a lifetime of solitary study. Yet we must not suppose that only those may abide with Jesus who are shut off from the outward world. Abiding in Christ is the privilege of every believer, even while most busily engaged in the earthly calling wherewith he may be called.

3.—An attractive Saviour.—Jesus was passing by. He did not call these two men by any outward voice, but being lifted up to that faith by John the Baptist, who made him so lovely, as the Son and Lamb of God, "he drew them to himself" (i) by his person and office. When we know who Jesus is, the Son of God, and what he is, the Lamb of God, there is such beauty in him, such need of him, and such longing for him, that we cannot but follow after him. (ii) He was an observing Saviour, too, for he took notice of these two followers, and immediately turned to ask them, "What seek ye?" It is well to know what we seek Jesus for. They soon made it apparent *whom* and what they sought; they sought *him* as the Lamb of God, and they sought in him their salvation. If this be so with us, we too shall hear the same words from Jesus as these disciples did. (iii) "Where dwellest thou?" "Come and see." The secret dwelling-place of Christ is revealed to those, and to those only, who closely follow him. His dwelling-place is not in the visible Church; not in the creed of the Church; not in the forms of the Church; not even in the ordinances of the Church; but in that secret place which he shows to all those who follow him with a true heart. We cannot tell it to the world. That place of union and fellowship in which the believer dwells with Christ all may find who truly desire to "follow on to know the Lord."

III.—A BROTHER'S LOVE.

The true disciple drinks deep at the well of salvation that he may have to give out to others. The Gadarene demoniac went back to his own home to tell them of Jesus; the Samaritan woman went back to her own city and told all the men; Mary rose from the sepulchre whence Jesus had risen, and "fled" to the disciples to tell them the good news. Now, this is ever the first impulse of the truly converted man. He desires "to tell to others round what a dear Saviour he has found." In Andrew we find this prompt, quiet, loving impulse immediately developed.

1.—A brother's love.—Andrew's first thought was for his brother and partner in business. We are told that it is harder to speak to those of our own household of the things of Christ than to any one else. However that may be with those who have grown cold and whose lives at home have been inconsistent, it is not so with a newly converted soul. There is no fear in love, but a holy zeal. It is natural that our tenderest thought and desire should be for our own household. God has planted in us the love of kindred above all other love, and it is right that we should obey its instincts.

2.—A brother's message.—He first found Simon, and then told him that he had found the Messiah. What a find was that! Blessed is the man who has found the Christ, and blessed is the man who, having found Jesus, finds a sinner to tell him the good news and share his discovery with him. He did not tell Simon that he had found "religion," or "a happy experience," but that he had "found the Christ." Who has found *him* has found all in him.

3.—A brother's service.—"And he brought him to Jesus." This is still the way the Lord gathers his people. One saved sinner finds another and brings him to Jesus. So the four men brought the palsied one; so after that Philip brought Nathanael. No better service to Christ or to man than to find and bring sinners to him. If every sinner who has found Jesus should bring but one sinner to Christ in the course of a year, fifty years would see every sinner in this great world rejoicing in the Lord. And what a mighty work it was to bring Simon! Andrew was not one of the greatest disciples. He never wrote a gospel, nor even an epistle. He never founded a church. He was not a great preacher (if he ever preached at all). But he was a quiet, zealous winner of souls. He found Simon Peter, one of the greatest of the apostles, who afterward by one sermon won three thousand souls to Christ. So Andrew was a great preacher after all. It was Andrew who brought the little boy with the loaves and fishes to Jesus, and so helped to feed the multitude. It was Andrew to whom the Greeks came, saying, "Sir, we would see Jesus." There must have been something winsome about him, as well as quick and ready.

XXXIV.

THE FIRST MIRACLE OF JESUS.—John ii, 1-11.

(1) And the third day there was a marriage in Cana of Galilee; and the mother of Jesus was there: (2) And both Jesus was called, and his disciples, to the marriage. (3) And when they wanted wine, the mother of Jesus saith unto him, They have no wine. (4) Jesus saith unto her, Woman, what have I to do with thee? mine hour is not yet come. (5) His mother saith unto the servants, Whatsoever he saith unto you, do it. (6) And there were set there six waterpots of stone, after the manner of the purifying of the Jews, containing two or three firkins apiece. (7) Jesus saith unto them, Fill the waterpots with water. And they filled them up to the brim. (8) And he saith unto them, Draw out now, and bear unto the governor of the feast. And they bare it. (9) When the ruler of the feast had tasted the water that was made wine, and knew not whence it was: (but the servants which drew the water knew;) the governor of the feast called the bridegroom, (10) And saith unto him, Every man at the beginning doth set forth good wine; and when men have well drunk, then that which is worse: but thou hast kept the good wine until now. (11) This beginning of miracles did Jesus in Cana of Galilee, and manifested forth his glory; and his disciples believed on him.—John ii, 1-11.

John has shown Jesus to us as the "Eternal Word," as the "only begotten Son," as the "Son of God," as the "Lamb of God," as the "Son of man," as the "Ladder that unites heaven and earth," and as the "King of Israel." Now he introduces him to us as the divine-human-Saviour-Jesus, who "manifested forth his glory" in that he used his divine power for the comfort and happiness of the children of men. Though not of us as to his original nature, he becomes one of us; and though used to the presence and homage of the highest angels in the glorious abodes of light, he gladly and freely mingles as a guest, and even as a servant, with the lowliest of human beings. Surely in all this we begin to see the manifestations of his glory. The study before us to-day is crowded with suggestive and helpful lessons.

THE FIRST MIRACLE OF JESUS.

I.—JESUS AT THE WEDDING FEAST.

It was three days after his interview with Nathanael, that Jesus, with his five disciples and his mother, went to the wedding feast at Cana of Galilee, a little town in the hilly country, probably about sixty miles away from the scene of his baptism and the calling of these first disciples. How Jesus and they came to be bidden to this marriage feast does not appear. They were probably all friends of the bridegroom. It seems indeed certain that both Mary and Jesus were intimate with the family. Mary's quiet authority with the servants would indicate that she was well known and highly respected there. It may be that originally only Jesus and Mary were invited to the feast, and that he presumed on the custom of the country to bring the disciples with him, or secured invitations for them. This, however, is not material. The fact that Jesus was there, and that there he chose to work his first miracle, is the fact of importance and significance to us, from which we learn, among other lessons—

1.—**That Jesus was no ascetic.**—The first thought on reading this story is one of gladness at seeing our Lord, at the very beginning of his ministry, taking his place easily, familiarly, socially, nay, fraternally, among other men. John the Baptist was an ascetic from the beginning, and his disciples likewise. There was good reason for this. But "the Son of Man came eating and drinking," for he was, during all the time of his ministry, socially related to men. It was charged to him on this account that he was "a man gluttonous, and a wine-bibber"—a false charge, based on the blessed fact that he accepted readily the invitations of both rich and poor, high and low, Pharisees and publicans; and we may believe that he enjoyed more than one social gathering of friends at the house of Mary and Martha at Bethany. While he pursued his Father's business with unwearied diligence, he did so among men, always keeping in touch with them, and that in no austere way, but as their friend and companion. Always in touch with men, he was, in the truest and best sense of the word, "our brother." On the other hand, he never gave himself up to sociability for its own sake. He never lost sight, in the midst of social pleasures, of the fact that he was the Son and Servant of God. It was impossible to banish God or the thought of him, or conversation concerning divine things, wherever Jesus was found. That he took his disciples to this feast with him should teach us that it is not his will that we should withdraw from men and hold ourselves aloof from them in a gloomy or Pharisaic manner, but that, imitating him in this respect, we should be social with men, while true to God. The danger in our day is not that disciples will withdraw from the social scenes of life, but that, mingling with them, they will forget what Jesus *never* forgot, that he "must be about" his "Father's business."

2.—He sanctified the marriage relation with his presence. —He himself is "a bridegroom." It was meet that he should thus, at the beginning, while rejoicing over the finding of these first disciples, set his seal by his presence to that human institution ordained of God which is the parable of his relation to believers; for, says Paul, speaking of marriage, "This is a great mystery: but I speak concerning Christ and the Church." (Eph. v, 32.)

3.—No marriage is perfect without the presence of Jesus.—Let those, therefore, who enter into that state (and Jesus seems to encourage men to do so) never fail to invite him to be present, as their most honored guest and divine patron.

4.—Jesus sanctions innocent pleasures.—The Jewish marriage festivities sometimes spread over a whole week, and were the occasion of all social pleasures. We can scarcely conceive of Jesus attending a marriage feast during the last week of his earthly ministry, when the dark clouds of death and judgment were hanging over him, and when his soul was being pressed with the burden of human sin and sorrow. But now, at the beginning of his ministry, he enters easily and benignly into the pleasures of these happy young people, who are just beginning life under the most propitious circumstances. There comes a time in our lives when scenes of social conviviality are out of harmony with our spirits; but it is not for us, who have passed the halcyon days of youth, to look frowningly down upon those who are just stepping across the threshold of life. If we cannot partake with them in all their pleasures, let us sympathize with and sanctify them by our loving presence, and seek to furnish them with that better wine, even the wine of the kingdom, without which, perhaps, their good wine may degenerate, as it too commonly does, into the worse.

II.—JESUS AND HIS MOTHER.

Whether the feast had lasted longer than usual, or the company was larger than anticipated by the bridegroom, or his hospitality was larger than provisions made to grace it, we do not know; but on the arrival of Jesus and his disciples, probably toward the close of the feast (maybe the third or fourth day), it was discovered that the wine was exhausted. Mary, the mother of Jesus, had probably been there before him, and as soon as he arrived she stated this fact to the Lord. She either was expecting that on this his first appearance in public after his formal dedication of himself to his life-work, he would signalize it by working some sign, or else she desired it. She was his mother, and was anxious for some display of his power. She evidently knew already that to do signs and wonders would be a part of his work. His allusion to his "hour" seems to suggest this. She was, however, in part mistaken, though not wholly so. In answer to her hint (for it was not more than that), he seems to have rebuked her by the terms of his answer.

1.—Jesus' address to his mother.—It is common, to young people especially, to be surprised at the term which he used toward her. (i) "Woman." The term "woman" is not one of disrespect, nor was it so intended by Jesus. It is only so with those who have allowed this noble word to be abused, and made to mean something less and lower than it really does. Indeed, this term is the noblest one by which either wife, mother, or full-grown maid can be addressed. What can be nobler in this world than a true "woman"? Every true woman is a lady in the best sense of the word, but there are many "ladies," in the world's sense of that word, who are by no means true "women." When Jesus was on the cross, in the last hours of his agony, his filial thought and love turned toward his mother, and when he committed her to John's care he again used this term of high respect and endearment: "Woman, behold thy son." When we speak of our mothers, we do not say, "She was the best lady that ever lived," but "She was the best woman that ever lived." We are glad that Jesus sanctified, by his use of it to his mother, this noblest term by which we designate ours. (ii) "What have I to do with thee?" Here there seems something harsh, yet on Jesus' lips we can never conceive it to have been so. Hitherto he had been in complete subjection to his parents, and there never was so obedient a son on earth as Jesus. Now, however, the time was come when he assumed a different relation both to his mother and to the world. No longer were his actions to be guided by any human rule or authority. Presently, at a later period, Mary sought to interfere with his work and to call him away from some duty. Again Jesus reminds her that his relation to her was now changed. He was bound to all men. "Whosoever shall do the will of my Father which is in heaven, the same is my brother, and sister, and mother." (Matt. xii, 46–50.) From this hour Jesus knows no man and no woman after the flesh. Even now he first intimates that he draws away even from her in earthly authority (though never in his love). So must we come to know higher natural relationship than even our own flesh and blood. (II. Cor. v, 16.) (iii) "Mine hour is not yet come." This expression is to correct Mary's thought concerning the time when his full glory should be manifested. "My thoughts are not your thoughts, neither are your ways my ways." Understanding her desire, his thoughts fly away to the time, three years hence, when his "hour" would be upon him in all its fullness. (John xii, 27; xvii, 1.) Mary had pondered the things which the angel had told her, and was hoping that every occasion, even this first one, might be the time when his glory should be manifested forth in fullness, and Israel would see him as he was. But this was not his hour.

2.—**Mary's submission.**—If there was a touch of rebuke (though we cannot think there was) in his words, it was more suggestive of instruction than rebuke, and Mary accepted it quietly. As Luther says, "She nevertheless read 'yes' in his 'no,' and between the lines of his refusal she found, at least for herself, an assurance of the request granted." He would not now do what was in her thoughts as to himself, but he would do what she suggested in furnishing the guests with more wine. Though she was not to have all she hoped for, she nevertheless went quietly to work to prepare for the lesser gift. Our Lord is very gentle also with us. We make many petitions, we ask for many things which are not in harmony with his will, and yet no heart's desire ever went up to him that did not in some way bring back an answer. To the humble and trusting child of God there is a "yes" in every "no" that comes from him, and if the supreme hour which we desire is not yet, there will be an earnest of it in some lesser thing which God will do for us.

3.—**"Whatsoever he saith unto you, do it."**—Thus said Mary to the servants, anticipating that Jesus would work the miracle which he did immediately after. What a word is this for us, who are also his servants. By doing "whatsoever he saith" we become his "brother, and sister, and mother." It is delightful that One has come into the world who has the final authority for the direction of our lives, and to know that that authority is guided not only with infinite wisdom, but exercised in infinite love; and moreover, that "his commandments are not grievous." His "yoke is easy, and" his "burden is light." Let us lay these words of Mary to heart, for in them we find the secret of a happy, peaceful, and useful Christian life. By breaking up this sentence and laying emphasis on each word, we find a whole compendium of the Christian's law of life wrapped up in it. (i) "Whatsoever he saith unto you." He is our Master. (ii) "Whatsoever he saith unto you." Let us be sure that we have his word for the rule of our faith and conduct, and not some fancied spiritual impulse or foolish human wisdom to guide us, and which is most apt to lead astray. "If they speak not according to this word, there is no light in them." (iii) "Whatsoever he saith unto you." Let our obedience be marked in all things, and not only in some things. Does he bid us do or undertake a great thing? Let us undertake it with humility. Does he bid us do a small thing? Let us do it with alacrity and zeal, counting it an honor to serve him in the little thing as well as the great, just because it is his will. (iv) "Whatsoever he saith unto you, do it." Don't stop to think about it, and to debate whether it is worth while, or convenient, or agreeable, but do it! Do it promptly, do it freely, do it gladly, do it "as unto the Lord."

III.—JESUS AND THE MIRACLE.

Over this first miracle of Jesus there has been much discussion. All sorts of theories have been advanced by all sorts of theorists. Some hold it, as they do all other miracles, to be pure myth. Some rationalize it, and say that there was no real miracle, but that, by his influence over the guests, he made them believe that they were drinking wine, when, in fact, they were but drinking water; that, in fact, Jesus simply "hypnotized" them. Some urge that it was a mere trick, and there are many other theories. But how any one can seriously discuss this story in the light of the whole gospel and descend to these shifts, passes ordinary understanding. Jesus either did or did not work a miracle. If he did work the miracle, then he did just what the record says. If he did not work the miracle, then the record is false, and it is not worth while puzzling over the various possible explanations of what was or was not done.

1.—The water was made wine.—This is the simple statement of the apostle. The Lord seems to have guarded against any supposition of a trick by commanding that the firkins be filled to the brim, and then the servants were immediately commanded to "draw out." John again declares that the water was made wine. (John iv, 46.) The ruler of the feast recognized it as wine, and commended its quality. Whether it was fermented or unfermented wine is not the question now. It was wine, not spirits; not the vile poison that goes under that name and destroys men, but wine; that kind of wine that makes glad the heart of man (Ps. civ, 15); that kind of wine with which the prophet Isaiah (Is. lv) used to portray the goodness of the gospel, and which was as wholesome to man as the milk with which he associated it; such wine as our Lord used at the Last Supper with his disciples, only, if possible, it was better, as it came directly from the hands of the Creator, without even being filtered through the ordinary creation; better wine than was ever expressed by man from the best of grapes; better than the very best wine with which the bridegroom had regaled his guests at the beginning of the feast, when their palates were keen and sensitive as to quality; the wine which sets forth the grace of God; the wine of the kingdom given to his guests by the King himself. How he made it we do not know. It was by an act of his creative power. It was not a development out of water, but by the addition of something to the water, called up by the will of him by whom "all things were made, and without" whom "was not any thing made that was made." It is not necessary that we should know *how*. Out of his fullness, by an act of his power wine was made and of such high quality that it could not be compared to the best existing wines.

2.—There was an abundance of it.—Not only enough, but more than enough. Many gallons of it. So our God supplies our need. Perhaps Jesus was exercising that abundant benevolence which ever characterized him. He would even reimburse the kind, hospitable, but perhaps poor host who had invited him to this feast. We may be sure that, with Jesus in our house, our need will be supplied richly (Phil. iv, 19), and that we shall ever receive from him infinitely more than we have given or ever can give to him.

3.—Better than the best wine.—When this wine which Jesus had made was supplied to the governor of the feast (who knew nothing of the miracle, though the servants knew whence it had come), he at once detected its superior quality and flavor, and complimented the host on the exceeding riches of his hospitality. No complaint had been made of the quality of that which had been at first supplied to them according to custom, but here, out of the usual way, was the best wine reserved to the last of the feast. Is there not in this a lesson for us, that that which the world, or even nature, has to give us, is best at first and grows worst at last? The pleasures of youth finally degenerate, while they also degenerate us toward the close of life, if they be but the pleasures of this world. The way of the transgressor may at first be strewn with roses, but soon the roses fade, and nothing but the thorns remain for the weary feet to travel over. But God reserves his best to the last. His pathway "shineth more and more." The declining days of a sinner are usually miserable and hard, but the closing days of a Christian are soft and mellow, peaceful and happy. The best wine of life is the last that comes to him, and he looks gladly forward to even better still at "the marriage supper of the Lamb." Even the rulers of the feasts of this world have come to recognize that that which Jesus has given is the best. His coming into the world lightened it when it was very dark, and brought a new and sweeter life to those who were ready to perish from drinking the bitter dregs of that cup which the world had to give.

4.—**The materials and the instruments used.**—In working this miracle Jesus used water, but he cast into it something which was not in it before, and which could not be taken out of it. So in the salvation of our souls: he works on an existing personality and spiritual nature, but he casts into it eternal life, which he came to give, and to give abundantly. The unregenerated man is not made *another* man, but a *renewed* man, made so by that which comes to him from above. And note that in working this miracle he called "the servants" to his help. Jesus might have filled the empty firkins with water as easily as he turned the water into wine, but it pleased him to use men to help him. So in turning sinners into saints he calls upon us, his servants, to set them before him, and so to assist him in doing his blessed work. When he raised Lazarus he bade those who were standing by, "Take ye away the stone," though his word would have sent the stone flying away as easily as his word called back the soul into the body of the dead Lazarus.

5.—**Possible mystical significance.**—(i) Contrasting this miracle with the first miracle which Moses wrought, we see a suggestion of the two dispensations. Moses turned water into blood—a sign of the death which God was about to bring upon the people and the land of Egypt; but Jesus turned the water into wine—a type of the life and blessings which Jesus came to bring to us. "The law [death] was given by Moses; but grace and truth [life] came by Jesus Christ." (ii) This was one of the two creative miracles which Jesus wrought. It was early noticed by the Fathers of the Church that the two creative miracles of Jesus set forth the materials for the Eucharist. First, he turns water into wine, and after, he turns a few little loaves into a great supply of bread for the people. Jesus is both bread and wine for us, and in the eating of his flesh and the drinking of his blood we live.

IV.—MANIFESTING HIS GLORY.

At first this seems to be an extravagant characterization of this simple miracle, wrought in a little town in the poor district of Galilee, and among a few peasant people. It was not the full glory that was manifested forth, as he told his mother concerning "his hour" not yet come, but it was the beginning of that manifestation of his glory which would culminate at Calvary's cross. The first little shoot that springs up from the "corn of wheat" planted in the ground is not the full glory of the harvest, but the guarantee of it. In this miracle Jesus manifested forth his power, his goodness, his tender love, and his abundant fullness. So it was understood by his disciples, for they "believed on him." They had already believed on him, but now they believed on him again, and more than before. So with every new unfolding of the glory of Jesus to us in the Scriptures, and by the Spirit, we believe on him, and we believe on him again and again. Let us put these words together: "And of his fullness have all we received, and grace for grace." "For therein is the righteousness of God revealed from faith to faith." (John i, 16; Rom. i, 17.)

XXXV.

JESUS CLEANSING THE TEMPLE.—John ii, 13-25.

(13) And the Jews' passover was at hand, and Jesus went up to Jerusalem, (14) And found in the temple those that sold oxen and sheep and doves, and the changers of money sitting: (15) And when he had made a scourge of small cords, he drove them all out of the temple, and the sheep, and the oxen; and poured out the changers' money, and overthrew the tables; (16) And said unto them that sold doves, Take these things hence; make not my Father's house an house of merchandise. (17) And his disciples remembered that it was written, The zeal of thine house hath eaten me up. (18) Then answered the Jews and said unto him, What sign shewest thou unto us, seeing that thou doest these things? (19) Jesus answered and said unto them, Destroy this temple, and in three days I will raise it up. (20) Then said the Jews, Forty and six years was this temple in building, and wilt thou rear it up in three days? (21) But he spake of the temple of his body. (22) When therefore he was risen from the dead, his disciples remembered that he had said this unto them; and they believed the Scripture, and the word which Jesus had said. (23) Now when he was in Jerusalem at the passover, in the feast day, many believed in his name, when they saw the miracles which he did. (24) But Jesus did not commit himself unto them, because he knew all men, (25) And needed not that any should testify of man; for he knew what was in man.—John ii, 13-25.

After the peaceful and beautiful beginning of his work in Galilee in the little village of Cana, Jesus passed on and spent a few days in Capernaum. The season of the passover feast was at hand, and Jesus with his disciples went early up to the Holy City. Though Jesus' coming into the world was practically the closing of the old dispensation, it was not actually closed till after his resurrection. In the meantime he would faithfully fulfill all the ceremonial rites connected with the ancient typical worship. We have reason to believe that from the time of his twelfth year he had never missed a visit to Jerusalem on the occasion of this great feast. His first public entrance upon the scene of his testimony was at the passover feast, and his last gathering with his disciples was at the passover also. Thus did Christ our Passover identify himself with the feast that for centuries had been prophesying of him to the people, keeping in remembrance the great redemptive act of God in connection with the deliverance of his people from Egypt, and pointing through it to the great redemptive act of God by which he would deliver all people from the bondage, corruption, and guilt of sin.

I.—PURGING THE TEMPLE.

We have said that this was Jesus' first public appearance; and it was fitting that it should take place in the Temple, the central place of worship for the Jews and for all nations; for though the Temple was peculiarly the center of Jewish worship, yet it was from the beginning the center of worship for all nations. (Is. lvi, 7.) This fact was in a sense recognized by the Jews themselves, notwithstanding the intensity of their bigoted exclusiveness, in the fact that they had built a great court for the Gentiles, divided from the court of the Jewish people by "the middle wall of partition," beyond which they would not suffer a Gentile to come. It was in this court of the Gentiles that the events described in our lesson were enacted. The scene here described was the fulfillment and commentary in the first instance of the great prophecy of Malachi. (Mal. iii, 1–3.) How suddenly the Lord had come to his temple! How little they were prepared for his coming, though they were constantly professing to seek and desire it, and notwithstanding his messenger had already appeared and prepared the way for him by preaching repentance in the wilderness and publicly introducing him as "the Lamb of God." (John i, 29.) The coming of Jesus to the Temple at this time was the fulfillment of that other prophecy of Haggai. "The glory of this latter house shall be greater than of the former." (Hag. ii, 9.) The glory which Jesus brought to this Temple was not material but moral.

1.—**The desecration of the Temple.**—The great feast of the passover involved many sacrifices offered by the people—sacrifices of sheep, oxen, and doves, according to the ability of the offerers. It was inconvenient for them to drive their cattle and sheep from their distant homes, so they bought them after coming up to the city, as did the residents constantly visiting Jerusalem for purposes of worship. For the accommodation of these and all worshipers markets had been established where the necessary animals could be purchased. (John v, 2.) But now an abuse had grown up, and the court of the Gentiles had been partitioned off for the traders, for which they paid a rent to the reigning high-priest and his family, thus introducing a corrupt practice in connection with the Temple, and turning the Temple, which was only for worship, into a "house of merchandise." In addition to these traders there were greedy hordes of money-changers, who had their tables near by, to change larger sums into smaller ones and foreign or current coin into Temple money. In all this there was corrupt collusion between priests, traders, and money-changers. The selling of beasts and birds for sacrifice was legitimate and necessary; but to turn the Temple into a market-place, and make it a place of barter and gain, to the scandal of the worship of God, was a desecration which aroused all the honest and righteous indignation of Jesus. We are here taught a necessary lesson, viz., that however legitimate trade may be, and however necessary it may be to transact business in connection with the worship of God and the prosecution of the work of his kingdom, to make religion the cloak of covetousness and use the service of God as a sordid means of gain is desecration, and will not be tolerated by the Lord of the Temple or the great Head of the Church. This bears on all corrupt practices of high and low degree that have more or less in all ages fastened themselves on the Church of Christ. It is lawful for a minister to receive wages for his service (Luke x, 7), but to enter the ministry for the sake of the wages is a desecration. Indeed, to make use of religion as a means of gain at all is a desecration and profanation of God's holiness which will surely be required at our hands. Jesus characterized these things in burning words: "Make not my Father's house an house of merchandise;" and again: "My house is the house of prayer; but ye have made it a den of thieves." (Luke xix, 46.) This was not only an allusion to the general profanation of the Temple by turning it into a common market-place, but doubtless to the practice of extortion that was carried on in connection with the traffic, in which the traders took advantage of the necessities of the people to exact exorbitant sums for their wares.

2.—**Judgment beginning at the house of God.**—It was prophesied of Jesus that when he came to the Temple he would "purify the sons of Levi" "like a refiner's fire and like fullers' soap." (Mal. iii, 2, 3.) It was this greed of gain which had afflicted the entire priestly fraternity and made it impossible for them to "abide the day of his coming." The Jews were expecting and desiring—expecting because they desired—a temporal king under whose government they might again aggrandize themselves and build up an earthly estate; but Jesus came to them according to the Scriptures, as a mighty

Reformer, whose reign should be one of righteousness, and whose government should be of the spirit and not of the flesh. The natural man seeks after the things of the flesh always; but Jesus comes to purify us of all carnal and covetous lust and to build us up in righteousness and true holiness. This indeed is the burden of all the Scriptures. (Gen. xxxv, 2; Josh. iii, 5; vii, 13; so all the prophets; so Jesus, Matt. xv, 17-20; so the apostles, Gal. v, 19-23; Rom. viii, 5-10, etc.) The law of Christ's kingdom is that "judgment must begin at the house of God." (I. Pet. iv, 17.) So Jesus began his public ministry, not by miracle, not by proclaiming himself the Son of God, but by purging out the leaven of covetousness and extortion (corrupt selfishness) from the Temple. If we really desire Jesus to come and make his abode in us, we must be prepared to hear him say, "Take these things hence," and, more than that, we *must* take them hence; for if we live after the flesh we shall die, in spite of any profession of faith we may make. The hope of glory is also the hope of righteousness.

3.—The scourge of small cords.—The scene before us is so vividly described that it stands out with a sharpness in which every detail is manifest. Jesus suddenly stands in the midst of these hucksters and money-changers, accompanied by a few of his disciples. Lying on the floor are the remnants of the bark thongs or cords with which the sheep had been led or tethered. Without words or preliminary action Jesus picks up some of these fragments, and then, turning upon the traders, his whole soul stirred with the pent-up and accumulated indignation of years (for he had been a witness of these desecrations year after year, all his life), his eyes blazing with a strange and terrible fire, his hands uplifted as though to strike with the scourge, he drove them out, sheep, oxen, traders, money-changers, and all. Looking upon them, he charged them with desecration, quoting the words of Isaiah, "My house shall be called an house of prayer for all people" (Is. lvi, 7), and added, as on a later occasion, "Ye have made it a den of thieves." (Luke xix, 46.) There was an authority, a majesty, a look of such holy anger in the Lord's face that both men and beasts fled before him. Then Jesus, a look of scorn and wrath upon his face, overthrew the money-changers' tables, and scattered their coins upon the floor. It was a miniature judgment in which these sinners fled from the face and "the wrath of the Lamb." We are not told that he struck them with the scourge of cords, but just uplifted it as a sign of authority and a symbol of warning. They did not need to be beaten. Their own consciences, awakened by the presence of the Judge standing before them, scourged them instead. Indeed, the conscience of sinners is the best scourge a reformer can have, if only he can arouse it. And moreover, as they had furnished the scourge which Jesus used, so it shall be with all sinners—they shall be beaten with their own sins. Have we not often trembled before Jesus, who has stood over us as a Judge, and fled from him scourged by our sins which he has held up before us? There is but one salvation for sinners who are thus confronted by Jesus, and that is to flee to him and to fall at his feet and confess their sins.

> "To thee, whose blood can cleanse each spot,
> O Lamb of God, I come."

4.—Quickened memories.—"Then his disciples remembered that it was written, The zeal of thine house hath eaten me up." How many obscure Scriptures have been filled with light and meaning by Jesus, either in person, word, or deed. Jesus is indeed the light in which all Scripture must be understood. Without him the entire Old Testament is insufficient, and the great bulk of it absolutely meaningless; but with him it is plain, simple, and rationally intelligible and full of meaning. A knowledge of the letter of Scripture when standing with Jesus in full sympathy and fellowship with him, as these disciples did, fills the letter with life and makes it to be the instrument of our regeneration. (James i, 18; I. Pet. i, 22, 23.) The particular passage which was thus suddenly brought to their remembrance was first spoken of by David (Ps. lxix, 8, 9), but was clearly Messianic, and had its highest and only true fulfillment in Jesus, as can be seen by referring to it. So great was his zeal for God and his house, or his people and cause, it fairly consumed him—that is, it enlisted his whole being and called forth his entire energy. In Jesus we see the highest and only perfect type of consecration. This passage is the antithesis to that saying of his to his disciples on a later occasion: "My meat is to do the will of him that sent me, and to finish his work." (John iv, 34.) So also let these two Scriptures find a measurable fulfillment in us.

II.—THE CHALLENGE OF THE JEWS.

The report of this singular and tragic cleansing of the Temple came quickly to the ears of the Jews, that is, to the rulers (for such is John's invariable use of this term), and hurrying to the spot, they rallied the terrified traders and others standing by, and demanded of Jesus his authority for this singular and drastic work.

1.—"**What sign showest thou unto us?**"—The doing of the thing they did not challenge. This work of reform was so right, so in accordance with what even *they* must have admitted to be a true function of the Messiah, that they dared not challenge it. They did not attempt to justify the desecration, though they had allowed it and were sharing with the traders the spoils of the traffic. They were content to challenge the authority of Jesus, who assumed to do such a work. That they had heard of his advent, baptism, public announcement by John, and possibly of his visit to Galilee, there is little doubt. His sudden appearance in the Temple, and his boldness in assuming authority there, now brought them face to face with his claim to be the Messiah. This challenge they had a right to make; and this challenge Jesus met.

2.—"**Destroy this temple.**"—The spirit in which Jesus answered them, as well as the manner, was benignant though severe. He did not appeal to the Scriptures directly, or to anything in the past; nor did he do any mighty work to demonstrate his authority. He appeals to the future—to something which they would do and something which he would do. He might have appealed to the very act itself which was the ground of their challenge. That he had purged the Temple of these merchants and thieves was in itself a proof of his authority. The power to work a great reform is always the authority for doing it. But Jesus had done more; he had done it in the name of his Father. He said, "My Father's house." In this he asserted his Messianic right and relation. Moses had been faithful over the house of God (the people of God) as a servant, but Christ, as "a son over his own house" (his Father's house), had now assumed authority (Heb. iii, 1–8), and did "these things." They might have understood this if they had not already hardened their hearts against him; for they hated him because he had come to rebuke them for sin and selfishness as well as unfaithfulness, and to take away their place. Jesus, however, does not go back to this now that he was challenged, for he knew well that they would not heed this moral certificate of authority. He therefore said, "Destroy this temple, and in three days I will raise it up." It is supposed by some that at the time of this speech he pointed his finger to his own body; but this is doubtful. That he spoke of his body is certain. That the Jews possibly understood the reference is suggested by the fact that they afterward remembered that he had said, "After three days I will rise again." (Matt. xxvii, 63.) They must have referred to this declaration, for Jesus had never in any other way announced to them his resurrection. The exactness with which they quoted his words to Pilate is almost sure proof that this was the word or saying they referred to. The taunts of the passing priests (Matt. xxvii, 40-43) also go to show that this saying had sunk into their hearts, and more deeply than into the disciples' hearts, for it was not till after his resurrection (ver. 22) that they recalled this and other sayings to the same effect, spoken to them privately. The spirit of guilt and enmity is often of quicker perception than that of love.

3.—"I will raise it up."—In this saying Jesus asserts his own power over life and death. He does not say, "My Father will raise me up," but "I will raise it up." He "is the resurrection and the life." Death could not hold him, for he was and is the Master of death. He foresaw and knew what they would do to him, and thus early he charges and warns them of the crime already beginning to be contemplated by them against himself. In all this there is an infinite compassion manifested; for by this parable of the Temple, Jesus sought to put them on their guard against the crime then suggested in their hearts. Jesus never allowed his enemies to abide in the darkness, but always exposed them and their motives to themselves, that if they persisted in sin they must do it with their eyes open, and thus be without excuse when they came to reap the consequences. Warning and entreaty always go before judgment. This is as true to-day as it was then, and ever will be.

4.—The Jews harden their hearts.—Catching his meaning expressed in this parable, their quick hatred led them to affect a bald literalism which they would turn against him even then. Two things occurred to them. First, that they might turn this saying into ridicule by simply intimating its absurdity from the point of a literal application of his words. It could only be the ravings of a madman who would pretend that he could reconstruct in three days the Temple that had been forty and six years in building. The people would see this, and at once repudiate his claims. Second, they saw here a chance to turn his words into blasphemy, and thus give them cause against him by which they could destroy him. As a matter of fact it was on this trumped-up charge based on a deliberate perversion of his meaning that they suborned witnesses to testify. (Matt. xxvi, 61.) The willful misunderstanding of the Word of God, the willful hardening of the heart against Jesus Christ, is the dreadful danger to which men expose themselves who are set to continue in sinful ways. It is especially against this sin that we are warned in Hebrews iii, 7, 8. It was this willful misunderstanding of Jesus which led to their utter blindness later on, and left them to doom.

III.—SUPERFICIAL DISCIPLES.

On the feast day Jesus continued to teach the people and did many miracles, most likely simple miracles of healing. The result of this day's work was that a multitude of people proclaimed their belief in Jesus. "Many believed in his name, when they saw the miracles which he did." "But Jesus did not commit himself unto them"—that is, he did not trust them, for he saw how superficial and unreal their attachment was. It was not because of his teaching, not because they perceived his moral glory or were awakened to a real hunger and thirst after righteousness. It was a mere fanatical enthusiasm caused by his wonderful works. There are always those who are carried away by popular movements, by signs and wonders, who have no real appreciation of the real work or meaning of the mission which is attested by these outward signs of power. Jesus was safeguarded from these superficial believers by three facts.

1.—"He knew all men."—Jesus, who is Lord of all, knows all men. There are none so wise but that he can fathom their deepest thoughts. There are none so densely ignorant but that he can pierce through their mental darkness or obtuseness. Naked and exposed unto the eyes of him are even the secret thoughts of all men, and there is no "creature that is not manifest in his sight." (Heb. iv, 12, 13.) Blessed Saviour! that knoweth our hearts and can search out and cleanse our sins. Awful Judge! before whom we must stand if we have not come to him as Saviour.

2.—"And needed not that any should testify of man."—We are largely dependent upon the testimony of others for our knowledge of men; but Jesus has no such need.

3.—"He knew what was in man."—We know what men do and how they appear; but Jesus knows what is in each man. We take knowledge of deeds; he, of thoughts and motives. These superficial disciples could not deceive him. So neither can we, by formal, false, or even superficial professions of faith. We may deceive ourselves and others, but we cannot deceive him. If we really commit ourselves to him, he will commit himself to us. But there can be no union between Christ and a sinner without truth and sincerity.

XXXVI.

JESUS AND NICODEMUS.—John iii, 1-16.

(1) There was a man of the Pharisees, named Nicodemus, a ruler of the Jews: (2) The same came to Jesus by night, and said unto him, Rabbi, we know that thou art a teacher come from God: for no man can do these miracles that thou doest, except God be with him. (3) Jesus answered and said unto him, Verily, verily, I say unto thee, Except a man be born again, he cannot see the kingdom of God. (4) Nicodemus saith unto him, How can a man be born when he is old? can he enter the second time into his mother's womb, and be born? (5) Jesus answered, Verily, verily, I say unto thee, Except a man be born of water and of the Spirit, he cannot enter into the kingdom of God. (6) That which is born of the flesh is flesh; and that which is born of the Spirit is spirit. (7) Marvel not that I said unto thee, Ye must be born again. (8) The wind bloweth where it listeth, and thou hearest the sound thereof, but canst not tell whence it cometh, and whither it goeth: so is every one that is born of the Spirit. (9) Nicodemus answered and said unto him, How can these things be? (10) Jesus answered and said unto him, Art thou a master of Israel, and knowest not these things? (11) Verily, verily, I say unto thee, We speak that we do know, and testify that we have seen; and ye receive not our witness. (12) If I have told you earthly things, and ye believe not, how shall ye believe, if I tell you of heavenly things? (13) And no man hath ascended up to heaven, but he that came down from heaven, even the Son of man which is in heaven. (14) And as Moses lifted up the serpent in the wilderness, even so must the Son of man be lifted up: (15) That whosoever believeth in him should not perish, but have eternal life. (16) For God so loved the world, that he gave his only begotten Son, that whosoever believeth in him should not perish, but have everlasting life.—John iii, 1-16.

In our first study from this gospel we were embarrassed by the greatness and importance of the subject-matter handled by the Evangelist; and no wonder, since it had to do with the birth of the "Eternal Word" into the natural world. We are confronted in this study with a difficulty of almost the same kind and degree, for here we have to do with the birth of a human soul into the spiritual world. For our redemption Jesus became flesh, and for our salvation we must become spirit. For our redemption he took hold of our human nature; for our salvation it is necessary for us to be made partakers of the divine nature. God appeared among men by the incarnation; man only can appear before God by a new birth. John anticipates this address of Jesus to Nicodemus by his reference to the fact of the new birth in connection with those who received Jesus as the Incarnate Son of God. (i, 12, 13.) But space does not allow for preliminary observations, and, at best, we must be satisfied with the merest outline here, where every verse affords matter for a complete study.

I.—CONCERNING NICODEMUS.

The presence of Jesus in Jerusalem, and especially the excitement produced among the rulers of the Jews consequent upon the purging of the Temple, together with his increasing fame as a teacher and worker of miracles, which had reached Jerusalem from the hill country where Jesus had been, led to this famous interview. Nicodemus, with others, had been in discussion over the matter, and he, at least, determined (whether his purpose was known to others or not is not clear) to satisfy himself concerning Jesus by a face-to-face interview. Without going into too minute particulars, we shall treat Nicodemus as a typical man, and get our lessons from this point of view.

1.—**Who he was.**—(i) He was a man. Besides his religious opinions, his social and ecclesiastical position, and his moral character, he was simply a man born of a woman, and one of the fallen race of Adam. We must remember that fundamentally the revelation of God's law and grace has to do with men as such, and not with any special class or degree of sinners. Whatever else we are, common or noble, rich or poor, official or private individuals, cultured or ignorant, gifted with genius or merely mediocre people, we are each one of us but men, and as such God deals with us, and we must deal with him. Jesus died for every man, and God commands all men everywhere to repent. In this great matter God is no respecter of persons, for "all have sinned and come short of the glory of God." If only this truth could be gotten into the heads and consciences of sinners, how it would simplify things for them! The poor, obscure, or desperately wicked man would not feel himself to be specially outcast from grace; and the rich, the mighty, and the outwardly moral would not esteem themselves on this account to be specially exempt from the necessities of grace. (ii) He was a Pharisee—that is, as to his religious convictions and practice he was one of the strictest men. Religion was the main thing in his life. It was his constant endeavor to keep himself approved of God and separate and undefiled from all contact with "sinners." We should keep this fact in mind, in view of what follows. To him the Jewish Church, its ordinances and rites, was the sum and substance of all religion. As the Pantheist confuses and confounds God with all creation, so the Pharisee confused and confounded God with the visible Church and its rites and ceremonies. (iii) He was a ruler of the Jews—that is, a master or teacher of Israel. He was more than an ordinary Pharisee; he was officially a representative of "the theocracy," and one who exercised religious authority among and over his people. Thus he was an exalted personage, and supposed to have been clothed with, or possessed of, special sanctity and knowledge of God. Yet bear in mind that it was to this man that Jesus addressed his tremendous declaration, "Ye must be born again."

2.—**What he was.**—We have referred to his personality and position among men. Now we must point out his character as a man. So far as we can make out from the few details we have in the Scriptures, we feel warranted in saying that he was (i) a good man. By this we do not mean absolutely good, but relatively so, as compared with other men. He was moral, upright, and given to no gross acts of sin. Perhaps he could say, with one of his contemporaries, that he was free from the common sins of men (Luke xviii, 10, 11), especially those sins which often characterized "publicans and sinners." He was moral and religious rather than immoral and profane: he was what a respectable churchman is as compared with what an ordinary unbeliever is. (ii) That he was quite sincere his subsequent life proves, for we find that he so far yielded himself to the teachings of Jesus as to become a true disciple; this he could not have done if he had not been sincere. (iii) He was an earnest man. This is evident by the fact that he took the trouble to come to Jesus for instruction. (iv) He was a timid and cautious man; we will not say "a coward," as some do, for his subsequent actions testify to the contrary. (vii, 50; xix, 39.)

3.—**What he did.**—This man came to Jesus by night to interview him with respect to his mission. He so far recognized him as a teacher as to address him as "Rabbi." Jesus was reported to be the Messiah. John the Baptist had so designated him, and his disciples believed and received him as such, but Nicodemus was not ready to go so far. He also acknowledged that his right to teach was based on admitted great works done by him. His caution is remarked in this admission. He will deal fairly with Jesus, but will not accept him as Messiah without being further satisfied. So far all is right, and we believe Jesus at once recognized in him a sincere inquirer, and not a disguised enemy. When a sincere inquirer comes to Jesus he will not be cast out, and his difficulties will be fairly and patiently dealt with.

II.—THE NEW BIRTH.

Jesus at once saw and measured the man before him. He had come not only to get information, and possibly teaching, but probably with a view to examining Jesus. Jesus promptly brings him to a point beyond his thought or purpose, by abruptly breaking in upon his courteous address: "Verily, verily, I say unto thee, Except a man be born again, he cannot see the kingdom of God." By this he at once sets before him that it is not teaching which he needs, but the ability to understand teaching. Not more light, but sight. Further, he says that, so far as the kingdom of God is concerned, there is a necessity for qualification before it can be entered into. He thus lifts the question of the kingdom of God and man's relation to it out of the temporal into the spiritual realm. Nicodemus's thought was: "This young teacher claims to be the Messiah; I will question him and get his ideas as to what the kingdom of God is, and upon what grounds he claims to be the Messiah." Jesus, instead, informs him that his thoughts are all wrong, and instead of being a special favorite of God, he is so far from the kingdom that in his present condition he can neither see it nor enter into it. This, indeed, is the state in which all men are by nature.

1.—The universal necessity of the new birth.—This Jesus states in his words "except" and "ye must be." The kingdom of God is not for natural men, but spiritual men, and therefore a new birth or a spiritual birth is necessary. Natural birth introduces men into this world, and so a spiritual birth is essential to an introduction into the kingdom of God, which is not of this world, though in it. "That which is born of the flesh is flesh; and that which is born of the Spirit is spirit." Here is the whole matter in a nutshell. All men are but flesh as to their present condition, and so all men must be born again. The disqualification for heaven is not in some specially gross transgression of the law, but in the fact of a carnal and sinful nature which is common to all. Comparing one man with another, we do not say one is good and the other is bad, but only one is bad and another is worse. All are bad, but some are worse, and "none is good, save one, that is, God." Therefore, Nicodemus, take your place along with the "publican and sinner," and know that you, too, must be born again as well as they. At the bottom of their being, they lack spiritual sight and qualifications, and so do you, for you are naught but a man "shapen in iniquity and in sin . . . conceived," and no amount of mere religious knowledge and moral improvement, or ecclesiastical relation, can alter the fact of your nature.

2.—**What is the new birth?**—Manifestly it is not knowledge, for a man must be born again before he can "see" or know the kingdom of God. It is not religious improvement or reformation, for "that which is born of the flesh is flesh." It is not, as Nicodemus suggested, a second birth, but a different birth. It is not baptism or submission to ordinances, for baptism is something entirely different from the new birth, and not identical with it. If the reference here is to baptism, Jesus would remind him that John had clearly taught that, while he baptized with water, there was One who baptized with the Holy Ghost. Then what is the new birth? (i) It is something that comes from above. It is not a potency in us to be developed by any process, but a gift shed on us abundantly by the Holy Ghost. (Titus iii, 3-6.) For men are not born again by descent from man, or by the energy of the flesh itself, nor by the favor of man (John i, 13), but by the grace, energy, and favor of God. (ii) It is an entirely new creation. (II. Cor. v, 17.) In conferring the new birth upon us, God does not simply energize the old man by bestowing upon it new power. He introduces into us something entirely new. Man by nature is as dead and incapable of seeing and entering into the kingdom of God, or into living communion with God, until he is born again, as a blind and deaf mute is incapable of seeing and enjoying the material creation. We do not attempt to describe or define the new birth beyond this, that it is "a new creature," amounting to the gift of eternal life which Jesus comes to confer upon man. Perhaps it is just God himself coming into the soul of man (originally created with capacity for him), and taking possession of his own, and giving expression to his own life in and through man. Perhaps it is another incarnation repeated over and over again in every individual who surrenders himself to God to be his habitation. As the Holy Ghost overshadowed the Virgin Mother and Jesus was conceived in her, so, perhaps, the new birth is just Jesus Christ formed in us, "the hope of glory," by the overshadowing of the same Holy Spirit. (Col. i, 27.) Here we want volumes in which to write rather than a single page, and so must leave the matter, or this part of it, with this single suggestion: God was revealed *to* us by the incarnation of Jesus, and he is revealed *in* us by the new birth.

3.—"**How can these things be?**"—Here is the proof of the fact that Nicodemus needed a new birth: "The natural man receiveth not the things of the Spirit of God: . . . neither can he know them, for they are spiritually discerned." He could not see, much less could he enter in. When Jesus spoke of the new birth, Nicodemus at once thought of being born a second time, by entering "the second time into his mother's womb," and he could not see how that could be done, especially by an old man. What blindness! What stupidity! A ruler of Israel, and he did not know that the natural man could not inherit the kingdom of God! How carnal he was! With what carnal eyes had he studied the Scriptures! He was essentially a materialist in religion, and a materialist always asks "How?" Then Jesus tells him plainly that he utterly misconceives, and again says, "Ye must be born again." Jesus seems by a parable to explain that the operations of the Holy Ghost are as mysterious as to the "how" of them to the knowledge of man, as the operation of the wind is to our senses. We note the effects of the wind in its sound, but cannot tell by that "whence it cometh, and whither it goeth." A thing is not impossible or incredible because we do not understand how it is done. It is as much folly to stand out against this great truth because of our inability to explain the mystery underlying it as it would for a sailor to refuse to trim his sails to the wind because he did not know "whence it cometh, and whither it goeth." The wind is, no doubt, directed and controlled by law, and is not capricious, as it may seem to be to the unintelligent; so, though we may not understand the law of the Spirit's operation, it is never capricious or arbitrary. But if it is impossible to understand these "earthly things," how shall one hope to understand these "heavenly things"? Or, perhaps, Jesus may have meant, too: "If you have failed to understand the nature of the Messianic kingdom on the earth, that is to be composed of spiritual men, and not merely descendants of Abraham, how may I hope to explain to you the profounder truth of the operation of the Holy Spirit in creating spiritual men? If, being a master in Israel, you have not understood that there must be a new birth, how can you understand how that new birth is accomplished?" Here Jesus asserts his perfect and intimate knowledge of all mysteries as being at their source; naturally, no man can understand these things save one who is in heaven, and as for him, he is in heaven (though for the present he was on the earth). When you become a spiritual man, and so are a heavenly man, then you will understand, and not till then. No man can understand the mystery of the new birth till he himself is born again. The only way of knowing what the taste of a fruit is, is to taste it. So Jesus proceeds to give Nicodemus practical instruction as to how to be born again.

III.—THE NEW BIRTH IN RELATION TO THE ATONEMENT.

Turning the attention of Nicodemus away from a mere fruitless discussion of these mysteries, Jesus proceeds to open the way to the new birth by showing him the relation which he himself held to it, and how he was the way to it for every sinner.

1.—The uplifted serpent.—Here is a well-known fact, one upon which both Jesus and his inquirer could meet as on common ground. The children of Israel were dying under the poisonous bites of "fiery serpents." In their extremity God directed Moses to make an image of one of these, and to lift it high upon a pole in the midst of the camp, and then make proclamation to all Israel, that whosoever would look to it should be healed of the plague of the serpent's bite. As a matter of fact, those who looked toward it on the faith of that proclamation were healed, while those who refused and struggled to overcome the deadly bite themselves, perished. Now, as to how the healing was accomplished, the only answer is that "God healed them according to his word." Here was a mysterious process in connection with a practical well-known fact. The saving object was set before their eyes, they looked, and God's power went forth to heal in that connection. This, we may suppose, Nicodemus would readily admit, and with this for a practical starting-point Jesus refers now to his own relation to the healing of sinful souls.

2.—The Son of man lifted up.—That Jesus makes the brazen serpent of Moses a type of himself as a Saviour for men, goes without saying. By this typical parable Jesus teaches Nicodemus several most important things: (i) That he was the object of the Old Testament types. (ii) That whatever the Messiah was to the Jewish people with respect to a temporal kingdom, he was also the Saviour of all in respect to their sin. (iii) That there is a close, necessary, and vital relation between the new birth and the atonement which he came into the world to make, for there can be no doubt that Jesus alluded to his sacrifice on the cross when he said,

"So must the Son of man be lifted up." That relation is simply this: Man, as a sinner, must either die in his sins, as the bitten Israelites died of the serpents' poison, or he must be saved by the interposition of one who stands for him. Sin is guilty and must be punished. The death of Christ for us on the cross expiates our sin, whereof God has given us witness by his resurrection from the dead. But the death of Christ, even though it is an expiation of sin, is not sufficient to heal the disease of sin within us. Healing must actually pass on to the sinner for whom Jesus has died. Therefore we "must be born again." Here these two "musts" come together. Jesus "must" be lifted up to expiate our sin, and we "must" be born again in order to escape the punishment. (iv) That faith in Christ is the means by which we avail ourselves of the benefits of his sacrificial death and justifying resurrection. For as the bitten Israelites must needs look toward the serpent and rest their eyes upon it, so must we believe in Jesus Christ, the crucified Son of God, who became man for us that he might put away our sin. That the way to the new birth is by Jesus Christ is apparent from all the Scriptures, but we refer to two passages in particular—John i, 12, 13; Titus iii, 5, 6. John tells us that "as many as received him . . . were born" again; and Paul tells us that the "washing of regeneration and the renewing of the Holy Ghost" is "shed on us abundantly through Jesus Christ." (v) That eternal life, which is "the gift of God . . . through our Lord Jesus Christ," is identical with the new birth, or at least is at the foundation of it. For, says Jesus in his application of this parabolic type, as they looked and lived in the wilderness, so "whosoever believeth in him should not perish, but have everlasting life."

XXXVII.

JESUS AT JACOB'S WELL.—John iv, 5-26.

(5) Then cometh he to a city of Samaria, which is called Sychar, near to the parcel of ground that Jacob gave to his son Joseph. (6) Now Jacob's well was there. Jesus therefore, being wearied with his journey, sat thus on the well: and it was about the sixth hour. (7) There cometh a woman of Samaria to draw water: Jesus saith unto her, Give me to drink. (8) (For his disciples were gone away unto the city to buy meat.) (9) Then saith the woman of Samaria unto him. How is it that thou, being a Jew, askest drink of me, which am a woman of Samaria? for the Jews have no dealings with the Samaritans. (10) Jesus answered and said unto her, If thou knewest the gift of God, and who it is that saith to thee, Give me to drink; thou wouldest have asked of him, and he would have given thee living water. (11) The woman saith unto him, Sir, thou hast nothing to draw with, and the well is deep: from whence then hast thou that living water? (12) Art thou greater than our father Jacob, which gave us the well, and drank thereof himself, and his children, and his cattle? (13) Jesus answered and said unto her, Whosoever drinketh of this water shall thirst again: (14) But whosoever drinketh of the water that I shall give him shall never thirst; but the water that I shall give him shall be in him a well of water springing up into everlasting life. (15) The woman saith unto him, Sir, give me this water, that I thirst not, neither come hither to draw. (16) Jesus saith unto her, Go, call thy husband, and come hither. (17) The woman answered and said, I have no husband. Jesus said unto her, Thou hast well said, I have no husband: (18) For thou hast had five husbands; and he whom thou now hast is not thy husband: in that saidst thou truly. (19) The woman saith unto him, Sir, I perceive that thou art a prophet. (20) Our fathers worshipped in this mountain; and ye say, that in Jerusalem is the place where men ought to worship. (21) Jesus saith unto her, Woman, believe me, the hour cometh, when ye shall neither in this mountain, nor yet at Jerusalem, worship the Father. (22) Ye worship ye know not what: we know what we worship; for salvation is of the Jews. (23) But the hour cometh, and now is, when the true worshippers shall worship the Father in spirit and in truth: for the Father seeketh such to worship him. (24) God is a Spirit: and they that worship him must worship him in spirit and in truth. (25) The woman saith unto him, I know that Messias cometh, which is called Christ: when he is come, he will tell us all things. (26) Jesus saith unto her, I that speak unto thee am he.—John iv, 5-26.

In our present study we have an incident, recorded only by John, so deeply interesting that we must account it one of the most precious records in all the New Testament. Jesus is still "making disciples"; and these records of his method and grace, preserved to us by the Holy Spirit, have been the means of making thousands more through all the centuries since. John and Philip, Andrew and Simon, Nathanael and Nicodemus, had been won to Jesus, and others besides, and now he adds to the number a poor, nameless, sinful woman, who, in her turn, brings all the men of the village to hear him, who, when they hear, believe also. It is most interesting, indeed, to turn from the consideration of the conversation between Jesus and the learned ruler of the Jews to this interview between him and this Samaritan woman. John the Baptist had now been put in prison; the fame of Jesus was rising and growing, and his disciples were making more converts to him than John had done. The Jews were becoming uneasy, and Jesus foresaw that to stay in Judea any longer would but imperil his life and the cause which he came to represent and secure. He will be ready to die when his hour comes, but in the meantime he will be as careful of his life as then he will be ready to lay it down. He determines to return to Galilee, and in so doing "must needs go through Samaria," as that was the shortest, most convenient, and usually traveled way. Contrary to custom and to the bigoted prejudices of the Jews, when he arrives at a little Samaritan village, instead of pressing on through it, he stops by the well-side, and sends the disciples into the town to buy food. It was while they were gone on that errand that he met the woman who, with himself, is the subject of our study.

I.—JESUS AND THE WOMAN.

It would be difficult to group two persons so utterly removed from each other, and at the same time so closely bound together, as Jesus and this woman, as does the evangelist who records what took place by that historic well. But does not this same grouping occur whenever any sinner is converted to God? Were we not so brought together with Jesus when we met him first by the well of salvation?

1.—The divine-human Saviour.—It is not the divinity that appears to the eye of sense, but the humanity of Jesus. Can we picture to ourselves the Eternal Word who was made flesh for us— so poor that he journeyed on foot from Jerusalem up to the hill country, and so footsore and weary with the walk on that hot Eastern day that he sits all alone on the well-curb of a poor little Samaritan town and asks a drink of water from one of the most abandoned women of the town. And this is what we see. "Jesus therefore, being wearied with his journey, sat thus on the well." It was high noon, and the hot Eastern sun was striking his vertical javelins down upon the head of the Creator. What a picture of the voluntary humiliation of the Son of God is this! What gracious condescension is here! How our hearts ought to thrill at the remembrance that such was the love of God toward us sinners, and such was the Saviour who was sent into the world to reveal that love, and by it to bring us back to himself! How really he became bone of our bone and flesh of our flesh! Had he appeared by the well-side in the dazzling glory of the archangel, the woman would have fled, not daring to approach. But he comes to her as a man, as he comes to us, accessible by reason of his human kinship. "For we have not a high-priest which cannot be touched with the feeling of our infirmities; but was in all points tempted like as we are, yet without sin." (Heb. iv, 15.) Behold the Man! Yes, in all points he was touched with the sense of human infirmity. He wearied, he hungered, he thirsted, he slept, he wept, he rejoiced, he sorrowed, he sighed, he was angered, he compassionated, he marveled, he was tempted *in all points* like his brethren, yet without sin. Such, thanks be to God, is the Saviour who was sent, and who delighted to come, to seek us and bring us back to God.

2.—**The sinner.**—Now look at the other person, his companion at the well. (i) *She was a woman.* The Jews did not think it worth while to teach women, but Jesus saw in a woman a soul as precious to his Father and himself as was the soul of the master in Israel to whom he had, a little before, taught the mysteries of the kingdom of God. With him there is neither male nor female, but human beings whom God loves, and for whom he came to die and rise again. (ii) *She was a Samaritan.* The Samaritans were a mongrel race, made up of five heathen nations sent by the king of Babylon to occupy the land after he had carried the Israelites away captive. They intermarried with the poorest of the people (Jews), who alone were left, and mixed up their idol worship with that of Jehovah. In after-years they adopted the five books of Moses as the basis of their worship, and claimed Jacob and Abraham as their ancestors. The Jews (post-exile) held them in supreme contempt, hated them worse than they did the Gentiles, and had "no dealings with" them whatever. But here again Jesus rises above Jewish prejudice and fanatical hatred. Even a Samaritan was a human being, and one for whom he came to die. He would not pass *one* by who came in his way while journeying through the land. He is "the Saviour of all men." (iii) *She was a poor woman.* Not a Rebecca, the daughter of a chieftain, but a poor woman. For at this time it was not common for women of rank and position to go to the wells to draw water; only the poorest of women or servants did this. But Jesus is the Saviour of the slave as well as of the master, and came to save the poorest. With him "there is no respect of persons." In Christ there is neither rich nor poor, "bond nor free." (iv) *She was a sinful woman.* So sinful, indeed, as to be shunned even by the commonest and poorest of her sex. For hours before, at early morning, the respectable women of the city had been out to get their daily supply of water. This woman did not venture in their company, but now comes alone in the noonday heat, when she would meet none of them. Moreover, the Saviour knew her character, how fallen and how depraved she was. Yet he does not turn away from her in disdain, but all the more eagerly presses upon her the gift which he came to bestow, and which she so much needed. "Jesus came into the world to save sinners," and "not to call the righteous, but sinners to repentance." She was a sinner! The disciples would have passed her by without a word, though they were sinners themselves. Jesus did not pass *her* by, and he will not pass you by.

II.—THE MISSION OF JESUS.

Jesus loses no time in opening up to her the message and mission he has for and toward her. By asking her for a drink of water, and this in tones and manner of courtesy and kindness, he awakens an interest in himself. He at least was not moved by the bitter prejudices which she had been wont to encounter in other Jews. Her expression of surprise that he, being a Jew, should ask her, a Samaritan, for a draught of water, drew from him the remark, "If thou knewest the gift of God, and who it is that saith to thee, Give me to drink; thou wouldest have asked of him, and he would have given thee living water." In this answer of Jesus to the woman we have opened to us his mission to this world of sinners.

1.—**To communicate the gift of God.**—That is, to bring living water to thirsty and dying souls. Under this figure of living water Jesus sets forth that gift of God which is eternal life, and which is administered to us by the Spirit, and which, when received by us, is true spiritual life. (John x, 28; iii, 15, 16, 36; vii, 37-39; Rom. vi, 23.) Notice these particulars concerning what Jesus has to bestow on us: (i) *It is a gift.* Salvation is not something which a man has in his own power, nor is it an evolution from his own nature. It is not something which he can work out for himself; it is not something which comes to him as a reward; but it is a gift pure and simple, and is bestowed freely upon sinners, irrespective of their merit or ability. (ii) *It is a divine gift.* It comes not from man to man. (John i, 13.) He says, "Whosoever drinketh of the water that *I* shall give him shall never thirst." In the conclusion of his conversation he tells her plainly that he is the Messiah (whom all believed to be Jehovah himself), who should come into the world as the Saviour of sinners. It is the gift of God. (iii) *It is a gift of life.* Man by nature and sin is without spiritual life. By sin he is dead, but Jesus came that we might have life. "You hath he quickened, who were dead in trespasses and sins." A closer study of this matter reveals the fact that the life which Jesus pressed upon this sinner was the same which he pressed upon Nicodemus. It was only another way of preaching the new birth to her. The new birth was a birth of the Spirit from above. This water of life also comes from above from the same source. (iv) *It was an inward and upspringing life;* not a mere outward effort, or a spasmodic movement of the old life under an outward impulse, but a well of water opened within, which, like a living spring, bursts through all resistance, and comes up to the surface, living, flowing, and springing up toward God. The possession of this gift distinguishes a Christian from a formalist. The formalist is detected by his minute observances of mere outward *rites;* the Christian is known by the fact that out of him flow rivers of living water, going forth in streams of love, joy, peace, long-suffering, gentleness, goodness, faith, meekness, temperance, and such things. (v) *It is a satisfying gift.* "Whosoever drinketh of the water which I shall give him shall never thirst." Man has a spiritual capacity which can never be satisfied, except with this gift of life, for which, indeed, he was created. Whatever the world may have to give will only leave the soul thirsty again. But when Christ is in the heart there is a soul-satisfying, thirst-quenching river always springing up. (vi) *It is an everlasting gift.* Whatever else we have perishes with the using. Death cuts us off from all earthly gifts. But this gift goes on in spite of death. It cannot be cut off, because its source is God himself, and it is *in* us, and beyond the reach even of death. It flows to us from the other world, and when we die we only follow the stream up to its source. (vii) *It is a personal gift.* This water is not given to mankind *gen-*

erally, but to sinners *individually*. Luther says that "religion is in the pronouns": "Whosoever will, let him take the water of life." If I am to live, I must come to him; I must seek him out; I must ask him to give this water to me. So must you; so must we all, each for himself.

2.—To inaugurate true worship.—In the course of the conversation with the woman she evades the direct issue between the Lord and herself about the "living water," and raises a question touching the true place of worship. Jesus takes advantage of this to set the matter of worship right. (i) *As to the true object of worship.* "God is a Spirit." The time has now come when this must be distinctly understood. True worship, which is faith in Jesus Christ and love to God, is not limited by external things or rites. The temple or the mountain cannot contain him. No ordinance must be confounded with him. God is a Spirit, and he must be worshiped in spirit. The spirit that is in man must rise into communion with God, who is a Spirit. Not that true spiritual worship can never express itself in acts or words, but that its object must not be in anything local to this world, nor its essence in any external action. They only are true worshipers who so apprehend Jesus that anywhere and without rite or ceremony they can commune with God. (ii) *As to the true place.* Time was when God had "set his name" in Jerusalem, and limited his earthly habitation to the Temple; but now it is neither in Jerusalem nor at Gerizim. God is everywhere present, and true worshipers have not to journey to any earthly spot to worship him aright; neither do they have to turn to the right or left, to the east or west, to find him. In view of this, what supreme folly and wickedness is that theory of worship which binds and limits the true worshiper to this place or that, to this sectarian church or that, to this rite or that form! God cares not for Romanist, Episcopalian, Presbyterian, Methodist, Baptist, or Congregationalist, but only for true worshipers who worship him in spirit and in truth—that is, by the Spirit of God, and in accordance with the truth which came by Jesus Christ.

3.—To conduct a divine search.—"The Father seeketh such to worship him." That we sinners should seek after God seems perfectly natural, for we need him, and must have him or perish. But to be told that God seeks after us is most astonishing. Does God need us? Perhaps in the name "Father" (which first occurs here) we have the secret of this need in God. There is in him a divine Fatherhood which craves after his children, and, we might also say, a divine motherhood also. Yes, he needs us, and rejoices over us with joy and singing when he finds us and wins us. (Zeph. iii, 17; Luke xv, 6–10, 32.) "God was in Christ reconciling the world unto himself." (II. Cor. v, 19.) How does he conduct this search? (i) *By the incarnation of himself in Jesus*, by whom he revealed himself to us. (ii) *By putting away our sins*, which without atonement prevented our coming to him, and him from receiving us. (iii) *By declaring his gracious purpose to us.* (iv) *By sending forth the Spirit* of his Son into our hearts, regenerating us, and crying in us, "Abba, Father." All this by means of his Word, which is freely preached unto us and to all men.

III.—THE METHOD OF JESUS.

Even a superficial study of this most delightful incident suggests to us many helpful hints as to the method of Jesus in winning sinners to God, in which we find great encouragement for our own faith and wonderful instruction as to how to work for the Master in the same field of gracious endeavor.

1.—He meets the sinner on his own ground.—He does not require the sinner to approach to his lofty place as the Son of God, but condescends to our "low estate," and comes to us as the Son of man, weary and travel-stained, and asks a favor of us. He draws near to us, and on our own ground offers us salvation. This Samaritan woman was one whom most of us would have passed by, but not he! He knows her through and through; yet he speaks to her, and seeks to win her, and so he did. He is not ashamed to be found in her company and to be talking with her when the disciples return. He is never "ashamed to call" us sinners his "brethren." (Heb. ii, 11.) He does not patronize her or oppress her with lofty and proud condescension. He even goes the length of asking from her a favor before pressing upon her his gift. This would put her at ease, and show her that he did not despise her, as the Jews did. He was as easy and even more gentle with her than with Nicodemus. In all this we see the matchless kindness and graciousness of God toward sinners. Would that we might imitate Jesus in dealing with those who, like ourselves, need this gift so much!

2.—He uses a common opportunity to open up an uncommon subject.—Nothing could be more commonplace and incidental than a thirsty man asking for a drink of water, and yet by means of this apparently insignificant incident Jesus was enabled, easily and naturally, to turn the attention of the woman to the greatest of all subjects. The wise soul-winner need never be at a loss either for an opportunity or a method of introducing the great subject of salvation to sinners. A cup of water is a good enough text. God does not require great things with which to accomplish his testimony. A sling and a stone, an ox goad, a lamp and pitcher and trumpet, even a shepherd's crook, is good enough for him to use in delivering his people. It is not the instrument, the words, or the occasion, but the power of God that makes weak things mighty.

3.—**He sought to awaken in her a sense of deeper needs than those of the body.**—As a rule, all men are so deeply set upon supplying themselves with the things that minister to the body only, or at least to the life that now is, that they have forgotten that within them is a nature much higher than that which is represented by the body, and whose needs are unsupplied. Jesus seeks to awaken that deeper nature to her remembrance. So he tells her of "living water," and reminds her that, though she drew from Jacob's well never so cool a draught, it will not permanently satisfy her thirst. We should ever keep this before our mind, both in the direction of our own life and in seeking to win others to Christ.

4.—**Jesus exposed her sin to her, and so awakened her conscience.**—In speaking of the living water he awakened a spiritual curiosity, and in asking her to go fetch her husband he roused her conscience, and in such a natural way, and so gently, that she did not take offense. She perceived that he was a prophet, and knew her whole life. Ah, here is the wonder of the Eternal Word! "He knew what was in man." He knew these two disciples who were following him, and what they wanted. He knew what was in Peter, he knew what kind of a man Nathanael was, he read Nicodemus's heart like an open book, and now he turns over the leaves of the book of this woman's sinful life and reads them in her own sight. So it is now; "the Word of God is . . . sharper than any two-edged sword, piercing even to the dividing asunder of the soul and spirit, . . . and is a discerner of the thoughts and intents of the heart." (Heb. iv, 12.) We need only to preach the Word in order to find the heart and conscience of the sinner. But in exposing the sins of men and women to their consciences we should imitate the gentleness of Jesus with this woman. He showed her that, while he knew her, he did not either hate or despise her, but longed to do her good. It has been well said that "sin and punishment should only be preached with tears in the preacher's eyes, and tenderness in his heart."

5.—**His zeal in his Father's work.**—In presence of the Master we need, all of us, to be ashamed of our cold-heartedness. Weary and worn out as the Lord was, sitting thus on the well, he nevertheless turned eagerly to the work of saving this one poor sinner. So intent was he in this work that when food for his body was brought by his disciples, he turned away from it, and said, "I have meat to eat that ye know not of," namely, to do his Father's will, and to finish the work he had given him to do. There never came a time in the life of our Lord on earth when he said to any one in need, "I am too tired," or, "The time is not favorable." It was always time for him, and every occasion was a welcomed opportunity. Let us first as to ourselves be as the woman before him, and then toward other sinners *as he was toward the woman;* so shall we be saved ourselves, and be also the means of saving others.

XXXVIII.

DANIEL'S ABSTINENCE.—Daniel i, 8-20.

(8) But Daniel purposed in his heart that he would not defile himself with the portion of the king's meat, nor with the wine which he drank: therefore he requested of the prince of the eunuchs that he might not defile himself. (9) Now God had brought Daniel into favour and tender love with the prince of the eunuchs. (10) And the prince of the eunuchs said unto Daniel, I fear my lord the king, who hath appointed your meat and your drink: for why should he see your faces worse liking than the children which are of your sort? then shall ye make me endanger my head to the king. (11) Then said Daniel to Melzar, whom the prince of the eunuchs had set over Daniel, Hananiah, Mishael, and Azariah, (12) Prove thy servants, I beseech thee, ten days; and let them give us pulse to eat, and water to drink. (13) Then let our countenances be looked upon before thee, and the countenance of the children that eat of the portion of the king's meat: and as thou seest, deal with thy servants. (14) So he consented to them in this matter, and proved them ten days. (15) And at the end of ten days their countenances appeared fairer and fatter in flesh than all the children which did eat the portion of the king's meat. (16) Thus Melzar took away the portion of their meat, and the wine that they should drink; and gave them pulse. (17) As for these four children, God gave them knowledge and skill in all learning and wisdom: and Daniel had understanding in all visions and dreams. (18) Now at the end of the days that the king had said he should bring them in, then the prince of the eunuchs brought them in before Nebuchadnezzar. (19) And the king communed with them; and among them all was found none like Daniel, Hananiah, Mishael, and Azariah: therefore stood they before the king. (20) And in all matters of wisdom and understanding, that the king inquired of them, he found them ten times better than all the magicians and astrologers that were in all his realm.—Daniel i, 8-20.

According to our syllabus of study this one is marked for a "Temperance Lesson," by which I suppose is meant that Daniel (according to the modern theory of total abstinence) refused to drink the wine which was provided for him from the king's table because he was in principle a total abstainer from the use of wine. But it is not fair to wrest the Scripture in this way, even for the purpose of supporting so good a cause as total abstinence. On the same principle of interpretation we would have to make out that Daniel was also a total abstainer from meat, that is, flesh, and was also a strict vegetarian! The merest glance at the text will show that it was not the drinking of wine or the eating of meat in itself to which Daniel objected, but the eating and drinking of wine and meat which had been before offered to an idol. It was not wine and meat in general, but the wine and meat which came from the king's table. The first verse in our study gives us the key. "But Daniel purposed in his heart that he would not defile himself with the portion of the *king's* meat, nor with the wine which *he* drank." The Babylonish kings were "religious," and all their food and drink were first solemnly dedicated to the idols which they worshiped before they ate it, just as it is the custom with Christians to offer their food to God for blessing before they eat. To eat meat and drink wine offered to idols would be to acknowledge the idol and defile himself with the unholy food; therefore Daniel determined that he would not dishonor the God of Israel by so doing. The lesson of the text is the unswerving loyalty of this young man to his God, the God of his fathers, the God of Israel. If only we could inspire our young men with this spirit of loyalty to God and his honor, we should lay the foundations for self-control, temperance, and every other virtue which goes to sanctify the character and ennoble the life.

Our study has to do with Daniel and his companions, but especially with Daniel and the circumstances in which he found himself when first carried away captive to Babylon. We are accustomed to think of Daniel and the other great prophets of Israel as old men with gray locks and flowing beards. So indeed most of them had become in the end; but here we are introduced to a prophet of the Lord in his tender youth; for it is evident that the spirit of prophecy was in him at the very beginning of his career, as recorded in this history. Daniel was probably a lad not beyond sixteen years of age when he is introduced to us. Yet all the signs of a prophet are present—piety, courage, wisdom, together with the power of foretelling future events. There is a striking similarity between the history of Daniel and that of Joseph. Joseph was the first distinguished man of his house—that is, of the house of Jacob; and we may say with truth that Daniel was the last man of great eminence, especially among the prophets. In their youth they were both captives, and both equally true to God and their own consciences in circumstances of a very trying character. Both obtained favor with their kingly masters, and attained to places of great honor and power in the kingdoms whither, in the providence of God, they had been sent as captives. It is both interesting and surprising to note how often young men, even lads, have played great parts in the world's history; especially in the history of the kingdom of God upon the earth. Moses and Joshua were comparatively young men for the age in which they lived; David and Solomon were young men when they were called upon to assume the gravest responsibilities. Joseph and Daniel were mere lads when God began to use them. John the Baptist and Jesus were young men when they began their ministries, Jesus being only a lad of twelve when he first undertook his "Father's business." Saul of Tarsus was a young man when Jesus met him "on the way," converted, and commissioned to be the great apostle to the Gentiles. Timothy was hardly more than a boy when Paul chose him for his companion in apostolic labor, adopting him as his son. What encouragement is here for young men, and even lads, to enter at once into the work and service of God. Daniel was one of four young men who were carried away by Nebuchadnezzar in the third year of the reign of Jehoiakim, before the final captivity of Judah. We do not know who his parents were, but we know that he was one of the princes royal. It was the custom of eastern monarchs to select from their captives the most noble, the fairest, and the cleverest, and train them up for their own service, often attaching them to their persons, as Nehemiah was attached to his king as "cup-bearer." This policy was probably dictated by the consideration of conciliating their enemies, as well as of availing themselves of the wisdom, tradition, and learning of the nations around them. In accordance with this custom, Daniel and his three friends (all Jewish princes) were selected to be specially trained for government service. They were placed under the particular care and instructions of the chief eunuch of the king's household, to be educated and fitted for future positions. It is our duty to consider the history of Daniel under the circumstances here detailed, and to draw from that history such lessons as may be helpful to us.

I.—DANIEL UNDER TEMPTATION.

Whether it was a part of the policy of the king to corrupt these young men by feeding them from his own table with the meat and drink which he had offered to his idol-gods, and so to wean them away from the religion of their fathers, or whether we are to consider these circumstances as the providential occasion for the development of the faith and character of Daniel and his companions, is not a question of much moment. We are inclined to think that the king had no thought of corrupting them. It is certain that amidst all the idolatrous customs of his own country Daniel had been carefully taught and trained in the way of faith and righteousness by godly parents, perhaps under the supervision of Jeremiah himself, and had so escaped the prevailing unbelief and apostasy of his house. When he was called upon to eat meat and drink wine offered to idols, he and his friends entered their protest and sought to be free from that compromise of their religious principles. Daniel was from the very beginning of his career a faithful witness for the truth. His temptation was all the more severe from the following circumstances:

1.—**Because of his youth.**—It would not have been so remarkable that he declined to compromise his conscience had he been a full-grown man with religious principles and character strongly established by reason of maturity and long habit of righteousness. Youth is indeed purer than manhood, but then, as a rule, it is weaker and more easily led by those under whose power and influence it is brought. Now Daniel was but a lad, yet in a most manly fashion he withstood the temptation offered him. He demonstrated the possibility of one even so young as he standing by a purpose loyally and firmly, and the importance of doing so at the very outset. Had Daniel yielded here to this first temptation, he would hardly have recovered his faith or strength at a later time. If we win the first fight with the tempter we may assure ourselves of victory all along the line of our life.

2.—**Because he was away from home.**—One of the worst situations for a young man to find himself in, is to be away from home and home influences, in a strange city; especially when surrounded by those who have no sympathy with the religious training and principles of his home life. In this situation Daniel was placed. What had become of his father and mother, his brethren and kindred, we are not told. Possibly they had been killed in the siege, or carried away captive to some other province. At any rate, it was an hour of weakness and desolation with the lad, and in such a time the tempter is sure to be present to spread his net and shoot his fiery darts. Daniel's courage and faith under these circumstances are all the more remarkable.

3.—**Because of his helplessness.**—He was not only in a strange land and among strangers, but he was a captive and wholly at the mercy of the king and his servants. He might have said to himself, and not without some show of reason, "I am not responsible for the things which I do under the command of the king, whose prisoner I am." We have heard young men who justified themselves in wrong-doing because "they were carrying out the orders of their employers." On the other hand, I once knew a lad of fourteen who threw up a position which it had cost him two years of hard work in the establishment where he was employed to attain, rather than make out a false shipping invoice at the command of his employer. Daniel was made of the same kind of stuff, and had the courage of the older men and apostles who at a later time said, "We ought to obey God rather than men."

4.—**Because of the subtlety of the temptation.**—It was a great compliment to Daniel that the king had selected him to fill a high place in his personal service, and he had further given orders that he should be fed with meat and drink from his own table. This high distinction would be recognized by the other captives and by the king's officers themselves. To have refused this distinguished mark of the king's favor would have been both ungracious and impertinent. There is no surer approach to the citadel of man's moral nature than by the gateway of vanity and with the instruments of flattery, especially if the agents be rich and great. What we might refuse from our inferiors, or even our equals, is not so easily declined if offered by our betters. But Daniel was proof here too; for he considered the favor of God as being of greater worth than the flattery of kings.

5.—**Because of the peril of his position.**—Sometimes we can brave the sneer of the ungodly and the arched brow of the less conscientious where we would not be willing to stand up at the peril of life itself. Yet this was Daniel's danger. To have absolutely refused to eat the meat and drink the wine appointed by the king would have been to have imperiled his life. Even the king's servant who had charge of the matter said that to concede Daniel's protest and petition would "endanger my head to the king." But Daniel counted not his life dear to himself in this emergency. The favor of God to him was more than life. We do not wonder, after this, that at a later period in his life he calmly went on praying with his face toward Jerusalem, even though the den of lions was appointed to be his portion for so doing.

II.—STANDING BY A PURPOSE TRUE.

In accounting for Daniel's firmness in this matter it will be profitable to look under the surface and inquire into the secret of his strength.

1.—He was true to a godly education.—We do not know who his parents were, nor are we in possession of any of the details of his early education; but we are morally sure that he had been carefully trained in the fear of God by somebody. Perhaps the low state of religion in his own land tended to increase in himself the sense of responsibility for an absolutely true course in the matter now before him. He had pondered the matter and had "purposed in his heart" what he would do. No lad would have withstood this temptation unless he had been thoroughly well taught; not in the external ceremonies of religion, but in its true essence and power. In this there is a message of great importance, both to parents and sons. If we parents wish to be absolutely sure of the course which our sons will take when the time comes to send them forth into the world to fight life's battle for themselves, let us be sure that they go out from us rooted and grounded in the truth and established in the faith of God and his Christ. Better sacrifice everything else than fail to send forth our children thoroughly equipped Christians, able to "work out" their "own salvation" in the face of a hostile world. If boys expect to stand in the face of temptation when away from home, and have the favor of God in all their undertakings, let them see to it that they, like Daniel, have a purpose true not to defile themselves with the world's meat and drink, whether it come in the form of ungodly indulgences or unrighteous pleasures and profits.

2.—He was true to his conscience.—It was not only loyalty to his home training, but loyalty to conscience, that stood him in this hour of trial. In leaving home we leave behind home influences and restraints, but if we have a conscience which has been trained in the fear of God we may always have that with us for a monitor. Home training may keep us a little while, but a sensitive conscience will prove to us a never-failing guide. Daniel dreaded defilement of conscience more than aught else which might befall him during his captivity; and his extreme sensitiveness in the matter of eating or not eating the portion from the king's table shows how really he was a child of God. To have eaten the food set before him, knowing it to have been first offered to idols, would have been an act of sacrilege from which his conscience would not have easily recovered. That is a happy boy or man, whether rich or poor, prince or peasant, who has a conscience like Daniel's. It will stand by him and strengthen him in many an hour of trial and perplexity.

3.—He was true to the Word of God.—It was contrary not only to the whole religious training of Daniel that he should have any fellowship with the heathen rites and religions, but he evidently had in remembrance the special teaching of God's Word (Lev. ii and Deut. xii), where any conformity to idol worship or heathen religious customs is specially forbidden. By taking heed to the Word of God a young man may cleanse himself from all evil ways; but will also be enabled to do something even better than that: he will escape the defilement altogether.

4.—He was true to his brethren.—Daniel seems to have been the spokesman for the other three young princes, as he was undoubtedly by nature (and possibly by rank) their leader. Should he give way, his brethren would hardly stand, and so a double responsibility rested upon him. If he stood fast, they, encouraged by his example, would stand by his side. Moreover, there were many other captives in Babylon who would naturally look up to these young princes, already marked out by the king's favor, for examples to themselves. Daniel was therefore rightly jealous of his own conduct, as in that stood his influence. He must be a true witness for the sake of others. It is not only our business to keep our own souls free from taint and harm, but we must also keep our influence upon others untainted, for every Christian man becomes his "brother's keeper." It is this conviction which often serves as a help to ourselves, and enables us to stand firm for others' sake where we might yield if only we ourselves were concerned.

5.—He was true to God.—When Daniel requested permission to decline the king's meat and drink and live upon a simple vegetable diet such as was never offered to idols, the king's officer protested that the result would be disastrous to the best physical condition of these young men, unfitting them for king's favorites. However, Daniel pleaded for a trial of this simple diet. He believed that God, for whose honor he was acting, would not desert him, or allow his act of piety to go unvindicated. A true Christian may always appeal to the results of a Christian walk for its justification. Daniel only asked a trial of ten days. He believed that in this brief space God would demonstrate the wisdom of his course, and even prove to the eunuch that in every way it was better to serve God than to compromise with idolatry. Like Paul, he was ready by an experimental test of the truth to commend himself and his brethren to the judgment of men. In all this Daniel was not forward in making any great profession of faith or arguing in favor of God. He was not stubborn or conceited, but courteous and gentle throughout. Perhaps his gentle spirit and courtesy had as much to do in influencing the eunuch to trust him, as his firm purpose not to yield. It is always best to win a point by persuasion if possible, before resorting to a declaration of war. We may always be sure that God in the end will honor those who honor him. (I. Sam. ii, 30.)

III.—DANIEL VINDICATED AND REWARDED.

God stood by his young servant in this matter as he did also by Joseph in Egypt. God's favor was seen in three things.

1.—In the favor he gave Daniel with the eunuch.—He had already brought him "into favor and tender love with the prince of the eunuchs." When there is a purpose in our hearts to be true to God, he does not wait for it to be worked out before he comes to our help. There must have been something very charming and winning about Daniel from the very beginning. Real faith should always develop a character which is attractive to unbelievers, sometimes in its gentle courtesy and sometimes in its rugged manliness. Let us not be afraid of losing the favor of man by being true to God. It was because the early Christians were true to God that they won the favor of the people.

2.—By giving the young men greater physical beauty.—At the end of the ten days' trial "their countenances appeared fairer and fatter in flesh than all the children which did eat the portion of the king's meat." No doubt there was special interposition of God in this matter; but no doubt, on the other hand, the result was in part owing to the very fact that they had abstained from the luxuries of the king's table and the deteriorating influence and effects of the wine which was appointed them to drink. In the long run, the man who lives on simple fare will show more physical beauty than he who fares sumptuously every day on rich food and wine and all manner of dainties. Chrysostom says of these four young men who stood to their purpose that "they had better health for their spare diet, and their good consciences and merry hearts were a continual feast unto them." They also had God's blessing on their coarser fare, which was the main matter that made the difference. It is said of the Scotch that they owe their well-known superiority, both intellectually and physically, to their training in the Shorter Catechism and their diet of oatmeal.

3.—By their superior intellectual ability.—At the end of the three years which had been assigned for their special education, they were brought before the king, and in all matters of wisdom and understanding . . . "he found them ten times better than all the magicians and astrologers that were in all his realm." There is scarcely a doubt that if the facts were known and tabulated it would appear that both the intellectual and physical life of Christian people is far in advance of those of the people of the world who reject God and his counsel both as to spiritual and temporal things. It is not only things offered to idols in the specific and formal way stated in the lesson, but things offered to the great idol of this world—sacrificed on the altars of appetite, lust, and mere carnal pleasure, from which we must abstain. The general and well-known superiority of the Anglo-Saxon race is due most of all and first of all to the influence of the gospel of Christ. God has trained that race for the evangelization and civilization of the world. Woe to them if they prove unfaithful to their trust, and woe especially to them who break down their spiritual and physical constitutions by indulging in a life of luxury and dissipation.

XXXIX.

REVIEW.

Golden Text: "The kingdom of God is at hand: repent ye, and believe the gospel."—Mark i, 15.

XL.

JESUS AT NAZARETH.—Luke iv, 16-30.

(16) And he came to Nazareth, where he had been brought up: and, as his custom was, he went into the synagogue on the sabbath day, and stood up for to read. (17) And there was delivered unto him the book of the prophet Esaias. And when he had opened the book, he found the place where it was written, (18) The Spirit of the Lord is upon me, because he hath anointed me to preach the gospel to the poor; he hath sent me to heal the broken-hearted, to preach deliverance to the captives, and recovering of sight to the blind, to set at liberty them that are bruised, (19) To preach the acceptable year of the Lord. (20) And he closed the book, and he gave it again to the minister, and sat down. And the eyes of all them that were in the synagogue were fastened on him. (21) And he began to say unto them, This day is this Scripture fulfilled in your ears. (22) And all bare him witness, and wondered at the gracious words which proceeded out of his mouth. And they said, Is not this Joseph's son? (23) And he said unto them, Ye will surely say unto me this proverb, Physician, heal thyself: whatsoever we have heard done in Capernaum, do also here in thy country. (24) And he said, Verily I say unto you, No prophet is accepted in his own country. (25) But I tell you of a truth, many widows were in Israel in the days of Elias, when the heaven was shut up three years and six months, when great famine was throughout all the land; (26) But unto none of them was Elias sent, save unto Sarepta, a city of Sidon, unto a woman that was a widow. (27) And many lepers were in Israel in the time of Eliseus the prophet; and none of them was cleansed, saving Naaman the Syrian. (28) And all they in the synagogue, when they heard these things, were filled with wrath, (29) And rose up, and thrust him out of the city, and led him unto the brow of the hill whereon their city was built, that they might cast him down headlong. (30) But he, passing through the midst of them, went his way.—Luke iv, 16-30.

There are some difficulties in fixing the chronology of this visit of Jesus to his own town of Nazareth. If we had only Luke's Gospel we should think that he went immediately to Nazareth from his triumphant battle with Satan in the wilderness; but by reference to Matt. xiii, 54, Mark vi, 1, and especially to John iv, 43, 44, it would seem that this visit was not until after the close of his first

Judean ministry, various incidents of which are recorded, particularly by John; such as the calling of the first disciples (John i, 35-51); Jesus' first miracle (John ii, 1–12); first passover (John ii, 13-23); his conversation with Nicodemus (John iii); his interview with the woman of Samaria (John iv, 1–26); also his second miracle in Cana of Galilee (John iv, 43 *et seq.*). After this he returned to Galilee, and preached his first sermon in Nazareth. It has been supposed by some that he twice preached in Nazareth, but it is not likely. So far as we can make it out, the Lord only once revisited his own town, at which time he was so violently rejected by his old neighbors and friends that he never returned again.

Still in the power of the Holy Ghost, he made his way back to Nazareth, which some months before he had left to present himself to John for baptism. It must have been with much gladness that he went back to his early home, and not without a great and happy anticipation that they would be as glad to accept the good tidings which he brought them, as he was to publish them. His success and the power which God had given him, not only in Judea but in the neighboring city of Capernaum, would be sufficient introduction and guarantee to them that he came not in his own name, but in the name of the Father and in the power of the Holy Ghost. His disappointment is not unlike that which has met many a one of his disciples who has been rejected where he might have hoped to be most welcomed. The story of this visit to Nazareth is simply told. We read it with wonder, and turn away from its conclusion with sadness, repeating the golden text attached to this lesson with a fresh emphasis: "He came unto his own, and his own received him not."

I.—THE DIVINE PREACHER.

Never was such a preacher on earth before. Jesus is yet the model of all the best preachers, and the elements of his methods should be found in every one who preaches or teaches in his name. We indicate some of the leading points noted by the evangelist.

1.—**He was in the power of the Spirit.**—He went "in the power of the Spirit" (Luke iv, 14), and again, "The Spirit of the Lord" was upon him, because the Lord had anointed him to preach the gospel. (ver. 18.) It is interesting, and of the utmost moment, to notice how the Holy Ghost was the ally of Jesus in all his ministry. He received the Spirit without measure at the time of his baptism; he went in the power of the Spirit to his conflict with Satan in the wilderness; he was in the power of the Spirit all through the interval between his leaving the wilderness and his coming again into Galilee; and now he goes to Nazareth and ascends the platform in the little synagogue there, and declares himself that the Spirit is upon him in special anointing power. It must not be understood that this presence and power of the Spirit (which first came upon Jesus at his baptism) is the same *in manner* as the Spirit dwelling *within him* as the Son of God. This is a special gift of the Spirit for service. If any disciple doubt that it is for him also to be thus anointed with power from on high, let him only remember that it was for this very purpose that our Lord would not suffer his disciples to go forth to their work until, at Jerusalem, they also should be so endued. This is the most important element in our ministry, whether it be as preachers, teachers, or private disciples testifying and working for God. If we may not have the Spirit as Jesus did, without measure, we may yet have him in such measure that our words and our work may be in the power of God. It was thus Paul preached in Thessalonica, not "in word only, but also in power, and in the Holy Ghost, and in much assurance." (I. Thess. i, 5.) The gospel is the power of God unto salvation only as it is preached "with the Holy Ghost sent down from heaven." (Rom. i, 16; I. Pet. i, 12.) Much stress is laid in these days upon the importance of well-prepared sermons and lessons. No minister or teacher would be long tolerated who neglected thorough preparation for the pulpit or the class. It is not, however, so carefully insisted on that they must also be in the power of the Holy Ghost. A minister would feel at a loss in his pulpit if he had failed to prepare his sermon, or, having prepared it, had forgotten to bring it with him. It is not so certain that all of us feel the same embarrassment because of the absence of the Holy Spirit. It is hard for the minister to try to preach without the holy anointing, but it is harder for the people to listen to sermons that are not preached (or children to listen to lessons that are not taught) in the power of the Holy Spirit. Let Jesus be our model in this respect.

2.—**He reverently read the Scriptures, taking his text from them.**—It is deeply significant that in this first sermon which we have from Jesus he bases it upon the Word of God. He did not take the last sensation in society or politics, the last discovery in science, or the last new novel criticising Christianity, for his text, but the Word of God. Nor did he begin by expressing a doubt as to the authorship and genuineness of the Scriptures he read to the people. It is no wonder that such a preacher succeeded at once in attracting and riveting the attention of his audience. For "the eyes of all them that were in the synagogue were fastened on him." (ver. 20.)

3.—**He preached the gospel unto them.**—There is a singular significance in the fact that, at a certain point in his reading, "he closed the book." (ver. 20.) By a reference to the place in Isaiah from which he took his text (Is. lxi, 2), it will be seen that he stopped, not at a period, but at a comma, the whole sentence being, "To proclaim the acceptable year of the Lord, *and the day of vengeance of our God.*" The words we print in italics he did *not* quote, for the reason that the day of vengeance was not yet at hand, and his present purpose was to announce and press upon his hearers the gospel. Jesus knew rightly how to divide the truth. There is a divine art in reading the Word of God to a congregation, and we should study that as thoroughly as we do the sermon we are to preach. Having taken his text, he begins to unfold it to his hearers. (i) He makes the startling announcement that the Scripture he had read to them was fulfilled now, in their ears. (ver. 21.) When the prophet spoke those words he spoke them with reference to the promised Messiah. "This day," says Jesus, "is this scripture fulfilled," for as he said to the Samaritan woman (John iv, 26), so now he says in effect, "I that speak unto thee am he." Of course, when we preach or teach we cannot appropriate the Scriptures to ourselves, but we can identify them with Jesus. Jesus preached *himself* as the substance of his doctrine; "we preach *not ourselves*, but Christ Jesus the Lord." (II. Cor. iv, 5.) (ii) He proceeded to open up to them the wonders of the gospel. The acceptable year of the Lord had come —that is, the universal jubilee of God was now announced. Of old, once in every fifty years God proclaimed (on the basis of a special atonement) a universal decree of deliverance, liberty, and return to all who were in debt or enslaved. (Lev. xxv, 10; xxvii, 24.) So Jesus now, himself our atonement, proclaims, on the basis of the sacrifice he is about to make of himself, universal forgiveness. The words "deliverance" and "liberty" are in the Greek the word which is elsewhere translated "forgiveness." This reminds us of the Apostle's great sermon, in which, after having set forth Jesus as the Son of God crucified and raised again, he makes this proclamation: "Be it known unto you therefore, men and brethren, that through this man is preached unto you the forgiveness of sins." (Acts xiii, 38.) This is what Jesus now preached to the people of Nazareth, himself being at once the preacher and the atonement; on this basis the proclamation was made, that it was preached "to the poor." That it was preached to the "broken-hearted" was an announcement that it was to those who were penitent and stricken under a sense of their sins. That it was "deliverance to the captives" was a declaration that Satan, who had long held them in his power, was overcome and compelled to let them go. That it was preached to the blind was an announcement that might come to them "in whom the god of this world hath blinded the minds of them which believe not." (II. Cor. iv, 4.) It was preached to "them that are bruised" by the galling chains of sin, that cut so deeply and sorely into the soul. In a word, it was the same gospel which Jesus afterward commissioned Paul to preach: "To open their eyes, and to turn them from darkness to light, and from the power of Satan unto God, that they may receive forgiveness of sins, and inheritance among them which are sanctified by faith that is in me." (Acts xxvi, 18.) Such was the sermon which Jesus preached. What a message it was, and what a message it still is to all sinners to whom the gospel is still preached by the grace of God! This is the acceptable year of the Lord. "Behold, now is the accepted time; behold, now is the day of salvation."

II.—A CONTROVERSY.

A crisis had come to the Nazarenes. Their Lord was present with them, preaching the gospel in power and in sweetness. Would they hear the glad tidings and receive Jesus as Christ? Two things are affirmed of them: they "all bare him witness, and wondered at the gracious words which proceeded out of his mouth." They were astonished at his power in preaching, and filled with wonder at the sweetness of his manner, and the gracious message he delivered, for we must suppose that our Lord commented on these words of Scripture, explaining and pressing upon them the love and grace of God. It appears, however, that they were more taken up with the manner than the matter of his sermon. This is too often the case. Many people go to church and are charmed with the eloquence of the preacher and the manner of the message, but pay no heed to the matter of the address. Then again we learn that, instead of discussing the message of God, they fell to criticising the preacher. "Is not this Joseph's son?" Here their prejudices came in. "How can it be possible that this carpenter, whom we have known all his life, can be the Messiah?" Not only was prejudice, but jealousy, present in their hearts. These two common but evil passions come in between many souls and God's salvation. His brethren sneered at David and mocked him when he stepped forward to accept the challenge of Goliath, and bade him go back to his sheep and not aspire to be a man, much less a champion, in their presence. The brethren of Joseph were prejudiced and jealous of him, and sold him to the Midianites. Not only does this prejudice extend to the Lord himself, but to some of his disciples. Can it be possible, men say, that God would send his gospel to the poor and oftentimes to the ignorant of this world, and pass by the wise? Can that be true which women and children accept, and "the wise and the prudent" reject? "Even so, . . . for so it seemed good in thy sight." A great crisis had come to these people. They acknowledged his singular power and authority in unfolding the Scriptures, and the graciousness of the message; but he was a carpenter! If they accepted his message they must accept him, and if they accepted him then they would have to exalt above themselves a common man whom they but little esteemed. What would they do? Jesus perceived what was going on in their hearts, and at once laid open their thoughts to them.

1.—"Physician, heal thyself."—The meaning of this seems to be: "You are claiming great things for yourself; make some demonstration of your power; lift up yourself out of your lowly position, and by mighty works show yourself to be a Great One. It is reported of you that in Capernaum you did mighty works, and you come to us with words only. Do here, in your own town, what you are said to have done elsewhere. Make a display." This was substantially the third temptation of the devil over again. It was what he met on the cross later on: "If thou be the Son of God, come down from the cross." There also they cried out in effect, "Physician, heal thyself." "He saved others, himself he cannot save." He came to them with gracious words, not with his own, but with the Father's message; he came himself, the Father's servant, to save them; but they demand signs and wonders. Perhaps they were jealous of the reputation of their little town. He had done wonders in Capernaum, and made that place famous, and now will he not do as much for them? Here their pride and selfishness came in also. But Jesus never did anything merely for display. He would work no miracle before Herod, even to save his life; he would not open his mouth before the Sanhedrim or Pilate to exalt or defend himself. We may learn from this that when God's Word is rejected (from whatever cause) no mighty work will be done merely to gratify pride or assuage prejudice. Nathanael was prejudiced against Jesus because of his town, but he was so frank and sincere that he was ready to come and see for himself.

To him Jesus then gave satisfactory signs of his Messiahship. We are reminded of what our Lord said on another occasion: "If they hear not Moses and the prophets, neither will they be persuaded, though one rose from the dead." If we would have a fuller revelation of Christ, we must lay aside prejudice and put away jealousy and pride from our hearts.

2.—A dishonored prophet.—Jesus accepts the situation. He came with the Word of God in the Spirit and power of a prophet— the Prophet of all prophets—but they would not hear him because he was their own townsman. Had he been a stranger, they would have heard him. He decides upon his course, as they had decided on theirs. They would not receive him without signs and wonders, and he decides to take a prophet's reward. They were insincere in their demands, seeking not for truth, but only making excuses. This spirit he cannot condone by yielding to their demands. Had they received him and his message, he would have wrought wonders, but it is said that "he could there do no mighty work" "because of their unbelief." (Mark vi, 5; Matt. xiii, 58.) The honor of God and his Word was at stake; for in the power of the Holy Ghost they had heard his Word and been smitten with it, but they would not yield. In this case he must accept rejection, and they must accept the consequences of their unbelief.

3.—Mercy passes by the unbelievers.—Jesus reminds them of a similar state of things in Israel in the olden time. In the days of Elijah, though there were many widows who needed his power, yet, because they rejected him as the prophet of the Lord, the mercy that might have been theirs passed them by, and fell on a poor Gentile. In the days of Elisha there were many lepers in Israel, yet because of their unbelief none of them were healed but a Gentile. Now it is about to happen after this fashion. Salvation had come to them, but since they would not accept their Messiah that salvation would pass them by in like manner. How serious a thing it is for any soul to cavil at the Word of God, or to treat God's salvation with prejudice and pride. What might have been life to them thus becomes death. We are reminded of Paul's last words to the Jews at Antioch: "It was necessary that the word of God should first have been spoken to you: but seeing ye put it from you, and judge yourselves unworthy of everlasting life, lo, we turn to the Gentiles." (Acts xiii, 46.) What a fearful responsibility they undertake who reject the Word of God!

III.—CHRIST REJECTED.

Their selfishness, pride, prejudice, and unbelief all flame up into hatred and passion at these solemn words of warning uttered by Jesus. This is the manner of unbelievers. They reject Christ themselves, and then become angry because their sin is exposed and that which they have despised is promised to others.

1.—The violence of unbelief.—"And all they, . . . when they heard these things, were filled with wrath." It is most noteworthy that they who reject Jesus become angry with him. The second stage of unbelief, especially after conviction, is wrath, as the third stage is violence. In this scene we have a prophecy of that which Jesus experienced at the hands of the whole nation. For, not content with rejecting him as Messiah, they could not rest until they had murdered him on the tree. Unbelief has not changed since then; for though Jesus himself is beyond the reach of violence, and for the most part his disciples are beyond the reach of persecution, yet do men vent their hatred against his cause, and do everything they can to assail it. Satan first sought to tempt Jesus to cast himself down from the Temple, and so destroy himself by sinful presumption and pride; and failing in that, he begins at once to effect his death by stirring up unbelievers to cast him down from a precipice.

2.—Jesus escapes out of their hands.—The crowd surrounded him, and were rushing him on to destruction, when he managed to escape out of their hands by slipping through the crowd. His hour was not yet come, and so he saved himself. In less than three brief years he will not resist the crowd that come to deliver him up to death, and yet will he escape out of the hands of his enemies. Indeed, by death and resurrection he has triumphed over them all, and is forever beyond their reach. The "heathen rage and the people imagine a vain thing," and "the kings of the earth set themselves, and the rulers take counsel together," but God has set his king upon his "holy hill."

3.—A Saviour lost.—But what a loss was the Lord's departure to that little town and to its foolish and sinful inhabitants! He went from the midst of them—never to return again. So will he depart from all unbelievers. Once he is thoroughly rejected and leaves, he may never return again. How careful should we all be how we hear the Word of God, and how we reject the Son of God!

XLI.

THE DRAUGHT OF FISHES.—Luke v, 1-11.

(1) And it came to pass, that, as the people pressed upon him to hear the word of God, he stood by the lake of Gennesaret, (2) And saw two ships standing by the lake: but the fishermen were gone out of them, and were washing their nets. (3) And he entered into one of the ships, which was Simon's, and prayed him that he would thrust out a little from the land. And he sat down, and taught the people out of the ship. (4) Now when he had left speaking, he said unto Simon, Launch out into the deep, and let down your nets for a draught. (5) And Simon answering said unto him, Master, we have toiled all the night, and have taken nothing: nevertheless at thy word I will let down the net. (6) And when they had this done, they inclosed a great multitude of fishes: and their net brake. (7) And they beckoned unto their partners, which were in the other ship, that they should come and help them. And they came, and filled both the ships, so that they began to sink. (8) When Simon Peter saw it, he fell down at Jesus' knees, saying, Depart from me; for I am a sinful man, O Lord. (9) For he was astonished, and all that were with him, at the draught of the fishes which they had taken: (10) And so was also James, and John, the sons of Zebedee, which were partners with Simon. And Jesus said unto Simon, Fear not; from henceforth thou shalt catch men. (11) And when they had brought their ships to land, they forsook all, and followed him.—Luke v, 1-11.

There are great but not insuperable difficulties in harmonizing the accounts given by Matthew, Mark, and Luke of the calling of the first four apostles. (Matt. iv, Mark i, Luke v.) It has been supposed that there was more than one call; but it seems not possible that Christ should have called the same men twice under the same circumstances, and in substantially the same words, and that the same incidents should have occurred on both occasions. It is not our purpose to attempt to settle the harmony, either in the matter of chronology or in detail. Luke is never chronological, that is, not strictly so; and as for the others, they, as well as Luke, relate incidents with a particular end in view, and not as having to satisfy the modern critic. We are content to leave these questions to those who have the time and inclination to investigate them.

Hitherto Jesus had a few disciples and friends; but no one man was bound to him by any special tie or command as from him. But now the time had come when it was necessary that he should gather about him a chosen band of men, who should both hear his words and be eye-witnesses of his work, and also come under his constant daily instruction, as to the divine purpose and method of grace in the salvation of men, in order to fit and prepare them to take up his ministry where he must lay it down, and carry it forward till the end of the age. Our lesson deals with the very important matter of calling the first four apostles, for though Andrew's name is not mentioned by Luke, we are informed by Matthew that he was one of the four—Peter and Andrew (who were brothers and partners in the fishing business), and James and John, the sons of Zebedee (who also were engaged with their father in the same work). (Matt. iv, 18–22.) We have met these brethren before—at least, three of them. Andrew and John were the first two disciples of Jesus. (John i, 35, 40.) We know that Andrew went and found Peter, and brought him to Christ, and not improbably John did the same for his brother James, though we have no particular account of James's conversion. It is most likely that these were the disciples that were with Jesus in Capernaum, mentioned in the last chapter in connection with the healing of Peter's wife's mother, though Luke does not call them by name. If Luke is correct in his chronology, they seem to have parted company with Jesus after that Sabbath in Capernaum, and returned the next day to their daily business, while Jesus continued to preach in the neighborhood. They meet together again at the lakeside (the sea of Galilee). Jesus probably went down to the place where they were engaged, for the purpose of calling them, being followed there by a vast concourse of people, who sought to hear and see more of this great prophet's words and deeds. These are probably the circumstances that face us in this lesson.

I.—PREACHING TO THE PEOPLE.

Jesus already had excited a vast interest among the people by his preaching, and his wonderful miracles of healing. Even the rulers and chief men of the nation were being stirred with interest. "Who is this strange man?" they were asking one of another. "He is evidently no mere agitator; and yet his appearance and manner are not those of one who seeks to lead a rebellion or head a party for national deliverance. But this cannot be the Messiah, for surely that glorious One would never come in so humble a manner, and consort so entirely with the poor." For the vast congregations, or rather crowds, of people that followed him were of the common people—what we would call, in our day, the rabble. He was no sensationalist, and yet his words produced a sensation whenever he spoke to the people. "Never man spake like this man." His message was of salvation, the love of God, righteousness, mercy, justice, and judgment. He preached the "Word of God" unto them. Jesus was a close preacher of God's Word. Though he said many things not written in the Old Testament, yet the seed and root of all his teaching was in the ancient Scriptures. He came not "to destroy the law or the prophets," but to expound and illustrate them by his own coming, and the fuller revelation which, in himself, he gave of God's will toward men.

He was so pressed by this multitude that he was constrained to step into one of the fishing-boats. Thus it was that he at once borrowed and extemporized a pulpit. We have seen how at home Jesus was in the synagogue on the Sabbath-day; how easily and naturally he went about his Father's business in the home of Simon, ministering to and healing the sick; how equally prompt he was to carry his blessed and gracious help to the crowd of poor, sick, and demon-driven people that crowded about the door of Simon's house. Now we see him outside the city, down at the lakeside, preaching to a mass of people—a mixed multitude—making the seashore his church and a fisherman's boat his pulpit. Jesus was far removed from the conventional type of religious teacher. He availed himself of the usages of the Church establishments, but was never bound by them. Like all his disciples who in subsequent ages have led great revivals, he set usage aside, and did the thing which his hand found to do, apart from the cold, formal, and dead services of the synagogue. Wesley abandoned the churches, and took to barns, coal-pits, and open fields. In a later day Moody took to halls and theaters, and even to the market-places, old warehouses, and machine-shops. This was a part of our Lord's power, humanly speaking; he was not bound. The people had been neglected by the priests and Levites, and no longer came to their ministrations, so he left the priests and Levites, and went out to the people, and they heard him gladly. Paul and Barnabas did the same, preaching in the synagogues on the Sabbath-days, and in the market-places between the Sabbaths. Some movement of that kind waits upon us now. Religion is too much shut up in the churches; it needs to get out into the open air. It is too much confined to the Sabbath; it needs to be manifested on the week-days. It is too much shrouded in the "dim religious light" that scarcely gets in through stained-glass windows; it needs to come out into the sunlight. It is too much bound by conventionalities; it needs to be preached from fishermen's boats and extemporized pulpits.

II.—THE GREAT DRAUGHT.

Having finished teaching the people, the Lord now turns to Simon, in whose boat he was, and who had been his companion and listener during this discourse. Doubtless he had this purpose in mind all the time; the preaching to the people was by the way and along the line of it. There were two seas before him and before Peter: the sea in which fish were swarming, and the sea of humanity, in which sinners were swarming. Both were waiting for the net to be let down among them. The Lord would now give Peter and his brethren an object-lesson in the great business of catching men. Our Lord's parables were sometimes spoken and sometimes enacted. This was an acted parable—a "miracle parable."

1.—The command of Christ.—"Launch out into the deep, and let down your nets for a draught." They had toiled all night and had taken nothing. It seemed to Peter a useless thing to begin again, especially in the morning, when it was not customary to catch fish. But here was a command, simple and straight. The work of winning men to God is based on the command of Christ. His way and his time may not be ours, but his word must be law to his disciples, as it contains all wisdom and is grounded in perfect knowledge. Whether Jesus saw with the eye of omniscience a shoal of fish in the offing, or whether, by the power of his omnipotence, he commanded them hither at the time, is not material; the miracle of omniscience is as great as that of omnipotence. The fact of more moment to Peter, and to us, is the command, both as to its authority and detail. In the latter we have two items worthy of attention. (i) *"Launch out."* The fish were not inshore, but out in the deep. This is a command we need much to heed. We are often fishing too near the shore—confining our labors to the immediate precincts of our churches when there is a great deep beyond the confines of our parish, or lying between our parish and the next—a "deep" of neglected districts and classes of people, where there are shoals of souls awaiting our net. And still beyond, there is the vast heathen world, in which there are so few fishermen and such multitudes of perishing souls. Perhaps in this there was an intimation to Peter that the Lord had chosen him to be the apostle to the Gentiles. At any rate, there is the deep still before us, and if we would obey the command of Christ we shall launch out and away into it. (ii) "*Let down your nets for a draught.*" We cannot catch fish unless we let our nets down amongst them. There are many preachers who do but display their nets to the fish, turning them over and describing them, but never letting them down. Sometimes they cast them high up into the air, where there are no fish, and sometimes they let them down and never draw them in, as when a preacher declares the gospel and never stops to inquire if any have believed it, or calls no after-meeting for the purpose of drawing his net to shore to see if there be any fish caught. But our Master has bidden us both to "launch out into the deep" and to "let down your nets for a draught." Note that the careful drawing in of the meshes of truth is as important as the launching out and the letting down. These are wondrously good lessons our Lord is teaching Peter, and necessary for us too. Shall we be wise to learn, whether we be ministers, teachers, or simply private lay workers for Jesus?

2.—**Peter's faith.**—We say his "faith," for his obedience was but his faith, and his faith was his obedience. There are three things observable in it. (i) *The warrant of his faith.* This was the word of Jesus. "Nevertheless *at thy word* I will let down the net." He would never have dreamed of doing this, under the circumstances, at his own suggestion, and perhaps it would have been folly to do so but for Jesus' word. No man becomes a true fisher of men but at the command of Christ; and no man who does let his net down at Christ's command but will catch men. Perhaps he may not get so many as Peter caught at this time; even Stephen caught only one, and that not until after he had laid down his life, yet that one was a great catch, for it was the great apostle Paul. Let us take courage by reason of Christ's command, which is our warrant. Be sure the Lord either sees fish ready for our nets or will cause them to come to them. He would not command us to preach if he did not know the certainty of the result. (ii) *The obedience of faith.* Peter mentions to the Lord that they had toiled all night and caught nothing. He was already discouraged as far as present success was concerned; besides, it was the morning, and that was not the usual time to fish. Night is the time that men go out to let down their nets. Now Peter was skeptical as to this venture; his own judgment and experience were against it, yet he obeys the word of the Lord. In doing this he did two things. First, he put away discouragement from him. He would not allow his past failure to hinder him from trying again when the Lord bade him. This is a great lesson for us. Nothing so hinders the Lord's work as the discouragement that overtakes his workers. Jesus left us a good example in this respect. What an apparent failure he had made in Nazareth, for he not only caught nothing in his own town, but was driven away from the fishing-grounds by the neighbors among whom he had been brought up. Nevertheless, he launched out into the deep places of Capernaum, and there he incloses a multitude of souls. "Let us not be weary in well doing: for in due season we shall reap, if we faint not." (Gal. vi, 9.) He bids us "go preach." If we have not been successful at one time or in one place, let us launch out again, either in the old ground or elsewhere. Faith does not wait for sight, but just obeys orders, and does whatsoever the Lord bids. Second, he surrendered his fisherman's judgment to the Lord's command at once, though at first he seemed to say, "There is no use launching out at this hour or in these circumstances; it is not regular or according to good judgment or experience; nevertheless at thy word I will let down the net." He, however, forgot this lesson at Joppa, when the messengers of Cornelius came to him, and had to be taught it again by a vision from heaven. Indeed, Peter's ministry was afterward somewhat spoiled just because he did not always give up his judgment and prejudices at the simple word of God. It is by no means sure that it was not on account of this very failing that he was set aside, or at least superseded, by Paul in the apostleship to the Gentiles. (iii) *The reward of faith.* Taking Christ at his word and simply obeying, he was speedily rewarded by a great draught of fishes such as he had never known before. So great was the draught that their nets gave signs of breaking; and Peter and Andrew, finding themselves unable to manage the "haul" alone, called for James and John, who were their partners, to come out to their help. This was a most blessed experience. We wonder if Peter thought of this on the day of Pentecost, when he inclosed three thousand souls in the first net he ever let down among men in the name and at the command of Christ. The calling of the brethren to help is like a minister greatly blessed in his work calling in Christian workers to assist in the inquiry room. Nor did the helpers lose anything by the help they gave, for there were fish enough to fill both the boats. How we would like to see such times in our churches and schools, or in some deep place of fishing! This were reward indeed!

3.—Peter's humility.—As soon as they got the fish into the ship, and the ships to the shore, Peter saw the whole wondrous result of that draught, and he fell at the Lord's knees and entreated him to depart from him, saying, "I am a sinful man." Two things are noticeable in this. First, Peter calls Jesus "Lord" here, whereas before he addressed him as "Master." He begins to recognize something in Jesus higher and more divine than he had hitherto done. Second, we are not to understand this expression too literally (that is, according to the English rendering). It was nothing more than an expression of profoundest humility. "Lord, why hast thou wrought this great miracle for me? I am a sinful man; it were far more becoming to me, at least, if thou shouldst depart from me. I am not worthy of such great favor." Humility usually overcomes us more when great blessings are poured out upon us than at any other time. Well might we all say this to the Lord, in view of blessings he has vouchsafed to us in connection with work done at his command. If any one wonders at the amazement which seized Peter and his companions at the sight of this miracle when they had been witnesses of possibly greater ones in the healing power of Jesus and in the casting out of demons, we answer that now the power of Jesus had come home to them as never before. Here was a miracle wrought in their own peculiar sphere of labor, in their own boats, and with their own nets. What God does to us and for us individually always seems more wonderful than that which he does for others. That he should save and honor other sinners is a marvel, but that he should save, use, and bless us individually in work is an amazement.

III.—THE CALL TO THE MINISTRY.

It is true that Luke speaks only of the call of Simon, and yet we are led to infer, even from his own account, that it extended to the others also, for "they forsook all, and followed him"; but Matthew tells us distinctly that first Simon and Andrew were called, and then immediately James and John. Let us glance at some facts in connection with this important call of these four men to the ministry.

1.—Who they were.—Of course they were believers; but it is noticeable that they were men from among the common people. Jesus came as a common man, and not as a prince, into this world. They were neither rich nor poor, but belonged to the well-to-do middle class, as he himself did. But they were men of character and parts. They were hard-working, energetic, patient workers, and no idlers or visionaries. So does God usually select men for his servants. Now and then one from the higher classes is taken from idleness to service, but usually he calls those who are at their work in this world to take up his work. Moses was tending his sheep, Gideon was threshing out wheat behind the wine-press, Saul was looking for the lost asses, David was watching over sheep, Elisha was plowing with oxen in the field. God wants for his ministers men trained and accustomed to work.

2.—**How he encourages them.**—Luke says, "Fear not." Another evangelist says, "Follow me:" or, "Follow me" and "fear not." "Doubtless there will come times when your courage will be put to the test, but remember it is I who have called you, and that I am able to give you success, and that I promise to stand by you."

3.—**What he calls them to.**—"From henceforth thou shalt catch men." What a noble calling! None on earth is so great as to "catch" and rescue men from sin and bring them back to God; to ennoble them from being slaves of Satan to be children of God. The greatest works of man in this earth will finally perish with time and the judgments of God, but he that wins a soul for God has done a work which will abide in both worlds, and will be a source of joy throughout eternity alike to God, to the soul-winner, and to the saved soul.

4.—**Their prompt response.**—"They forsook all, and followed him." They made no parley about it. They left their ships, their great draught of fish, their father, and all. The decision was instantaneous and complete, and it was a good exchange. What is worldly wealth to the heavenly treasure they would lay up for themselves? If there was sacrifice in it, there was also great gain. If they were separated more or less from their friends, occupations, and homes, they were constantly in company with him "whom angels praise." As Galilean fishermen, they would have long ago been forgotten, or never known out of their town or beyond their generation; but as the apostles of Jesus Christ their fame and name have outlived kings and heroes who have come after them. They followed Christ in the true spirit of entire consecration. If we would be like them in public ministry or private service, then we must "hear when Christ speaks, labor when Christ commands, believe when Christ promises, and follow whither Christ leads." So "when the chief Shepherd shall appear, ye shall receive a crown of glory."

XLII.

A SABBATH IN CAPERNAUM.—Mark i, 21-34.

(21) And they went into Capernaum; and straightway on the sabbath day he entered into the synagogue, and taught. (22) And they were astonished at his doctrine: for he taught them as one that had authority, and not as the scribes. (23) And there was in their synagogue a man with an unclean spirit; and he cried out, (24) Saying, Let us alone; what have we to do with thee, thou Jesus of Nazareth? art thou come to destroy us? I know thee who thou art, the Holy One of God. (25) And Jesus rebuked him, saying, Hold thy peace, and come out of him. (26) And when the unclean spirit had torn him, and cried with a loud voice, he came out of him. (27) And they were all amazed, insomuch that they questioned among themselves, saying, What thing is this? what new doctrine is this? for with authority commandeth he even the unclean spirits, and they do obey him. (28) And immediately his fame spread abroad throughout all the region round about Galilee. (29) And forthwith, when they were come out of the synagogue, they entered into the house of Simon and Andrew, with James and John. (30) But Simon's wife's mother lay sick of a fever; and anon they tell him of her. (31) And he came and took her by the hand, and lifted her up; and immediately the fever left her, and she ministered unto them. (32) And at even, when the sun did set, they brought unto him all that were diseased, and them that were possessed with devils. (33) And all the city was gathered together at the door. (34) And he healed many that were sick of divers diseases, and cast out many devils; and suffered not the devils to speak, because they knew him.—Mark i, 21-34.

After his baptism, Jesus was "led up of the Spirit into the wilderness to be tempted of the devil"—that is, tried—preparatory to his more public conflict with all the evil agencies of the devil. Then he came forth and began to preach, and called to himself four disciples—Andrew and Peter, James and John. With these four he journeyed to the city of Capernaum, and, it being on the Sabbath-day, he and his disciples proceeded at once to the synagogue, where he astonished the people with his teaching. The synagogue was an institution of late adoption by the Jews. It was a kind of church where the people resorted on the Sabbath-day to hear the law read and expounded by some recognized teacher, or by any one, even a stranger, if he seemed to have the gift of speech and learning. The service was very free, so that any one entering was at liberty to rise in his place and speak, or, if he seemed to be a man of intelligence, he might be requested by the ruler to take part in the discussion or to deliver an original address. In accordance with this custom Jesus either volunteered or was asked by the ruler to speak. From the first Jesus availed himself of this privilege and custom to teach the people and bring to the attention of the dwellers in both cities and villages the good news of the kingdom. We learn from Luke that it was his habit, before he entered upon his formal Messianic ministry, to teach in the synagogues of his own town and those of the surrounding villages. (Luke iv, 16.) During his first two years of public ministry this was his wont—that is, until the open rupture with the rulers by reason of the hatred which his teachings aroused.

I.—JESUS TEACHING WITH AUTHORITY.

Whether before his baptism the teaching of Jesus had been marked with singular authority or power does not appear from the record; but it is more than probable that he had hitherto confined himself to a reading of the law and the prophets, and a simple exposition of them. From Luke's account of his first appearance after his baptism in the synagogue in Nazareth, where he was well known, there was then a marvelous change in his teaching. He announced himself as being especially anointed, and his teaching produced such a commotion among the people that he had to escape out of their hands for his life. (Luke iv, 14–30.) From Nazareth he went at once to Capernaum, and his preaching was attended with similar power, as our story tells us. It is for us to inquire as to the particular characteristics of the power or authority here spoken of.

1.—His self-assertion.—"He taught them as one that had authority, and not as the scribes." The scribes were the recognized teachers of the nation. They were mere pedants. They had made void the commandments by their traditions. (Mark vii, 13.) They had smothered the Word of God with innumerable refinements: adding to and taking from it; elaborating a cumbersome and senseless system of casuistry which entangled rather than relieved the conscience. They were mere religious speculators and doctors. Their teaching was vague and involved, so that the people, as a whole, neither understood nor cared for it. But now Jesus appeared and began to teach as one "that had authority"—that is, he taught from a new standpoint. He declared, first of all, that the Spirit of the Lord was upon him, and that he was specially anointed to preach the gospel. (Luke iv, 18.) In this he asserted also that he was the very Messiah whom their prophet predicted should arise. (Is. lxi, 1.) He taught as being authorized by his own right and power to teach; not as Moses taught, who always prefaced his communications with the usual formula, "Thus saith the Lord," as also did all the prophets. The scribes did not even profess to have any authority directly from God, but repeated what Moses had said, and then proceeded to give their opinions. Jesus, on the other hand, with a single stride put himself above the scribes, the prophets, and even Moses, for he began his address with a formula peculiarly his own: "Verily, verily, I say unto you." He not only had a message which had authority in it, but "he identifies himself with the message." The scribes had "constructed cisterns in which to store truth which they had gathered, or aqueducts to convey truths from higher levels"; but Jesus announced himself as the very source and substance of the truth. The divine self-assertion of Jesus was something entirely new and unheard of. "I am the way, the truth, and the life." "I am the door," "the true vine," "the bread of life," "the good shepherd," "the resurrection": yea, "before Abraham was I am." Such self-assertion must have astonished the people beyond measure. "They never heard it on this wise." This characteristic of the teaching of Jesus was peculiar to him. No other teacher, either before or since Jesus, ever identified himself with his teaching—that is, made himself the substance of his doctrine. "Come unto me, . . . and I will give you rest." "He that hath the Son hath life, and he that hath not the Son of God hath not life." "I am the Son." It follows from all this that no one can accept the teaching of Christ without accepting him, for he is the substance of his teaching.

2.—**The matter of the Lord's teaching.**—We may judge something of the matter of his teaching by examining the sermon which he preached at Nazareth just before he came to Capernaum. Perhaps he repeated that sermon. It is not unlikely that he did. He preached the gospel to the poor; he declared that God had sent him "to heal the broken-hearted, to preach deliverance to the captives, and recovering of sight to the blind, to set at liberty them that are bruised, to preach the acceptable year of the Lord"—that is, the "Jubilee" year, in which God proclaims forgiveness of sins and deliverance to sinners; and that this blessing comes, not by attending to ceremonials or by works of righteousness—religious performances—but by believing on him and uniting their lives with his life. He intimated, also, that this grace of God was not to be confined to the Jews only, but that as of old the Zidonian widow was made a subject of grace and Naaman, the Syrian leper, was healed, so now through him the whole Gentile world was to be included in the benefits of the "acceptable year." This teaching was at once so simple, so gracious, and so comprehensive, that it produced a marked sensation of astonishment. The droning of the scribes, their senseless hair-splittings about mint, anise, and cummin, the length of the fringes on their garments and the breadth of their phylacteries, were swept away as so much rubbish, and the great truths of the gospel were at once brought to their attention. We can well imagine, also, that he announced some of those mighty truths afterward gathered up in what is known as the Sermon on the Mount, in which he cleared the law of the rubbish which the scribes had heaped upon it, and showed them that it was the spirit as well as the letter (if not rather than the letter) which God held to be of account. His preaching must have both cut and bound up, wounded and healed, the conscience.

3.—**The energy of his teaching.**—This was a new element in teaching. His word was "in power, and in the Holy Ghost, and in much assurance." The teaching of the scribes was in word only. It did not affect either the conscience or the life. It was mere speculation, the tossing about of opinions, which the people caught and cast back, or played with as children play with a ball. Their teaching smote no conscience, touched no heart, regenerated no life. It was but the chaff of wheat blown about with the breath of words and definitions. But our Lord's teaching was in power. His words were as a fire, a hammer, and a sword. (Jer. xxiii, 28, 29; Heb. iv, 12.) His words went like a coal of fire to their consciences; it smote their hearts like a hammer falling on the rock; and as a sword it pierced even to the dividing asunder of the soul and the spirit, and the joints and the marrow, and discerned—that is, exposed to their consciences—even the thoughts and intents of their hearts. It took their thoughts away from mere external conduct to internal motive, and showed them that it was not that which went into a man that defiled him, but that which came out of his heart. (Mark vii, 18, 20.) Not clean hands made so by much washing, but a pure heart which withheld the hands from sinful actions; not whole burnt-offerings, but obedience to God; not sacrifices, but judgment and mercy. Thus did Jesus preach, and set us all an example of how to preach. He preached thus because he was anointed by the Spirit of God, and if we are to preach or teach like unto him we must be similarly anointed.

II.—THE UNCLEAN SPIRIT.

One of the effects of his preaching was that it stirred up to an agony of wrath and fear some demons who were in possession of a man present in the synagogue. They recognized in Jesus "the Holy One of God," who they somehow knew came to destroy them. The unclean spirit, as he is called, was one of several or many who had possession of this man, and was spokesman for them all; so that sometimes he speaks in the singular and sometimes in the plural. Who these unclean spirits were is a matter that has occasioned much debate. They are called devils, but they are demons. There is but one devil: there are myriads of demons, *i.e.*, subordinate spirits. It seems utter folly to attempt to identify these demons with mere physical and mental infirmities. They are always spoken of and dealt with as intelligences, evil spirits who, by some means, had power to enter into and assimilate with both the minds and bodies of men. There is no doubt in my own mind that these demons are the same in kind that have operated in all ages since the fall of man in connection with every form of false religion, especially paganism. They were the witches and gods of the Egyptians, and the inspiration of all the bestial and wicked worships and ceremonies of the Philistines and other nations that filled the land before God gave it to his people. I believe these demons are the inspiration and evil power of all paganism to-day. Whether they are potent now with men or not is a question. It is held by some, not without good reason, that one of the permanent acts of Jesus in the direction of destroying the works of the devil was to cast these demons out of men where the gospel had come. They themselves asked, "Art thou come hither to torment us before the time?" (Matt. viii, 29.) That is, in advance of the final overthrow of the devil and all his hosts of darkness. On the other hand, it sometimes appears that these wicked spirits yet possess men, for there are some forms of wickedness which it seems impossible to conceive of except by supposing that men are driven to them by demons from the very pit.

There are several things worth noticing in the interview between the Saviour and the demons. The presence of Jesus stirred them up—they could not keep still in his presence. This is always so.

Evil can ill maintain itself in the presence of goodness; it must fly out against it and manifest itself. They were evidently well aware of him, and who he was. The demons from the pit know him and confess him, though wicked men affect not to recognize in Jesus Christ the Son of God. They were afraid of him, and in this they were wiser than many sinners are who have neither faith in Jesus as the Saviour, nor dread of him as the final Judge of living and dead. They confess him, either in defiance or deprecation of his wrath. This confession of the demons sounds more to me like the wicked and impious blasphemies of sinners who take the name of Jesus in vain. Finally, we see that Jesus was master of them and cast them out. What a blessing this suggests to us! There is come One who can not only teach with authority and rebuke sin, but also can cast it out. If we hear his word and yield to him, he will say to us, "Be thou clean," and with such power that we shall be saved. It was the power of Jesus over the unclean spirits that so profoundly impressed the people with his authority. Our preaching and teaching does not go forth with the seal of power until it is efficient in transforming the lives of sinners into saints.

III.—SIMON PETER'S WIFE'S MOTHER.

Leaving the synagogue, Jesus repaired with his four disciples to Simon's house, where, with his brother Andrew, he lived: the house which afterward became his own home as much as any he ever had on earth. Here we find several points of interest.

1.—A sick woman.—In the house lay the mother-in-law of Peter, sick with a fever. This is another evil effect of sin—not necessarily her sin, but entailed sin. Sin brought all manner of evils into the world. Demons and diseases follow in its wake. Perhaps the evil spirits have something to do with disease of the body as well as with the maladies of the mind. At any rate, sickness was one of the things which Jesus came to cure. He "bare our sicknesses" as well as our sins. (Matt. viii, 17.) He is the healer of our diseases. (Ps. ciii, 3.) When he was on earth he delighted to heal all manner of sicknesses, and when he sent forth his seventy he gave them power to cast out devils and to heal diseases. (Luke ix, 1.) Certainly it is difficult to separate sickness from sin, either as a direct or an indirect result. Sickness is the forerunner of death, and death is the wages of sin.

2.—Sympathetic friends.—When Jesus entered the house, the disciples—probably Simon and Andrew—at once told him of the sickness of their relative. They had not known of his ability to heal the sick, for hitherto that power had not apparently been displayed; but they reasoned from his power over the devils that he might heal the sick, especially as it was a common belief among the Jews that certain forms of sickness, particularly fevers, were the result of demoniacal agency. Having, therefore, witnessed Jesus' power over the unclean spirits, they said to themselves, "He will be able to heal her." This application to Jesus in behalf of the sick woman was, in effect, their "prayer of faith" for the sick. It is a blessed thing that we may resort to him for everything and in every time of need. It is a comfort to the sick to know that there are sympathizing friends who will speak to Jesus concerning them. No class of sufferers is more in need of our tenderest sympathy than the sick. Jesus specially commends the sick to our care, and specially recognizes those as being his disciples who identify the sick with himself and as unto him visits them. (Matt. xxv, 39, 40.)

3.—**A compassionate Saviour.**—Jesus needed no urging, but immediately went to her, and, taking her by the hand, lifted her up, and "the fever left her." We have already spoken of his compassion for the sick as well as the sinful, and remarked that his mission is to the diseased body as well as to the sinful soul. Whether or not we are warranted in expecting that in every case Jesus will heal the sick for whom we pray, is by no means clear, either from the teaching of Scriptures or from experience. Certainly we are warranted always in bringing our sick ones to him in prayer. This much we know, that "he is the Saviour of the body" (Eph. v, 23); and that when he comes he will raise the bodies of his saints, dishonored by disease and death, and fashion them "like unto his glorious body." He came to destroy death, but the time is not yet. He came to heal all our diseases, but the time is not yet. These occasional manifestations of his power over sickness and death are rather to be taken as the promise of his final victory over both, when the resurrection is accomplished. Let us wait upon him, but not dictate to him in this matter.

4.—**Grateful recognition.**—No sooner did this good woman rise from her bed than she set to work ministering to the wants of Jesus and his disciples. This should teach us that all the blessings we receive from God are to be employed in blessing others. He ministered to her, and now it is her grateful privilege to minister to him.

IV.—JESUS HEALING A MULTITUDE.

It is not surprising that the news of the appearance of this marvelous teacher, who also had "power against unclean spirits," should literally fly over the country. The people soon found where he was, and came in crowds to the house. The sick and the demon-possessed were there in multitudes. Jesus was "not weary in well-doing." He was instant in season and out of season: in the synagogue, in the house, and about the street-doors of the house. Wherever there was need he was present to meet it. With this multitude he did as he had done with the two individuals. He healed the sick among them and cast out the devils. There were divers diseases and many devils, yet he was able to cope with them all. How blessed the thought that he is over all, and that all power in heaven and in earth is given unto him, and that he holds and uses it all for man's sake. There is here an intimation full of suggestive interest. The demons, as they were brought into his presence hidden away in the bodies of their victims, were prone to cry out as did the unclean spirit in the synagogue. They would have confessed him also and remonstrated with him. But he suffered them not to speak, "because they knew him." He commanded the unclean spirits to hold their peace—literally, to muzzle their mouths. Why would not Jesus suffer these demons to speak and confess him? Would it not be a good testimony for even the devils to acknowledge his Godhead? No! Jesus revolts at the idea of receiving honor from these filthy and wicked demons. He will not be helped on by them. Any help which might have come to him from the lips of hell was shocking and revolting to him. There are men in the world who will not gain an advantage by doing wrong themselves, but who will not hesitate to accept an advantage that comes to them by the wrong-doing of others. There are churches who allow themselves to be patronized by men whose patronage is little short of the favor of demons. Jesus will neither take testimony nor a kingdom from the devil, any more than Abraham would be made rich by the king of Sodom. He will wait for Peter to give him the full confession of his name when he shall be moved thereto by his "Father in heaven," and he will wait until "the kingdoms of this world are become the kingdom of our Lord," when it shall please the Father to give him the full victory and glory purchased by his sacrificial life and atoning death.

XLIII.

A PARALYTIC HEALED.—Mark ii, 1-12.

(1) And again he entered into Capernaum after some days; and it was noised that he was in the house. (2) And straightway many were gathered together, insomuch that there was no room to receive them, no, not so much as about the door: and he preached the word unto them. (3) And they come unto him, bringing one sick of the palsy, which was borne of four. (4) And when they could not come nigh unto him for the press, they uncovered the roof where he was; and when they had broken it up, they let down the bed wherein the sick of the palsy lay. (5) When Jesus saw their faith, he said unto the sick of the palsy, Son, thy sins be forgiven thee. (6) But there were certain of the scribes sitting there, and reasoning in their hearts, (7) Why doth this man thus speak blasphemies? who can forgive sins but God only? (8) And immediately, when Jesus perceived in his spirit that they so reasoned within themselves, he said unto them, Why reason ye these things in your hearts? (9) Whether is it easier to say to the sick of the palsy, Thy sins be forgiven thee; or to say, Arise, and take up thy bed, and walk? (10) But that ye may know that the Son of man hath power on earth to forgive sins, (he saith to the sick of the palsy,) (11) I say unto thee, Arise, and take up thy bed, and go thy way into thine house. (12) And immediately he arose, took up the bed, and went forth before them all; insomuch that they were all amazed, and glorified God, saying, We never saw it on this fashion.—Mark ii, 1-12.

Having made his tour of Galilee, Jesus returns with his disciples to Capernaum. His presence in the city was soon noised abroad, and presently a great multitude of people came together about the house where he was. The house was filled directly, the passage-ways blocked, and the house surrounded. We do not hear that at this time Jesus wrought any miracles of healing among the multitude, but "he preached the Word unto them." What would we not give to have heard one of his discourses in full, and to have beheld his face as he spoke to the people! If there was life in his words, there was benediction in his looks and manner. Yet we have the sure word of teaching in the "Book he has given," and which tells us of his love, and of that of the Father who sent him; and if we search the Scripture we shall find in it all that he at any time said to the people. And since he is not dead, his words are still full of spirit and life, and are just as potent to bless now as then. In the house with those who were gathered there, occupying the chief seats, no doubt, as their custom was, and with cold, formal, and jealous interest criticising all he said and did, watching for an occasion to catch him in his talk, were the scribes and Pharisees. This is the first time we hear of these formal religious teachers taking any notice of the Lord Jesus, and this interview is the beginning of that long series of verbal conflicts which Jesus had with the Jewish teachers and rulers, which ended in his death and our salvation. A familiar method of treating this lesson is to divide it under these three heads: The Healer, the Helpers, and the Hinderers. We shall not follow these divisions exactly, but they may serve to guide the thought of the student into the heart of the subject before us.

I.—THE SICK MAN AND HIS FRIENDS.

God has, in his providence, so ordered that we are all related to each other in bonds of helpfulness or dependence. It is a question whether the joy was greater of the healed man or that of his four friends who were so potent in their instrumentality in securing his double blessing. Certainly the joy that comes into the heart of a sinner who hears the blessed words of Jesus, "Thy sins be forgiven thee," is beyond that which can be awakened by any earthly blessing; and it is equally true that the joy that comes into the heart of the soul-winner is akin to nothing else on earth. We envy the joy of the soul-winner and we pity the barrenness of soul (for the lack of such joy) of the man or woman who has never been consciously and purposely instrumental in bringing any one to the feet of Jesus.

1.—The sick man.—There is before us a man who was a palsied paralytic—a disease at once painful in its perpetual restlessness, and miserable in its hopeless helplessness—a fit type of that deeper disease of which it is so suggestive. Sin is a trouble in the human soul; a disease which is like the worm that "dieth not and the fire is not quenched." To the unforgiven and unsaved sinner there is no peace either on earth or in hell. Like the evil spirit, it is ever seeking a dry place for rest, and finding none. Palsy is a disease which the natural forces of the body are unable to throw off, and that is not amenable to the curative arts and science of medicine. So neither can the sinner of himself, nor by the help of any human power, expel sin from his soul. How wretched, to be ever doomed to this restless, shaking misery! Back of this physical infirmity our Lord hints that there was a guilty origin. (John v, 14.) In the case of this man, as well as the one healed at the pool of Bethesda, the paralysis may have been the immediate result of some moral transgression. In all cases sickness cannot be traced immediately to actual transgression, but back of all disease, without doubt, sin is the fruitful cause. Therefore we are told by God that he who forgiveth our sins also healeth our diseases. (Ps. ciii, 3.) No doubt this man who came to Jesus, helped thereto by his sympathetic friends, found a cause of brooding bitterness in the remembrance of some sin which produced his paralysis. Many another sinner is preparing for himself a miserable bed of sickness, the pain and agony of which will be more in mind than in body. Whether this sick man had faith in Jesus to cure his palsy we are not directly told, but the fair inference is that he was a willing visitor to Jesus. His friends would scarcely have brought him against his will. On the other hand, he would scarcely have come, even if he could have done so, without the help of their faith. There are multitudes of sinners who do not and will not, nay, cannot, move toward Jesus without the stimulus, encouragement, and help of some others' faith. If we but look about us we shall be able to find them, and, finding them, they will cheerfully, willingly, be brought to Jesus.

2.—**The sick man's friends.**—This is one of the most interesting groups of faithful helpers whose good work is brought to our attention in the Bible. There were four of them; who they were, or how they came to have such sympathy for their palsied friend and such faith in Jesus, we do not know. It is not difficult to imagine or believe that they were of those whom Jesus had healed on his first visit to Capernaum. Certain it is that none are so ready to help others *to* Jesus as those who have been helped *by* Jesus. Several interesting particulars are suggested by their action in this matter. (i) *They had faith in Jesus.* This is apparent by the words of the historian, who says of Jesus, when the sick man was laid or let down at his feet, that "when Jesus saw their faith, he said unto the sick of the palsy, Son, thy sins be forgiven thee." It is only men of faith who can truly do good to others. If we do not believe in our hearts and souls that Jesus Christ can forgive and heal sinners, we shall certainly never bring any such to him. But faith does not attach only itself to Jesus; it goes out in profound sympathy to others than ourselves, who have needs similar to those in ourselves which Jesus has met. A man who says he believes in Jesus Christ and has been saved by him, but who yet is not moved with compassion toward those who are not saved, belies his faith and is not a true disciple of the Son of man. The Spirit of Christ in us, which comes by faith in him, is certain to awaken a compassion for sinners akin to that which Jesus himself felt for *them*. No man can love God or be moved by his love without also loving his neighbor. The sympathy of these helpers went out to their friend on account of his physical suffering; but the man or woman who knows the blessedness of forgiveness and reconciliation looks deeper than the temporal miseries which beset men. They see in sin a worse affliction than any bodily disease, and in the holiness of life which comes from spiritual contact with Jesus a greater blessing than even bodily healing. They see in sin not a remote calamity, but a present one, even spiritual death; and in salvation not an ultimate heaven, but a present restoration of character, which is heaven begun. Therefore they are in haste to get men to Christ at once. (ii) *Theirs was a practical faith.* Faith is not merely a sentiment which believes something to be, but a vitalized affection which starts all our faculties into action and sets us to work to accomplish something. That is not a true faith which simply longs to see people saved and spends itself entirely in prayer, any more than that is true sympathy which is contented with some tender feeling of compassion. True faith, like true compassion, materializes in practical help. It was so with these men; it ought to be so with us. (iii) *Their faith was resourceful.* There were difficulties in their path. No one of them could have brought the sick man to Jesus; therefore they combined and wrought together. The work of faith in this world is of such a nature that it requires and brings about fellowship and joint action. We are not only "workers together with" God, but with each other. After having begun together this good work, the sick man's friends found fresh difficulties in the press about the house, so that it was impossible to get in by the ordinary way of access. They were not discouraged, but took to the roof of the house by the outer stair that led thither. Again they were met with difficulty. The little opening in the roof was too small to let down the bed on which their friend was lying into the court below, where Jesus was. Though the lifting of the tiles involved some damage to property, some violation of conventional usage, and would entail expense and invite criticism, they were not deterred. What though it was irregular and would provoke the rebuke of the scribes below, and, perhaps, scatter the *débris* of the roof down upon the heads of the company who had the monopoly of our Lord's presence. They went ahead, as a quaint old writer has put it, "confident that Jesus would be more pleased to have this sick man at his feet than disturbed by the falling mortar," and "convinced that it were better to get their friend healed first and settle the bill for the broken shingles afterward." This was real enthusiasm of faith. Such a faith is more needed to-day than anything else in the Church of God. While the scribes are "reasoning in their hearts," the disciples of Jesus ought to be on the housetops, tearing up the tiles and getting sinners down at his feet. This kind of faith "wins a blessing, and none the less wins it though it is the free gift of Christ."

II.—JESUS AND THE SICK MAN.

It is true that Jesus spoke only to the sick man. Nevertheless, he did not overlook the faith of his friends. Indeed, it was when he saw "*their* faith" that he spoke to the palsied sufferer. What he did for him is beautifully brought out in the single sentence: "Son, thy sins be forgiven thee." Matthew tells us that Jesus first said, "Be of good cheer." What a heaven of help there was in those words to the poor man!

1.—**The divine fellowship of Jesus.**—Here was a poor man; perhaps one who had largely lost the kindly and tender love of earthly parents; perhaps he had by a course of sins (like some poor drunkard) alienated the sympathies of man from him; a man of desolate spirit as well as suffering body. It must have been like a breath of heaven falling on his spirit to hear that tender appellation, "Son." Jesus was the Son of his Father. He knew what that means, and so now he would impart by his very first words a comfort which should go to his very heart, and assure him that he was not cast out of the heart of God. As the Father loved him, even so did he assure this sinner that he was loved. He is not ashamed to call us brethren. "You too," he seemed to say, "are a son of God; not because you have honored him in your life, but because he has sent this wondrous 'manner of love' into the world, that calls us and makes us to be the sons of God." (I. John iii, 1, 2.)

2.—"**Be of good cheer.**"—Ah, what good cheer does Jesus bring into the world! This was a favorite expression of our Lord's. He spoke it often to those whom he healed. He spoke it to his disciples in their troubles. He spoke it to Paul when he was sore perplexed and in danger of his life; and Paul afterward passed it on to the shipwrecked crew who were sailing with him to Rome; and when he met the brethren on the Appian way "he thanked God, and took courage." These four blessed words were the prelude to that heavenly symphony which followed, and which has since filled a sin-cursed and sin-burdened world with the joys of salvation.

3.—"**Thy sins be forgiven thee.**"—Here was the word of power never before spoken by man on the earth. The poor man came for the healing of bodily infirmity, but he who knoweth what is in the heart of man saw a deeper need than was confessed; a need which perhaps the sick man did not dare to hope might be removed. If there was nothing else in store for him, this might make him blessed indeed. The grace of God is deeper than man sees. They who come to Jesus always get more than they come for. The world is ready to acknowledge the outward benefits of Christianity, ready to part the garments of Christ, even while they see not the higher benefits of the cross. This was the first time that Jesus spoke direct words of forgiveness of sin to man, and it is noticeable that it is the first word he spoke to this man. In the fuller unfolding of the gospel after the resurrection, we learn that it is the first word spoken to the world in the gospel message of reconciliation. "Be it known unto you therefore, men and brethren, that through this man is preached unto you the forgiveness of sins." Jesus did not wait for this man to unbosom his soul to him, to pour out his bitter confession and give proof of contrition, but at once spoke the word of power to him, which assured him of the deep, eternal love of God. This is God's argument with the sinner—his appeal for our reconciliation (II. Cor. v, 20), not his response to our penitence.

4.—"**Arise, and take up thy bed, and go thy way.**"—Forgiveness is not all. Whoever receives the forgiveness of sins shall hereafter receive the entire healing of the body. It may not be now, but in the resurrection all forgiven sinners shall arise from disease, and even death itself, and, with bodies transformed and "fashioned like unto his glorious body," shall go their way into the Father's house and home in glory. If we receive the forgiveness of sins from him, we may patiently wait for the healing of the body. It will certainly come.

5.—**A new fashion.**—"We never saw it on this fashion." They were all amazed, and well they might be; and well might they glorify God on this behalf. Thank God for this new fashion which Jesus has brought into the world. Not a mere doctrine, not the logic of a religious philosophy, but burning words of love and sympathy, spoken with power that dissipates sin like mist before the rising sun; with such power as sends a new stream of life flowing through soul and body. Man is not left comfortless in his sin and death, but God has come to him in the likeness of sinful flesh, to put away sin and to restore him to health both of soul and body.

III.—JESUS AND THE SCRIBES.

Luke tells us that scribes and Pharisees and doctors of the law out of every town of Galilee and Jerusalem were there. They had come to investigate, and doubtless to put down this rival teacher. They had come in force to overawe and intimidate the people. Pedantry, formalism, and the wisdom of this world were then, as now, sitting in cold, heartless, critical, and jealous judgment upon the doctrine and grace of Christ. How little they understood either the real needs of man, or the great, dear love and grace of God! The interview is full of instruction.

1.—The scribes and Pharisees reasoned in their hearts. —So the world reasons to-day; but God's blessed gospel is something better than the product of human reason. It is a heavenly revelation. They said, when Jesus spoke the word of forgiveness to the man, "This man blasphemes." So they said of him to the last, and hanged him on the cursed tree; but God raised him from the dead, and answered their blasphemy. They said, "Who can forgive sins but God only?" In this they were right, but they knew not that he who spake this blessed word was God manifested in the flesh. To them forgiveness of sins was but a formal doctrine of their cold and word-splitting orthodoxy. They knew nothing of God's heart, and cared nothing for man's misery of sin. To them religion was mere doctrine and form. That grace could reach the heart without the interposition of their washings, fastings, prayings, processions, and phylacteries, they never dreamed. Indeed, they knew naught and thought not of grace at all, nor of the power of God acting through his love. Acceptance with God was a reward of their own merit, and not the fruit of a divine compassion that reached deeper than hell and higher than heaven. They thought he was playing them a trick and eluding their watchful eyes. He would not, and could not, they thought, heal the body, as was reported of him, and, instead, would put them off with a declaration of something done for the man which no one could see or know. And this they said he would do, even at the expense of blasphemy. It was a trick, a crime, and an imposture! Thus does the world reason to-day of the gospel and its sweet message. It is either a blasphemy, a fraud, or a fanaticism. "The Jews require a sign, and the Greeks seek after wisdom." Unbelief demands a miracle or a syllogism; and were both given, unbelief would make answer that the one was not true because impossible, and the other insufficient because not comprehensible to reason.

2.—**Our Lord's answer.**—While they reasoned in their hearts and muttered among themselves, Jesus, who perceived the deep secret of the palsied man's soul, also perceived the selfish jealousy and hypocrisy of their hearts. In his answer he lays bare their thoughts to themselves, and in that very fact gives them proof of his supernatural authority, and proceeds to overthrow all their reasoning by the act which followed. "You think I am evading your scrutiny; you think it is easy to say, 'Thy sins be forgiven thee,' and that this is nothing but an empty word. Do you think it easier to forgive sins than to heal a body? That you may know, therefore, that my words are not empty, I will now do that which in your hearts you think I cannot do." Therefore he spoke the word of power that sent the man forth healed and well in body as in soul. So comes the answer to Christ's word to-day in the healed souls of men—which healing is impossible to explain apart from heavenly grace and power; and in the day when he shall raise the dead (even as God raised him from the dead) shall the unbelieving world know that "the Son of man hath power on earth to forgive sins." As the healed and forgiven man went out from their presence through the crowd which would not give way for him to come into the house, so shall the forgiven and healed disciples pass through the crowd of unbelievers on their way to their home in heaven.

XLIV.

JESUS LORD OF THE SABBATH.—Mark ii, 23-28.

(23) And it came to pass, that he went through the corn fields on the sabbath day; and his disciples began, as they went, to pluck the ears of corn. (24) And the Pharisees said unto him, Behold, why do they on the sabbath day that which is not lawful? (25) And he said unto them, Have ye never read what David did, when he had need, and was a hungered, he, and they that were with him? (26) How he went into the house of God in the days of Abiathar the high priest, and did eat the shewbread, which is not lawful to eat but for the priests, and gave also to them which were with him? (27) And he said unto them, The sabbath was made for man, and not man for the sabbath: (28) Therefore the Son of man is Lord also of the sabbath.—Mark ii, 23-28.

No subject of controversy between the Pharisees and Jesus occupied a larger place than that concerning the Sabbath. The Jews after their return from the captivity became rigidly puritanical—that is, they concentrated their attention upon a careful attention to the letter of God's law. The shameful neglect of the law had led to their captivity. Now they are determined that idolatry shall henceforth have no place among them, but that the law shall be observed in the most particular manner. We cannot blame them for having taken this high stand in respect to observing the law of God. Jesus also says to his disciples, "If ye love me, keep my commandments." But as time went on, the ceremonial observances of the law became a substitute for spiritual worship. The letter of the law took the place of the spirit. And as mere ceremonial without spirituality must ever be unsatisfactory, the leaders gradually increased the yoke of service in the matter of ceremonials, by adding to them things which God had never ordained, and forcing upon the commandments interpretations which they would not bear. It was for this that Christ rebuked them, saying, "Ye have made the commandment of God of none effect by your tradition." (Matt. xv, 6.) Among all the ceremonial observances, that of the Sabbath was marked out for very special care. On the other hand, Jesus seems to have interpreted the law of the Sabbath rather in the light of its spirit than of the letter. We do not infer from this that Jesus treated the Sabbath lightly, or would teach men so to do; but as it was kept by the Jews in his day it was but a dry old bottle out of which all the wine had gone. Jesus, as it were, sought to put new wine into this old bottle, with the result that he broke it. He did not mean that the Sabbath should (like wine running out of a broken bottle) be lost, but he designed a new bottle in which to put the new wine. In other words, Jesus fulfilled the spirit of the old Sabbath law only to carry it into a higher law, viz., that of the Christian's "Lord's day." We have our Sabbatarians to-day, and also our anti-Sabbatarians; and the great difficulty with many earnest Christians is to keep the mean and true Sabbath, and at once to avoid the Phariseeism of the Jews and the license of the anti-Sabbatarians. That it is entirely outside the pale of the Christian's law to observe the Levitical Sabbath is as evident as it is that the old Temple service, with its feasts and sacrifices, are done away in Christ—that is, fulfilled in him, so that he alone becomes the object of our worship. On the other hand, there is a spiritual and real time of rest and worship which every Christian is bound to recognize. If we could but keep in mind the spirit rather than, or at least besides, the letter of the law, we would be saved from grave mistakes in this matter. Two sayings of the Master kept side by side in mind and heart constitute the safeguards of the Sabbath: "The Sabbath was made for man, and not man for the Sabbath;" and, "The Son of man is Lord also of the Sabbath." Within these two sayings the Sabbath lies, and within them we shall find the true law of observance. We come now to consider the occasion and outcome of the present controversy.

I.—WHAT JESUS AND HIS DISCIPLES DID.

It was on a Sabbath-day, and Jesus and his disciples, perhaps on their way to the synagogue, or on some other errand of worship or mercy, passed through a field of corn, and being hungry began to pluck and rub out in their hands some ears of corn and eat them. There were following them a company of Pharisees, intent not on worship or Sabbath rest, but with hearts full of jealousy and bitterness, and bent upon watching Jesus to see if he would venture a foot beyond the limits of what *they* had prescribed as a "Sabbath day's journey," or whether he would do aught which they would declare a violation of the Sabbath, even some work of mercy, such as healing a blind or a lame man. (Luke xiv, 5.)

1.—Plucking ears of corn.—The Pharisees did not protest against plucking the ears of corn and eating them, though they were growing in another man's field. This was perfectly lawful (Deut. xxiii, 25), for it was allowed to any hungry man to help himself to as much as ever he could eat, only he must not put a sickle into his neighbor's corn. So this was not their complaint, but that they did it on the Sabbath-day. Now, God no more forbade a hungry man to eat on the Sabbath-day than he forbade him to pluck his neighbor's corn. Hunger is not confined to the six working days of the week. But the Pharisees had added a commandment to God's Word which interpreted the plucking of corn to be reaping, which was secular work, and the rubbing out of the ears in the palms of the hands to be threshing, which was also secular work, and therefore a breach of the Sabbath.

2.—The accusation of the Pharisees.—Promptly these hypocrites (Luke xiii, 15) pounce upon him, and by way of a question charge the Lord with violating the Sabbath. Now, it is evident that their care was not for the Sabbath, but to get an occasion against him so that they might either discredit him with the people as a lawbreaker or despiser of Moses' law, or that they might bring him before the Sanhedrim and condemn him. This is why he denounced them as hypocrites. They were pretending one thing while they meant another. They were in fact gratifying their hatred under a cloak of religious zeal. This is one of the worst forms of vice which prevails in the religious world. Pretending zeal for God and his Word, there are those who to gratify spite use God's law as a weapon of destruction against an opponent, and substitute their own enmity and passion for the zeal of God. This spirit is most hateful to God, and most damaging to one's own soul. There is, it is to be feared, much of this spirit and practice in the present state of religious controversy in the Church of Christ. How little these wretched enemies of Jesus knew of the Sabbath they were pretending such zeal for! Sabbath means rest—rest of spirit as well as of body; rest from all that is carnal and selfish, and the surrender of the whole being up to God in spiritual worship. But these zealots were restless in their endeavors to overcome one whom they hated, and their hearts were rankling with jealousy and envy instead of swelling with praise and prayer. How poor a substitute is an outward form for an inward spiritual state! "The hour cometh, and now is, when the true worshipers shall worship the Father in spirit and in truth." All the ordinances of God were given to man in order to help him in worship, and not to bind him to a ceremonial, which is the merest mockery unless it is subordinated to the spirit. The worship of "the lips when the heart is far from God" is hateful to him. The most punctilious observances of feasts and fasts and all offerings are loathsome to God when they are not the true expression of a heart throbbing with love and desire toward him. Many a man breaks the Sabbath in keeping it. Jesus kept it in breaking it, even supposing his present action was a breach of the letter of the law, which it was not.

II.—THE DEFENSE OF JESUS.

We cannot but be struck with the matchless tenderness and forbearance of our Lord in dealing with these rancorous critics and accusers. He might have turned upon them, as at a later time, and charged them with violating God's commandments and profaning them by their additions and traditions. But now, in this early time, his heart was set on winning them to himself and to a better understanding of God's Word. So he defends, or rather justifies, himself by an appeal to an incident in the life of David, their great and ideal king, which at once offered a justifying precedent and illustrated the spirit of the law of the Sabbath. In addition to the incident cited on this occasion, we shall also introduce other incidents to which our Lord appealed, as given by the other recorders in connection with this as well as at other times when this controversy was in debate between him and the Pharisees.

1.—What David did.—He cites the occasion when David, fleeing from Saul (I. Sam. xxi, 1-6), went into the Temple with his little band and asked bread of the priest; who, when there was no common bread found, gave David and his young men the hallowed "shewbread," which "is not lawful to eat but for the priests." The priest gave them this bread in defiance of the letter of the ceremonial law, because there was a higher law present which made it necessary for him to feed the hungry. Better break the letter of a hundred ceremonial laws than that a child of God should go hungry in a time of need like this. This case was exceptional, but it illustrated the point. Now, even had Jesus broken the Sabbath (which he had not), he was justified in feeding the hungry disciples or allowing them to feed themselves. Works of necessity are lawful on the Sabbath-day, as, for instance, the leading forth of the oxen to water. This is a technical violation of the Sabbath because it involves labor. Yet no one ever thought of calling in question that work because of the law of the Sabbath. (Luke xiii, 15.)

2.—What the priests do on the Sabbath.—In Matthew's account of this incident he says that Jesus cited to them the fact that the priests on the Sabbath profane that holy day and are blameless (Matt. xii, 5, 6), because without slaying the sacrificial animals it would be impossible for the worship of God to go on. Here two laws come in to modify *their* Sabbath law. First, it was required by law that these animals should be slain on the Sabbath, though ordinary slaying would have been a breach of the Sabbath. Then there is that general and higher law that compels men to worship God, and sanctifies whatever manual labor or exertion is involved in so doing. It is lawful, then, to do work in connection with the worship of God. My work is more arduous on the Sabbath than on any other day in the week; yet surely I do not violate the Sabbath in thus serving God. Even the necessary travel involved in God's service is lawful to me. If I take a horse to ride or drive, it is lawful. Many say it is not lawful to drive or ride to one's work on the Sabbath, but that one must always walk. Well, my judgment is that man is of more value than the horse, and so I spare the man and use the horse when it is necessary. Again, it is urged that it is not lawful to require one's coachman or a cabman to drive you to church or to carry you to your work. But I cannot see the difference between employing a coachman or cabman and the beadle of the church or the blower of the organ or the man who attends to the fires. All necessary work in connection with the worship and work of God is lawful on the Sabbath-day.

3.—What may be done for mercy on the Sabbath-day.— Once Jesus healed a poor woman who had been bound for many years with a deformity which caused her to go bent in a painful and constrained position. He was fiercely denounced for breaking the Sabbath in doing this work of mercy. He justified himself by an appeal to what all would admit to be a work of necessity. If, for instance, one's ox or ass should fall into a pit, or a sheep get turned over on its back, it would be lawful to pull out the poor beasts, no matter how much labor was involved in it. Is it not much better to help a human being than a beast, or at least as lawful? (Luke xiii, 14-16.) Then all works of mercy are lawful on the Sabbath-day. Mercy is never ceremonial, and must always take precedence of every ceremonial on every and all days of the week. Matthew tells us that the Lord, having used these illustrations, added: "If ye had known what this meaneth, I will have mercy, and not sacrifice, ye would not have condemned the guiltless." (Matt. xii, 7.) There is much significance in Jesus' words (ver. 25), "Have ye never read?" Either some people do not know the Scriptures, having never read them, or they have not read them aright, and so they fall into mistaken and narrow interpretations of God's blessed Word, which, like his mercy, has in it "a wideness like the wideness of the sea."

III.—THE SABBATH AND MAN.

Our Lord concluded his address to the Pharisees by defining the relations of the Sabbath to man, or, perhaps better to say, the relations of man to the Sabbath.

1.—"The Sabbath was made."—The Sabbath—that is, the consecration of a seventh day or portion of time—is not an institution which is founded on anything observed in nature, such as the division of time into years, months, and days, according to the astronomical movements of the planets. Man left to himself would not have discovered the beneficent law of rest inaugurated by the creating or setting apart of the seventh day as a day of rest. The Sabbath is a revelation of God, and was ordained of God from the beginning of creation. Without that revelation it would never have had existence. It is therefore a divine and not a natural or human institution. This at once invests it with a peculiar sanctity and authority.

2.—It was ordained for man.—The object of the Sabbath institution was for the benefit of man. "The Sabbath was made for man," as the earth was. The earth was made first, and thoroughly fitted for man's residence and the sphere of his training and development, and I may say for his final enjoyment. In like manner the Sabbath was ordained for man as a means toward the end of his development and training for God and the enjoyment of God forever. Man therefore is greater than the earth, as the owner and occupier of a house is greater than the house. So also is man greater and of more importance than the Sabbath. The uses of the Sabbath and the proper observance of it are to be studied from the point of view of man rather than from anything inherent in the day itself. Our Lord impressed this upon his hearers when he said, "The Sabbath was made for man, and not man for the Sabbath." All ordinances are made for men, and not men for the ordinances. It is therefore a violation of the divine purpose when man is made the slave of the ordinance. The essence of ritualism is to subordinate man to ordinances, rather than to keeping ordinances in subordination to man. The Word of God was given for man in order that he might come to know Christ (John v, 39); but when the Word of God became the object of worship it killed by its letter instead of giving life by its spirit. (II. Cor. iii, 2.) So of the Sabbath: it was given to help man in his relation to God; but when men made an idol of the Sabbath, then it became a taskmaster, and not a servant of man to minister peace and rest to him through faith in God and his Christ. The three great ends for which the Sabbath was given were: (i) That man might be reminded that God was the Creator of the world and that man owed him allegiance and thanksgiving. (Gen. ii, 1-3.) (ii) That God was the redeemer and deliverer of man. (Deut. v, 14, 15.) In that great Egyptian redemption and deliverance, man was taught that God delivered him without his help or on account of his work; pointing to the great redemption and deliverance which is in Christ, and not "by works of righteousness which we have done." Therefore we remember and rest from our works, and give glory to God. (iii) That we might know that in Christ the people of God have come into an eternal rest from the bondage and service of sin; and that labor, as one of the curses which came by sin, is turned into a holy rest which is the gift of God. Therefore in Christ man rests from his works as God did from his. (Heb. iv, 8-11.) The Sabbath of God fully entered into by Christ puts man into the paradise of God as sin turned man out of God's Eden. It is also suggested by Jesus in this saying that the Sabbath was made for man as such, and not for Jews or Gentiles, but for all men. Therefore the Sabbath, rightly interpreted, is in itself a gospel as universal as the race.

IV.—THE SON OF MAN AND THE SABBATH.

Jesus seemed to say to the Jews, that as the Sabbath was made for man and not man for the Sabbath, man was not therefore to be bound by the Sabbath as a slave to his chain; but that it was rather to be used by man in any way which would best conduce to his good. But lest this larger interpretation of the Sabbath should be construed into license, he added, "Therefore the Son of man is Lord also of the Sabbath." As God is the Lord of creation, so Jesus is the Lord of the Sabbath. As the creation is to be used by man for his good and enjoyment under God's Lordship, and not abused as a mere instrument for selfish gratification, so the Sabbath is to be used by man for his spiritual good and not abused for selfish and idle ends. If men who plead for the free use of the Sabbath as a mere holiday, and quote the words of Jesus to the effect that it was made for man, would only also quote this other declaration of Jesus, that "the Son of man is Lord also of the Sabbath," it would check their license. The Christian Sabbath is the "Lord's day," and therefore we may not steal it for ourselves or misuse it, seeing that it is his, and is lent to us for a high and holy purpose. Let us every one remember that Jesus is "Lord also of the Sabbath," and then there will be no fear that we shall abuse the privilege and trust, break the Sabbath and forget God's example and commandment.

XLV.

THE TWELVE CHOSEN.—Mark iii, 6–19.

(6) And the Pharisees went forth, and straightway took counsel with the Herodians against him, how they might destroy him. (7) But Jesus withdrew himself with his disciples to the sea: and a great multitude from Galilee followed him, and from Judea, (8) And from Jerusalem, and from Idumea, and from beyond Jordan; and they about Tyre and Sidon, a great multitude, when they had heard what great things he did, came unto him. (9) And he spake to his disciples, that a small ship should wait on him because of the multitude, lest they should throng him. (10) For he had healed many; insomuch that they pressed upon him for to touch him, as many as had plagues. (11) And unclean spirits, when they saw him, fell down before him, and cried, saying, Thou art the Son of God. (12) And he straitly charged them that they should not make him known. (13) And he goeth up into a mountain, and calleth unto him whom he would: and they came unto him. (14) And he ordained twelve, that they should be with him, and that he might send them forth to preach, (15) And to have power to heal sicknesses, and to cast out devils: (16) And Simon he surnamed Peter; (17) And James the son of Zebedee, and John the brother of James; and he surnamed them Boanerges, which is, The sons of Thunder: (18) And Andrew, and Philip, and Bartholomew, and Matthew, and Thomas, and James the son of Alpheus, and Thaddeus, and Simon the Canaanite, (19) And Judas Iscariot, which also betrayed him: and they went into a house.—Mark iii, 6-19.

The controversy concerning the Sabbath continues. Having answered the Pharisees as to the lawfulness of his disciples plucking the corn on the Sabbath-day to appease their hunger, the Lord passes from the open fields into the synagogue in Capernaum and there finds a man with a withered hand. The watchful Pharisees followed him and set a watch upon him, for they pretty well knew that his compassion would lead him to heal this poor man, and they might have opportunity in that to renew their attack upon him. Knowing their thoughts, and himself taking the initiative this time, he commands the man with the withered hand to "stand forth." Then, turning upon them, he forestalls their attack by propounding a question to them: "Is it lawful to do good on the Sabbath days or to do evil? to save life, or to kill?" This was an unanswerable question to them. If they said, "It is lawful to do good on the Sabbath days," then they gave away their whole argument; but if they said, "It is lawful to kill but not to do good," then they would put themselves in so ridiculous a position that even their own party must have laughed at and despised them. So "they held their peace." Jesus did not reply by words to their silent confession of insincerity, but, looking about upon them, scorched them with the anger of his eyes; and even yet he had an infinite pity for them. The anger of the Lord at the willful hardness and perverseness of heart of deliberate sinners is very great; yet at the same time his compassion is equally great, because it grieves him to see men so utterly blinded and deluded to their own destruction. To the end Jesus was full of pity and compassion for his rejecters and murderers. He wept over Jerusalem and lamented the sad end of those who would not receive him, and when at last they murdered him he prayed that they might be forgiven.

The opening verse of our study presents us with a sad and melancholy picture of the baseness of the human heart when it is deliberately set against Christ. After Jesus had healed the man with the withered hand, and they were compelled for very shame to keep silent because of the dilemma he had put them into by his searching questions, they left the synagogue. It became too hot for them there, and so they went out—not, as Peter did, full of penitence to weep over their sin, but full of rancorous hatred to plot how they might destroy him. "They could not silence him, so they would slay him." They feared to do anything openly, because they saw that "the people" were on Jesus' side, and so they must plot secretly what they dared not do openly. Those who begin by criticising Jesus usually end by trying to destroy him. There are those who to-day cannot resist or answer his words, and so they go round about to slay him through his Word. The modern critic who seeks to discredit the Word of God seeks to do so not in the interests of truth, but that they may thereby get rid of Christ. For if his Word can be impeached he is impeached and his influence and authority gone. Let the modern Pharisee answer to himself and to God for the work he is seeking to do under the specious pretense of love for the truth.

I.—JESUS WITHDRAWS HIMSELF.

Jesus knew full well what was in the hearts of these Pharisees, and also what their "counsel" was concerning him (Matt. xii, 15, 16); and as his business was not controversy (or more especially conflict with these cavilers), he withdrew himself and retired out of the city to the seaside. His method was not to strive or cry in the streets (Matt. xii, 19), and so he left the streets and went away. Not because the Lord was afraid of their "counsel," or because he dreaded the result; but because for the present his business was with the people, to preach the kingdom of God and teach them the things belonging to their peace. His hour for suffering and death had not yet come, and until it did Jesus was bound to avoid all hazard to himself. Besides, the raising of a great crowd was foreign to his purpose and would seriously interfere with his present work of teaching. No noisy debater or agitator was our gracious Lord, but meek and lowly, rather giving way than contending, knowing as he did what the final end would be: that when he had finished his teaching work he would be given up to die for sinners, and then from on high carry on the blessed work of salvation. Jesus was fond of retiring to the mountains if they were near, or to the seaside. He loved the quiet of nature, and always seemed to be nearer his Father when he was away from the crowded city or thoroughfare.

1.—The following multitude.—But Jesus could not be hid. The multitude followed him out of the city to the seaside, whither he and the disciples retired. These were men from every part of the land—from Galilee and Judea; from Jerusalem and from beyond the Jordan; from Idumea and from Tyre and Sidon. Even the Gentiles were beginning to rejoice in him. In this following multitude we see a prophecy of the great truth that he should draw all men unto him. There is that about Jesus which compels attention and causes men to seek after him. He is the real magnet of men. It is even true that when he is the most condemned he becomes attractive to the multitude. The assaults of enemies only cause the multitude to think more of him.

2.—The impelling motives of the crowd.—The question at once arises, Why did this multitude follow after Jesus? What was there about him that men sought him out so persistently? No doubt the motives of the multitude were as mixed as the crowd was. We know full well what some of their motives were, and may judge this crowd which thronged after him much as we would judge a crowd of to-day. (i) There was the careless crowd of people who were merely curious to see and hear what he might do or say further. He was a unique figure in the land. He had a new doctrine, and he spake not "as the scribes" (their regular teachers). He had a strange and wonderful power, and his miracles had excited universal curiosity. They were not necessarily interested in his mission, but were curious as the Athenian crowd was to hear what "this babbler" might say, or to see what this Nazarene miracle-worker might do. (ii) Then, again, his teaching, his miracles, and especially his wonderful personality; his fearless impeachment of the Pharisees and scribes; his exposure of their sophistries and the unmasking of their hypocrisies, together with his wonderful words of sympathy and love; his tender compassion also upon the sick and friendless was beginning to tell upon the hearts and consciences of not a few; and we may hope that there was a dawning faith among them and they longed to see and hear more from this man who took the part of the poor against the pharisaical rich, and of the outcasts against these religious aristocrats. So they came after him, eager for more light or for a fuller draught of that water of life of which they had gotten a taste. These were they in whom had been awakened the first serious impressions, which if they followed "on to know the Lord," would lead to their conversion and salvation, but which if they did *not* follow up would leave them in a worse state than if they had never seen or heard of him at all. How many are like them to-day! They are interested and attracted, and something in their hearts is stirred; for a moment they believe that in Jesus there is the hope of those better things of which they have thought and dreamed, but who are (alas, many of them!) checked and hindered by some saying of his which touches their selfishness, worldliness, or pride, and they follow him no more, and then lay the blame of their own superficiality and lack of earnestness upon him, saying, as we have often heard them say, "We have tried religion, and it did us no good." (iii) Then there were those who were moved by self-interest—at least by a kind of immediate selfishness growing out of some pressing bodily infirmity which they desired to be cured of. "When they heard what great things he did," they "came unto him," "for he healed many, . . . as many as had plagues." We cannot blame these poor plague-stricken people who came to get their bodies healed, only we would that they came to know the plagues of their own hearts. Jesus cures all the plagues which have fallen upon man because of sin. When upon the earth he healed their bodily plagues first, as a pledge of his love and power; but now his method is first to heal the soul, and then in the resurrection he does more than heal this "vile body"; he changes it and fashions it "like unto his glorious body," which is forever impervious to sickness.

3.—**The unclean spirits.**—Among the remarkable testimonies to Jesus were those given to him by the unclean spirits. "And unclean spirits, when they saw him, fell down before him, and cried, saying, Thou art the Son of God." A number of incidents of this kind are recorded in the Gospels. In the first chapter of this Gospel, at the twenty-fourth verse, we have one such, who cried out, "What have we to do with thee, thou Jesus of Nazareth? art thou come to destroy us? I know thee who thou art, the Holy One of God." The demons recognized Jesus before the afflicted multitude did; nay, even before his own disciples did. But he sought not testimony from devils, and so he commanded them to hold their peace. Again we have another incident. (Luke iv, 41.) In this case also they confessed and declared that he was "Christ the Son of God." In this case also he rebuked the unclean spirit and forbade him to speak. He will not have men believe on him on devils' testimony, but on the testimony of God in his Word, by the works which he did, by his own word, and by the Spirit revealing this knowledge from the Father. (Matt. xvi, 17; John xiv, 11.) Again, we have the case of the demoniacs of Gadara, who confessed him to be the "Son of the most high God." Surely these devils put many a man for whom Christ died to shame in this matter. They believe and tremble (James ii, 19), because for them there is no mercy. Jesus did not come to save devils, for they sinned after such a manner that left for them no room for repentance. In believing and knowing him they had no hope, and did not even ask for mercy, except that they might not be tormented before their time, or that their torments might not be exaggerated. (Matt. viii, 29.) When a devil believes he trembles; but when a sinner believes and confesses Christ he is declared to be a "blessed man," and rejoices. In heaven there is no unbelief concerning Jesus, for there the angels of God worship him; in hell there is no unbelief concerning Jesus, for there the devils believe and tremble. It is only on earth among men that we find unbelief. These human unbelievers will all be converted from and cured of their skepticism, either in heaven among the angels or in hell among the devils. Would God that all men might believe unto life everlasting and escape this devil's faith which leads not to life.

4.—**Jesus preaching from a small ship.**—Having reached the seashore, the throng which followed the Lord was so great that he could do nothing because of the great press about him. So he bade his disciples provide a little ship or boat, and, putting out a little way from the shore, he sat or stood in it as a kind of pulpit, and spoke to the people, and even healed them; for Jesus could heal by a word as well as by a touch, and we are told by Matthew, who relates this same incident with added particulars, that "he healed them all." (Matt. xii, 15.) This putting off from the shore and separating himself from the crowd suggests to us a larger fact in the life of Jesus. He has gone away from the earth now to heaven, but he did so that he might the better save us. We know that in a vast throng only a few could even see him, much less get at him to touch him. So we cannot help thinking how disadvantageous it would be for us had Jesus remained on the earth. How many of the poor plague-stricken men of earth could have gone to him, or rather *how few* could have gone to him. But now that he is removed from the earth to heaven, he is where we may all see him by faith, even from the ends of the earth, and "his word is nigh thee, even in thy mouth and in thy heart," and all who hear his words and believe on him are saved. In fact, just as Jesus was practically nearer to the multitude, both for sight and hearing, in that little boat than on land, so he is nearer to us now than if he had remained on earth. As near to the man in China, in India, or Africa as to us, and "all who call upon him" are heard and saved. The throng which pressed upon him out of idle curiosity does not hinder the earnest ones who come to him for salvation. It is the man who out of his heart calls upon him who is saved rather than the man who throngs him with a multitude of curious people who do not really want him.

5.—**Jesus commands that he should not be made known.** —This was to avoid a mere carnal popularity or a curious throng. But he does not now command us not to make him known. No. On the other hand, he bids us go to the very ends of the earth and preach the gospel and make disciples of all nations. Says the late Mr. Spurgeon, commenting on this passage: "*We* are under no charge to conceal his gracious wonders, and therefore we would joyfully enlarge upon that glorious record, 'He healed them all.'" What an encouragement this is for sin-sick souls!

II.—THE APOSTLES ORDAINED.

Having left the seaside, Jesus retired to a mountain, and called to him special ones from among his disciples, and ordained them to be his apostles.

THE APOSTLES ORDAINED.

1.—The sovereignty of his choice.—"And calleth unto him whom he would." "No man taketh this honor unto himself." Even the most worthy disciples must not run until they are called and sent. Hitherto these disciples were content to follow Jesus whithersoever he went and do that which they were bidden, but they were in no wise distinguished from all other believers, so far, at least, as any special claim to precedence was concerned. They were all simple brethren together. But now the time had come to select a special number who should in a more particular and official way be his representatives. It is true that Jesus called "whom he would," that none were nominated to him, but he exercised his own right and sovereignty in selecting this company of apostles. "Ye have not chosen me, but I have chosen you, and ordained you, that ye should go and bring forth fruit, and that your fruit should remain." (John xv, 16.) There was sovereignty but no arbitrariness in the choice which Jesus made. All the choices of God have love and reason in them. In fact, I think we may say that God never does anything out of mere arbitrariness. Certainly he never calls men to special service unless there is that in or about them that makes the choice specially fit. Who that recalls Abraham, Joseph, Moses or Joshua, Elijah or Elisha, David or Solomon, John the Baptist, Peter or Paul, but that must say, "These were the best men that could possibly be found for the work they had to do"? No doubt the work developed the men, as the grace of God fitted them, but there was that in them that was capable of such development as to natural gifts, not to speak of the disposition in them by grace.

2.—The response of the disciples to the Master's call.—"And they came unto him." No doubt they had long before in a very true sense consecrated themselves to his service. He had before called Peter (after the first call to salvation) to follow him as a fisher of men. And Levi the publican (whom we know as Matthew) had already left all to follow Christ. Now again when the Master calls them they go to him, ready each one of them to say, "Here am I, Lord; send me." This is a mark of a true apostle, that he is henceforth ready to come or go at the call of Christ. "Lord, what wilt thou have me to do?" was the first word of Saul of Tarsus after he found Jesus. This should be our attitude toward Christ, for though we may not be apostles we are all his sons as well as his servants, and are liable to be called and sent at any time.

3.—The apostles ordained.—In what consisted this ordination beyond the word of Christ telling them of their being chosen and giving them instructions? The word used means simply to make, to appoint, to set forth. It has no special or sacred sense. It is almost certain that there was no ceremony other than the mere communication of the fact of his choice of them for the office to which they were called. The laying on of hands in the early Church upon those selected or appointed for special service was but the formal expression of the ordination or appointment and did not *constitute* the ordination. The word of Christ was their warrant and authority. This, and this only!

4.—**Their preparation.**—Their preparation was to "be with him." And this still must ever be our best preparation for service for Christ: To be with him. To learn of him, and to catch and absorb his spirit—this is preparation either for public service or private living.

5.—**Their chief business.**—"That he might send them forth to preach." This must ever be the chief business of apostles of whatever sort. A great apostle, even Paul, charged a young preacher whom he had ordained after this fashion: "I charge thee therefore before God, and the Lord Jesus Christ, who shall judge the quick and the dead at his appearing and his kingdom, *preach the Word.*" In those days apostles were not occupied with altars, candles, incense, reredoses, vestments, postures, and genuflections; but with the serious and glorious business of witnessing for Christ, testifying of his resurrection and his second coming. Perhaps those who are so sure that they are in the direct succession would make better proof of their ministry in following in the steps of the apostles in this respect than by proving their descent through a long line of spiritual ancestors, many of whom were but corrupt flesh-loving men. In addition to this chief business these first apostles were endued with special power for healing sickness and casting out devils. We have never heard of these modern so-called successors of these first apostles doing these apostolic works. To visit the sick, to pray for them, to do all we can to relieve their sufferings, and to fight against the devil's work as it is manifested in a thousand deplorable sins, is the privilege of all believers in our day, and all who love our Lord Jesus Christ should be ranged in this succession.

6.—**The men who were chosen.**—The three first evangelists give the names of the men who were chosen, but not in the same order. Matthew, who gives the most orderly arrangement, sets them forth by twos, and in three groups of four each (Matt. x, 1–4); but that is not the point of importance. They all agree in naming Peter first, and Judas the traitor last. Peter first because he was the man who by nature and temperament was the natural leader, and not because he was the primate in the modern sense of that word.

THE APOSTLES ORDAINED.

Leaders take their place naturally in the Church of Christ if the Church is free and not bound by external authority or organized into a hierarchy. Let us all strive to be first, not as a matter of ambition, but first in devotion, first to speak and to act for our Lord; and then we shall all be primates. The story of each of these twelve men affords matter of interest, but we have neither time nor space to follow them. Few of them ever became very conspicuous, at least as far as we know, even in their apostolic office. Their record is on high. Tradition tells us that all of them (save the beloved John) at last found for themselves martyr-deaths, crowning patient, devoted lives.

XLVI.

THE SERMON ON THE MOUNT.—Luke vi, 20-31.

(20) And he lifted up his eyes on his disciples, and said, Blessed be ye poor: for yours is the kingdom of God. (21) Blessed are ye that hunger now: for ye shall be filled. Blessed are ye that weep now: for ye shall laugh. (22) Blessed are ye, when men shall hate you, and when they shall separate you from their company, and shall reproach you, and cast out your name as evil, for the Son of man's sake. (23) Rejoice ye in that day, and leap for joy: for, behold, your reward is great in heaven: for in the like manner did their fathers unto the prophets. (24) But woe unto you that are rich! for ye have received your consolation. (25) Woe unto you that are full! for ye shall hunger. Woe unto you that laugh now! for ye shall mourn and weep. (26) Woe unto you, when all men shall speak well of you! for so did their fathers to the false prophets. (27) But I say unto you which hear, Love your enemies, do good to them which hate you, (28) Bless them that curse you, and pray for them which despitefully use you. (29) And unto him that smiteth thee on the one cheek offer also the other; and him that taketh away thy cloak forbid not to take thy coat also. (30) Give to every man that asketh of thee; and of him that taketh away thy goods ask them not again. (31) And as ye would that men should do to you, do ye also to them likewise.—Luke vi, 20-31.

There is probably no more difficult portion of the teachings of our Lord to interpret than that which we know as the Sermon on the Mount. We have but a fragment of it for our present study. Whether the address recorded by Luke is identical with the longer discourse given by Matthew, it is difficult to determine. Possibly our Lord repeated the substance of the famous address more than once. Certainly its importance is such that it would warrant repetition many times. We, at least, have need to ponder it, and inwardly digest it, by means of many readings and much prayerful meditation. *The time* of its delivery, in our judgment, was soon after the call of Levi (Matthew). Perhaps it was the first formal address he had heard from Jesus, and for that reason, as well as from the fact that he had just been called and honored by Jesus' selection as one of his apostles, it made a most profound impression on his mind. The *occasion* of its delivery is to some extent conjectural, and yet it may be determined with comparative certainty. Already Jesus had, by his teaching, his authority, evident power, and influence, come in conflict with the ruling classes, and especially with the scribes and Pharisees, the professional teachers of religion, and the dominant sectarians, who assumed to be the only true interpreters and exemplars of Moses' law. It was clearly evident that there was no single point of agreement between Jesus and the Pharisees; but it was not yet evident that Jesus was opposed to Moses, though this was what the Pharisees were insisting on and endeavoring to make appear. Their assumption was that to teach anything contrary to *their* exposition of the law and *their* religious practices was necessarily to be opposed to Moses.

Jesus had already a vast following, some of them deeply and sincerely attached to him by a powerful spiritual tie, some of them by one of popular and political expectancy, and more by idle curiosity. *Who is he?* and *What will he do?* were the prevailing questions. Is this the Messiah? Is he only a prophet, and as such will he lead a new departure in the religious life of the nation, in opposition to Pharisees and Sadducees? What does he mean by the kingdom of heaven and of God being at hand? If he is to lead and establish a new order, how will he do it? What are to be the principles of the kingdom he represents, and by what means will he accomplish his purpose? As to the controversy between him and the Pharisees and the rulers, wherein do they differ? These were probably some of the thoughts that were in the minds of the people. A favorable opportunity now offered itself for him to answer the questions uppermost in the minds of these followers. The Sermon on the Mount contains a digest of the principles upon which the new order is to be built. It is not in opposition to the law as given by Moses, but rather in exposition of it, and even an advance upon it. Christ came not to destroy, but to fulfill the law and the prophets. If he in any wise destroyed or set aside the old order, he did so by fulfilling it, just as the forming of the fruit destroys and sets aside the blossom, which was the prophecy of its coming. The law of Moses, given on Mount Sinai, was an exposition of the whole duty of man *according to righteousness*. The Sermon on the Mount was an exposition of the whole duty of man *according to love*. Now since "love is the fulfilling of the law," then the Sermon on the Mount must be not in opposition to, but in fulfillment of, this law. The law shows a *condition* of life; the Sermon on the Mount, the *outcome* of it. The law says, "Do and live"; the sermon says, "Live and do." The Sermon on the Mount is the apotheosis of the law. As Moses delivered the law, it was a rule of righteousness outside of us to be *lived up to;* as Christ interpreted it in his sermon, it was a living principle or law of love inside of us *to be worked out.* This agrees with the whole teaching of the New Testament. "The law was given by Moses, but grace and truth came by Jesus Christ." The law was truth, but the gospel is *"grace* and truth." Christ came at once to fulfill the law and impart grace. "What the law could not do, in that it was weak through the flesh, God sending his own Son in the likeness of sinful flesh, and for sin [or by a sacrifice for sin], condemned sin in the flesh: that the *righteousness of the law might be fulfilled in us*, who walk not after the flesh, but after the Spirit." (Rom. viii, 3, 4.) The Pharisees sought to fufill the law by overlaying it with innumerable glosses and commandments, "urging the letter of the precept to such a degree as to make it contradict the spirit." They had "stifled morality under legalism." They had wrapped the corn of the law around with innumerable husks of small observances, and were feeding the people on chaff. Jesus, with a bold hand, tears off this mass of husk, blows it aside, as with a breath from heaven, and lays bare the true corn and wheat of righteousness. He breaks through the letter of the law, and reveals the spirit of it throbbing with life and love. "Ye have heard it said." That is, ye have heard the Pharisees and scribes say. "But I say unto you." These words are the key by means of which we are to unlock the truth of the Sermon on the Mount in relation to the law. Matthew gives the sermon, with the evident intention of showing the Jews that Christ did not deny the law, but spiritually interpreted it. Luke is not so much, or, we may even say, not at all concerned with the Jews, and gives the sermon as containing the true principles of the kingdom of God, or Christ's law of love.

I have spoken of the difficulty of interpreting the various precepts of the sermon in respect to a practical application of them in daily life. This difficulty is a twofold one: if we accept them as being binding statutes, to be literally fulfilled, it must be seen that, in a very true sense, they are *impracticable;* on the other hand, if we say they are not to be carried out literally, then we are in danger of making void the commandments of Christ. It seems to me that we must not so much regard them as statutes, but as containing the fundamental principles of the law of love, to be held in mind and heart in all our dealings with men, and to be applied in every case and to the last extent of possibility. They are neither to become the foundation of a new legalism, nor to be regarded as the expression of an unattainable idealism. They are, in the whole reach of them, to be interpreted by the key which Jesus himself has given us in these expressions: "Be ye therefore perfect, as your Father which is in heaven is perfect." (Matt. v, 48.) "Be ye therefore merciful, as your Father also is merciful." (Luke vi, 36.) Put his Spirit into all that you do, and show by all your intercourse with men that you are not acting from personal and selfish motives, but as "the children of your Father which is in heaven." With this somewhat lengthy preface, which seems necessary in order to a comprehensive judgment of this great discourse, we are prepared to look more in detail at that particular portion which is the immediate object of our study.

I.—BLESSINGS AND WOES.

The company gathered about Jesus at this time was a mixed one, with his immediate disciples in the foreground and the more or less interested multitude gathered around, in which the Lord perceived some of those enemies which were already beginning to organize themselves into a band of resolute persecutors, who had determined on his death, and would, for the hate they bore him, pour out their wrath on his disciples for his sake. In Matthew's report of this discourse, Jesus speaks of the disciples in the third person, saying, "Blessed are *the* poor"; but Luke reports his discourse as having been delivered directly to his disciples, and to their enemies, saying, "Blessed be *ye* poor." There are four beatitudes here, and four woes—the first pronounced upon the disciples, and the second upon their and his enemies.

1.—The beatitudes.—These were pronounced concerning four several conditions in which he beheld his disciples. (i) "Blessed be ye poor." We are not to understand that poverty in itself is a ground and condition of blessedness, or that they were blessed and of necessity heirs of the kingdom of God because of their poverty; but he speaks to them in their present actual condition. They were, as a matter of fact, poor, and that poverty tended to bring about in their minds a humble estimate of themselves, which in its turn prepared them for the good news which the Lord had brought them. Matthew describes them as "poor in spirit." Luke here emphasizes their actual outward condition. The world hated and despised them because of their poverty, and especially because they had compensated themselves with the riches of his grace, and an appropriation of the promised kingdom of God. This made them independent of earthly riches and constituted them heirs of a kingdom which the wealth of this world could not give, or the favored position among men which their enemies boasted. Our Master bids them be of good cheer and be no longer cast down because of their poverty and insignificance, but to rejoice in that which he now gave them, not because they were poor, but because they had chosen God's riches in him. "To this man will I look, even to him that is poor and of a contrite spirit, and trembleth at my word." (Is. lxvi, 2.) Compare this with what James says of the poor who have chosen God for their portion. (James ii, 5; I. Cor. i, 27, 28.) Why has God chosen the poor and the weak and the base? Not because of these conditions, but because men in these conditions are the most likely to look to God for help and mercy, as having nothing to hope for or expect or to make life worth living in this world. Outward poverty tends to humbleness of mind, and leads to that state of spiritual poverty which makes men glad to accept spiritual wealth. Such shall have their compensation in the kingdom of God—that is, both now, in the consciousness of God's love, and hereafter, when all the world is brought under the sway of divine righteousness, when men shall be estimated for what they are and not for what they have. (ii) "Blessed are ye that hunger now." Matthew adds, "after righteousness," but Luke would show that those who, having chosen Christ, even though outwardly they be in straits for temporal things, in view of that full supply of every need which God has prepared for them that love him, are to be congratulated above those who are full in this world, yet have no portion in the final distribution of God's measureless bounty. The heir of a vast fortune who is fitting himself worthily to take possession of it, even though he be at present in great need, is a man rather to be congratulated than a spendthrift who has his fortune and is rapidly wasting it, with nothing further in store but the misery he is providing for himself, both in character and condition. (iii) "Blessed are ye that weep now." These poor disciples of Christ had much in this world to distress them, which caused oftentimes tears to come into their eyes, even like many of his disciples at this day. Let them be cheered! There is coming a time when their mouths shall be filled with laughter, and their sorrows shall flee away forever. Let them be patient under their trials and affliction. They shall forget them all very soon in the fullness of their coming joy. (iv) "Blessed are ye when men shall hate you," etc. Some of them were even then hated, had their names erased from the synagogue roll, and were cast out and separated from the respectable (?) people of that day, their names reproached, and themselves denounced as evil-doers, for Christ's sake. So Christ's people have suffered (some of them) in all ages, and so will they continue to suffer, some in a greater and some in a lesser degree, as they are true and faithful to Christ; but let them rejoice in that day which is coming, and leap for joy, for God has prepared something so great and good for them, in token of his appreciation of their love and loyalty to him, that will be infinitely better and beyond everything they have suffered for Christ's sake. Moreover, let them encourage themselves with the thought that they are treading in the paths of the holy prophets, those chosen men of all ages who have stood for and with God, and who represented all that was best in the kingdom of God on earth. No new and strange thing had come upon them, and God would not forget their testimony.

2.—The woes.—Turning from his disciples for a moment, he addressed himself to a company of proud, self-indulgent, worldly-minded men who were now the leading spirits in fomenting opposition and organizing persecution against him and his disciples. He tells them plainly that they had already received their consolation. They had gotten already all there was to get out of their high social positions, out of their carnal fullness, and their evanescent pleasures. A time of soul-hunger was coming to them—a time when they should desire but not have, a time of weeping and mourning, when there would be none and nothing to comfort them. This not because they were rich, but because they found in their riches a worldly sufficiency which led them to reject the better things which God was offering them, and made them angry with "the poor in spirit" and in worldly goods, because they had learned how to be happy and independent of these things in spite of their persecutions. It is characteristic of the worldly spirit that it hates others who can be contented without riches and position, and have a secret source of happiness which is unknown to the world. This discourse of Jesus is the commentary upon the story of the rich man and Lazarus set forth in the sixteenth chapter of this Gospel.

II.—THE LAW OF LOVE.

As has been already pointed out, the underlying principle of this law, in its manifestation, is to do nothing to any man from a mere personal and selfish consideration. If we will carry this thought in our minds, it will help us much in understanding the following precepts.

Luke does not use the words, "Ye have heard that it hath been said, Thou shalt love thy neighbor, and hate thine enemy," for the reason that he is not concerned with the bearing of this law of love on the controversy with the Pharisees and scribes, but only as it is the new law of the kingdom of God, and for the disciples of Christ. There are three parts to the manifestation of the law in the first summary, though later on others are added.

1.—Its active manifestation.—"Love your enemies." This is not the rule of nature, nor in a certain sense of law, but it is the rule of love. "God commendeth his love toward us, in that, while we were yet sinners, Christ died for us." (Rom. v, 8.) We are henceforth to deal with men, not as though there were no God, nor as though God had put law into *our* hands. We are to regard them (our enemies) as sinners against God, and yet as the objects of his divine love and compassion, and think of them as desiring to win them *to* God, and *from* their sins. If we can win them to God, we will reconcile them to ourselves. It does not bid us to love their sin, or to approve, justify, or even excuse their wrong-doing, but to regard them as objects of love—that is, of our good wishes. We are to lose sight of our personal wrongs in view of their more wretched estate. The man who wrongs another does more harm to himself than to him he injures, and is therefore the greater object of pity. The second precept is to "do good to them which hate you." This is to carry love beyond a mere sentiment. It is to embody it. We may often be inclined to forego vengeance and leave that to God, but it is a higher exercise of love to do good to them which hate us. "Therefore if thine enemy hunger, feed him; if he thirst, give him drink: for in so doing thou shalt heap coals of fire on his head. Be not overcome of evil, but overcome evil with good." (Rom. xii, 20, 21.) This is the vengeance of love. Yet more than this: "Bless them that curse you." If one should, in wrath and blasphemous hate, call on God to "damn you," as often wicked men do, then do you counteract that curse with a devout prayer, "*God bless you.*" This were the manifestation of love. But yet this is not all. "Pray for them which despitefully use you." Not only are we to exert our power of love upon our enemies, but we are to go beyond ourselves and our own resources, and call on God's help by praying for them. This is the climax of love. Such love as this can only emanate from the heart of him who prayed for his murderers. And yet that *it is* possible for his disciples to exercise it, is attested by Stephen's prayer for his murderers, and in the cases of hundreds of others, who have so prayed for them who have most cruelly injured them.

In this spiritual realm it is possible for us to fulfill the law in both the letter and the spirit.

2.—Its passive manifestation.—Love is both active in the exercise of its sentiment, and passive in its power of suffering wrong. "Unto him that smiteth thee on the one cheek offer also the other." Here there is no doubt a rule that has its qualifications. There are circumstances in which this may be done, but it surely does not mean that under all circumstances we are to submit to and encourage personal injuries and indignities. When the Nazarenes sought to thrust him over the brow of the hill, he did not tamely submit, but escaped out of their hands. When he was under arrest and they smote him on the cheek, he did not offer the other, but remonstrated with them for so doing. (John xviii, 23.) It must mean just this: that love not only does not revenge itself, but is ready, if needs be, to go to any extreme length in the exercise of patience and forbearance. It is in charity that the disciple of Jesus yields when he yields; it is in charity, also, that he resists when he resists. *Charity has no other limit than charity itself*—that is to say, it is boundless. "When he was reviled" he "reviled not again." "And him that taketh away thy cloak forbid not to take thy coat also." This surely is not a direction that we are to stand still and be plundered by every robber that chooses to stretch out his hand against us—to open our houses and expose our goods to every idle, vicious vagabond that comes along, and say, "Help yourself. I will not only not resist you, but will not forbid you." It must be understood in the light of such Scriptures as these: "Now therefore there is utterly a fault among you, because ye go to law one with another. Why do ye not rather take wrong? Why do ye not rather suffer yourselves to be defrauded?" (I. Cor. vi, 7.) "If a man will sue thee at the law, and take away thy coat," etc. (Matt. v, 40.) In a small matter it is far better to give way than contend. If a creditor be uncharitable to the extent of taking the very coat from your back, better to go to the extreme of charity and voluntarily surrender your cloak, than to resist him in the same spirit that he shows toward you. For charity's sake go to any length—only act in charity and not in defense of mere personal rights. (Rom. xii, 19–21.)

3.—Its benevolent manifestation.—"Give to every man that asketh of thee." This clause brings us to consider our relation to men, neither in respect of their enmity nor their oppression, but in respect of their need, and our ability to supply it. Does this mean that we are indiscriminately to give to every one that asks us? Surely not, for this would defeat the very ends of charity, by presently destroying the very means of helping those who were really in need. To interpret this clause without comparing it with Scripture would be to put all industry at the mercy of idleness. It would be sometimes, and not infrequently, to make charity the accessory of vice. Would it be charity for me to give money to a man whom I knew would go straight to a tavern and spend it for drink, or in vicious indulgences? Nay, true charity would require me to withhold, not to save my purse, but to save the one who asked me. The same would be true of other things we might have to give besides money. Should a robber ask me to give or lend him help in accomplishing his evil deeds, does this law compel me to give him aid in sin? By no means. The rather let it be interpreted in the light of Deut. xv, 7–11: "If there be among you a poor man, . . . thou shalt not harden thine heart, nor shut thine hand from thy poor brother. . . . Beware that there be not a thought in thy wicked heart, . . . and thine eye be evil against thy poor brother, and thou givest him nought. . . . Thou shalt surely give him, and thine heart shalt not be grieved when thou givest unto him. . . . For the poor shall never cease out of the land: therefore I command thee, saying, Thou shalt open thine hand wide unto thy brother, to thy poor, and to thy needy, in thy land." "He that hath pity upon the poor lendeth unto the Lord." But these are neither the idle nor the vicious poor, for we read again: "If any would not work, neither should he eat." The Pharisees were a hard and covetous race, and it was against the grasping avarice which led them to despise and oppress the poor, rather than to help and relieve them, that our Lord leveled these words. Luke takes them up into the general law of charity, and passes them on to us for our guidance. The measure of our giving must be so liberal, that we must neither give nor withhold out of regard to ourselves, but according to the law of love; sometimes not giving much for charity's sake, and sometimes heaped up, pressed down, and running over, even to the point of personal deprivation, if charity command and sanction it.

4.—*Its law.*—In this famous law, called the Golden Rule, we have the sum and substance of all Christ's teaching with reference to our relations to each other. Space does not allow anything like a full discussion of it. As a saying it raises heaven high above any conception which man has ever had of disinterested and loving regard for our neighbor. It is not negative, but positive. "It covers the whole breadth of our conscience in its manward direction." Others have had gleams and glimpses of this law of love, but never a full, clear, shining beam of light fell athwart human conscience until Christ uttered this. How is it that not one out of a thousand persons can quote any one of the so-called "silver rules" that have been put in competition and comparison with this? Just because when the sun is shining the stars disappear from sight. With this rule in our heart we can measure every human action as between man and man, and especially our own daily lives, and see if they come short of Christ's law of love.

XLVII.

OPPOSITION TO CHRIST.—Mark iii, 22-35.

(22) And the scribes which came down from Jerusalem said, He hath Beelzebub, and by the prince of the devils casteth he out devils. (23) And he called them unto him, and said unto them in parables, How can Satan cast out Satan? (24) And if a kingdom be divided against itself, that kingdom cannot stand. (25) And if a house be divided against itself, that house cannot stand. (26) And if Satan rise up against himself, and be divided, he cannot stand, but hath an end. (27) No man can enter into a strong man's house, and spoil his goods, except he will first bind the strong man; and then he will spoil his house. (28) Verily I say unto you, All sins shall be forgiven unto the sons of men, and blasphemies wherewith soever they shall blaspheme: (29) But he that shall blaspheme against the Holy Ghost hath never forgiveness, but is in danger of eternal damnation: (30) Because they said, He hath an unclean spirit. (31) There came then his brethren and his mother, and, standing without, sent unto him, calling him. (32) And the multitude sat about him, and they said unto him, Behold, thy mother and thy brethren without seek for thee. (33) And he answered them, saying, Who is my mother, or my brethren? (34) And he looked round about on them which sat about him, and said, Behold my mother and my brethren! (35) For whosoever shall do the will of God, the same is my brother, and my sister, and mother.—Mark iii, 22-35.

The passages parallel with the portion which is the basis of our present study are found in Matt. xii, 22-32, and Luke xi, 14-22, and should be carefully studied in connection with this lesson. Matthew gives the more circumstantial account of this remarkable dispute between Jesus and the scribes and Pharisees. The controversy between Jesus and the leaders of the people had now reached its culminating point. Indeed, this was practically the last meeting he had with them. Henceforth he speaks only to his own disciples, and leaves the Jews to go their way and do their worst. He does not leave them, however, without uttering a most solemn warning, for they were standing on the edge of an awful spiritual precipice, which if they fell over, or rather stepped over, there would be for them nevermore any deliverance, but they must plunge headlong into perdition.

(Mark iii, 29.) This dispute concerning the power of Christ, or rather the source of it, arose after he had delivered a poor captive whom the devil had made both blind and dumb (Matt. xii, 22), thus shutting him completely out from the gospel, for he could neither see the Saviour nor hear his word. This indeed was a masterpiece of satanic work; but Jesus was stronger than the strong man who bound him, and set him free with a word, just as he is able to-day to destroy the works of the devil in any sinner who is brought to him. So extraordinary was this masterful work of Jesus, that, taken together with everything else which he had both said and done, the conviction was forcing itself upon the people that he must be the Messiah. It was a conviction not altogether complete, but it was both deepening and growing, insomuch that "they were amazed" and were saying, "Is not this the Son of David?" (Matt. xii, 23.) Or rather, more correctly, "Is this the Son of David?" for the word "not" is not in the original, and in the revised version it is properly omitted. (See also Matt. vii, 16; xxvi, 22, 25; Mark iv, 21; xiv, 19; Luke vi, 39; etc.) It is as though they were saying, "Can this be the Messiah? It must be. And yet it cannot be. Still it must be he." This conviction was also taking strong possession of the leaders themselves, but they had taken up such strong grounds against him, that to have accepted him would have been not only to step down out of their high worldly places, and to have confessed that all along they had been not only wrong in their teachings but wicked in their actions. Their pride, their greed of power, their covetousness, their envy and hatred of Jesus the man, were so great, that they, added to that natural pride which revolts against any humbling confession of wrong, prevented them from willingly admitting their fast-dawning conviction. So, gathering up their hatred and fanning it into a flame, they determined to fling themselves upon him in a last desperate attempt to overthrow his claims and hopelessly prejudice and discredit him with the people. This they sought to do by boldly accusing him with being in league with the devil himself and working his wonders by satanic power. (Matt. x, 25; xii, 24, 32; Luke xi, 15, 18.)

I.—THE ACCUSATION AND ITS REFUTATION.

They had before slandered the Son of man by many evil, false, and vile charges, such as that he was "a gluttonous man and a winebibber," and that "he hath a devil," and was even Beelzebub himself; but hitherto Jesus had taken no notice of these vile charges and epithets, either being too busy to notice them or leaving them to die with the poison of their own malice. Now, however, the charge was a little different, and revealed to his mind such a depth of depravity in them, and such appalling peril, that for their sakes (and for the sake of all future generations) he called them to account for their terrible accusation, and pointed out both the absurdity of it and the horrible peril in which they were placing themselves by making it.

1.—**The horrible charge.**—"He hath Beelzebub, and by the prince of the devils casteth he out devils." They did not deny his mighty works; they could not do that, but they would discredit the work by charging upon him that he was in league with the devil—in fact, a very incarnation of the devil; Beelzebub himself in the garb of an angel of light, and therefore to be abhorred and shunned rather than received and worshiped as the Messiah. The charge was that he and Satan were joined in a kind of incarnation, so that he did his works by Satan working through him. The designation Beelzebub was an epithet the most loathsome and horrible they could apply. Beelzebub was the name of the god of the Ekronites (II. Kings i, 2, 3, 16), and signifies the Fly-god—that is, the god who sent plagues of flies, which communicated all kinds of horrible and filthy diseases. By a kind of derision and satirical play upon this word, they came to apply the name to Satan—the loathsome evil spirit, the chief of the hierarchy of the bottomless pit, the very extremest opposite from God. They charged Jesus with being one with this foul devil, and in league with him, and of appearing among men but to deceive and destroy; that all his wonderful works of loving kindness and all his words of tender grace and sympathy for men, and all his claims of fellowship with the Heavenly Father were devilish, false, and blasphemous. This is what they would have had the people to believe of Jesus, and, so believing, turn from him with loathing, scorn, and hatred.

2.—**The charge refuted.**—In answer to this foul calumny Jesus simply called them to him, and made answer by a series of parables which exposed the fallacy and absurdity of their accusation. In order that we may get the fullest benefit of this matchless defense of Jesus, we shall incorporate Matthew's version of the interview with that contained in our text. (See Matt. xii, 25-29.)

(i) "How can Satan cast out Satan?" "If Satan cast out Satan, he is divided against himself; how shall then his kingdom stand?" (Matt. xii, 26.) That he was destroying the works of the devil had to be and was admitted. Is it, then, true·that Satan is destroying his own work? Is he fighting himself? Here is an absurdity. Is Satan divided against himself? If so, then his kingdom cannot stand. An earthly kingdom at civil war with itself cannot stand. If the war goes on it must fall. A house divided against itself cannot stand; the family must be broken up and come to destruction. So would it be with the kingdom of darkness. But alas! there is no division in that dark kingdom. It has rather remained for divisions, strifes, and contentions to come among "the children and servants of a better Master." Would God that we might hear of strife and contentions in the ranks of the kingdom of darkness. If the public-house keepers might rise up against the gamblers; if thieves and swindlers might but take each other by the throat; if the managers of the horse-races might but begin to make war upon the organizers of the lottery schemes; if drunkards and seducers would but fall out; if only Satan might fight against Satan, and his kingdom fall into bitter, relentless, and uncompromising internecine strife, asking and giving no quarter—then would it be a good day for this poor devil-ridden world. But no such good thing as this is happening, or ever will happen. That argument or charge falls to the ground when only it is once fairly stated. "If Satan rise up against himself, and be divided, he cannot stand, but hath an end."

(ii) "If I by Beelzebub cast out devils, by whom do your children cast them out?" (Matt. xii, 27.) There seem to have been many even of the very children of the Pharisees, or at least members of their sect, who were by profession exorcists, who sought by prayer, by fasting, by the strong exercise of their own wills and high moral purpose, as well as incantations and the calling upon the name of God, who succeeded in expelling evil spirits from men and reclaiming them from the power of the devil in some cases of special possession and disease. Jesus puts it to them whether they were ready to go the length of saying that they, too, succeeded in their work by going into league with the devil. "This would impale them upon the horns of a dilemma, and prevent them from uttering that malicious slander again."

(iii) "But if I cast out devils by the Spirit of God, then the kingdom of God is come unto you." (Matt. xii, 28.) Jesus not only refutes their slander but presents to them a new aspect of the whole case, and would awaken in them, if possible, a better and more thoughtful mind. There seems to be no doubt but that certain men among the Jews were able in a measure to cast out evil spirits and work many cures among the afflicted people. This they did both by the use of remedies and by the powerful exercise of a better will and by faith in God. The power of spirit over spirit is well known; the superior power of a pure spirit over an evil spirit is also fully recognized. It is not at all either true or wise to condemn and deny wholesale the power of the ancient exorcists. No doubt in connection with this good work there had sprung up many charlatans and impostors who assumed to work these cures. Just as to-day we have doctors who can cure, to a certain extent, disease; professors of "Christian science" who in many cases do accomplish wonderful things; "faith cures" which are undoubted. And also alongside of these all manner of impostors, quack doctors, and men and women who trade in the name of God and of Jesus to carry on their nefarious deceptions. All the curative properties of medicine, all the undoubted power of good men over evil men, is a prophecy of the final and only effectual work of Christ. These medical and faith efforts are all blows at the kingdom of darkness, disease, and death, though none of them have succeeded beyond the farthest outworks. "Now," says Jesus, "if I by the Spirit of God, by the finger of God, by the Father that dwelleth in me, have come among you, and do by a word actually cast out devils and heal the sick and raise the dead, then the kingdom of God has come among you. If I do it by the Spirit of God, then the power has come among men, and to them, that will finally destroy the power of Satan. Unless this is the work of God, then Satan is not overthrown and his kingdom taken." Thanks be to God that the kingdom has come to us, and that there is One even now on earth by the Spirit who can say to devils, "Hold thy peace and come out of him," "thou unclean spirit."

(iv) "No man can enter into a strong man's house, and spoil his goods, except he will first bind the strong man." (ver. 27.) Satan is the strong man who has taken men captive by the cords and bands of sin, and holds them as a spoliating warrior does his goods. Now, it is impossible to recover the stolen goods from a great robber unless the robber be first overcome. The devil is that robber of souls. Christ is the Stronger than the strong man, who has bound Satan and spoiled him of his spoil. This is the true statement of the case.

II.—THE SIN AGAINST THE HOLY GHOST.

Having refuted the foul slander against himself, our gracious Lord now proceeds to speak his last gracious and solemn words to these deliberate slanderers and rejecters of him as the Messiah.

1.—**A gracious declaration.**—"All sins shall be forgiven unto the sons of men, and blasphemies wherewith soever they shall blaspheme." Matthew adds, "And whosoever speaketh a word against the Son of man, it shall be forgiven him." (Matt. xii, 32.) What glorious revelation of truth this is! "All sins"—this is the generic offense and trouble. Nothing can go beyond this in grace. All sin, every kind of sin, no matter what its nature; even blaspheming the Son of man, which is a specific count in the indictment against men; the calling of him "Beelzebub"; besmearing his holy name; even this may be, nay, shall be, forgiven to men. Did not our Lord pray for even his murderers, who were also reviling and blaspheming him even in the hour and agony of death? Oh, thanks be to God for this infinite grace! We would fain dwell upon it and illustrate it, but must leave it to make its way into the hearts of our readers. But why did Jesus say this? It was in order to make the one exception to this universal proclamation of forgiveness stand out the clearer and more terrible.

2.—**A solemn warning.**—"But he that shall blaspheme against the Holy Ghost hath never forgiveness." What is this terrible sin which excludes from the otherwise universal reach of the divine forgiveness, and consigns men to eternal damnation? Whole libraries of books have been written on this subject. Thousands of souls have been shut up for years in prison-houses of despair over this saying of Christ. It can only be understood in the light of the previous verse concerning forgiveness of all manner of sins and blasphemies. The thirtieth verse seems to give an answer: "Because they said, He hath an unclean spirit." This would indicate that their blasphemy was against him rather than against the Spirit. This was but the expression of the blasphemy, and not the substance. Jesus came to bear to the world the news of his love, and his purpose of grace toward all men and for all manner of sins. The Holy Spirit in him, and by whom he both spake and wrought, is the only revealer of this grace to men. To attribute to the Holy Spirit, by whom Jesus made his revelation, the nature and attributes of Satan (or Beelzebub, the foul and unclean spirit of the deep and dark pit) blasphemes the Spirit as a liar and impostor, and shuts out from the heart the word of salvation which the Spirit came to reveal to men by testifying to Jesus that he is the Son of God and Saviour of men. Jesus came to reveal the propitiousness of God toward all men and for all sins. To reject the testimony of the Spirit either in the words or works of Jesus, for he both spake and wrought by the Spirit, is to blaspheme that Spirit. He only can convince of sin, of righteousness, and of judgment. He only can work intelligent faith in the soul, by taking the things of Christ and showing them to us; he only, in a word, can reveal to us, as he did to Peter, that Jesus is the Christ. Now when this Holy Spirit works such a conviction in our hearts, to turn upon that Spirit and "smear him over" with Satan's vilest name and treat him with this foul and deliberate contempt is of course to shut the soul out from all knowledge of salvation and cut it off from all faith and repentance, and so to leave it hardened and confirmed in sin. There is no salvation for a soul except through faith and repentance, and there can be no faith and repentance except they are wrought by the Spirit. Therefore, to blaspheme that Spirit is to leave the soul forever without forgiveness, and thus put it beyond the pale of the gracious propitiousness of God. This awful offense is the final maturity of sin, and leaves the soul dead to all further influence for good. Let it be remembered that this sin can only be committed by those who have been enlightened by the Spirit. It is not a sin of ignorance or even of presumption, but of *defiance.* Hebrews vi, 4-6; x, 26-29, ought probably to be interpreted in the light of this fatal offense. To the man who has been enlightened and then turns away willfully and deliberately from the revelation of God, trampling "under foot the Son of God," counting "the blood of the covenant, wherewith he was sanctified, an unholy thing," and doing "despite unto the Spirit of grace," there can be no place for repentance, seeing there is nothing to repent toward, nothing to cleanse from sin, and nothing to move him either to faith or desire for good. He has put all good from him deliberately and of choice.

3.—A fearful end.—"Eternal damnation." This is the precipice upon the edge of which these Pharisees were standing, and from which Jesus would even then rescue them. The term "eternal damnation" does not refer so much to eternal punishment, though that is involved in it, as to the eternal fixedness of the soul in sin and alienation from God. The revised version properly renders the phrase "eternal sin." God sent his Son into the world to save his people from sin, to destroy the works of the devil. If that revelation is rejected and the Holy Spirit blasphemed, sin must remain and become the fixed condition of the soul. This indeed *is* eternal damnation. From this there is no deliverance, since Jesus, in whom the Father is reconciled and the Holy Spirit sits enthroned, is put away by the blasphemy. May God in his infinite mercy save us all from this fearful end.

III.—THE KINSFOLK OF JESUS.

It is one of the most remarkable facts in connection with the life of Jesus, and it shows how dull and stupid the wisdom of the flesh is, that even the kinsfolk of Jesus did not understand or fully appreciate him. We are told in one place that "neither did his brethren believe on him." That is, before the resurrection, after which we are certain that James (the brother of the Lord) fully gave himself up to him and became his great disciple. Mary must have always tenderly loved him and cherished highest hopes of and for him; but she and they were all in the dark as to the true nature of his mission, supposing, no doubt, that if he was indeed and in truth the Messiah, his glory would be manifested in earthly pomp and splendor, according to the expectation of all the Jews. They could not understand his self-abnegation, his close friendship with publicans and sinners; they deplored the widening breach between himself and the ruling classes; they were in perpetual fear during these last days for his personal safety. Hence they were anxious to get him away from this angry crowd of Pharisees and take him away from the place of danger.

1.—Outside kindred.—They were without—that is, not in the inner circle of the crowd standing by him and with him, but on the outside of the crowd, loving him, but wanting to get him away from his present surroundings. They no doubt thought him unwisely carried away with enthusiasm, and that he was spoiling or hurting his cause as well as imperiling his life. Jesus has many outside kindred—those who admire him, and appreciate to some extent his sublime teaching on ethical points; but they do not understand him as the world's Saviour; especially they do not understand the significance of his death and his relations to all men irrespective of persons, and the nature of that new kingdom of men and women "born not of blood, nor of the will of the flesh, . . . but of God." Nor do they understand the dogged enthusiasm of his disciples who persist in going down to the slums fishing for souls, and to far-off heathen lands to seek out and recover those who are sitting "in darkness and in the shadow of death" there. They would withdraw all such to the quietness and respectability of home and home lands. They are without the spiritual circle, however well-intentioned they may be.

2.—Inside kindred.—Jesus answered their message by looking about him on those who had left all to follow him and were then seated about him, and announced the new kinship. "Behold my mother and my brethren! For whosoever shall do the will of God, the same is my brother, and my sister, and mother." Thus it is that we come into the new kinship of Christ. "Henceforth know we no man after the flesh." The strongest and highest point of union in this world is that which binds us to God by Christ. All other ties will fail, but this is eternal. Let us claim kin with Jesus by accepting him as God sent him to us, and by henceforth doing the will of God prove our family relationship with him. To "as many as received him, to them gave he power to become the *sons* of God." (John i, 12.)

XLVIII.

CHRIST'S TESTIMONY TO JOHN.—Luke vii, 24-35.

(24) And when the messengers of John were departed, he began to speak unto the people concerning John, What went ye out into the wilderness for to see? A reed shaken with the wind? (25) But what went ye out for to see? A man clothed in soft raiment? Behold, they which are gorgeously apparelled, and live delicately, are in kings' courts. (26) But what went ye out for to see? A prophet? Yea, I say unto you, and much more than a prophet. (27) This is he, of whom it is written, Behold, I send my messenger before thy face, which shall prepare thy way before thee. (28) For I say unto you, Among those that are born of women there is not a greater prophet than John the Baptist: but he that is least in the kingdom of God is greater than he. (29) And all the people that heard him, and the publicans, justified God, being baptized with the baptism of John. (30) But the Pharisees and lawyers rejected the counsel of God against themselves, being not baptized of him. (31) And the Lord said, Whereunto then shall I liken the men of this generation? and to what are they like? (32) They are like unto children sitting in the marketplace, and calling one to another, and saying, We have piped unto you, and ye have not danced; we have mourned to you, and ye have not wept. (33) For John the Baptist came neither eating bread nor drinking wine; and ye say, He hath a devil. (34) The Son of man is come eating and drinking; and ye say, Behold a gluttonous man, and a winebibber, a friend of publicans and sinners! (35) But wisdom is justified of all her children.—Luke vii, 24-35.

The earthly ministry of Jesus was drawing to a close. The bitter antagonism of the officials was coming to its wicked head. The dignified, still gentle and pathetic pleadings of the Christ with the people, who were rejecting him to their own destruction, was being punctuated by occasional stern and piercing discussions, in which he charged home upon them the wickedness and mad folly of their course. John the Baptist had for months past been imprisoned by Herod because of his faithful and stern ministry in rebuking him for his sin in having taken his brother Philip's wife for his own. John in prison had been hearing through his disciples of the sayings and doings of Jesus, but it seems that during the time of his imprisonment Jesus had sent him no message nor put forth any effort or power to release him. His work was over, and the time of his departure was at hand. Yet John, who had introduced Jesus to the people as the Messiah, seems now, if not to have lost faith, to have at least wavered a little in regard to Jesus. Perhaps he, too, had expected that Jesus as Messiah would have fulfilled the popular ideal by manifesting forth his glory in temporal pomp and power, restoring again the glorious kingdom of David; and since he only heard of his spiritual preaching and his benevolent work among and for the people, he may have wondered, after all: "Can this be the Christ of the prophets, the glorious Lord for whom the nation had been looking for so many long centuries, and to herald whose coming he had been sent?" We must not wonder at this, for John was a great prophet—yea, more than a prophet; yet he too was a man of like passions with us and liable to seasons of depression, as was even his great prototype Elijah, yea, even as we to-day are. It seemed to him that the curative ministry of Jesus, which kept him in company with the sick, the diseased, the publicans and sinners, the lepers and the devil-possessed, was too lowly a mission for the great Messiah. It was probably to correct this thought that Jesus said to those standing by, "Blessed is he whosoever shall not be offended in me." (ver. 23.) The answer Jesus sent to John was not categorical, but by way of an appeal to the Scripture and the corresponding facts in his ministry: "Go your way, and tell John what things ye have seen and heard: how that the blind see, the lame walk, the lepers are cleansed, the deaf hear, the dead are raised, and to the poor the gospel is preached." (ver. 22.) This was an appeal to Isaiah xxxv, 5-6; lxi, 1, and this is the glory of the Messiah! Tell John that, and let him put these things together. The glory of Christianity is not in its splendid cathedrals, pomp and ceremonial, political sway and power, but just in that it is still doing this work among the afflicted and putting the glad tidings into the hearts of the poor. Let us not glory in the outward and accidental splendors of Christianity, nor be offended or scandalized because of its work among the poor and the lowly. Christ's kingdom is not of this world, but his credentials as King are found to-day as when John asked his question.

I.—A REMARKABLE MAN.

Having sent his answer to John, Jesus turned upon the people, and, with John still in his mind and heart, he proceeded to pay a great tribute to his "forerunner." No doubt the question asked by

John's disciples of Jesus had strongly agitated the multitude, who, perhaps, were asking the same question and wondering at the answer given by Jesus. Taking advantage of this interest, Jesus turns to them and asks them a question concerning John, the proper answer to which would lead their thoughts back to himself. This crowd, or at least a large part of it, had, during John's ministry, gone out to see and hear him. John was a striking figure, appearing as he did in the wilderness clothed in the traditional prophet's garb, and preaching his gospel of repentance in stern and uncompromising tones. So great was the impression which he had made, that it compelled the attention of all Jerusalem and Judea. He did not have to seek an audience, but they sought him. Even the king had gone out to hear him, perhaps more than once, and "heard him gladly." Jesus now seeks to awaken in their minds some clear analysis of their motives in going to hear him.

1.—"A reed shaken with the wind?"—Was John such a character? A man of vacillating speech, subject to every stress of influence that blew upon him? Was he such a shiftless man as that? A man of mere words, and these uncertain and inconsistent? Would you have gone out to hear a mere babbler, such as had again and again appeared in the land, giving out that he was some great personage? But had John been such "a reed," the people would never have gone in crowds day after day to listen to him and behold him. The obvious answer to this question is a negative—certainly not! This the people themselves would have confessed had they been allowed to speak, and so Jesus takes their answer for granted, and proceeds to put another negative.

2.—"A man clothed in soft raiment?"—"But what went ye out for to see?" If it was not to see a reed shaken in the wind, was it to see one of those "dilettant" philosophers who clothe themselves in soft and luxurious raiment such as the courtiers do who seek audiences in kings' houses, and are patronized by the great and the worldly? Again, certainly not! One hearing of John, one sight of that rough, stern man preaching repentance and proclaiming the ax at the root of the trees, and the coming of One with a winnowing fan in his hand, would have dissuaded from any such a false thought. John, who denounced the king's sin, was not a soft man. He who spake to the rulers and the great of the city as a "generation of vipers," and did not hesitate to warn them "to flee the wrath to come," was not such an one as that. And yet ye went out again and again in greater crowds to see this preacher of righteousness. The putting of these two questions, which carried their answers with them, cleared the way for what was to follow. John was no ordinary man, and had no ordinary message. Who, then, was he? What was he? He did not proclaim himself. He was no leader seeking to gather a crowd of disciples about himself. He was no politician preaching a crusade against an existing order. He was no revolutionist stirring up the people against their Roman masters. To the rulers he said he was but "the voice of one crying in the wilderness." More than once the people had been puzzled and the rulers silenced concerning John. The people indeed believed him to be a prophet, and the rulers dared not say from whence he received his commission. (Mark xi, 29–33.)

3.—"A prophet?"—"But what went ye out for to see? A prophet?" Jesus now both asks and answers a question, not with an implied negative, but containing an affirmative, which he reinforces by a direct answer to the question which he puts: "Yea, I say unto you, and much more than a prophet." Let us now look at this declaration. (i) What is a prophet? A prophet is a man who has received a message from God, and delivers that message. In this respect John abundantly fulfilled his calling. "He stood consciously before the invisible God, and spoke for God, God communicating with him; and he gave utterance in the ears of men to the communicated ideas of God." Each of the four evangelists give testimony to the prophetic office of John. At the time of his birth, Zacharias, his father, "being filled with the Holy Ghost," gave this testimony to him: "And thou, child, shalt be called the prophet of the Highest: for thou shalt go before the face of the Lord to prepare his ways; to give knowledge of salvation unto his people by the remission of their sins, through the tender mercy of our God; whereby the dayspring from on high hath visited us, to give light to them that sit in darkness and in the shadow of death, to guide our feet into the way of peace." (Luke i, 76–79.) That John was personally conscious of his prophetic calling is evidenced by what he himself has said: "And John bare record [of Jesus], saying, . . . And I knew him not: but he that sent me to baptize with water, the same said unto me, Upon whom thou shalt see the Spirit descending, and remaining on him, the same is he which baptizeth with the Holy Ghost." (John i, 31–33.) To these testimonies of Zacharias and John, Jesus now adds his own. (ii) He was more than a prophet. That is, he was doubly a prophet, from the fact that he was himself the subject of prophecy, as well as the bearer of a message from God. "This is he, of whom it is written, Behold, I send my messenger before thy face, which shall prepare thy way before thee." (ver. 27; Mal. iii, 1.) Of no other of the prophets was this ever said. Therefore Jesus adds: "Among those that are born of women there is not a greater prophet than John the Baptist." This is said not of John personally, but of him as a prophet. He was personally a great man, a very great man—great in the sight of God. But his greatness stood in this, that being the subject of prophecy, being filled with the spirit of prophecy, standing in the immediate presence of the great Messiah, and personally introducing him to the people, the honor thus conferred exceeded that given to any of his predecessors. Abraham and Moses and all the succeeding prophets spoke of Jesus, the Coming One, being yet afar off; but John as it were took the Messiah by the hand and introduced him personally. He was the last of that long line of men whom the Holy Spirit had moved to speak of the coming of Christ; the last and the greatest—at least, there was none ever greater. Therefore Jesus would warn the people, that, clothed with this authority and standing in this greatness, his message must be heeded. As they heeded the words of Abraham and Moses, even so must they heed the words of John. On the authority of the older prophets they were looking for the Messiah; on the authority of John they must believe that the Messiah had come, and was even now before them, yea, speaking to them.

4.—**Those greater than John the Baptist.**—Jesus proceeds to say after this splendid tribute to John, "But he that is least in the kingdom of God is greater than he." What does this mean? Does it mean that John was not in the kingdom of heaven? Certainly not, for the kingdom of heaven and of God is confined to no age or dispensation. Does it mean that the least Christian or believer in Christ is greater in character than John? No, certainly not, for we know that there are thousands who believe in Christ and are in some sense following him who are infinitely less than John was in nobility of character, in humility, in courage, in intellectual grasp of the truth, in magnanimity and nobleness of soul, in purity of life and devotedness to the work of God. It means simply that great as was John's privilege as the last and greatest of the prophets, the privileges of the least believer are greater than that of a prophet. Theirs was the privilege of seeing and hearing the Son of God with their own eyes and with their own ears. This the prophets and wise men of all ages had desired to see and hear, but had not been given their desire. (Matt. xiii, 17.) The least of those in the kingdom of heaven enjoy a privilege of fullness of the gift of the Holy Ghost which even John did not enjoy. (John i, 16.) Happy for us if, enjoying greater privileges than even this greatest of prophets, we do not yet fall too far behind him in greatness of soul, in devotion of life, and utter disinterestedness of service.

II.—A PARABLE.

Jesus now proceeds to make an application of the whole matter by referring first to the various ways in which John was received by the people and the rulers, and then illustrating the whole situation as it referred to the rulers by a striking parable.

1.—The common people received the prophet's message.— The preaching of John was received by a large number of the common people, especially by publicans and harlots, and other outcasts of society. In fact, John's ministry was remarkably successful so far as the people were concerned. They at least "justified God." That is, they recognized in John, God's prophet, and in his message God's words to them; in the salvation which John preached to them through Jesus, God's salvation; in the doctrines of repentance and forgiveness, the true doctrines of God; in the announcement of judgment to come, the judgment of God; and in Jesus, the true Lamb of God, the very Messiah.

2.—The Pharisees and rulers rejected both the prophet and his message.—"But the Pharisees and lawyers rejected the counsel of God against themselves, being not baptized of him." This was a true statement of the facts in the case. The people are for God and Christ; the upper classes in particular are against God and Christ. And being against the counsel of God, they seek to discredit it. The only result is that they reject it against themselves. The opposition of sinful men to God and his gospel, no matter how high their position in this world, only reacts against themselves. They cannot alter his counsel, nor defeat the general purposes of his grace.

3.—"Children sitting in the market-place."—Jesus now, as his wont was, illustrated the whole matter by a striking parable. There was a game played by children in those days something like our modern charades. They would divide themselves into groups. One party, for instance, would troop out playing upon pipes (or pretending to do so). The music played or imitated would in one case be glad and happy as the music played at a marriage feast. The other party of children, questioning the import of the charade, would rise up and respond by dancing. In another case the one party would walk forth mourning, with heads covered and hair disheveled, as a funeral party. The other party of children, discovering the meaning of the play, would respond by mourning, as those who had also been stricken with some great grief. Sometimes these charades would be enacted and the party to whom they were played would not respond, either through their inability to discover the meaning or possibly through pique or mere willfulness. Jesus now applies these childish games to the case before him. John the Baptist came as an ascetic, living in the wilderness, faring on common coarse food, and avoiding the haunts and companionships of men. The Pharisees, hearing his message of repentance, would not mourn over their sins. Jesus preached the glad tidings of salvation and they would not be glad. They would not have either teacher or teaching. They would neither dance in joy nor mourn in sorrow. They gave as a reason for their rejection of John that he had a devil. They attributed his severe and ascetic life, his stern and uncompromising message, to the possession of a devil. On the other hand, Jesus came eating and drinking, showing himself friendly with men, moving about among them, dining with both publicans and Pharisees, and declaring the love of God and the forgiveness of sins; but they rejected him and his message also, giving as a reason (falsely) that "he was a gluttonous man and a wine-bibber." "Ah," they said, "John cannot be a prophet of God, for he is too exclusive, too severe, too stern. We want a salvation that is more humane, more genial. We cannot all be ascetics and go sorrowing and gloomy all our lives." Then came Jesus, and they said, "Ah, he cannot be of God; for look, he eats and drinks like other men, and associates with all kinds of people. We must have a religion that is more serious and solemn than that." Hypocrites! They simply would not have God in any way God came to them. These Pharisees have their followers to-day. If a minister preaches seriously to them of their sins, if he be a man in dead earnest, having himself a deep conviction of the sinfulness of sin, and warning men "to flee from the wrath to come," especially if he is a serious-minded man and withdraws himself from the world and the ways of the world, they cry out and say, "Oh, that is too severe and gloomy. Religion should be made more attractive, more cheerful. We can never become long-faced like him! Why, such doctrines would take all the gladness out of life and fill the world with groans and tears." Well, another minister sees the joyous side of religion; preaches almost always the love of God, the gladness of forgiveness, the freeness of salvation, paints the glories of heaven, and so, in possession of all the good things of God, paints life with the color of the rose, and goes in and out among men, eating dinners with them, and attending their feasts and social gatherings. These Pharisees declare, with uplifted eyes, "Oh, we can never receive a message from God at the lips of such a man. He is too worldly; he lacks solemnity; he is a self-indulgent, pleasure-loving man—in fact, a wine-bibber and a glutton. Religion is a serious and solemn matter, and is only brought into scandal by such frivolous and self-loving, ease-loving preachers as this." So, whether the gospel is piped unto them they dance not; or whether it is mourned unto them they weep not. They will neither be sorry for sin nor glad for forgiveness.

4.—"**But wisdom is justified of all her children."**—This is a somewhat obscure and difficult passage. Its simplest meaning seems to be that the divine wisdom of God is justified, whether in the ascetic life and stern preaching of John, or in the social life and glad and hopeful preaching of Jesus. God's messages are not all of one kind, nor delivered in the same way. God chooses a messenger suitable to the message, and in the end the wisdom of God will be justified in the ways of God. It may also carry with it the idea that the children of wisdom justify God's wisdom by accepting God's messages by whomsoever and in whatsoever ways they are sent. Happy shall we be if we attend to the messages of God, whether by ascetic prophet or social preacher, and repent because of our sin and rejoice because of his great salvation.

XLIX.

CHRIST TEACHING BY PARABLES.—Luke viii, 4-15.

(4) And when much people were gathered together, and were come to him out of every city, he spake by a parable: (5) A sower went out to sow his seed: and as he sowed, some fell by the way side; and it was trodden down, and the fowls of the air devoured it. (6) And some fell upon a rock; and as soon as it was sprung up, it withered away, because it lacked moisture. (7) And some fell among thorns; and the thorns sprang up with it, and choked it. (8) And other fell on good ground, and sprang up, and bare fruit a hundredfold. And when he had said these things, he cried, He that hath ears to hear, let him hear. (9) And his disciples asked him, saying, What might this parable be? (10) And he said, Unto you it is given to know the mysteries of the kingdom of God: but to others in parables; that seeing they might not see, and hearing they might not understand. (11) Now the parable is this: The seed is the word of God. (12) Those by the way side are they that hear; then cometh the devil, and taketh away the word out of their hearts, lest they should believe and be saved. (13) They on the rock are they, which, when they hear, receive the word with joy; and these have no root, which for a while believe, and in time of temptation fall away. (14) And that which fell among thorns are they, which, when they have heard, go forth, and are choked with cares and riches and pleasures of this life, and bring no fruit to perfection. (15) But that on the good ground are they, which in an honest and good heart, having heard the word, keep it, and bring forth fruit with patience.—Luke viii, 4-15.

Jesus is still in Galilee. Every day his popularity with the whole mass of people is on the increase. Not only are his real disciples increasing, but crowds of more or less thoughtful and curious people follow him. He has become the fashion, as well as the object of serious interest. As he journeys from city to city, preaching the kingdom of heaven, healing the sick, and casting out devils, the crowd of followers increases. Every city furnishes its contingent, until at last a vast throng of people are in his train. It was a mass of "all sorts and conditions of men." There were his chosen disciples, and a company of closely clinging, devout women (among whom were Mary Magdalene and Joanna and Susanna), who "ministered to him of their substance"; outside there were the curious, superficial, enthusiastic crowd who had been excited by his preaching, and perhaps much more by his popularity; then there were the careworn people, with whom were mixed the worldly ambitious and the pleasure-seekers; and last of all, a few thoughtful and earnest souls who were thirsting and longing for the words of life and ready to receive them from Jesus, whom they were hoping was that great Prophet spoken of by Moses, who was to come and teach them all things.

This parable of the sower was the first of a series which Jesus delivered on this occasion (but not all at one sitting), in which he gave a prophetic and panoramic view of the whole progress of the kingdom of heaven, from the beginning of his ministry down to the latest time of the present dispensation, when the judgment (parable of the draw-net) should bring it to a close, making a final separation between the good and the bad. Luke contents himself with giving us the parable of the sower, though he is generally much more rich in his record of parables than either Matthew or Mark, who both give the whole series of which this is the initial one. The accounts of this parable, as given by the three evangelists, differ in detail but not in substance. The omissions by one, the additions by another, and the reversal of the order of development, are only signs of independence in the three records, and point out clearly that the three Gospels are not copies of each other, nor of some document to which all the writers had access.

I.—GENERAL OBSERVATIONS.

For a comparatively full exposition of this parable, we refer our readers to our *Bible Studies for* 1889, page 33. Instead of taking up the whole parable in detail, we shall first of all call attention, by some general observations, to the parable as a whole, and to the meaning of this particular one, and the significance of parabolic teaching.

1.—**The occasion.**—The multitudes following Jesus were now so great that he must deal with them in a practical way to sift them. He had once done this when he gave the Sermon on the Mount. The people then, but especially his disciples, were made to see that his kingdom was not one of temporal power, but of far-reaching righteousness, the spread of which among men would bring them into characteristic relations with God, rather than bring in a splendid temporal dynasty. Here he seeks to show them that not those who hear the Word merely, and follow him about with their bodies, are to be counted as his disciples, but those who take heed to his Word, give it an honest and deep entrance into their hearts, and bring forth fruit to God. Jesus was not deceived by this vast following. He saw then, as we have seen ever since, that among the many hearers of the gospel there are but few sincerely devout doers of the Word. The Word which he spoke to them was indeed spirit and life, but its power to save was dependent on its reception by the hearer. It is not only *what* men hear that saves them, but *how* they hear. John the Baptist had warned his disciples that it was not baptism by water, but by the Holy Ghost only, which would save; that though they might receive the one, unless it was supplemented by the other it would not answer for their salvation. Jesus now warns his hearers that the good seed so liberally broadcast over all hearts, while it had in it all the "power and potency of life," would not give life unless it was cordially and deeply received and cherished. Those only who heard and kept it would bring forth fruit. Thus was Jesus already purging his floor with the fan in his hand. He also warned his disciples that in time to come they must not be deceived by mere outward adherents to their ministry, but must look for deep inward results of their preaching. They must not be discouraged if, out of a multitude of hearers, only here and there one would be found who truly and honestly received the good seed; and that even among those who received it there would be those (besides the wayside and stony-ground hearers) who, while they received it, would be so divided between worldliness and spirituality that their Christian lives would be choked and fruitless.

2.—**Prophetic significance.**—No doubt the entire series (see Matt. xiii, 35) contains a prophecy unfolding of the whole progress of truth in connection with the opposing forces of error. This particular parable contains the germ and seed of all. In it we have a hint of the resistance which the gospel meets with from human hearts themselves; of the active opposition and malignant interference of the devil himself (ver. 12); of shallow selfishness and moral cowardice; of the seductions of the world and the cares of life. Besides this, we are clearly taught that we need not expect that by the preaching of the gospel alone, and with the present measure of power, all men will be saved, or that all the world will be converted. While we do not suppose any such arithmetical proportion as one to three represents the number of the saved as against the lost, yet it clearly intimates that the true believers will be in a small minority as compared with the idle, careless, selfish, and half-hearted.

3.—The opposing powers.—In the fact that Jesus tells us that the devil himself will be at hand to catch away the seed from the hearts of the careless and indifferent, we get a glimpse of the awful fact that, while God is supernaturally working for the salvation of the world, there is another dark spirit counterworking to keep men in sin, and to prevent the operation of God's gracious word for their salvation. Whoever else does not believe in a personal devil, present and active in this world, Jesus believed it, and warned us in many ways to beware of him and his devices.

4.—" The mysteries of the kingdom of God."—By "the mysteries of the kingdom" (ver. 10) are meant those truths which lie beyond the reach of man's mere reason: those heavenly things of which Jesus spoke to Nicodemus (in contradistinction to the earthly things), and which the Son of man came down to teach, and which the world by its own powers of thought or investigation could never know, because "no man hath ascended up to heaven." (John iii, 12, 13.) There are many particular mysteries in connection with the main and all-comprehensive one included in the incarnation which it might be well for us to study in connection with this parable, since Jesus has told us it is given us to know them. (Matt. xiii, 11.) (We recommend a careful examination of this subject with the help of Cruden's Unabridged Concordance.) Of these mysteries we may say that they were ever unknown to man apart from the revelation of God; that they may yet be known by means of that revelation; but can only be known by those who give careful heed to God's Word, receiving it into good and honest hearts, and keeping it there. Those who are of the inner circle of honest and sincere hearers understand these things, while those without, among the careless and worldly hearers of the gospel, not only do not understand them, but even become hardened by them. God's gospel is a revelation to those who desire to know him, but it is a hidden mystery and a blinding light to those who refuse to see. Notice the difference of the relation of truth to those whom Jesus speaks to as "unto you," and those of whom he speaks of as "to others." (ver. 10.) Here is the whole matter in a nutshell. The gospel is a mystery or secret; it can only be known by revelation: first, by the revelation of it in Christ, and second, by the special revelation of it by the Holy Ghost, to those who have a good and honest heart to receive the Word. It is the entrance of that Word that giveth light to men.

5.—The parabolic method.—Parabolic teaching was not original with Jesus, but it was by him carried to perfection. It was prophesied of old that he should speak in parables when he came.

(Ps. lxxviii, 2.) The word "parable" comes from two Greek words, "para bola," which signifies, from the verb out of which it is compounded, to compare things together. "It is a simile taken from natural things, to instruct us in the knowledge of things spiritual." As we have already said, this method was used by Jesus for the double purpose of conveying and veiling the truth. The rays of the sun passing through space above our atmosphere make no light. It is only when they come in contact with the atmospheric veil surrounding this earth that they burst into light. Thus truth comes to us at once veiled and revealed in Jesus Christ. Should the whole truth of God burst upon our souls without a veil, it would so dazzle us that we could not see; but revealed as it is by parable, for "without a parable spake he not" (Matt. xiii, 34), it is softened and becomes possible for us to see. To the honest-hearted Jesus expounds them, but to those who have despised the truth the revealing atmosphere becomes a dense cloud which completely hides it. In this case parables are uttered and left unexpounded as a means of judgment (Matt. xiii, 13); but there is also a mercy in this use of parables, even to those whose hearts are hardened against the truth. (See *Bible Studies for* 1889, page 35.)

II.—THE SOIL.

The Master was seated in a little ship (Matt. xiii, 2; Mark iv, 1), which he had been compelled to extemporize into a pulpit to avoid the thronging multitude, as well as for the greater advantage it gave in addressing the crowd which stood on the shore. The picture is easily imagined: the shore which came down to the sea receded toward and up the hillside; a pathway was at the foot of a plowed field which covered the lower reaches, and also the upsloping side of the hill, from which a projecting rock stood out, upon which, however, there was a thin coating of soil. Every condition of soil which our Lord spoke of was doubtless represented in that field before his eyes and the people's. He thought to transfer the varied facts of nature before them to themselves. Perhaps there was a sower at that very moment busily engaged in broadcasting the good seed. Jesus was, of course, the sower of whom in fact he spoke; the people whom he addressed were the soil; the harvest was yet to appear, accordingly as they received or rejected the good seed. The Master spoke of four kinds of hearers: the wayside hearer, represented by the hard-beaten pathway; the stony-ground hearer, represented by the hard rock covered by a thin layer of soil; the thorny-ground hearer, by a portion of the soil which was, indeed, good, but from which the seeds and roots of thorns and briers were not thoroughly exterminated; and the good-ground hearer, by that rich deep soil well and thoroughly prepared and cleaned by the husbandman for the reception of the seed. We have said there are four different kinds of soil. This is hardly the case, for the soil is the same in each case, only the difference is in the conditions in which it is found. The wayside was hard; the stony ground was thin; the thorny ground was dirty with preoccupation by the seed and roots of evil weeds; the good ground was in splendid condition, as we have said. We will look in detail at these four conditions of soil, as indicating the various spiritual conditions in which the Word of God, as it is sown broadcast by the preacher or teacher, finds the human heart.

1.—The wayside soil.—This represents the merely outward religious hearers, whose hearts are beaten hard by worldliness. They have no interest in spiritual things, though they go to church and apparently listen to the Word, while in fact their thoughts are on other things. Sometimes they are spoken of as "gospel hardened," but this is incorrect, for the gospel itself hardens no heart, though the gospel *rejected* may leave an already hardened heart more hard than it was before. Thoughtless and indifferent to spiritual things, and given up to worldly interests, they are impervious to the gracious influences of the gospel. This class of hearers stood before Jesus, and they sit in every congregation. One can almost pick them out of the mass of hearers as he preaches, by the hard indifference and blank vacuity expressed in their unreceptive faces.

2.—The rocky soil.—This represents those hearers whose religious natures are thin and shallow. They are oftentimes, indeed usually, both enthusiastic and emotional. They listen with eagerness, and even with delight, to the gospel, especially those phrases of it which are calculated to excite the merely emotional parts of our nature. They are quick to receive the promises, forward to profess a faith they really do not have, and, so long as there is nothing that calls for self-denial or that interferes with their personal comfort or pleasure, they endure well. But underneath there is a hard rock of selfishness that resists the rooting tendencies of the truth. If any persecution arises on account of Christ, if they are called upon to deny themselves, or to sacrifice their ease or comfort, they wither away like seed that has sprung up on a piece of rocky soil. They have no deepness in themselves. They are a kind of "Galatian" hearers, who run well for a season, but because they lack perseverance or patience, soon fall out of line. These are they who say, "We have tried it, and it does not last." Yes, they have tried the sentiment of religion, but have never taken Christ thoroughly into their hearts and lives, "rooted and grounded in love." Here we have "another instance of partial conversion," which has effect only in the sphere of the intellect, imagination, or mere feeling; which, indeed, may to a certain extent affect the action of men under favorable circumstances, but which has never penetrated the will and carried it over to Christ. "Much may go on in the heart without its becoming in truth a partaker of the new life." Such followed Christ for the loaves and fishes; such are as the scribe who turned back when he heard of foxes which had holes, and birds which had nests, but that the Son of man had not where to lay his head. They will follow Christ if they are sure of a "hole" or a "nest," but not if there is prospect of trouble or want, like the young man who would have life, but rejected it at the cost of selling what he had and giving to the poor.

3.—**The thorny soil.**—These are they whose lives are mixed and unseparated. They are not hard-hearted, nor shallow, but they have not surrendered themselves wholly to Christ; that is, they are attempting the difficult and impossible task of compromise. They would serve both God and mammon. They accept Christ, and go forth into the world, not to antagonize it, but to have fellowship with it. They surrender to the cares, the ambition for riches, and the fellowship and pleasures of the world. They are half-hearted, divided, mixed in all their affections, and double-minded, like Balaam. They would keep in alike with God and with the world. The result is, that what of grace there is in them, which, if they had come clean out on the Lord's side, would have made them strong and vigorous Christians, is choked and smothered with care, riches, and pleasures, and "they bring no fruit to perfection."

4.—**The good soil.**—These are they who with full purpose of heart receive the Word, and cleave to the Lord. They are patient endurers, keeping the Word and patiently working out their salvation in fellowship with God, who worketh in them to will and to do of his good pleasure. (Phil. ii, 13.) There is much in the Bible about the honest-hearted. They see the immense superiority of godliness over worldliness; of spirituality over sensuality; whole-heartedness over half-heartedness; and gladly sacrifice whatever there is in the world that interferes with growth in grace to the heavenly fruit which they see promised in the Word. With Paul they can say, "I count all things but loss for the excellency of the knowledge of Christ Jesus my Lord." They represent that true discipleship which denies self, takes up the cross daily, and follows Christ.

III.—THE FATE OF THE SEED.

The fate of the good seed is determined by the nature or condition of the soil, just as the fate of the hearer is determined by the reception he gives to the seed. It is worthy of great thought that in our Lord's exposition of the parable he identifies the hearer with the Word, or the soil with the seed. If any one hears the Word and is not saved by it, whose fault is it? Indeed, if out of the great mass of hearers of the gospel few are saved, whose fault is it? It is not God's, "who will have all men to be saved and to come to the knowledge of the truth." It is not the fault of the Word, which is able to make men wise unto salvation. (II. Tim. iii, 15.) It is not the fault of the sower, who preaches the gospel, and, as though God did beseech men, prays in Christ's stead to be reconciled to God. (II. Cor. v, 20.) It can only be the fault of the individual, for God's message miscarries in the case of each kind of hearer who fails to receive it in a good and honest heart, as follows:

1.—**The wayside hearer.**—By the voluntary condition of carelessness as to divine things. In his case the Word of God is "trodden down"—that is, by the worldly interest to which he wholly surrenders himself. Moreover, these are the hearers who are specially watched over by Satan, who "taketh away the word out of their hearts, lest they should believe and be saved." The devil can only do this in the case of those who voluntarily refuse to hear with attention and purpose the word of the kingdom.

2.—**The stony-ground hearer.**—He fails because of his supreme central selfishness, being unwilling to endure any trial, but must be "carried to the skies on flowery beds of ease," or not at all.

3.—**The thorny-ground hearer.**—He fails because he will go forth into the world, lusting after and living in the fellowship and indulgence of those things which choke the good seed. Here is the man who will give up nothing for Christ, but tries to worship God and at the same time to serve his own idols.

4.—**The good-ground hearer.**—This is he who hears the Word, keeps it, and patiently works it out.

The prepositions used are suggestive. Some fell "by," some fell "upon," some fell "among," and some fell "*into*" (Matt. xiii, 8) good ground. Only when the seed gets *into* good ground—that is, cleared of briers and thorns—can it bring forth a hundredfold.

L.

THE TWELVE SENT FORTH:—Matthew x, 5-16.

(5) These twelve Jesus sent forth, and commanded them, saying, Go not into the way of the Gentiles, and into any city of the Samaritans enter ye not: (6) But go rather to the lost sheep of the house of Israel. (7) And as ye go, preach, saying, The kingdom of heaven is at hand. (8) Heal the sick, cleanse the lepers, raise the dead, cast out devils: freely ye have received, freely give. (9) Provide neither gold, nor silver, nor brass in your purses; (10) Nor scrip for your journey, neither two coats, neither shoes, nor yet staves: for the workman is worthy of his meat. (11) And into whatsoever city or town ye shall enter, inquire who in it is worthy; and there abide till ye go thence. (12) And when ye come into a house, salute it. (13) And if the house be worthy, let your peace come upon it: but if it be not worthy, let your peace return to you. (14) And whosoever shall not receive you, nor hear your words, when ye depart out of that house or city, shake off the dust of your feet. (15) Verily I say unto you, It shall be more tolerable for the land of Sodom and Gomorrah in the day of judgment, than for that city. (16) Behold, I send you forth as sheep in the midst of wolves: be ye therefore wise as serpents, and harmless as doves.—Matthew x, 5-16.

The sending forth of the twelve apostles, formally commissioned to preach the gospel of the kingdom of heaven, reminds us of that noble and wonderful stream which Ezekiel saw in vision proceeding from under the threshold of the Temple, at first but a small rivulet not more than ankle-deep, but which, as it went on its way, increased to a stream knee-deep, then up to the thighs, and afterward to a great river for a man to swim in, and carrying healing in its blessed waters whithersoever it flowed. Jesus is the true Temple of God, and in him this stream of life rises, and through his apostles and disciples it flowed forth, at first a very small stream, but it has gone on widening and deepening until its waters have filled the whole earth, and whithersoever it has flowed it has carried life and healing. (Ezek. xlvii, 1-9; Rev. xxii, 1-7; John vii, 37, 39.) To human judgment nothing could be more insignificant than these twelve Galileans, ignorant of the learning of the schools, unprovided with money or support from men, going out to preach the gospel of a rejected Messiah who was but a few months hence to be crucified as a common malefactor. On the other hand, nothing in all history has developed so much power and influence among men as that same gospel, rising in Jesus Christ and spreading abroad throughout the world at the hands of men for the most part chosen and called from the ranks of the common people. Its onward flow (sometimes an onward rush) has been a torrent which has carried all before it. To-day it is the mightiest moral force in the world, and there are none to sneer at it except fools and knaves (though many still oppose its onward flow), while millions all over the world and among all peoples live to bless God for his love and for his unspeakable gift in Christ Jesus.

I.—THEIR FIELD OF LABOR.

At a later period, subsequent to the death and resurrection of Jesus, the commission given to the apostles and to all disciples was, "Go ye into all the world and preach the gospel to every creature;" but now for this present time their commission was tentative and their field of labor was restricted. This first commission restricted them to a very narrow territory, and to one people, viz., the Jews.

1.—Not among the Gentiles.—"Go not into the way of the Gentiles." This was not because Jesus had not at that time any thought of winning the Gentiles to God, or because he was himself of a narrow mind and had but a limited and local purpose. All that concerned Jesus in his birth and earthly ministry demonstrates that his coming into the world was on a mission to the world. He was not the Saviour of the Jews only, but was born a Saviour which should be for the joy of all people. (Luke ii, 10; John iii, 16.) We also know that the coming of Jesus was the publication of that secret of God which had been hid from other ages, but was now revealed to his "holy apostles and prophets by the Spirit; that the Gentiles should be fellow-heirs, and of the same body, and partakers of his promise in Christ by the gospel." (Eph. iii, 5, 6.) But for the present, until the sacrifice for the sins of the whole world should be accomplished and formally accepted and proclaimed by the resurrection, the message was to be confined to the Jews, to whom Jesus came first as the Messiah of God. While he was yet on earth, and until the redemption in Christ could be fully proclaimed, it was useless to preach to the Gentiles. In his coming as the Messiah the Gentiles had no interest, but as the Messiah he was of all importance to the Jews, to whom he had been promised for centuries by their holy prophets. Besides this, it was necessary that a base of operations for a world-wide mission must be established within the narrower circles of the Jews. To them pertained the Scriptures, and to them was both naturally and practically given the first offer of the gospel. This was the order preserved even by the great Apostle to the Gentiles. "To the Jew first and also to the Gentile," was the standing order of apostolic missionary operations.

2.—**Not among the Samaritans.**—"And into any city of the Samaritans enter ye not." The Samaritans were a mongrel race who inhabited a tract of country lying between Galilee and Jerusalem. Their origin may be ascertained by consulting II. Kings xvii, 24, and Ezra iv, 2. They were the descendants of intermarriages between apostate Jews and Assyrians. Originally they were an idolatrous people, but gradually, like the Jews themselves, they were weaned away from their idols, accepted Moses as their prophet, and worshiped the true God. There was a perpetual and irreconcilable feud between them and the Jews, which had been handed down since the days of Ezra. The Jews had no dealings with them (John iv, 9), and scorned them with an utter hatred and contempt. They on their part returned the hate and scorn which was heaped upon them by the Jews. There are still a few hundred of these miserable people living in their ancient land, who still profess to be the original and pure people of God. When Jesus forbade his apostles to go among them, we are sure that the Lord was actuated by no prejudice against them, though he denied their claims to be the covenant people of God, as is learned by his interview with the Samaritan woman recorded in the fourth chapter of John's Gospel. That same interview also shows that Jesus, though he sided with the Jews in their religious controversy, did not share the Jewish prejudices against the Samaritans, but himself with great kindness and gentleness introduced them to the favor of God, bringing to them the water of life as freely as he offered it to his own kinsmen according to the flesh. But, much for the same reason as we have assigned for forbidding the apostles to go on this preliminary mission to the Gentiles, he excluded the Samaritans also from their labors. Besides, it would have been a great tactical mistake, so far as his purpose to win the Jews was concerned, had he aroused their deep and bitter prejudices by putting the Samaritans on the same level with them in proclaiming himself as their Messiah. Neither the Jews, the Samaritans, nor the Gentiles were yet ready for the universal proclamation of the gospel. In the whole development of the scheme of grace God has always had regard to fitness as to times and seasons, and also to the preparation of people to receive the gospel. It was not until the "fullness of time" that Jesus himself came into the world, and so not until another "fullness of time" could the gospel be preached to Samaritans and Gentiles; but now, thank God, the time *is* fully come when God "commandeth all men everywhere to repent" and believe the gospel.

3.—**But to the house of Israel.**—"But go rather to the lost sheep of the house of Israel." "He came unto his own" (John i, 11), and though his own received him not, yet his yearning love for them never grew cold. To him the Jews were "the house of Israel"—nay, more, they were "the lost sheep of the house of Israel." Professing themselves to be the flock of God, they had lost their way in the wilderness of formalism and materialism. Their shepherds had turned out to be but wolves, and the people were torn and bleeding with the wounds inflicted upon them by the selfish rulers of their own people, as well as suffering under the cruel oppression of the Romans, their political masters. Our Lord had more than a thought of divine order in the publication of the gospel, more than an eye to tactical wisdom; his heart longed for them, and though he knew they would reject and murder him, still he wept over them, and would fain gather them under the divine protection of his brooding wings. They were ignorant, having been misled by their teachers, who were now but "blind leaders of the blind," and all were falling into the ditch together. Before the Gentiles were called, before the Samaritans were summoned to repentance, he would lead poor lost Israel back to God.

II.—THE APOSTOLIC MESSAGE.

In order to save these lost sheep, which consisted of the whole house of Israel (for all were lost sheep, leaders and people alike), the apostles were charged with a message to them from the Christ. They were his heralds, going before to announce his advent among them, and the grace and help he had come to bring them. Throughout the land, up and down and across it, they were to go and make public proclamation. As for the substance of that proclamation, Jesus gave it to them in very simple but most comprehensive words: "Go preach." The world is moved by preaching more than by reading or by thinking. The prophet and the preacher have ever been the leaders and movers of the people. "It pleased God by the foolishness of preaching to save them that believe." Among men, preachers of the gospel are not held in highest esteem; but more than any other class they are the honored servants of God, holding commission as ambassadors of heaven itself. And as for influence, after all is said, there is no class so influential as the preacher of the good tidings, and just in proportion as the herald or preacher is a worthy servant, his influence is increased.

1.—"**The kingdom of heaven is at hand.**"—There is little doubt that our Lord meant to take up exactly the message which John heralded forth to the people, when he preached, saying, "Repent ye, for the kingdom of heaven is at hand." (Matt. iii, 2.) The kingdom of heaven was the blessing announced, and repentance was the condition of entering into this kingdom. The Jews were looking indeed for the establishment of the old theocratic kingdom of David, and they expected when Messiah came he would at once reëstablish that kingdom, deliver them from the political power of the Romans, and make them the masters, not only of their own political destinies, but also of that of their enemies. It was largely because they had misread the Scriptures that they did not recognize in the meek and lowly Jesus the glorious prince they were looking for. They were looking for a political king and kingdom. Jesus was indeed a king, but his kingdom was not of this world. His kingdom was from and of heaven, and not from or of men. His was to be a reign of righteousness, and its power was in righteousness and not in physical force. Not national relation, but spiritual character, was the qualification for citizenship in this kingdom. This feature of the preaching and teaching of Jesus was repulsive to the ambitious, non-spiritual leaders of the people, and led them to reject him. Nevertheless, he would still call the people to this better hope of a reign of righteousness in fellowship with God. This kingdom was now at hand, and the King was here! And where the King is, there is the kingdom. Already citizens were pressing into that kingdom through the door of repentance. Jesus would have the whole nation so incorporated into his kingdom, but they could only enter one by one, and that by the appointed door. The proudest Pharisee, the most exalted personage in the land, could not be received except he repented of his wrong thoughts of God, and turned from his sins, and sought unto righteousness. On the other hand, the most wretched harlot, the most utterly outcast publican might enter that kingdom by the same door. The cry was practically this: God has come nigh to you with truth and grace; all sins and iniquities shall be forgiven you, and you shall become the children of God indeed, through faith in Christ, the true Messiah and Saviour. Therefore turn to God and forsake your wicked ways. "Let the wicked forsake his way, and the unrighteous man his thoughts: and let him return unto the Lord, and he will have mercy upon him; and to our God, for he will abundantly pardon." (Is. lv, 7.) That kingdom is still among us, and the terms of entering into it are the same now as then. Blessed are they who enter in!

2.—The power given unto them.—They were to preach the immanence of the kingdom, and at the same time they were given a seal to their commission which would accredit them as true ambassadors, in a sign which should tell the people of the benevolence and grace of God. Jesus demonstrated his Messiahship to John by appealing to his works of mercy and healing. These apostles would demonstrate themselves as the authorized and accredited ambassadors of the King of heaven by doing the works of the Messiah. Of old an Eastern king gave to his accredited ambassador his signet-ring. So Jesus gives his signet-ring to his apostles. That token was the power to heal. "Heal the sick, cleanse the lepers, raise the dead, cast out devils: freely ye have received, freely give." God gave to Moses a rod wherewith he demonstrated the authority of his mission. He gave the apostles power over disease, death, and devils. He gives to us not only power over our own sins and a life begotten of God, but still he bids us deal with sickness, death, and devils. Throughout all the centuries Christians have been following in the footsteps of Christ in their ministry to the sick, the diseased, the devil-ridden, and the dying: thousands of hospitals for every manner of disease and affliction; nurses everywhere to care for the suffering; the white cross on the battle-fields; remorseless warfare against every form of evil, and successful warfare, too. A Christlike life, sympathy, active and tender, with the suffering poor under all conditions, are the credentials of authority which Christ gives to us all now. Just so far as we demonstrate our fellowship with Christ in his love for men we have the seal to our ministry. But mark! It is not philanthropy pure and simple which demonstrates our fellowship with heaven. We are to preach the gospel and heal the sick. To preach the gospel and not stretch out a hand to the poor and suffering would be to demonstrate our insincerity. To stretch out a hand to the poor and yet not to preach the gospel is to demonstrate our impotency so far as affording any real help to the world is concerned.

III.—BILL OF INSTRUCTIONS.

Having given them their commission, our Lord next proceeds to instruct his disciples as to how they are to set about their work and bear themselves among those to whom they deliver their message.

1.—**Make no provisions for the journey.**—"Provide neither gold, nor silver, nor brass [or rather copper] in your purses," etc. Our Lord bade them go forth as they were, without making elaborate preparation for their journey—in fact, without making a provision for it at all, except the clothes they wore. This was a tentative mission. They were to avoid any appearance of making a trade out of their work, or of being in any wise above the poorest of the people to whom they went. The spirit of this charge is still binding upon all missionaries and preachers, but the letter of it was temporary so far as this tentative mission was concerned. Jesus does not imply that ministers and missionaries are not to be fed and clothed as other men are; only that they are to avoid all appearance of making merchandise of the gospel. On the other hand, he distinctly says, "For the workman is worthy of his meat." He guarantees their support, and implies that their needs shall be fully met (no doubt by the free gifts of the people to whom they ministered). Freely they had received the blessings of the gospel themselves, freely they were to give. Jesus provided nothing for himself, yet he accepted freely the ministries of his disciples. He lived in their houses, partook of their meat, and allowed many noble women to minister unto him of their substance. (Luke viii, 3.) Paul affirmed his right to support at the hands of the churches among whom he labored, but waived it lest any one should charge him with making gain out of the gospel.

2.—**Conditions of accepting hospitality.**—They were to go into the cities and towns of the country, inquiring who in the place were well reported of and favorably inclined toward righteousness, go to them, and declare their mission. They were to salute the house with the Oriental "Salaam" of peace; and if received, they were to abide there during their mission, and not go about from house to house. If the family to whom they applied would not receive them, their salutation of peace (which was an authorized benediction) should return to them again. What a solemn and awful thing it is to have God's peace pronounced upon one and then because it is not welcomed to have it return to him. God has spoken peace to this world. His proclamation of forgiveness is universal. Those who receive it are saved. Those who reject it suffer the mercy of God to be withdrawn and themselves to be left to their sins. He that hath an ear to hear, let him hear, for in this we have a solemn lesson for the present time.

3.—**Solemn warning.**—In the event of their being rejected, and their words likewise, on leaving the city they were to shake off the dust of it from their feet. How awful for men thus to suffer God to depart from them! Our Saviour tells us that the sinners of Sodom and Gomorrah shall be less guilty in the Day of Judgment than are those who reject the gospel of Christ. They in much darkness and ignorance gave themselves up to wickedness. The rejecters of the gospel, in the full light of Christ's glorious day, deliberately choose sin and despise God and his mercy. Therefore to them is the worse condemnation.

4.—Authority and caution.—In the first place, Jesus assures them that they go forth with his authority. "Behold, *I* send you forth." This is immense comfort and strength. He identifies us with himself, and virtually promises to be with us in all our work for him. He then warns them that as sheep among wolves, so will they find themselves in the prosecution of their work. They will be "hated of all men" for Christ's sake and the gospel's. All manner of devices will be brought into activity to destroy them. They will be slandered, vilified, persecuted on every hand. Therefore he cautions them to be "wise as serpents and harmless as doves." The wisdom of the serpent consists in its adroit ability to hide itself from danger, not in slyness, but simply in an instinctive wisdom as to self-defense. They were to imitate this wisdom, and be prudent in regard to their own safety, and not needlessly or rashly provoke the wolves to bite and devour them. On the other hand, they were to be "harmless as doves." The word really means guileless. They were to be sincere, without craft in the bad sense of that word, and demonstrate by their conduct their entire honesty of purpose. "They were to be ingenuous throughout, pure, truthful, through and through—in fact, as 'unwily' as doves." A mingling of "wariness and guilelessness." I conclude this comment by quoting Dr. James Morrison's keen and comprehensive remark: "The Saviour's 'therefore' must not be overlooked. It hangs on the emphatic 'I' of the first clause. 'It is I who send you forth as sheep in the midst of wolves; become ye *therefore* as apostles charged with my commission, wary, but qualify that wariness with dovelike guilelessness. The presence of the wolves demands that ye be wary; the fact that ye are my apostles demands that ye be guileless.'"

LI.

THE PRINCE OF PEACE.—Isaiah ix, 2-7.

(2) The people that walked in darkness have seen a great light: they that dwell in the land of the shadow of death, upon them hath the light shined. (3) Thou hast multiplied the nation, and not increased the joy: they joy before thee according to the joy in harvest, and as men rejoice when they divide the spoil. (4) For thou hast broken the yoke of his burden, and the staff of his shoulder, the rod of his oppressor, as in the day of Midian. (5) For every battle of the warrior is with confused noise, and garments rolled in blood; but this shall be with burning and fuel of fire. (6) For unto us a child is born, unto us a son is given: and the government shall be upon his shoulder: and his name shall be called Wonderful, Counsellor, The mighty God, The everlasting Father, The Prince of Peace. (7) Of the increase of his government and peace there shall be no end, upon the throne of David, and upon his kingdom, to order it, and to establish it with judgment and with justice from henceforth even for ever. The zeal of the Lord of hosts will perform this.—Isaiah ix, 2-7.

The ancient people of God were organized into a nation under the rule of a king. From the first it was a people under the rule of God; but afterward, through lust of power and pride of nationality, they chose a king, to their own hurt as well as to the dishonor of God. Nevertheless, God yielded to their desire, at the same time prophesying for them trouble and disaster. He was their King, but him they repudiated. They were his people, but they chose rather to be a nation among the nations of the earth than a people of God among nations. So they had their own way, and evils fearful and terrible came upon them. At the time of the utterance of this prophecy, the nation had been divided, and Judah and Israel were under separate kings. Ahaz was the king of Judah, and he was a false man and a traitor to God, and the people were no better than their king. Yet God would have spared both king and people according to his mercy, but neither of them would hear his Word; so the Lord gave them up to their own devices. The seventh and eighth chapters should be carefully read in order to appreciate the glorious promise of our text. The seventh gives us a view of a false king bent on his own way and refusing God. In this chapter there is the promise of "Immanuel" (Is. vii, 14), but to that no heed was taken. The prophecy, it is true, was vague, but it pointed to the coming of their true King. In the eighth chapter we have a picture of a false and unworthy nation, among whom there were a few individuals who took heed to the Word of God. (Is. viii, 16.) These disciples were bound to God, not by a national but a spiritual tie, and, spiritual in their allegiance, were a prophecy of a coming people who should supersede the nation. Together we have the prophecy of Immanuel and the people of God, or, as we read and understand it now, the king and the nation were to give place to Christ and the Church. The nation turned to false refuges religiously, as the king turned to broken reeds politically. Refusing God, this traitor-king made alliance with the heathen kings, who ultimately destroyed him; the people turned to witches and familiar spirits (Is. viii, 19), who of course did them no good. In the midst of this deep apostasy and dense darkness the prophet, with his heart still big with mercy and hope, born of the Spirit of God, looks forward and sees rising upon the dark horizon a great light. To him the full meaning in its ultimate spiritual significance may not have been fully plain. He saw only a nation delivered by the coming of a great Hero-King, and the people restored to heart allegiance to God. We, who have now the full meaning of this prophecy, see in it the advent of Christ, and the turning of the people from sin to righteousness, being converted to God by Christ.

I.—LIGHT OUT OF DARKNESS.

We are not left in doubt as to what the end of this great prophecy was. In Matthew iv, 15, 16, we have it expounded to us. During the awful afflictions which came upon the ancient nation the provinces of Naphtali and Zebulun (lying in Galilee) were the most terribly punished. Out of these lands came Jesus, first preaching to the people the kingdom of God.

1.—The great darkness.—The prophet first saw the people utterly overwhelmed by the ruthless hand of cruel and merciless war. It had been once a fair and prosperous land, but now darkness dense and deep had come over it till it was a veritable "shadow of death." Nevertheless, to them there appeared, as in prophetic vision, a great light arising and shining upon them. Now, turning from the immediate political significance of this to its spiritual import, we can easily see in it a picture of the spiritual condition of the world when Jesus came. The whole world was lying in the wicked one. The Jewish people, though they had the living Word of God, had in the darkness of their carnal ambition and lifeless formality lost all true vision of God. "The Light shineth in the darkness, and the darkness comprehended it not." Politically, they were bound hand and foot under the power of the Romans. From every point of view the land of Judea was a land of darkness and under the shadow of death. The people, that is, the masses, "were as sheep not having a shepherd." The rulers, without spirituality, and ambitious only to keep some semblance of power under the ecclesiastical reign which they were permitted to maintain, had utterly neglected the people; nay, they had bitterly oppressed them, grievously taxing them with avaricious usury and haughty contempt, so that life was a misery to them, existence a burden. Looking beyond the borders of that land of misery, political, social, and physical, the Gentile world was no better off. The Roman rule was oppressive and hard; the idolatrous religions were vile and degrading; the philosophy of the Greeks had utterly failed, affording no consolation to the people and giving no real light to the few who were learned and wise. The best which they had was on the one hand a sensuous and godless Epicureanism, and on the other a cold and hopeless Stoicism. Turning from the condition of the world at large at the time of the coming of Christ to the condition of the unconverted people of our own day, we see also only darkness and the shadow of death. What light for the soul has all our modern philosophical thinking and scientific research given? Doubt, all manner of skepticism, rank worldliness, and hopeless materialism are offered to the starving and dying people, as stones and scorpions in lieu of bread and eggs. Society without Christ to-day is as bad as it ever was in the dark days of Greece and Rome, "having no hope and without God in the world."

2.—**The great light.**—The darkness which the prophet saw was political, physical, and spiritual, all conspiring to lay the people down under conditions of almost hopeless misery. The darkness which this typified was that of the human spirit without God. The light which the prophet saw was the intervention of God for the deliverance of the people from political bondage and physical misery with some spiritual return to God. That which it typified or foreshadowed was the advent and work of Christ, who was, according to Matt. iv, 16, the fulfillment of the prophecy. "From that time Jesus began to preach, and to say, Repent: for the kingdom of heaven is at hand." John says of Jesus: "That was the true Light which lighteth every man that cometh into the world." Jesus himself says: "I am the light of the world: he that followeth me shall not walk in darkness, but shall have the light of life." (John viii, 12.) How this Light shone upon the darkened world when it came! Rising out of that dark and afflicted land of Galilee and spreading gradually over the whole land of Judea, breaking across the borders into Gentile nations, it has since gradually filled the Western world with light, and, turning back upon itself, that light has now penetrated also the darkness of Africa and Asia, sending its bright rays into India and China, and across all seas to the Southern Pacific Islands. Truly it is a "great light." The light seen in the face of Jesus Christ is the glory of God, revealing his eternal purposes of grace to all sinful men. If any one should ask how Christ lights the world, we might answer, "By loving it"—that is, by revealing the love of God to sinners: "For God so loved the world that he gave his only begotten Son, that whosoever believeth in him should not perish but have everlasting life." Then he lightened the world by dying for it: "For in that he died, he died unto sin once." And surely this is a great light which tells us how our sins, which are many, are all forgiven us. What darkness is so great as that which clouds the conscience and fills the soul with all the evil, bitterness, and guilt of sin? Then he fills the world with light by his resurrection from the dead. This revelation of life and immortality floods the valley of the shadow of death with heavenly light, takes away the terror of death, and fills the soul with the sunlight of blessed hope. It is not necessary to tell how this blessed Christ has lightened us in our sorrows and afflictions; how he has lightened us in all ways which make for righteousness; dispelling the clouds of selfishness and mere materialism; giving us a better hope and a purer law and rule of life. How dark would the world be if the light of Christ should by some dire calamity be withdrawn from us! Every soul which has been brought by the blessed truth of the gospel to Christ knows what floods of light, entering the soul, he has shed upon the world—light for the understanding of spiritual things; light for living, and light for dying. Christ is indeed a great light, and we who believe on him are become the children of light and of the day, no more walking according to the course of this dark world, and no longer wandering on in darkness and to death.

 3.—**The great blessings.**—With the coming of the true light came wonderful blessings to the people. This is described in the language of the prophet in several ways, or under several figures of speech. (i) "Thou hast multiplied the nation." National prosperity is seen largely in an increased population. Israel came out of Egypt a comparatively feeble people; under the great reigns of David and Solomon, especially under Solomon, the nation was vastly increased; but, after all, the Jews or Israelites were never a very numerous people—small, indeed, as compared with some of the multitudinous nations around them. If we look to the real fulfillment of this prophecy, what a vast increase in the people of God there has been! From those few disciples (Is. viii, 16) the number of them that have been added to the "nation" or the Church of Christ has risen into hundreds of millions, and is still daily increasing—a vast multitude out of every nation and tongue and kindred and people; a great and mighty host which no man can number. In the Revelation we see the multiplication of the holy nation. (Rev. vii, 9–14.) (ii) "And increased their joy," for so the passage should be read. Of old the people of God rejoiced at their best periods in mere national prosperity—in well-watered fields, rich vineyard slopes, numerous cattle, and abundance of gold and silver. But under the spiritual reign of Jesus the people shall rejoice in better things. Theirs shall be a joy that will be independent of material prosperity. Their joy shall be "the joy of the Lord," a joy arising in God's own heart and flowing in upon theirs—the joy of sins forgiven; the joy of eternal life; the joy of salvation. Again we see in the Revelation a glimpse of the joy of the people. (Rev. vii, 16, 17.) (iii) "According to the joy in harvest." Of old the happiest festival of the Jews was the harvest feast, when the fruits of the earth were all gathered in, and the people blessed God and rejoiced in their riches. But now he gives us a new and better harvest, the ingathering of souls, the first-fruits of which were gathered on the day of Pentecost. Then the people rejoiced. "And they, continuing daily with one accord in the temple, and breaking bread from house to house, did eat their meat with gladness and singleness of heart, praising God, and having favor with all the people." (Acts ii, 46, 47.) This "joy in harvest" is the greatest we know in this world. There is no such pure joy as that which arises in the heart when God's salvation is being accepted by men and women, and his harvest is being gathered. What will it be in that day when the glad harvest home is accomplished? (iv) "And as men rejoice when they divide the spoil." This is a figure borrowed from the triumphant joy of the victorious warrior, who, having overthrown the enemy, and taken possession of the enemy's goods, divides them as spoil among the victors. Well, so shall, and so do, God's people rejoice over the victories which the gospel wins over "the god of this world," and the "spoil" of souls which are taken out of his power. By and by they shall see the "ransomed of the Lord . . . return, and come to Zion with songs and everlasting joy upon their heads: they shall obtain joy and gladness, and sorrow and sighing shall flee away." (Is. xxxv, 10.) (v) "Thou hast broken the yoke . . . and the staff." Hitherto the people had been under the iron yoke of their oppressors, and beaten by the rod of their taskmasters, as in the old slavery times of Egypt. How happy when that yoke shall be broken, and that cruel staff or rod done away! Under Messiah's reign the cruel bondage of Satan's yoke is broken, and the taskmaster's staff done away. Satan is no longer taskmaster to oppress and afflict. We are not under the power of sin any longer. Christ has delivered us by his grace.

4.—**How Christ delivers.**—In earthly conflicts battles are fought "with confused noise and garments rolled in blood." The captives were delivered of old by these terrible and sanguinary methods; but Christ delivers his captives by the power of the Spirit of God, "with burning and fuel of fire." The fire is the Holy Ghost, and the fuel of fire is the word of truth. The gospel preached with fire sent down from heaven, that is, the Spirit, is the power of God for the salvation of men. How glorious was the whole prophecy! How glorious has been its fulfillment in those who have in all ages accepted this wonderful deliverer, whom now the prophet goes on to describe.

III.—THE PRINCE OF PEACE.

This is one of the most wonderful of the Old Testament prophecies. It is a much fuller prophecy than that contained in Isaiah vii, 14, and seems to be the gathering up of all the more or less vague promises of the coming of a great Messianic Deliverer. I say vague promises only because there had not hitherto been a definite description of him beyond the fact that he should bring salvation to Israel, and be a king whose kingdom should never end. The Messianic hope of Israel was not an ideal but a personal one. It was altogether beyond them to comprehend an ideal king and kingdom. To them there could be no kingdom without a king, and they knew nothing of any kingdom except an earthly one, nor of a king except a personal one. Therefore they were always looking for the coming of some wonderful man who should have in himself the powers of God. They expected him to be born of woman, but could not much comprehend the supernatural side of the Saviour's nature, though they were not unfamiliar with the supernatural. The prophet now sets the Messiah more clearly before them. He speaks of him as having already been born. But this is characteristic of Hebrew prophets. They speak of future events as already accomplished! I suppose because they considered what God had promised so sure, that it was practically the same as an accomplished fact. "Unto us a child is born, unto us a son is given." This points directly to Jesus Christ, and we see the prophecy fulfilled in the account of the birth of the Saviour given in Luke's Gospel. This is so obvious that it is not necessary to dwell upon it.

1.—**His wonderful names.**—In the seventh chapter the son of the virgin was called Immanuel—"God with us"—which is also a title of Christ, and exactly tells the facts of his divine-human personality. (Matt. i, 18.) In the passage before us the prophet rises to a higher and fuller definition of the character and offices of the Messiah. Whether we consider these names as double ones or single ones is of little consequence so far as their significance is concerned. They are descriptive of his person and authority. (i) "Wonderful, Counselor." The term "wonderful" suggests all that is most glorious in his being and personality. We think of his eternal unity with the Father as depicted by John in the first chapter of his Gospel and the first verse. We are reminded of his wonderful advent into this world, the child of the Holy Ghost and the Virgin Mary; of his divine-human nature. We are reminded of his mission: to reveal the being and personality of the Father, "full of grace and truth." (John i, 14, 18.) We are reminded of his wonderful teachings, spoken forth to men as "never man spake" before or since; of his wonderful works among men, such as no other man ever did, not only in kind, but in spirit. I mean his wonderful love, pity, compassion, and tenderness of administration. We recall his wonderful death, his glorious resurrection, and ascension to the Father. Everything about Christ, so divinely human, proclaims him the Wonderful One—the One who stands absolutely *alone* as to comparison with any other human being ever born into the world. The other part of this double name, "Counselor," proclaims him as the Word or Wisdom of God. In him "are hid all the treasures of wisdom and knowledge." (Col. ii, 3.) He is "the Wisdom of God." (I. Cor. i, 24.) Of old it was written of him: "Counsel is mine, and sound wisdom; I am Understanding." (Prov. viii, 14.) He is well named "Counselor." No man ever sought him in vain for counsel. The man or woman who submits the ordering of his or her life to him is sure to "make straight paths" in this world, and go away to

God at the end of the life that now is. The whole eighth chapter of Proverbs is a wonderful setting forth of this glorious and Wonderful Counselor. Bind that chapter on your foreheads, and write it in your hearts. (ii) "The Mighty God." Some translate this, "Hero-God," in respect of the glorious achievements of his grace. He is the God who came to our rescue, and accomplishes, through his advent, life, death, resurrection, and second coming, our complete and everlasting deliverance from sin and Satan, from death and all the powers of the underworld, conferring upon us life and immortality. None can observe the works of Jesus without saying, Truly this is the Hero-God! Behold how he goes forth against all forms of evil and triumphs over them. He is Master of all the forces of nature, and the all-powerful Conqueror of sickness, disease, death, and devils. He is well named Hero-God. (iii) "Everlasting Father." If there is something which grates upon our ears when we call Jesus "Father," as though that blotted out his Sonship, let us remember that God the Father "was *in Christ* reconciling the world unto himself" (II. Cor. v, 19), and that he only is the revealer of the Father (John i, 18), because he dwelt in his bosom, and was and is one with him. He himself hath said: "He that hath seen me hath seen the Father," and "I and my Father are one." (John xiv, 7-11; x, 30.) Truly there ought to be no trouble in understanding this designation of Christ. The wonderful thing about it is, that the prophet should have been given to see this so many centuries before Christ came into the world. (iv) "The Prince of Peace." Truly this is a right designation of our blessed Lord—"The Wonderful One." "He is our peace"; he made peace for us by his death; he preached peace to us; he gives us peace in our hearts toward God, and in respect to the perplexing providences of daily life; he brings about peace between men in individual relations, and the preaching of his gospel tends to bring peace to the nations of the earth. When he was born into the world the angels sang the prophetic song: "Glory to God in the highest, and on earth *peace*, good will toward [and among] men." (Luke ii, 14.) In these names we have a revelation of (i) the mysteriousness of his person; (ii) the wisdom of his teaching; (iii) the mightiness of his power; (iv) the love and tenderness of his relations to men; (v) and the peace which he introduces to and among men.

2.—His government.—In the sixth verse we are told that "the government shall be upon his shoulder." He is the true King of men and of all the powers of the universe. In the seventh verse we are told that "of the increase of his government and peace there shall be no end." Not like human governments, which rise and fall, being constantly superseded by recurring and limited dynasties. It shall be characterized by "justice and judgment," in which also it shall be established. All this will be accomplished by "the zeal of the Lord;" that is, by his divine energy and his unfailing love and care for men, whom he has loved with an everlasting love, and whom he will, having loved them, love to the end. (John xiii, 1.) Amen.

www.ingramcontent.com/pod-product-compliance
Lightning Source LLC
Chambersburg PA
CBHW020545300426
44111CB00008B/796